The Wealth of Wives

The Wealth of Wives

Women, Law, and Economy in Late
Medieval London

BARBARA A. HANAWALT

OXFORD
UNIVERSITY PRESS

2007

OXFORD
UNIVERSITY PRESS

Oxford University Press, Inc., publishes works that further
Oxford University's objective of excellence
in research, scholarship, and education.

Oxford   New York
Auckland   Cape Town   Dar es Salaam   Hong Kong   Karachi
Kuala Lumpur   Madrid   Melbourne   Mexico City   Nairobi
New Delhi   Shanghai   Taipei   Toronto

With offices in
Argentina   Austria   Brazil   Chile   Czech Republic   France   Greece
Guatemala   Hungary   Italy   Japan   Poland   Portugal   Singapore
South Korea   Switzerland   Thailand   Turkey   Ukraine   Vietnam

Copyright © 2007 by Oxford University Press, Inc.

Published by Oxford University Press, Inc.
198 Madison Avenue, New York, New York 10016

www.oup.com

Oxford is a registered trademark of Oxford University Press

Library of Congress Cataloging-in-Publication Data
Hanawalt, Barbara.
The wealth of wives: women, law, and economy in late medieval
London / Barbara A. Hanawalt.
p.   cm.
Includes bibliographical references and index.
ISBN 978-0-19-531175-4; 978-0-19-531176-1 (pbk.)
1. Women—England—London—History—To 1500.
2. Women—England—London—Economic conditions.
3. Women—England—London—Legal status, laws, etc.
4. England—Social conditions—1066–1485.   I. Title.
HQ1147.G7H36 2007
306.872'309421'209023—dc22   2007011346

1 3 5 7 9 8 6 4 2

Printed in the United States of America
on acid-free paper

Preface

A preface is a time to reflect about the process of concluding a major project. This book was a particularly challenging one to write because the materials on London women are scattered through a number of archival sources, both printed and in manuscript. It is a study that involves the history of women, feminist theory, legal and economic history, and London's history. The project began as part of a larger study of London social and family history. In 1988–89 I had an ambitious project to do for London what I had done for the peasants in *The Ties That Bound: Peasant Families in Late Medieval England*. I had planned to do the life cycles of medieval Londoners from the cradle to the grave. Thanks to a fellowship from the Guggenheim Foundation, I spent that year in the London archives copying life-cycle events for men, women and children. In 1990–91 I was honored with a fellowship to the Wissenschaftskollege zu Berlin. A third of the way through the year I was still struggling with childhood when a friend suggested that I simply write a book on childhood in London. Brilliant, I thought, and finished that book within a year. Women would form a second book, and men will be considered in a separate study on dispute resolution. Writing on children and childhood was a delight, because the evidence was wonderful and a target as big as Philippe Ariès was easy to attack. But writing on women in London turned out to be far more complicated. I started the most complex part of the project at the National Humanities Center in 1997–98 on a grant from the National Endowment for the Humanities. This segment of the project was to discover the legal rights of women in inheritance, dowry, and dower in medieval London.

No comprehensive book or set of articles exists on the legal rights of women in London, which necessitated reconstructing this complicated system from laws and ordinances written at the time and from the actual court cases in which the laws were reiterated as they were applied or interpreted. It has been a challenge, and I hope that I have laid the groundwork that can be corrected with further research. Doing such original research is both challenging and daunting. As a graduate student, I admired the men who originally worked out the "grand narrative" of political history, but I have come to realize that I and others have worked on more difficult narratives, that of the people whose voices were absent, muted, or distorted in the chronicles and official records. For historians such as myself, it is the discovery of these voices and the creation of a narrative of their lives and the changes that they experienced that are so exciting. It is difficult work and involves long hours in archival materials that will never be easily microfilmed or put on a website. One must shuffle through the parchment and rejoice in the evidence found there. Sometimes it is an individual case, but if the social science researcher is lucky, it will be a long series of documents that can be quantified. Single cases are a problem, because they do not represent a general picture. They are engaging, but one wonders if they are a typical or an aberrant case. The quantifiable evidence is a statistical comfort, but one does not often get it in medieval records in England.

It is one thing to write about the social and legal history of London women, but another to engage in the feminist historiography that has evolved in the late 1990s and the early twenty-first century. Medieval London women were not feminists in these terms. I have, since the beginning of my serious career as a historian, been aware of the problems facing women as historians. I had excellent female professors at Douglass College who warned me that I would face discrimination as a woman historian. At Michigan I even had a male historian who warned me that I would have to publish twice as much as men to make it in the profession.

I have been a feminist for most of my life. My mother was a school teacher who made her own way until the depression ended and she married my father. She stood by me in my complaints about unequal salary, which she had also experienced. My father, a professor of psychology, had a great admiration for my academic career as a historian. I have served on many committees in universities that oversaw the promotion of women and tried to overcome prejudices against them. I sometimes won and sometimes lost, but it was a good cause. However, I have not tried to introduce into my own writing a present-day assumption that women in the Middle Ages could move significantly outside the boundaries of patriarchy. Women in my own family imbibed the assumptions of patriarchy and lived within the boundaries. But they had their own strengths and voices as well; they were not Victorian shrinking violets. One woman brought her four sons from England as a widow and settled in America. But the first conscious feminist voice I heard of in my family was a great-grandmother, a suffragette, who cut her hair and wore it in a snood. My mother, as a school teacher, bought a car in the early twentieth century to drive to her one-room school. When she married, she seldom drove, and reverted to the assumptions of a housewife and mother. Women accommodate to the situations they find, and I feel very lucky to have had a career in a period of women's liberation.

Although an active feminist, I do not try to find early feminists in London and do not set out to prove that late twentieth-century emancipation can be found in the Middle Ages. Single examples of exceptional women cannot be read as typical of society as a whole. Patriarchy was a strong force, and still is. Women knew, and know, the importance of it as well as men.

Women learned how to manipulate patriarchy for their own ends. They were not necessarily victims of the system. Although subject to the usual limitations of access to education, credit, magisterial position, and freedom of movement, London women had a number of legal advantages. They inherited equally with their brothers. Their marriage contracts protected their dower. They usually were selected as guardians of their children. The courts were readily available to women for redress of wrongs. London laws and the men who enforced them certainly upheld patriarchal authority, but in doing so they put limits on men's rapaciousness and protected their women and children from those who might do them or their property harm. The city put constraints on patriarchal domination.

I hope that this book will provide an appreciation of medieval women and their ingenuity in managing their lives. I also hope that readers will understand the skills that historians bring to understanding and reporting the voices of the past that are often muffled in the records.

Working on London has been a pleasure. The archivists in the Corporation of London and in the Guildhall have all been helpful and welcoming. They have all gone out of their way to point out books that might help me and suggest records that I might want to consult. The Public Record Office, now moved from Chancery Lane to Kew Gardens, has long been an archive I have used and enjoyed. Chancery Lane had its charms, but the new environment is certainly more pleasant. I have often consulted with the legal historian Janet Loengard about law relating to marriage, dowry, and dower in London. Her knowledge of these subjects is vast and she has guided me to archival material in London that I have used. Caroline Barron, the premier historian of London, has always been most helpful. When I could, I attended her London Seminar at the Institute of Historical Research and gained much from the insights scholars provided. Indeed, the Institute is among the institutions that has been a constant source of help to me in my research on English history.

The University of Minnesota aided my research in this project on London women with a McKnight Summer Faculty Fellowship in 1993 and Scholar-of-the-College grant in 1995–98. I also had Grants-in-Aid of Research from the University of Minnesota from 1988–90, and 1992–93. With this aid and a National Endowment for the Humanities Summer Research Grant, I made further trips to the archives, and I hired research assistants among my graduate students, who helped with taking notes from some of the printed sources and with quantifying archival materials. Douglas Biggs did the big project of quantifying the two volumes of printed wills from the London Husting court, and Katherine French provided her able skills as a researcher in going through the material on orphans and many other sources. Susan Burns Steuer, Anna Dronsek, Amy Brown Amelio, Kristin Burkholder, Christine Guidera, Jonathan Good, and several history master's students also lent their help. It has been a big project, and everyone was cooperative. Many dissertation topics spun out of my research interests on London women. These graduate students have moved on to their own careers and publications, and the reader will find them cited in this book. During the 1990s, I wrote articles and essays that were an outgrowth of my research. A National Endowment for the Humanities Research Fellowship in 1997–98 permitted me to begin writing this book. The National Humanities Center graciously offered me an office and Delta Delta Delta funds for travel. In this wonderful environment, I completed a collection of essays, including many on London. I began writing the legal history part of the current project.

In 1999 I moved to Ohio State University, where I was appointed to the King George III Chair of British History. The research stipend that came with this chair helped to pay for the assistance of my doctoral research student, Valerie Emanoil, who has seen me through the final stages of the work on this book and several others for Oxford University Press. Her work is close to mine, in that she has been studying medieval London widows. I regard her more as a colleague than as a graduate student, and have often consulted her about legal questions regarding London women. After completing the first draft of the book at Ohio, I was fortunate to have an invitation to the Netherlands Institute for Advanced Study (NIAS) to spend 2005–06 writing, which enabled me to make needed revisions. It was a wonderful environment in which to work, and my colleagues were most delightful.

I am in debt to my editor at Oxford, Susan Ferber, who took on the unwieldy manuscript before I went to NIAS and set me on the right track. She also sent the manuscript to two excellent reviewers who also pointed the way to revisions. I am deeply grateful to the reviewers and especially to her; she also read the revised manuscript. The personal attention of a good editor is hard to find, and I am extremely appreciative to have found such a gem.

Scholars always thank archivists, funding agencies, and editors for help with their research, but I want to reiterate how much the good editors I have had at Oxford University Press and other presses have meant to me. There were times in my career when I really needed free time to go to archives, and the funding agencies helped me to achieve this time in congenial places for research and writing. With a number of books, one goes through the usual dedications to parents, siblings, husbands, lovers, and so on, but what really makes the opportunities are the people who serve on the selection committees of funding agencies, and the kindness of editors. In all gratitude, this book is dedicated to these people.

Contents

Contents

5

Recovery of Dower and Widows' Remarriage 95

6

For Better or Worse: The Marital Experience 116

7

Standard of Living and Women as Consumers 135

8

Women as Entrepreneurs 160

9

Servants, Casual Labor, and Vendors 185

Illustrations

Illustrations

The Wealth of Wives

Introduction

Women in London were in a unique position to have an impact on the city's growing economy in the late Middle Ages. As London became a leading commercial city in Europe, women contributed to the household economy and the retail trade, but they also helped to provide the capital for London's expansion in the late fourteenth and fifteenth centuries as it became a leading commercial city in Europe. The city was a major participant in the international trade in raw wool to the weavers of Flanders and Italy and also established itself as a distribution center for goods such as wine, fine cloth imported from the Continent, and, increasingly, luxury items produced in London itself. Trade and merchant guilds gained in power, and—although revolts of the ordinary people occurred—London's government became more oligarchic and more stable. Major officers, such as the mayor, were selected from among citizens who were members of the most powerful guilds. International trade, the presence of the royal government in Westminster, and crafts (particularly in the production of luxury items such as silk weaving and goldsmithing) fueled the city's growing wealth. The Hundred Years' War contributed to London's importance, perhaps even providing silver and gold looted from France for the goldsmiths of the city to work and for wealthy Londoners to place in their homes. All of these economic and political roles involved men and seem to leave little role for women, but London's laws were generous to women in terms of inheritance, dower, dowry, and wardship of their children and their inheritances. Women had access to courts to preserve their rights, and city officials oversaw the administration of laws regarding women, their children, and their property.

The major thesis of this book is that the circulation of wealth, talent, and service through women contributed to capital formation in late medieval London and paved the way for the development of London as an international player. In arguing for the importance of the transmission of wealth through women and particularly through their marriages, I am departing from the traditional approach toward women's economic contribution in urban centers in medieval England, which has emphasized women's work as laborers and entrepreneurs.

London and its population experienced tremendous changes in the course of the fourteenth and fifteenth centuries, and these changes had an impact on women as well as men. London was a crowded city in the early fourteenth century—very crowded. Within its walls, which enclosed a little more than a square mile, and the wards that grew up outside them, perhaps eighty thousand people or more lived.[1] Although smaller than Paris, London was one of the large cities of Europe, and by far the largest in England. But the city's trade and England's agriculture could not sustain this population. In the first quarter of the fourteenth century, famines resulting from incessant rain and cold weather took their toll. Individuals froze to death or died of starvation. In the famine years, multitudes of paupers gathered for distributions of bread or pennies. Men, women, and children appeared at these outpourings of alms, and some were crushed to death trying to grab a penny or a loaf.[2]

These crises occurred before the appearance of the Black Death (bubonic plague and perhaps other variations of disease) in London in 1348. Within two years, the inhabitants of London died in such large numbers that the population shrank to half its size. The loss was enormous, but only a few laments remain. Deaths were so prevalent that bodies were buried in mass graves with little lead crosses on their chests, but the bureaucracy managed to continue recording wills and making sure that orphans got their due share, at least on a reasonable scale.[3] The plague continued to visit almost every generation in the fourteenth and fifteenth centuries, and other diseases also appeared. The overall effect was that the population of England and London remained low until the end of the fifteenth century. Women, of course, were affected economically by the reduced population—but how?

Early speculation suggested that women survived the plague better than men and that there was a surplus of women in the postplague era, but current evidence offers little confirmation of that. Several scholars have posited a "golden age" for women in the period of depopulation following the onset of the plague. They argue that the loss of population in the late fourteenth and early fifteenth centuries opened up more jobs for women outside the household. This "golden age" allowed women to have free entry into the workforce, positions as skilled laborers formerly open only to men, and opportunities to enter into a business or to continue the occupations of their deceased husbands. A further claim is that women increasingly delayed their age of marriage because they could earn good wages or chose to remain single. Late medieval England, these scholars argue, looked demographically more like early modern England, with couples marrying in their late twenties and a large portion not marrying at all.[4]

The applications of modern ideas about the meaning of equality do not apply to the Middle Ages. Medieval women did not think in terms of equal pay or equal say in the household. Demographic shortfall alone could not open employment to women, because patriarchy put limits on women's access to skilled training and business opportunities. Contrary evidence and arguments have suggested that women's role in the economy showed more signs of continuity than change in the late Middle Ages and that women never rose to prestigious positions. Indeed, women's economic role may have declined in the late fifteenth and sixteenth centuries.[5] The evidence in London's archives on women's specialized training, employment, and entrepreneurial roles, as explored in this book, does not suggest an open door for women, even in depressed demographic conditions.

The argument from demography is largely based on new opportunities for widows and single women, but the presumption of most of the medieval literary and archival sources was that a woman would marry and even remarry. Fourteenth- and fifteenth-century advice literature for women, letter collections, sermons, legal records, and individual bequests in wills were predicated on women's marriages.[6] England was not different from the rest of Europe in assuming that the household economy was based on a marriage that established an "economy" (from Greek *oikos*, house, and *nomos*, law or rule). While the contractual conditions of the marriage differed from northern to southern Europe and from northwestern continental Europe to London, the general assumption, as it had been from ancient times, was that the married couple and their children and servants were the basic economic unit. As for who had the *nomos*, this is a question I will discuss later in the book, but the *oikos* was clearly the household of a married couple.[7]

In addition to famines, plagues, and other diseases, London was heavily involved in the Hundred Years' War, the first year of which began in 1337, eleven years before the plague outbreak in 1348. London was pressured to give generously and raise troops. The war continued intermittently, and while it probably increased London's wealth in the long run, with the influx of royal money, increased trade, and loot from France, in the short run London women were sometimes left to run businesses on their own as their husbands were held for ransom or simply disappeared for years in the king's armies. London feared invasion, but the French never landed. Instead, in the middle years of the fourteenth century, Edward III invited the Flemish weavers of woolen cloth, who had a far advanced technology of weaving, to bring their skills to England. Men and even some women were able to find work as weavers, but this occupation did not become a major one until the sixteenth century. In addition to weaving, the Flemings brought their taste for beer and the technique for making it. Ale was the drink of the English, and many women engaged in brewing. Ale soured quickly, and women could make up batches of it for quick sale; in London they even had larger breweries. But the addition of hops (an herb) made beer a more stable beverage. Larger quantities could be made and kept longer. Women were squeezed out of the brewing business in the fifteenth century.[8] War and new technology did not benefit many women. Although Londoners adopted a taste for beer, as well as an industry to make it, and developed their own weaving industries, the presence of a large Flemish population caused tensions in the city that were manifested in the form of individual complaints and sometimes riots.

Rather than concentrating on women's work in weaving, brewing, and skilled and unskilled trades, this book argues that women's largest economic impact on London's economy, mercantile trade, and the stability of its government and society lay in the transfer of wealth through marriage. The market in real estate, valuable objects, and capital was a fluid one. London followed borough law which permitted all children, male and female, to inherit equally. The father's estate was divided in three ways with a third reserved to pay the testator's debt and for the salvation of his soul, a third was put aside for his children's inheritance, and a third was reserved as dower for his widow's life use. The widow could take her dower into another marriage, but after she died, the surviving children inherited her portion. These laws kept wealth circulating, and women became conduits of wealth, whether they had only small amounts of capital or skills as finishers or marketers of a husband's craft or were heiresses to real estate, jewels, and household goods. One of the effects of population decrease was, as this book shows, that widows and their minor children became increasingly wealthy. The accumulated wealth of widows, heirs, and heiresses who survived the plague became concentrated in the hands of fewer people by the late fourteenth and the first half of the fifteenth century. If the demand for marriageable heiresses and widows in London constituted a "golden age" for them personally, we will never know.

The liquidity of capital and women's access to it had implications for London's social structure. The city did not evolve patrilineal social structures that were typical to those English –nobles and other freeborn subjects—who were governed by common law. Nor did it follow the pattern of patrilineage that existed in many European cities. In English common law inheritance followed the rule of primogeniture so that the eldest son inherited the father's estate. Daughters received a dowry and widows had dower, but younger sons were lucky to get a monetary settlement or a military position. Daughters did not inherit in common law unless they had no male siblings. Property, titles, and wealth usually remained in the male line of descent.

Foreigners were very interested in London's household economies, as well as their inheritance, dower, and dowry practices, because they differed from those that were familiar to them. William Caxton, an Englishman returning after a long sojourn in Flanders in order to establish a printing business, was shocked to find that families in London existed for only three generations of inheritance from father to son.[9] In Flanders he had observed lineages that went back generations, even, he thought, a thousand years. A Venetian visiting England around 1500 made a similar observation and commented on the concentration of wealth and property in women's hands. He shrewdly observed that the inheritance system was the cause of this deficiency. Added to the partible inheritance of the father's estate was the dower right of widows which delayed or even deprived male heirs of paternal wealth.[10] London seemed to have a more horizontal social structure, compared to the vertical one in Venice or in Italian cities.

London law was clear about the rights of women in terms of property, but one of the questions raised in this study is to what extent city officials followed and enforced their laws in practice.[11] The mayor, aldermen, and chamberlain of London were charged with overseeing the wardship and inherited wealth of citizens' orphaned children (by London's definition, an orphan was a child whose deceased parent inherited the family wealth, usually that of the father). Chapter 1 discusses the extent to which young girls received an equal distribution of the family wealth and the care that was taken of their well-being, as opposed to that of their brothers. Some questions arise from the fact that, of the orphans appearing before the mayor and chamberlain, 60 percent were male and 40 percent were female. Were female children given equal treatment at birth and in their early years? Was their identity the same as that of males and were they valued equally in their families? Chapter 2 continues the theme of equal treatment of female children, raising the issues of investment in their education and apprenticeship. The possibility of abuse of female children must also become part of this discussion. For the most part, girls' education and training were directed toward an eventual marriage, not toward independent employment and lives as single women.

London preserved the dower and dowry in the marital contract, as was true of northern Europe.[12] The dowry was the bride's contribution to the marriage and could be money, household goods and clothing, fine objects of gold and silver, or even real estate. The dower, the husband's contribution to the marriage, was promised in a contractual arrangement and would come to the wife if she outlived the husband. She had use of the dower for her life, and then it passed to the heirs. The dower in London usually included living quarters, a trade or business, household goods, and so on. The two marriage portions were roughly equivalent in value. In contrast, Italy and much of southern Europe abandoned the dower in the twelfth century, favoring only the dowry.[13] London fathers were very concerned about providing dowry for daughters. Almost all the wills and some of the court cases point to the female inheritance being directed toward an eventual marriage. If the father was alive, a daughter would receive her portion of inheritance when she married. So important was the presumption of marriage that a favorite charity was money toward the marriage of poor maidens. Male inheritances emphasized apprenticeships, tools of the trade, and real estate. If a man and his family could afford it, the dower was promised in real estate. Chapter 3 discusses the rights of heiresses and the provisions for dower and dowry.

Marriage contracts were legally binding, since they involved an exchange of goods and promises of property, but social presumptions and religious constraints also accompanied marriage. The Church required that couples consent to marriage and not be forced into it. Marriage was a sacrament, and church courts regulated the validity of marriages. Divorce was very difficult to gain in a church court, so couples entered into marriage presuming a life commitment. Although marriages were arranged, a period of courtship and consent were common in London and elsewhere. But after consent came the negotiations on dower and dowry. While England did not have the strong notarial tradition to record these contracts such as existed on the Continent, some marriage contracts were entered in city records, and contested contracts appeared in London courts and provide an idea of what the arrangements were. Chapter 4 explores the formation of marriage, marriage contracts, and the partnership that the husband and wife entered into.[14]

The "partnership marriage" has been misinterpreted to mean equality of the couple, but not all economic partnerships are on an equal footing. London wives came under coverture of their husbands, and a wife's legal position was known as *femme coverte* (the wife submitted her legal identity to that of her husband, and he was responsible for her conduct and her finances). Marriage passed on wealth that came under the control of the husband, who could use it for his business, but he could not permanently alienate dower or inherited property. In addition to the financial arrangements, marriage involved the sexual "debt," as it was called. That is, husband and wife had the duty to be sexually available to each other and produce children. Finally, the couple was expected to cooperate in the household economy. Men's and women's tasks in marriage were well defined in the medieval economy, and both parties followed assigned economic roles. The partnership might work well, or it might fail horribly, as chapter 6 explains.

A dower, promised to a bride at the church door, was done in front of witnesses and sometimes was also written down. Since so many of the arrangements were verbal, a widow might find that she had to pursue her right to dower property in court. London provided a court for women to reclaim dower, and widows seemed to know how to use these courts to secure their claims. Their knowledge of court procedures in pursuing their dower, in securing the wardship of their children, and in contract cases make it clear that women had a good knowledge of the city laws and could be articulate in courts. Chapter 5 explores women's use of courts for dower and their successes and failures.

Whether or not a widow secured all of her dower, the court records show that widows were very desirable for remarriage. A man who married a widow secured a half of the former husband's estate from his new bride's dower if she did not have children. If she did have children, he had the use of a third of the former husband's estate during her life and the third that was the inheritance of minor children until they reached the age of majority. The amount could be in thousands of pounds sterling by the beginning of the fifteenth century. The new groom, of course, had to provide a dower in turn. The case of Thomasine Bonaventura, discussed in chapter 5, shows that women could accumulate considerable wealth through marriage and remarriage. She started as a high-class servant in a merchant house and married her master when his wife died. He died soon afterward, and she married another merchant. When he died, she again married. Since she did not have children, she had a considerable accumulation of dower property and became one of the wealthiest women in London. Another case is that of the Celys, who were traders in wool, buying wool in the countryside in England and selling it in Flanders. The family business was a profitable one, but when two brothers wanted to establish themselves in London and settle down, they both sought wealthy London widows as marriage partners. Widows not only provided an infusion of capital but also assured husbands of a prominent place in London society, a type of "social capital." The Cely letters illustrate the courtship of wealthy widows and the property the couples exchanged at marriage.[15]

The circulation of wealth through marriages suggests that women played a large role in the consumer economy of London. They helped to furnish houses, bought and received clothing and jewels, and kept the London goldsmiths and silversmiths busy ordering various ewers, bowls, silver spoons, basins, salt cellars, cups, and a host of other things to put on display in their houses. Even poor women might have silver spoons in their dowries. Purchase of food and drink for a household was also a major part of the consumption pattern of women as they sought to supply their households. Women needed a variety of services as well and were in charge of household servants. Chapter 7 looks at the standard of living of women, from the wealthiest to the poorest, and their participation in the consumer economy.

The final chapters of the book, chapter 8, on women as entrepreneurs, and chapter 9, on women as servants, casual laborers, and vendors, examine the extent to which women could participate in the economy alone, rather than through marriage. Widows left with real estate either as inheritance or as dower might choose not to remarry and to manage their own property. Some did, although the numbers cannot be known. Single women and widows were not active in purchasing or leasing property. Widows could take over their husbands' businesses, as Thomasine Bonaventure seems to have done for a brief period, but women in trades found it hard to collect debts, might not be able to control or train apprentices, or might be too inexperienced or too old to manage a business. The evidence for widows successfully carrying on their husbands' trades is limited. London did have a law that permitted married women to trade as *femme sole* and be responsible for their own businesses and for the debts that they incurred. Despite this law, which appears to have offered married women an opportunity for economic freedom, the records show that few London women took advantage of the status. Only women involved in silk working seem to have successfully established themselves as independent vendors.

London has no systematic records for investigating women who acted as servants, took positions as laborers, or acted as vendors. Many of these women were single—particularly servants—and were immigrants to London. If one were looking for a "golden age" for women, this could not be a more depressing place to look. Servants were in great demand, and the records are full of the problems of masters retaining servants in a period of low population and of servants being abused and kept virtually imprisoned in their positions by ruthless masters. While some married women sold products from their husbands' shops or from stalls that they rented, many street vendors were women who were involved in a resale trade. They bought ale, wine, food, and so on for resale on the streets or in stalls. They went by the general name of hucksters because they called out their wares and sold in the open. Their living was mostly a marginal one, and the records mention them because they were often accused of illegal activities. Sometimes they were accused of forestalling, that is, of buying goods before they came to market. The fallback for all women, married or single, who lived on the margins was prostitution. When other sources of income failed, women sold their bodies. These were not women who were involved in careers as sex workers but who seem rather to have used prostitution as a last resort or were forced into it.

While the exploration of the passage of real property and of lucrative marriages emphasizes the craft and merchant class, this book explores all classes, not simply daughters, wives, and widows of citizens with substantial wealth. The women appearing in these pages are contextualized within the framework of greater London's society and economy. They do not appear as isolated individuals, plucked out of a wealth of records, nor are they subsumed into the miasma of such general terms as family and household. They are actors in their own right, but they also participate in the legal tissue of London and are subjected to general societal attitudes toward women and the presumption that males dominated the government, society, law, and females. Men had the privilege of participating in government and being magistrates; women did not. Men were responsible for their legal actions at age twelve, but fathers were responsible for their daughters' behavior, masters for their servants', and husbands for their wives'. Only as widows did women have more freedom of economic action and personal choice. Perhaps they did not succeed in this role, and perhaps they found reentry into *coverture* a more comfortable role.

Much of the discussion surrounding women in history has revolved around the constraints men placed on them. The London women who appear in this book are sometimes victims of excessive male exercise of patriarchy—particularly female servants and powerless women. But the everyday limitations on women's behavior are perhaps better understood by looking at the ways in which women learned either to manipulate male dominance or became pliant in accommodating the prevalent social mores. Class differences as well as gender differences account for many of the disparities of power that are explored in these pages. The less privileged in a society learned to get along within the dominant culture and played the roles that would see them through. We would not expect, in medieval society, to see active feminist revolt against patriarchy.

London laws regarding women, the enforcement of the laws, and the active role women played in the economy suggest an alternative view of patriarchy in the city. The laws and those men who administered them were designed to protect their women from the predatory action of other males. London citizens did not want to see other males take inheritances from their orphans, male and female. They wanted their widows to be protected and provided for so that they could rear their children and be assured of such material comfort as was available. London's patriarchal ideology did include concern about passing property and wealth to heirs, male or female, but long lines of patrilineal descent, which preoccupied Italian or Flemish observers, did not seem to concern them. They had developed an understanding that keeping capital fluid and allowing widows to remarry was in their best interest for their trade and increasingly for the power of the guilds. They seemed to agree with the civic laws that limiting their own, immediate patrilineal ambitions was best for their guilds and community. As this book shows, medieval London created a "constrained" or "self-limiting patriarchy." London's government, guilds, and social conventions ensured that the head of the household had responsibilities as well as freedoms: he had to obey the laws of London, provide for his wife and children, and not use excessive correction on them. Men as well as women were bound by legal and social customs.

London archival sources offer rich information about women, but they can also be frustrating in their silences. The story presented in this book is pieced together from a vast range of sources, including cases from royal, mayoral and ecclesiastical courts, wills, and personal correspondence. In addition, popular literature has added to the interpretation of the legal records and letter sources. This study has used both printed and archival materials in a systematic way. It does not cover all the records; no single researcher could do that.

But the study does include a complete survey of all printed sources (often correlated with originals or complementary documents such as wills), a complete statistical analysis of the Mayor's court original bills, a sample of the Mayor's court of common pleas involving widow's suits for recovery of dower, a complete analysis of the Portsoken wardmoots (local pleas made against offenders for misdemeanors and property offenses for one city ward), and a complete survey of all the pleas from London for equity to the lord chancellor in the late fourteenth and fifteenth century. Coroners' rolls, both printed and in manuscript, have provided much of the local color and some of the statistical material. Ecclesiastical court records have been sampled, rather than systematically cited.[16]

Part of the research problem is that the data on women are so huge and amorphous that it is impossible to encompass them all. While some of the repetitive materials can provide quantitative analysis, much comes down to the experience of individual women. Yet anecdotal material does not tell the complete story either. One widow who takes up a trade does not make a measure for the widows who failed. One servant who did not suffer abuse and married the master does not account for all those who were sexually assaulted or could not force a master to honor a contract. The researcher is left with gaps that are hard to fill, even with vast amounts of material available. And a researcher is always looking for the voice of women, not of the court records of men who determine cases or record them.[17]

Women living in late medieval London had a full range of experiences. They were instrumental in creating the wealth of London men through inheritance, dowry, and dower, they produced children, and they remarried in order to pass on wealth and prosperity to London men and to preserve their own standard of living. Throughout it all, they had a remarkably steady and sure voice in the records. They pleaded their own cases in the various Mayor's courts. They were there when the property and the rearing of their children was discussed in the court of orphans. They pleaded their dower cases in the Husting court of common pleas. They were vocal when they were accused of creating a nuisance on their property or were brought before the wardmoot courts for infractions of ward morals. And they easily entered into the recording of deeds, into bills before the Mayor's court, and into petitions to the lord chancellor. We cannot think of London women as silent, subservient, and without a voice of their own. The records, as this book shows, are full of their voices, along with their successes and disappointments. They knew how to give utterance to their complaints, their grievances before the courts of law, and their petitions for redress. They seemed to know their way around the patriarchal system; not all women fell victim to it.

⟆⟅ **I** ⟆⟅

Daughters and Identities

A London girl's economic prospects in life depended on many factors. Simply being born female rather than male influenced the options open to her. She would, at birth, begin to experience the limits that patriarchy would put on her and other European daughters, and her early training would direct her to the route most appropriate to her sex and her social class. Daughters of London citizens, however, enjoyed the borough law of partible inheritance, that is, a daughter inherited equally with her brothers.

Londoners gained citizenship (known as "freedom of the city") by inheriting it from their fathers, by finishing apprenticeship in London, and by buying the right to citizenship. Women mostly became citizens through marriage to a citizen. Citizens ranged from poor to very wealthy, so that it was not simply merchant-class children who enjoyed legal protection. If the girl was an orphan, she could be assured that the mayor and aldermen would protect her inheritance. But laws can be broken and twisted, and this chapter investigates the degree to which female children had equal access to family wealth. Children of noncitizens did not enjoy these protections. Inheritance, however, was not the only matter that influenced childhood opportunities. The early life of London children can be reconstructed from the court of orphans and other city records about young children. They reveal information about their welfare, their families, their ages, and their survival. A disturbing set of statistics derived from these records indicates that female children were either undercounted or simply did not survive early childhood.

Naming and Identity of Girls

In the first moments after birth, the midwife determined the sex of the infant, and at that point the different paths for the lives of male and female children began. The father was informed of the birth and sex of the newborn, since it was his responsibility to select godparents and arrange for the baptism and celebration. The baptismal ceremony included naming, and a girl would be given a distinctively female name. When Elizabeth Bryan (de Birene in the Inquisitions Post Mortem) was born in the parish of St. Peter at Paul's Warf in Queenhithe ward on March 13, 1381, her father, Guy Bryan, was dining with friends at a house near the one in which his wife gave birth.[1] Five of the men present remembered the event eighteen years later when they testified about Elizabeth's age.[2] The mother remained at home and was not part of the baptismal festivities. A woman who had just given birth was considered unclean and could not enter the sacred space of a church until six weeks had elapsed.[3]

As was the practice in England, Elizabeth Bryan was baptized two days after her birth. The dangers of infant mortality and the fear that the child might die in original sin led to early baptism. On hearing the good news of his daughter's birth, Guy Bryan set about organizing the baptismal party. The vicar was summoned.[4] Three men agreed to hold wax torches beside the font. Four men carrying candles accompanied the baptismal party there.[5] The most serious problem was assembling three godparents, two women and a man for the baptism of a girl and two men and a woman for a boy. In selecting godparents, the father had a number of considerations. He would not want to choose someone who, by acting as a godparent, would be eliminated from future marriage alliances. The Church instructed that godparents entered into a spiritual kinship with each other, with the parents, and with the child. In forming this spiritual kinship, they became related in too close a degree to marry each other. Thus, the father of the child could not later marry one of the godmothers.[6]

Another qualification for godparents was that they be people of sufficient prestige to advance the family's honor and fortunes, as well as those of the child.[7] Usually the godparent who raised the child from the font and named it was the most distinguished member of the baptismal party. The father would, therefore, want to select a godparent for this role who had a name he wished to give to his child.[8]

Although godmothers are mentioned less frequently in the records, when they appear it is because of their prestige. A sixty-four-year-old man remembered that Albreda, the wife of Richard Sutton, a citizen and stockfishmonger (dried fish seller) of London, had been the one who washed and attended the baptism of a young heir. Another man had seen an esquire of the household asking a godmother to attend.[9] Two godmothers, Anne, the late wife of Edward le Spencer, and Maude atte Melne testified that the daughter of John de Beverley was of age and bore Anne's name.[10] Male witnesses had been impressed with the quality of the ladies who had been present as godmothers. For example, John Goldsburg saw the noble woman, Elizabeth le Despenser, at the baptism of John le Strange's heir.[11]

In addition to naming and baptizing the child, the ceremony provided witnesses who could be called on to testify, years later, that a child had reached the age of inheritance. A father wanted as many distinguished witnesses present as possible and so he often invited the sheriffs and mayor of London to the ceremony. They did not always come.[12] Since oral testimony was usual and the chances of early death were great, witnesses who could testify to the age of the child were important. An elderly or sick person might not be the best choice but rather someone who would survive until the child was of age. One man, however, mentioned that he had been present at the baptism of Maud, daughter and heir of Thomas Durant, and that he remembered that the vicar had written the day and hour of Maud's birth in a psalter and that it still remained in the church. In the case of Maud both an oral and written verification were available.[13]

The baptism ceremony had important social and economic implications for both the father and the child. The father, godparents, and other guests consolidated the social bonding with each other and with the child by gift giving and a feast. Two London men remembered general drinking among the male attendants at the church and that a servant of the father carried jugs of the sweet wine to the church.[14] Another man said that he had helped a father catch fish in the fish pond in Southwark for the celebratory feast.[15] Another witness had noticed that the Earl of Arundel presented a godchild with a gift at the baptism.[16] Gift giving became so extravagant for both the rich and the poor that the mayor and alderman issued an ordinance in the last quarter of the fourteenth century: "for as much as men of great estate had given large sums on the occasion of the baptism and marriage of their children and others of less estate had followed their example to their own impoverishment, it is ordained that no one of the City shall give at baptism of any child more than 40d., under penalty of 20s. to the Chamber."[17] While this was a laudable concern on the part of the city government, it was an ordinance that was impossible to enforce.

The institution of godparenting could have provided an opportunity for a close relationship with the godchild, but little evidence survives to indicate that such bonds were common, either in London or the countryside. The religious duty of the godparents was to instruct the child in saying the Pater Noster, Ave Maria, and Credo, and the priest asked them to recite these prayers at baptism on behalf of the infant.[18] No evidence shows that they gave religious instruction as the children grew older.

Only testamentary evidence gives us a hint about the relationship, and it does not indicate strong bonds. Only 3 percent of the testators appearing in the London Archdeaconry court wills from 1393 to 1409 left bequests to their godchildren, and in the Husting court wills, only 1 percent of the testators between 1357 and 1500 did so.[19] Some testators made a godchild one of the chief beneficiaries of their wills. For example, Christina Malying named her goddaughter, Christina, daughter of Ralph Bakelowe, as her chief beneficiary. Alice, widow of Robert Lyndiwyk, recognized two goddaughters named Alice and Mary Lodewyk (a variant spelling of the name) and specified that she was leaving a third of her estate to her goddaughter "who was named for me."[20] Others left sums of money. Christiana Reynewell, the widow of an alderman, left two goddaughters 20 marks for their dowries, but only 6s. 8d. (the customary gift to godchildren in London) to other goddaughters, and 20s. to yet another.[21] Most of those leaving bequests were widows and men without children of their own, particularly clergy. But William

Trippelowe, an armorer, who died in 1390, stipulated in his will that his executors (including his widow) were to provide his goddaughter, Elizabeth, with a living until she married.[22] On occasion a godchild left a bequest as well. An unmarried silkwoman left Isabel Fremley, her godmother, a small bequest in 1456.[23]

Godchildren would seem to be a source of adoption for childless couples, but neither English secular nor ecclesiastical law had provisions for adoption.[24] Likewise, one might assume that godparents would be natural guardians of orphaned godchildren, but, as we shall see, usually the mother was named as guardian in London.

Baptism gave the child a spiritual and legal identity. The "Christian" or first name was only one element of a child's identification. In legal records, the child was further recorded with the name of the father—and in some cases, particularly if the wealth was in the mother's name, the name of the mother. Designating a child "daughter of" or "son of," as in "Maud, daughter of Thomas Durant" let the world know who had responsibility for Maud. Thomas, son of Christina de Comptone, bore his mother's name, since his wealth came from her.[25] The designation of "daughter of" or "son of" was used until the young people had passed through a change of status. For young men it might be on reaching the age of majority, finishing apprenticeship, or marriage. For young women, the designation of who bore responsibility for them changed with marriage. At this point a woman assumed the husband's name, for example, "Amy, wife of Thomas Neweton." As a widow, she would be designated "Amy, widow of Thomas Neweton." Prostitutes often had simple descriptive names such as "douche Kate," "Bette le polde fote," or "haltingwoman," indicating a status that was so low that they did not have the dignity of a father's name.[26] Women listed only by a first name or surname might have been single.

Orphans and Guardians

Since London inheritance laws, following borough custom rather than common law, divided estates equally among the surviving children, daughters could assume they had an equal share.[27] In common law, by contrast, the eldest male received the family estate. London girls' portion could come in the form of a dowry from the family property while their fathers were alive (*inter vivos* settlement), as part of the inheritance to be shared with brothers and sisters, or as a sole inheritance if they were only children.[28] We know a great deal about the partition of wealth and the rearing of children who had not yet reached the age of majority from cases in the Mayor's court.

To ensure that minors received their just inheritances, London law gave the mayor and chamberlain oversight of orphaned children of citizens and their property. An orphan, by the city's definition, was a child who had lost the parent from whom her or his inheritance would come, usually her or his father. London law was designed to keep inheritances intact and did not use the modern definition of an orphan as one who has lost both parents. Such children became wards of the city and were protected by city laws. As heiresses, girls as well as boys came under this stringent protection. About a third of the adult males residing in the city were citizens.[29] Noncitizens' orphans did not enjoy the mayor's protection. Since most men became citizens through apprenticeship or by buying the rights of citizenship (redemption), the orphans who came into the Mayor's court were mostly daughters and sons of artisans and merchants.[30] One might presume that only the children of the well-to-do London citizens fell under the protective laws of the mayor and aldermen, but impoverished orphans of citizens were reared at the city's expense.[31] The Mayor's court of orphans reveals a remarkable amount of information about both female and male children.

London law stipulated that the testator's property be divided into three parts. One-third was for the testator, to be disposed of for the good of his soul, one-third went to his children or his heirs, and one-third went to his wife as dower for her life use. The widow could take the dower into another marriage, but it reverted to the heirs after her death. Unless the testator modified the legal provisions for his heirs by will, all the children inherited equally. One case restated the law:

> it was immemorial custom of the city that the children born in matrimony of freemen [citizens] of the city, if they had not been advanced in their father's lifetime, should on his death have a third part of their father's goods, chattels, and money, and that when one of the children had so been advanced [through an *inter vivos* settlement], the other [remaining] children or child should have the third part.[32]

For instance, the mayor and chamberlain settled the estate of Simon Godard and his wife, both deceased, making sure that all children inherited equally. The estate included a silk cope (ecclesiastical vestment) valued at £30 and £10 in cash, along with papers showing debts owed to Simon. The king wished to make a gift of the cope to the bishop of Worcester at his consecration. The mayor and chamberlain reimbursed the estate for its value and divided it by giving one married daughter one-quarter of the estate, another daughter now of full age another quarter, and reserving one-half for the two minor sons who were still in wardship.[33] Apparently, the oldest girl had not received an *inter vivos* settlement as a dowry on her marriage.

London laws were explicit about who could be a guardian and what would happen to the inheritance:

> A testator may bequeath guardianship of his [children] and his chattels to anyone he thinks fit; such guardians being bound to apply the proceeds of his inheritance to the use and advantage of such child until he comes of age. If arrangements are not made then the child is given to the side of the family from which his inheritance does not derive. If from the father, then the mother or nearest kinsman on the mother's side. If from the mother, then the nearest kinsman on the father's side.[34]

The law required the mayor, aldermen, and chamberlain to supervise the wardship of the children and their inheritance.[35]

Londoners had no illusions about the benign character of their fellow humans. The law required that no one could serve as guardian who might profit from the death of the child. Since a father's brother, sister, or elder children could inherit if the child died or was murdered, they were not eligible to be guardians. The widowed mother, however, could only have dower (life use) and could not inherit from her children, so she was usually the guardian. If she was dead, then her brother, who had no claim to the inheritance, was often selected as guardian. Thus Adam Ode, maternal uncle of Alice, daughter of Nicholas de Pecham, became her guardian, rather than a member of her father's family.[36]

When the mother was an heiress and had property, then the father or his kin became guardian. In one case, when a mother and her second husband claimed the wardship of her daughter, Jakemina, the court said that by city law, wardship of minors "ought not to be in the hands of a kinsman to whom the inheritance could descend." Since Jakemina had all her inheritance from her mother and none from her father, her wardship remained with her paternal aunt, the prioress of Kilburn.[37] In other cases in which the mother had the property, the father was given custody.[38]

To ensure that it had a full record of children's inheritances, the city hired a special common sergeant-at-law to record proceedings in the orphan's court.[39] He took an inventory of each child's inheritance. In assigning a guardian to manage the inheritance, therefore, the mayor and aldermen had a record to which they could refer when the child reached the age of majority, which was typically twenty-one but could be sixteen for females if they married. The city required guardians to find two to four sureties (men who would guarantee the arrangement with their own funds) so that the heir could be sure of payment. The court enforced the terms of agreement, sometimes requiring the sureties to pay when the guardian defaulted.[40] By the early fifteenth century, the city required the guardians to post bond for the child's wealth, and return it to the mature orphan with "2s. in the pound according to the custom," as "mesne profit."[41]

The careful accounting of orphans' goods and orphans themselves is apparent in a particularly full case. The plea was held in Guildhall chamber before James Andreu, the mayor, the aldermen, and the chamberlain in 1367. The common sergeant, "who prosecutes for orphans in the city," came and required Michael Ede de Cornewaille (Cornwall), draper and guardian of Johanna, daughter of Thomas de Welford, Senior, also a draper, to appear and account for her property and explain why he should not surrender the guardianship. The property consisted, among other things, of a great mazer (maple bowl), six silver spoons, an enameled silver cup, a long chest, and a circlet of gold and gems including scallops of peridot (green gemstone), and a gold fermail (clasp). Initially, Thomas had left three children, but two, a son and daughter, had already died. Michael Ede came and delivered Johanna and her inheritance into the hands of the chamberlain, who committed her and her property to another draper. After Johanna died in 1368, the chamberlain required the new guardian to appear with the property, which he did.[42]

The process of recording the property and guardianship is apparent in two cases. Alice, widow and executrix of William Lynne, a grocer, came to court March 1, 1324, with her late husband's will containing the provisions he made for her and their two sons and three daughters. On March 16 of the same year, the children and their portions were assigned to guardians.[43] In another plea, John de London, a barber, stipulated in his will that "his said children be brought before the Mayor and Sheriff of London for the time being at the Guildhall, so that the portion of each child may, with the assent of the said Mayor and Sheriffs be delivered to some honest and sufficient person in trust for them."[44] The mayor and chamberlain would certainly want to see the children in person, so as not to make a mistake about the number and sex of those needing guardians.

The court was full of people during the assigning of wardship. The mayor, aldermen, chamberlain, sheriffs, and sergeants would all be present in official robes. In addition to the mother and children, a group of about a dozen people directly involved in the case would also be present. Many women had remarried in the short interval between the reading of the will and the assignment of guardians, so a stepfather often would be present. Failing a stepfather, responsible men, perhaps designated by the father or members of his guild, were in attendance, as well as four or more men who stood surety for the goods of the child. The child may have met some of the men before the court session, but occasionally the child would be meeting the guardian for the first time.

A father could assign guardianship through his will. Only 210 fathers designated guardians for their children in Husting court wills. Their preference (55 percent) was for the mother to assume this role. After her, the testator looked to friends (27 percent), kin (8 percent), executors (6 percent), and, finally, apprentices, servants, and churchmen.[45] A typical will recorded in the orphans' court was that of John Greyland. He appointed his wife, Johanna, to be guardian of his daughters, Agnes, Avice, Matilda, and Johanna. In the event that she died before his daughters reached the age of maturity, Richard de Evere, an ironmonger, was to be guardian, and if he died, his late apprentice, William Chaumberlayn, was to assume the role.[46]

The mayor followed similar patterns when he selected guardians for citizens' orphans. Depending on the population dynamics of the period, the mother was selected in 30 to 57 percent of the cases. She acted alone or with a new husband. The lower percentage was in 1350–88, when a number of mothers must have died of the plague. The father alone as guardian does not appear until the end of the fourteenth century, suggesting that by that time more children had inheritances from their mothers.[47] The presence of so many stepfathers (57 percent from 1309 to 1458) indicates the lucrative nature of London's custom of dower and wardship. A widow with a third of her late husband's property for her life use and minor children who had a third of their late father's property made a very attractive package in the marriage market.

On the whole, the mayor and aldermen attempted to keep the children with kin. Until the onset of plague in the mid–fourteenth century, 61 percent were placed with relatives, usually mothers. The percentage fell to 36 percent in the worst of the plague years and only gradually recovered to 54 percent by the middle of the fifteenth century. Since some of the people in the nonkin category might have been distant kin or kin on the mother's side, the actual percentage of orphans who remained with relatives might have been higher. Furthermore, if the father was alive and the mother had died, there was no need for a court appearance. He would continue to hold his property and keep his children in the household. If London widows remarried rapidly, the widowers probably did so even more quickly, as this was a common pattern in preindustrial societies.[48]

The loss of a father was cushioned not only by the continuity of a mother's care but also by the practice of keeping siblings together. In only 54 cases (or 11 percent) were orphans dispersed to various guardians. Usually the separation of siblings occurred only when one of the boys reached the age of apprenticeship or a girl married. Separations of the siblings or disruptions of the guardianship arrangement were surprisingly rare. Between 1309 and 1428, only 8 percent required a move to a different guardian.[49]

The city's concern for the welfare of orphans extended to accounting for their upkeep. Guardians were to find food, linen and woolen clothing, shoes, and other necessities. The amounts spent on children's needs varied greatly. In 1376, the cost of providing for John, son of John Gartone, was committed to John Bas, a draper, whose daughter the boy had married at the tender age of nine. When the young wife died, her husband was still a minor, and the father-in-law rendered account for expenses that amounted to 2s. a week. The care of a cordwainer's invalid daughter for six and a half years in the 1380s cost about 12s. a year, or about 3½d. a week. Obviously, she lived less comfortably than the draper's daughter. Other guardians reported paying amounts of £1 a year, 6d. a week, one half a mark a year, and £7 19s. 3d. over a five-year period for a five-year-old goldsmith's daughter. The highest amount paid for maintenance of an orphan was 66s. 8d. annually, or over £3 a year.[50] The four surviving children (two boys and two girls) of Richard Toky, a grocer, were each allowed 1s. a week for their maintenance. When orphans came of age, the amount spent over the years was deducted from their inheritance.[51] But one grandmother agreed to pay for her orphaned grandson's food and upkeep as her own expense.[52]

The concern that the city, its officials, and citizen parents took for their orphans certainly grew out of anxiety for their survival, but the material circumstances of the children added urgency. Since many orphans had considerable property, one can understand the reluctance of the city fathers to leave these vulnerable innocents to the tender mercies of the unscrupulous. Here we see the constrained patriarchy in evidence. Fathers wanted no predatory males to benefit at the expense of their children. The heirs' wealth included real property such as houses, tenements, and taverns, as well as cash, silver and gold objects, clothing, and household goods. Since actual inventories do not survive for all inherited items, it is only possible to calculate when the cash value was recorded. Although the monetary value of an inheritance did not include items such as real estate, even the amounts given indicate that the wealth of London citizens, and thus of their orphans, was becoming increasingly concentrated as demographic catastrophes left a small number of survivors and as citizens intermarried. The average cash value recorded in the Mayor's court for orphans' inheritance before 1348 was only £80, but it rose steadily in the period following the onset of plague, to reach a high of £901 by the years of 1429–48.[53] The change may be partly due to greater care in recording orphans' property during the later part of the fourteenth century.[54] The increased wealth was probably also the result of the high mortality from the plague, which in London amounted to a loss of about half of the population in 1349.[55] Those who survived became heirs to greater concentrations of wealth, because the law required that the survivors receive the portion of any coheirs who died.

With so much wealth at stake, the city had reason to be concerned about abuse of wardship. Compliance with the law seemed to be generally good, since only 5 percent of the cases showed abuses of the privileges.[56] The most obvious abuse involved retaining the inheritance after the orphan came of age or married or of using it to make bad investments and then being unable to pay. A friend of the family, a city official, and sometimes the orphans themselves brought suit. Richard Odyham, the chamberlain, brought a complaint regarding the two daughters of John de Heylesdon, a mercer. He forced the guardians to pay the £400 owed to them.[57] When the original guardian could not pay, the sureties paid. John le Long's daughters complained through their mother's brother that their guardian had wasted their inheritance. The guardian fled because he could not afford to pay the £22 12s. 3d. he owed the girls. His two sureties paid, and the uncle was made guardian.[58]

Although both boys and girls were abducted along with their property, girls were more frequently mentioned. The object was to gain possession of the girls' inheritance rather than sexual assault. A man and his wife were charged with entering the house of John de Bergholte, a carpenter, and carrying off his ward, Agnes, daughter of the late Stephen atte Holte. In addition, they took silver vessels, jewels, wool, and linen valued at £10 that belonged to John. While John won his suit against the couple, Agnes was taken out of his wardship.[59] An eight-year-old ward, Alice, daughter of John le Leche, was left in the charge of her mother by her father's will. But this was 1349, the height of the Black Death, and her mother died soon afterward. One of the executors abducted her and stole her property.

The parishioners reported the missing girl to the mayor and alderman. A jury recommended that the abductor's property be taken into the hands of the city to make up the sum owed her.[60]

At least one attempted abduction of a ward became violent. Emma, daughter of the late Robert Pourte, became a ward of Gilbert de Mordone and his wife, Mabel. On March 25, 1325, Walter de Benygtone and seventeen companions came to Gilbert's brewhouse with stones in their hoods, swords, knives, and other weapons. They sat there and drank four gallons of beer, waiting for a chance to carry off Emma. Mabel, perceiving their intentions, took Emma upstairs to her chamber. Walter de Benygtone became violent, and a brawl began that spilled out into the High Street. The neighbors quickly came to Gilbert's rescue, and when they could not persuade Walter to drop his weapons, one of the neighbors hit him over the head with a staff.[61]

Marrying orphans without permission of the mayor and aldermen was another abuse of wardship. In addition to protecting the person and property of citizen's orphans, the court also made sure that the orphans suffered no loss of social status in marriage or apprenticeship; they did not want these children to be married below their social rank or put to apprenticeship in a baser trade than the father. The mayor had to approve of a prospective husband or wife and an apprenticeship contract. As in the selection of guardians, a rather negative view of human nature prompted the laws, because people would pay a bounty to a guardian to marry a well-endowed orphan. The guardian could take advantage of the orphan, marrying him or her below the correct social rank. A typical contract concerned Alice, daughter of William de Thele, whose guardianship was granted to John de Gildford, provided he would "maintain, treat and instruct Alice as he ought, and would not let her suffer disparagement [loss of social status] nor marry without the consent of the Mayor and Aldermen and her parents [or friends]."[62]

Examples show that the laws were needed. Often it was a stepfather who arranged a marriage without permission. Alice, daughter of John atte March, was an orphan twice over. Her mother had remarried and then had died. Her stepfather continued to hold her mother's inherited property, thus that of Alice, through curtesy of England (the right of the husband to hold his wife's inherited property for his lifetime.) In violation of the city laws, he married Alice to Thomas de Staunesby, a tailor. Alice's property was removed from his care, and he was sent to prison for not bringing the child into court. He was found to be in arrears of £4 and had to post a bond for £8.[63] Agnes, widow of John Laurence, and her new husband,

Simon de Burgh, were appointed guardians of Agnes, who was eight months old. The couple contrived to marry Agnes, who had inherited property worth 40 marks, to Thomas, son of Simon, who was eleven years old. The banns had already been read and the wedding garments purchased when responsible parties intervened and Agnes was removed from her mother's custody.[64]

Mothers with bastard children perhaps had more difficulty defending their daughters. Alison, a six-year-old bastard of John Rayner, was bequeathed 110 marks, mazers, two pieces of silver with cover, one "note" with foot and cover of silver gilt, and eighteen silver spoons. Her mother, for whom Rayner provided 40s. 4d., had been his servant, and he had no other progeny. He specified that his daughter should have an apprenticeship before marrying. But a fishmonger, John Bryan, begged the mayor to allow him to become the guardian of Alison and her funds. Later, her mother claimed in the Mayor's court that Bryan simply wanted the estate of the girl and had married her to one of his apprentices in order to get her inheritance to pay off his own debts.[65]

Because of high mortality, many London children grew up in families with a stepparent or even stepsiblings. The prevalence of such arrangements is probably not much different from today, though divorce rather than death account for most stepfamilies. Court records deal mostly with inheritances rather than the emotional relationship in families. Stepmothers were less likely to appear in the records as abusers of children's property and marriage rights, largely because they had few controls over the inheritance. Once in a while, however, strife appears. John Hammes petitioned against his father's widow, saying that she had arranged a forgery to try to convert the properties that he inherited from his father into an inheritance for herself and had attempted to force him to sign the forgery.[66] But stepchildren could cause problems as well. One woman complained that her stepson tried to prohibit her from trading in London, although she had enough merchandise in the city before she married to cover her trade and had made a covenant with her new husband about this merchandise.[67]

Stepfamily relations were complex. John le Seur wanted to leave all his tenements and rents in London to the children begot by both his first and second wife. While an equal division among the children of the two families was not allowed, he was permitted to sell part of the property and give the proceeds to his second wife and her children. The son of the first marriage contested this settlement, but the court upheld the father's will.[68]

Many cases indicate that stepfamily arrangements went smoothly. Richard Widihale left the guardianship of his son Thomas together with his inheritance to his second wife, Elizabeth. Four years later she delivered the inheritance.[69] John de Yieveneye and his wife, Theophania, widow of William de Medelane, were summoned to answer questions about properties left to Thomas and Juliana, son and daughter of William de Medelane. They explained that William provided for the children during their lifetime and that Thomas was paying the said William and Theophania an annuity of £10. The will was searched, and John and Theophania deposited two deeds with the mayor for safekeeping until the children came of age.[70]

Equal Treatment for Girls and Boys?

London laws and the administration of them indicate that girls and boys should have received equal treatment. But did they? At the time that children entered wardship, 780 (45 percent) of the orphans were female, and 951 (55 percent) were males. The disparity of the number of males and females varied greatly over the two centuries. From 1309 to 1348, or just before the outbreak of the plague, there were 14 percent fewer females than males in the wardship cases. During the years of the worst plague visitations, from 1349 to 1398, the disparity was only 8 percent. But from 1399 to 1448 it reached 22 percent, dropping to only 2 percent between 1449 and 1497.[71] A shortfall of 10 percent or more is a significant deficiency of young female population and needs careful consideration. The disparity in late medieval London was similar to that in fifteenth-century Florence.[72] Family size, equality of inheritance in law and actual practice, attitudes toward females and their early rearing, and early marriage could all be factors.

Medieval learned opinion emphasized female inferiority. The misogyny of this literature would suggest the neglect of female babies and, perhaps worse, their murder. The moral tracts on "the ages of man" gave women a limited personality, equating them with children.[73] Women, unlike men, remained underdeveloped and did not progress to maturity in reasoning power or bodily perfection.[74] Medical literature likewise portrayed women as incomplete humans.[75] Sermons, homilies, and vernacular literature spread these sentiments among the population at large. Women were aware of these attitudes and taught the same lessons to their daughters.

It is possible that these negative attitudes toward women influenced girls' survival in London, even if the law held that the all children inherited equally. But did girls and boys really receive equal portions of the estate? The question is difficult to answer, since the value of inheritances is hard to assess. The court of orphans usually did divide the estate equally, but occasionally an imbalance in the treatment of girls appeared. The mayor, for instance, arranged that the two sons of Thomas Hawkyn would receive £500 each when they came of age, but the two daughters were to receive only £200 each.[76]

Another source of information about the division of inheritance comes from wills. Wills were a legal instrument for overriding borough law, so they are a window onto actual practice. Those men and a few women who recorded their wills in the Archdeaconry Court divided their estates equally among their children. The testators in this court were mostly artisans and poorer people. For instance, a poulter who died in 1394 had two sons and a daughter and was able to leave them £20 each.[77] A brewer likewise left his two sons and one daughter 30s. each, and a baker whose son was a monk bequeathed him 100s. and the same amount to his daughter.[78]

London men who had real estate to dispose of recorded their wills in the Husting court of wills and deeds so that the city had a record of the transmission of property. These wills are less clear about equal division between sons and daughters because they do not necessarily include movable goods. Testators left real estate to 60 percent of their sons, compared to 44 percent of their daughters.[79] Women without brothers or with brothers who died before they came of age received all the real estate and chattels if any were mentioned. Changes in the custom of giving dower and dowry could influence the decision to give real estate or movables. Fifty-six percent of the offspring mentioned in wills were male, and 44 percent were female. Since the children could be mature at the time of the testator died, many of the daughters might have already received a dowry.

The will of William de Thame in 1357 shows the difficulty of evaluating the Husting court wills. After his debts were paid, his movable goods were to be divided into three parts, one of which would go to his wife, Christina, as dower, one to his children, and one to the church of St. Michael Queenhithe. He had three sons and two daughters surviving him, for whom he provided real estate as well. His wife got the capital tenement and shops for life, and her portion would go to John junior, his second son, after her death. John Senior, the oldest son, was to have other shops; William was to have rents and shops; and Agnes and Alice received a tenement, a shop, and granary. Since none of these properties had monetary values assigned to them, it is impossible to know if the inheritances were equal.[80]

The age of orphans appearing in the Mayor's court and the percentage of males and females in their families show when the shortfall of females occurred. While ages were not a routine part of the record, more than two hundred individuals can be identified and permit the conclusion that the children were mostly young, eight years old or younger. Between 1300 and 1349, 20 percent of the wards were under three years old, 15 percent were four to six years old, and 25 percent were seven to nine years old. In other words, these were young children. From 1350 to 1389, a period of prevalent plague, a similar pattern prevailed, with fewer infants and toddlers (6 percent) but more in the seven to nine age category (31 percent).[81] Of the orphans whose age was recorded, 63 percent were boys, and 26 percent were girls. The age of male children was, perhaps, more important than that of females, since boys were more likely to have to qualify for inheritance or apprenticeship by age. Apprenticeship for boys began at fourteen or older, and inheritance was at twenty-one or above.[82] Girls could be married at sixteen years of age and could inherit on marriage, but a strict record was less necessary. Perhaps girls' ages were kept vague in order to arrange early marriages or so that, should the information be necessary, officials and family could refer to witnesses at the baptism ceremonies. The meager attention to girls' age could also indicate less concern for them.

Family size and composition at the time the children were orphaned gives further insight into the imbalance of the sexes, indicating that the shortfall of girls appeared early in family formation. Seventy percent of the families had only one child.[83] In 61 percent of these families, only a boy is mentioned, while 39 percent mention one girl. Families with two children of the same sex showed a similar percentage of boys and girls, but when the family size grew to three to five same-sex children, females predominated.[84] The statistics indicate a balance in favor of male children in small families of one or two children.

Families with both boys and girls were only 30 percent of the total. In families with three children, those with one female and two males predominated. Only 19 percent of the families had four children. In these families, two male and two female children were most common. Larger families, some with eight and nine children, did not exhibit a sex difference. Most of the larger families were recorded for the late fifteenth century.[85]

The predominance of male children, particularly in families with one to three children, raises questions about the overall ratio of males to females appearing in the court of orphans. The most obvious explanation of the shortfall of female children is that the recording process simply neglected to mention girls as frequently as boys or that the girls were not present in the courtroom. But the court cases indicate that all children were present.

Urban centers in preindustrial Europe routinely had infant and child mortality rates ranging from 30 to 50 percent. In the court of orphans,

31 percent of the children died before reaching the age of majority. Mortality of the orphans accelerated following the Black Death and continued to rise in the fifteenth century.[86] Other children, of course, could have died before they became wards. Childhood mortality might have been greater in the general population. We know that the orphans were, on the whole, well off and well fed. We can assume that the children of prostitutes, laborers, hucksters, servants, beggars, and other lower-class individuals had higher mortality rates.

Of the children dying during wardship, 56 percent were males, and 44 percent were females. The figure is very close to the sex ratio of orphans appearing in the orphans' court, indicating that males and females were dying in proportion to the known number recorded. In other words, there is no evidence that the female orphans were more fragile than the males after they were recorded. Furthermore, in families with more than one child, the survivors were more likely to be females than males.

A particularly full entry regarding the children of Richard Toky, a grocer, illustrates both the death and survival of his children. At the time of his death in 1391, he had lost his wife and a son. He left as orphans Richard, William, Eleanor, and Matilda. William lived three years after his father. Eleanor was only in wardship for fifty weeks when she married a merchant from Bristol, Philippot Vale. Richard inherited at full age in 1398. Matilda became a nun at Kilburn in 1393. Of a family of three boys and two girls, only the girls and one boy lived to maturity.[87]

When a population shows a shortfall of female children, female infanticide is immediately suspected. London and English records, however, do not indicate either abandonment or killing of bastards and other unwanted babies, male or female. A London coroner's inquest for 1315 records the death of a female baby, "a quarter of a year old," who was found in a ditch by the Tower. But there is only a vague description of a woman with a kerchief placing her there.[88] The London Commissary court record has scattered unproven charges of infanticide. Christina was charged with drowning her child in a gutter in a street, but the sex of the child was not mentioned. Cecilia Clyffon and two other women were charged with taking a boy child to the Thames.[89] The Church was particularly concerned about the possibility of parents suffocating an infant that slept in their bed by rolling over on him or her (overlaying), but it was a rare charge.[90] In one London case, a woman was accused of overlaying two infants in different neighborhoods.[91] Accidental deaths of infants and children, likewise, do not appear to mask infanticide.[92] Perhaps because the infant mortality rate was so high, surviving children were regarded as a blessing rather than a burden in medieval society.

Deformity or illness might be an excuse for abandonment or infanticide,[93] but a London case indicates that disabled orphans received the same protections under London law as other children. Isabella was a deaf mute who shared an inheritance of a messuage (dwelling place) and shops with her sister, Alice. Isabella was in the custody of Simon de Iswode, beadle of the ward of Fleetstreet. When Alice reached the age of majority, she claimed her part of the inheritance and wanted also to take care of her sister. But as heiress of her sister, she could not have her as a ward.[94]

Bastardy, like deformity, could have been another reason for infanticide. Mayor Richard Whittington set up a lying-in hospital so that women bearing children out of wedlock could avoid shame and could eventually marry.[95] It is impossible to know the number of bastards born in London. Prostitutes, single women, and female servants were at risk of conceiving illegitimate children. Foreign merchants and those from outside London might have had second families in the city whom they visited regularly and for whom they provided. Even men in London could have two families, a legitimate one and an illegitimate one. Bastardy must have been common. A London church court, for instance, charged that Thomas Person impregnated a woman named Peryn. The woman stayed at a house in Holborn until the child was born. Three days after the birth and baptism the mother wandered away, and no one had seen her since.[96]

London laws regarding children tended to be protective rather than punitive. While bastards could not inherit the chief estate of the testator, the laws did not prohibit a father from making other bequests, such as the life use of real estate, rented or purchased property, or money and movable goods.[97] The status of bastard did not carry with it the slanderous meaning that it does today; indeed, it does not appear among the many terms of defamation that came before the London courts.[98] When it is mentioned, the term appears in connection with efforts to establish legitimacy in order to inherit property, rather than as slander.[99]

A number of such cases survive. When John de Gildesburgh, citizen, fishmonger, and bastard of London, died in the late fourteenth century, he made a bequest to his brother, Richard, and to Margaret, Isabel, and Juliana, his daughters by Isabel de Moleseye for life. All of these legatees were bastards themselves. After their deaths, the land reverted to the king.[100] Women with property fell under the same rules. Alice, daughter of Robert of Motoun, had a tenement with two cellars and three shops with solars (attic rooms) worth 100s. a year. The property went to Emma and her husband John Fraunceys, but at the Inquisition Post Mortem it transpired that Alice, Emma's mother, and John Vykery, her father, had been living together two years out of wed-lock when Emma was born. While they subsequently married, Emma was considered a bastard.[101] In one case, a man who had been mayor of London several times and was regarded as legitimate had the issue of his bastardy raised when his will was probated.[102]

Some bastard children had productive roles in the family strategy. A tanner with only daughters left his business to his illegitimate son. Tanning was not a trade that a woman could easily carry on by herself.[103] The Frowyk family supported two illegitimate sons, one of whom became a mercer (trader in textiles).[104] Thomas Albon, a woolmonger, had two bastard children, John and Elizabeth, as well as legitimate children. When John died, Elizabeth inherited his portion as well, and she made a very good marriage to Thomas Christofre, valet to the king.[105]

Bastard children of citizens, daughters as well as sons, received the same protections of their persons and property as did legitimate orphans. In 1370 the guardianship and inheritance of Thomas and William, sons of Christina, daughter of John Ippegravy, and mistress of the deceased Thomas Wirlyngworth, goldsmith, were committed to Christina and her new hus-band. In another case in 1372, the widow of Adam de Carille, a draper, was given wardship of his legitimate son and daughter as well as a bastard son.[106] Johanna, bastard daughter of John de Ashford and Johanna de Stodleye, came and claimed the inheritance of money her father had bequeathed to her. Her mother and another man had charge of the money and delivered it to her on her marriage.[107]

Even if the stigma of bastardy was not strong, the child's chance of survival depended on the social status of the mother and the willingness of the father to recognize and support the child. Our records do not per-mit an assessment of the deaths of illegitimate children of poor women, but the Commissary court indicates that unmarried women had surviving children, as did Margaret Clerk, who was said to have four boys by Frank Cornmonger.[108]

Perhaps the small number of female orphans came from more benign causes than infanticide. Simply a difference in the amount of care and atten-tion given to a sick male child, as opposed to a female one, could increase survival. The Florentine evidence shows that male children were nursed longer than female children and therefore probably did not suffer as many infectious diseases.[109] If the mother or nurse sat up with the sick male child, cooled his fevered head, and administered herbal drinks but did not do so for females, the male was more likely to survive. Miracle stories that were collected for the canonization of saints show that 78 percent of the miracles were performed for newborn males and only 22 percent for girls. Parents were more likely to seek the intercession of a saint in the case of male as opposed to female infants and were also more likely to make the pilgrimage to the shrine and have the miraculous cure recorded.[110] Modern studies of excessive female mortality have found that the attrition of females was not due to infanticide in medieval and early modern Europe.[111]

Court evidence indicates a general nurturing attitude toward London children. Since parents lived and worked in their shop, children had considerable surveillance. London streets were full of people who lived in the quarter or worked there. They had intimate knowledge of each other and seemed to be particularly concerned for the welfare of children. One of the most instructive cases is that of John de Harwe, a porter, who intervened when an unknown woman with a child in her arms were almost run down. The witnesses told the coroner that, after the hour of vespers, an esquire of the Earl of Arundel and another man were riding recklessly toward the Tower. They almost knocked down the woman and child. The porter, a burly man, used to carrying heavy loads, took hold of the esquire's bridle and "begged him to ride more carefully." The esquire drew his sword and inflicted a mortal wound on the good Samaritan, John de Harwe.[112]

Because of the dirt and danger in the streets, very young children were carried when they were outside, thereby lowering their risk of accidents.[113] One apprentice complained that he had not received any training in his craft because his master had forced him to carry his child in the streets for four years.[114] At least one of the miracles of Henry VI recorded that a boy nine months old was being carried in the arms of a "somewhat older boy." The child was playing with a circular, silver pilgrimage badge with an engraved image of St. Thomas of Canterbury. He put it into his mouth and choked on it, but Henry saved him.[115]

Nonetheless, children had accidents in streets and at home. Unlike those cured by saintly intervention, some of these children died. Three-year-old Petronilla, daughter of William de Wyntonia, was playing in the street when a strong and spirited horse got out of its groom's control and hit her on the right side with its hoof.[116] Boys tended to be further from home than girls and engaged in games, selling things, and going to school.[117] Girls were more likely to be home, as was the eleven-year-old Juliana, daughter of John Turgeys, who was so desirous of seeing what was going on in the High Street that she stood in an open window in a solar and fell out trying to get a better view.[118] A one-month-old girl died when her mother left her in her cradle, no doubt swaddled, when a sow wandered in off the street and "mortally bit the right side" of her head. The mother was able to keep her alive until midnight.[119]

Actual damage from corporal punishment of children appears in complaints by apprentices and their friends but is negligible in criminal records. The city and its citizens had a great sensitivity about protecting children from abusive behavior. They did not always succeed, of course, but it is difficult to know about cases that did not come to court. On March 21, 1373, Alice de Salesbury, a beggar, was placed on the pillory for an hour because on the Sunday before she had abducted Margaret, the daughter of John Oxwyke, a grocer, and stripped her of her clothes so that her family would not recognize her. She used little Margaret for begging, no doubt making the plea that she had to support the poor naked girl.[120]

While both learned and folk culture espoused a negative attitude toward females, London law tried to treat the daughters and sons of their citizens equally in terms of inheritance and legal protections. The city officials and men making wills wanted to give legal protections to their children and to limit the damage that other males could do to their children and fortunes. They practiced a self-limiting patriarchy. Although differences in distribution of real property and amount of inheritance—and perhaps the overall survival of female children—are discernable, the laws seem to have been enforced. The shortfall of 10 percent of girls in the court of orphans might have been the result of differential nurturing of male and female children. On the whole, however, sisters outlived their brothers. Since London law required that the surviving sibling inherit the portions of the other children, females could have considerable inheritances. As plague and other diseases decimated the city's population in the last half of the fourteenth century and the fifteenth century, the value of inheritances increased substantially. London's culture toward its women and children protected their inheritance rights and dowers and the right of the mother to rear her children. Because girls and women accumulated wealth, it made them very desirable in the marriage market. But did the prospect of marriage for women preclude education and apprenticeship of girls?

Education and Apprenticeship

Evidence from wills and from the court of orphans suggests that young women needed a dowry, since marriage was the most likely rite of passage from child-hood to adulthood. Advice literature presumed that women would marry. The author of one rare Middle English text drew a parallel between the seasons and the phases of a woman's life. Spring was "like a young girl adorned and resplendent before the onlookers"; in summer "the earth becomes like a bride laden with riches and having many lovers"; autumn was likened to "a mature matron who has passed the years of her youth"; and winter is "like a decrepit old woman to whom death draws near."[1] The advice poem directed to young women, "How the Good Wife Taught Her Daughter," emphasized the care that a nubile young female should take in preserving her virtue and preparing for marriage.[2] Young girls in London imbibed the same advice from mothers, fathers, priests, and nurses. Was there another track for these young women that included education and apprenticeship in London? A large city, if any place, might have provided an alternative. If the divide between rearing male and female children began to emerge in childhood, did the distinction become more obvious when children reached an age to be educated and apprenticed to learn a trade? The tasks that girls and young women performed, the schooling they received, their apprenticeships, and their sexual vulnerabilities could have differed substantially from those of males as they reached puberty. Puberty, whether defined culturally or biologically, provided cultural constraints that shaped girls' lives, compared to those of boys, as they prepared to enter the broader economy.

Education and Apprenticeship

The distinction between girls and boys became prominent in education and apprenticeship.[3] For boys, the advice manuals had injunctions on how to behave in school, with satiric poems about what happened to boys who misbehaved.[4] No such literature exists for girls, and, indeed, it is difficult to find information on their schooling. The apprenticeship for boys and girls also differed with regard to the ages of entry, prior preparation required, and the length of the apprenticeship.[5]

A statute passed in 1406 tried to limit the entrance into apprenticeship to those boys and girls whose parents had landed wealth, but the House of Commons added a clause assuring the right "of every man or woman, of what ever estate or condition they be, to set their son or daughter to take learning at any manner of school that pleaseth them."[6] The inclusion of education is curious and leads one to assume that education, even for girls, was becoming more common. One historian of London has argued that the statute should be read as an indication that girls were being educated and had complete access to apprenticeships.[7]

We have no evidence of girls attending grammar school, song schools, and other such establishments for the education of boys.[8] But it is entirely possible that some women as well as men ran schools for teaching reading and writing in English and doing sums, which would later be known as "dame" schools. For example, William Cresewyk, a grocer, left 20 s. to a "scholemaysteresse" in 1406. The fraternity of St. Nicholas recorded the name of Agnes, *doctrix puellarum*, among its members.[9] Again, the orphan's court is a good source. While most of the provisions for education were for boys, Alice Reigner, an illegitimate daughter of a corn dealer, was to have 1 mark a year toward her education. William Rouse, a mercer, left nine children when he died in 1486. Each of his children, four boys and five girls, were entrusted to William Mylburne, a painter, "to find them to school honestly for four years next after my decease."[10] A chandler's daughter attended school from age eight to thirteen at a cost of 25 s. for fees. Other evidence indicates an education of four or five years for girls.[11] Only two of the orphan girls entered nunneries, but they would certainly have had an education.[12]

While guilds in the fifteenth century required male apprentices to be able to read and write, no evidence suggests that girls needed these skills.[13] Some trades, however, were based on literacy. Alice and Matilda, orphaned daughters of John Shaw, a vintner, were apprenticed in 1420 to Master Peter Churche, a notary public. Presumably they had some writing skills before they were apprenticed.[14] Women had other needs for reading and writing skills. Some women carried on their own business; others took over their husbands' businesses when they were abroad or died, or needed to read communications sent about business. Women appeared frequently in court and seemed to have a very good knowledge of the law and various writs they would need to pursue their claims. But literacy cannot be narrowly defined. The writs would have been in Latin, which the women probably did not read, but they, like men, recognized the form that such a writ would take. In what was still largely an oral society, "recognition" literacy, that is, having a visual knowledge of the form, could be very useful. So, too, could the aid of someone who could read and write, such as a chaplain or a scrivener. Once something was read, someone accustomed to oral culture would hold it in her memory rather than rely on the crutch of a written record.[15] Some women certainly read for pleasure and edification and left books in their wills or inherited books.[16]

The parliamentary statute of 1406 also stipulated that no one should put his son or daughter to apprenticeship unless he had lands or rent to the value of 20 s.[17] The city found the 1406 statute too limiting in its property restrictions, and in a decisive case, a master won the right to keep his apprentice. He argued that, while the parents of the apprentice did not have land valued at 20 s., "nothing [was said in the statute] touching a son or daughter putting himself or herself as apprentice as they may please." The city petitioned the king to allow this loophole in the law, and the king granted their petition. Again, the language suggests equality: "every free person [*persone*] of the City may put his son or daughter as apprentice with any free man [*homme*] of the same; also that every free man of the city may take as apprentice the son or daughter of any such person."[18] City ordinances in 1432 directed that "all fines and fees for incoming and outgoing of apprentices, male and female," continue to be levied, suggesting that apprenticeships were available to both.[19]

The ordinances and statutes make it appear that male and female young people had equal access to apprenticeship, but record evidence reveals a paucity of females in apprenticeships.[20] Only about forty cases surviving in various London court rolls relate to female apprentices, a very low figure compared to over two hundred dealing with males. Most of the cases involving females are from the 1420s. Even if the court cases represent apprenticeships that have gone to litigation, we cannot assume that the overall numbers were the same but that females experienced fewer contract violations. The city required all men and women taking apprentices in the city to enroll them and the terms of their contracts with the mayor within the first year of their term or pay a fine. One reason was that at the completion of the term, an apprentice could become a citizen and trade freely in the city. Apparently, noncompliance was common, and the city periodically reissued this ordinance and had it proclaimed in the city, and many suits appear for neglect of this important procedure.[21] The enrollment of apprenticeship records do not survive. But the one extent medieval register of freemen (1309–12) lists 253 persons who became citizens by completing apprenticeships; not one of these was female.[22]

Official recognition of apprenticeship contracts, however, must have been as important for young women as men.[23] Families brought suits for nonenrollment.[24] Agnes Brown, daughter of Isabel Brown, a chandler, sued John Broke, a hat maker, complaining that she had apprenticed her daughter for nine years to him with the agreement that he was to meet all terms of the indenture, including feeding, clothing, and housing her, but he did not enroll her, to her damage of 20 marks.[25] At least one case mentions that the records were searched for an enrollment and, since the girl's apprenticeship was not found, the girl was exonerated from it. In another case, the indenture was "duly enrolled at Guildhall."[26] But London women, like continental women, gained their freedom of the city through being born there or marrying a citizen, rather than through apprenticeship.[27]

Since very few actual apprentice contracts are extant for medieval England, we can form no firm conclusion about differences for young men and women. Four contracts for women show that one was apprenticed to a tent maker and the other three were training as silkwomen. Two of these young women made their own contracts, and the other two were bound by their brother or father.[28]

A comparison of one London contract, that of Margaret, daughter of Richard Bissop of Sleaford in Sussex, to John Prechet, citizen of London and teldemakere (tent maker) and his wife, Burge, with the six male contracts preserved in the Westminister Abbey Muniment Room indicates that a general formula was used and special terms added at the end.[29] All of the young people agreed not to fornicate, get married, or frequent taverns. They swore to serve their masters diligently and not absent themselves. In addition, the contracts bound the master to teach his craft honestly and to provide room, board, bedding, and often some annual payment. Margaret's contract indicated that Burge was to teach her the secrets of her trade and pay her 12 d. a year. John and Burge were to find Margaret all necessaries in food and drink. Margaret made her own contract and apparently affixed her own seal. In addition to the usual provisions, she agreed to be "honest, competent, obedient and not to absent herself nor to frequent taverns." To secure the agreement Margaret put her heirs and executors and all of her goods as security that she would abide by the agreement for the seven years of her apprenticeship.[30]

Margaret's contract was similar to that of Francis Iwerst of Cirencester, save that he was to apprentice for ten years, while she would serve seven.[31] Robert Iden, an apprentice to a tailor, was to get 6 s. 2 d. for his labor after two years, and the amount spent on his food, drink, lodging went up steadily from 8 d. for the first year to 10 s. for the last year.[32] All contracts required some security to keep the agreement, either in the form of Margaret's pledge or in terms of a monetary payment, part of which would be returned at the end of the apprenticeship.

The infrequent references to female apprentices in the records probably arose from the lower expectations for a young woman's work career.[33] Since there were no female guilds in London, women tended to enter into male-dominated guilds, not through an apprenticeship system but as wives or widows of guild members. Silk makers, the predominately female craftspersons, did not have a guild, as they did in Paris. Brewing was another occupation in which many women participated, but although the brewers had a guild, they seem not to have had a regular apprentice system until the sixteenth century.[34] Perhaps women learned a craft in order to practice as *femme sole* (the term used for women in London who could run their own businesses even if married) or in order to have a skill, such as silk making, that would be a useful supplement to a household and further inducement to making an advantageous marriage.[35] A mercer or tailor with a wife who had skills as a silk maker, embroiderer, or dressmaker was in an advantageous position to offer extra services to customers. It is probable that unmarried daughters of guildsmen learned their craft at home without being apprenticed.[36] Servants may also have learned crafts in the home of employers.[37]

London borough custom made it clear that women could take apprentices, but the strong presence of male control appears in the custom.

> And married women who practice certain crafts in the city alone
> and without their husbands, may take girls as their apprentices
> to serve them and learn their trade. And these apprentices shall
> be bound by their indentures of apprenticeship to both husband
> and wife, to learn the wife's trade.[38]

While allowing for the *femme sole*, the rule seems to assume that all such women would be married and that an obligation to take on an apprentice was the primary legal responsibility of the husband.[39] Perhaps the tent maker to whom Margaret, daughter of Richard Bissop, was apprenticed would learn Burge Prechet's trade.

Court cases indicate that, as a rule, girls were apprenticed to married couples. Margaret Hardelowe, daughter of William Hardelowe, tailor, was apprenticed to John Baron, tailor, and his wife, Anneys, an embroiderer, to learn the trade of Anneys. Joan Bosoun was apprenticed to Richard Spenser and his wife, Anne, who was a silkmaker.[40] Only one of the girls was apprenticed to a widow: Agnes Chapman of Coventry was apprenticed to Johanne Davy, a widow and citizen. But even Johanne might not have been a widow when Agnes enrolled. Agnes Snell, daughter of John Snell of Hove in Kent, was apprenticed to Anneys Haunsarde, who became a widow after the apprenticeship began.[41] In addition to various aspects of silk making, thread making and embroidery, girls learned to become dressmakers and tailors, purse makers, card makers, weavers and scriveners.

Girls entered into apprenticeship by the same route as did boys. The arrangement was an intimate one, in that the master and mistress became *in loco parentis* for the apprentice. Apprentices in fourteenth- and fifteenth-century London came from a similar social background to that of their masters and mistresses. They lived closely together in the shop and house, which meant that the relationship could be either close or extremely unpleasant. Because of the importance of the bond between the master/mistress and apprentice, family and friends often made the inquiries and arranged the contract. The prospective mentors likewise wanted to be assured that the new person in their household was honest and capable of learning the trade.

Parents usually arranged apprenticeships for their sons and daughters. John Jurden arranged for his daughter, Joan, to be placed with a woman who was a purser, and John Sewyn had placed his daughter, Isabel, with an embroiderer. Mothers also made arrangements for their daughters.[42] Girls in guardianship might be apprenticed by their guardians, as was Matilda, daughter of Bartholomew of Astwode.[43] Other times it was a friend who helped to make the arrangements. Ellen Semy, daughter of John Semy, was apprenticed to learn coarse weaving by Elizabeth Thorne of Elstowe, a nun. Apparently the man and his wife to whom she apprenticed Ellen were kin, because his name was Thomas Thorne.[44] The father of one of the apprentices complained that a woman apprenticed his daughter without his knowledge and consent to a wiredrawer in the city for a term of fourteen years. The case involved a number of other irregularities that will be considered separately, but it does show that sometimes the parents were not vigilant enough.[45] Margaret, daughter of Richard Bissop, however, made her own arrangements.

The master and mistress had to be free of the city, that is, they had to be recognized as citizens. In one case, Thomas Glanton and his wife, Alice, pretended to be free of the city and had taken Alice Saumple and Agnes Saumple, daughters of two men (perhaps brothers) from Northumberland, as apprentices to teach them to be embroiderers. But the couple were not citizens, and the two girls were "fraudulently and deceptively taken as apprentices." They had made proper indentures, but they were exonerated from them because they could never become free of the city since their master and mistress were not.[46] A special inquisition showed that Margery Broham, embroiderer, "had retained a certain woman to dwell with her for a term of years as an apprentice," but Margery herself was not free of the city at that time and could not take an apprentice.[47]

Although the information is scant, a picture does emerge from the cases. The majority of apprentices came from London itself (nineteen), with one each from places like Hackney, Coventry, Reading, Northumberland, Warwickshire, Bristol, Norfolk, Northampton, and Kent. The length of their contracts varied considerably. A city ordinance of the early fourteenth century set the term of apprenticeship at seven years.[48] For male apprentices, the service time became longer.[49] Only sixteen cases involving women mention years of contract, which varied from four to fifteen, with seven being the most usual.[50] The city upheld the rule of at least seven years in a contested case involving the daughter of John Catour of Reading who had apprenticed his daughter to Elis Mympe, an embroider, for five years. Catour argued that Mympe had failed to provide his daughter, Alice, with food and had ill-treated her and beaten her. The parties agreed that the defendant would pay the complainant 13 s. 4 d. for her release from the apprenticeship. But the mayor and aldermen then intervened and asked why Elis Mymphe had only made indentures for five years, when the city stipulated seven, and why, furthermore, he had not enrolled the indenture. Elis had no defense, and the indentures were canceled.[51]

The city set the age of entry into apprenticeship at fourteen, but for boys it crept up to sixteen to eighteen in the fifteenth century. Possibly girls entered apprenticeship earlier, but the standard of fourteen was used for them as well. Two girls were said to be eleven, two were twelve, and one was fourteen. But Reginald Lightfot complained that his daughter, Katherine, had been apprenticed against her will and his to Thomas Blounvyle and his wife and that the girl was, in any case, under age. The mayor asked the court to find proof that she was under fourteen. They considered the evidence and concluded that she was under age fourteen and too young for apprenticeship.[52]

Apprenticeship fees for men became increasingly higher and more regulated by guilds in the fifteenth century, but female apprenticeships seem not to have been as well regulated. Apprenticeships for female orphans show varying amounts of payment. One girl had 40s. of her inheritance reserved for apprenticeship, but the maximum was a premium of £5.[53] We have scant information, but given the other evidence, it would seem that the fees for female apprentices were lower than for males.

The most common complaint of abuse of the female apprentice contracts was a failure to enroll the contract. These cases always end with the apprentices being excused without a fee from their contracts. Perhaps a certain informality crept into the arrangement so that the parents and master/mistress understood that the contract could be terminated should some other prospect, such as marriage, present itself. The apprentice would have learned perhaps enough of the craft, and the master and mistress would have had good work from their apprentice for a shorter period of time but also for less expense.

Some girls, however, complained of physical abuse. Joan, daughter of John Jurdan, went to the mayor claiming not to have been enrolled and that her master and mistress "unduly castigated and governed" her. Another girl brought suit to the mayor and, as a result, her master and mistress were to instruct her and "would find her food and drink, and would not beat her with a stick or a knife."[54] Medieval custom permitted physical punishment to train and educate a child, student, servant, apprentice, and even wife, but the custom also forbade excessive punishment.[55]

Complaints of sexual abuse were unusual among female apprentices compared to servants. Apprentices were closer in social class to their masters and mistresses and were protected by their contracts and maintained contact with kin. But "Alsoun Bostone [was] condemned to stand in the pillory three market days for an hour each day, being brought thither from prison with 'pypys' or other 'opyn minstralsy,' for having let to hire for immoral purposes her innocent young apprentice."[56]

The experience of Agnes, daughter of William Tikhyll, exemplifies the rather extreme problems that could arise in apprenticeship arrangements. First, the father complained to the mayor that a woman who was not free of the city enrolled Agnes against her will and his. William Celler, a wiredrawer, to whom she was apprenticed for fourteen years, left town and dismissed her before she had sufficient knowledge of the trade. She was in the custody of Joan, wife of William Celler, and the mayor set a date for her appearance. Joan appeared, as did Agnes, and they were separately examined. Joan admitted that a noncitizen, Thomasine March, had arranged the apprenticeship and that Agnes was underage and had not been enrolled. Joan was supposed to teach Agnes to make cards for carding wool and cloth. Agnes said that she had sealed the indentures "under threats of beating" and that she would rather go back to her father. Her indentures were canceled.[57]

Other problems arose when the status of the mistress changed. Agnes Wawton, daughter of Thomas Wawton, esquire, complained to the mayor that Alice Virly, her mistress, had withdrawn from the city and had not assigned her to anyone else.[58]

Not all of the blame rested on the side of the master and mistress. Elizabeth Peyton, who was late apprentice to John Westancotes, confessed that the bill of complaint she had brought against him was false. "On her bended knees and with raised hands she humbly begged pardon of the said John for her offences wickedly perpetrated against him." The offenses were not specified. He pardoned her.[59]

Despite the apparently equal treatment of girls that appears in the word-ing of statute, ordinances, and apprentice contracts, the impression one has from the court cases is that apprenticeship held a lower status for females than it did for males. The evidence suggests that apprenticeships for girls did not imply an independent career in the craft and that enrollment was lax. When the girls were not enrolled or were abused, the contract was usually voided, whereas boys were usually given to another master to complete their terms or were properly enrolled. It is probable that girls pursued an apprenticeship in order to have a supplemental income to take into a marriage or to make themselves more attractive on the marriage market because they had a skill to add to the household economy. Still, the evidence, scant though it is, shows that some women did achieve citizenship through completion of apprentice-ship and some did pursue trades as single women, wives, and widows. Perhaps completion of the full seven years was not necessary in order to learn enough of the craft to practice it at home. Agnes Coke made an agreement when she was bound to William Kaly and his wife, Joan, for seven years that if she wished to take a husband during her term, she might choose either to serve the rest of her term or pay the sum of 4 marks to be exonerated from her apprenticeship.[60]

Sexuality

If the presumption of parents and society as a whole was that young women would marry, then their sexuality became an issue. Even if young women did not marry or if they delayed their marriage, the neighbors, their employers, and the church took a great interest in controlling female sexuality. If we follow the prevailing literature and cultural expectations at the time, virginity would increase the chances of making a desirable marriage. According to the few court records we have, some parents and city officials regarded loss of virginity as a hindrance to marriage that required monetary compensation toward a dowry. But a girl's and a young woman's sexuality could also be exploited for economic benefits outside marriage. We have seen one mistress accused of prostituting her apprentice. Female servants were even more vulnerable to sexual exploita-tion. The records even indicate parental exploitation of their daughter's sexual-ity. Knowing the concern of London's government for female orphans and their stated intention to enforce statutes regarding apprentices, were they protective of young girls? Obviously, the importance of a father's social status, wealth, and access to courts influenced the protection a girl received.

Perhaps the first place to begin a discussion of sexuality and the need to protect girls is the cultural and legal assumptions about appropriate ages for sexual contact. For medieval Europe, the evidence for physical puberty is scant. The few cases available indicate a range of ages twelve to fifteen.[61] Canon law would permit girls to marry at twelve and boys at fourteen, which might have been close to the age of menarche for girls. The silence on menarche is not surprising. Menstruation made women "unclean" in the writing of theologians and among the general male population, so women chose not to call attention to the matter.[62] Medieval medical discussions put menstruation at fifteen.[63]

Legal responsibility began at the age of twelve for both boys and girls. Until they reached that age, they were regarded as not being mature enough to understand the difference between right and wrong in a felonious act. At twelve, a boy was required to become part of a frankpledge (a group of men sworn to keep the peace), but girls never reached this legal maturity and were the responsibility of their fathers or masters until they married, and then their husbands were legally responsible for their behavior. In the poll taxes of the late fourteenth century, fourteen or fifteen was the age at which boys and girls could be taxed. Inheritance in London, we have seen, was at twenty-one for males and single women, but could be at sixteen if a girl married.

The advice of the "Good Wife" to her daughter was to preserve virtue and virginity in order to enter into an appropriate marriage. The poem encouraged mothers to marry their daughters as early as possible. Daughters were told that they were to mold their lives in such a way that they could marry, particularly to avoid compromising their chances.[64] They were cautioned to walk without brandishing their heads or casting their shoulders about. They were not to speak to a young man on the street, "lest he by his villainy should tempt thy heart." Taverns and wrestling matches were dangerous places and could result in drunkenness and earn a woman the reputation of being a strumpet.[65]

If taverns and streets were pitfalls for young women's virtue, churches and priests could also be the snares of the devil. It was said of a curate, Sir Geoffrey, that

> After he had shryvyn yong women at Easter in the vestry and asayled them, then he wolde common with theme and kysse and put his handis under their clothis and commen with them to haue pointed with them, wher he and they might mete to do syne with theme and specially with Johanna the servant of Agnes Nele.[66]

In a popular Middle English verse, a young girl comments of her priestly lover, Sir John, that he is quite willing to pay for his pleasure and puts his offering in her "box."[67]

While cautionary tales about the risks of pregnancy and the problems of losing the prospect of a good marriage abound, few examples appear in records. The parents of Elizabeth Mappulton complained that a "Spanyard," Francis Derbyet, had come to their house for more than a year and "there craftily has moved and stirred their daughter to go with him." He has "persuaded her to be of vicious living of her body contrary to the laws of God and to the utter destruction of her body." He made her go with him to various parts of the city. She complained to her parents about it, but the only way they could control the situation was to keep her in the house. If they did that, they say in their petition to the lord chancellor, they could not get any benefit from her labor by sending her on errands. Derbyet threatened to have them imprisoned if they deprived him of their daughter.[68] Throughout their petition they refer to their daughter as a "maiden," so presumably they equated that status with being unmarried rather than with virginity. Sexual initiation did not change her status from adolescent to adult; only marriage could do that.

Some parents managed to get a settlement to compensate them and their daughter for her loss of virginity. Robert Trenender, a brazier, and his wife complained that Philip Rychard had deflowered their daughter. They took the matter to arbitration, and Philip bound himself by £100 to abide by the arbitration. He agreed that he would give their daughter, Agnes, a pipe and a half of woad (a blue dye for cloth) or £20 as compensation and agreed not to "vex" the family again. Agnes would have enough funds from the settlement to give her a good dowry toward a marriage.[69] Apparently, Rychard did not pay, and the parents petitioned the lord chancellor.

While the city tried to protect young urban girls from sexual exploitation, it was more difficult to control than marriages of orphan girls. Sexual abuse of boys never appeared in the records, perhaps because homosexuality was not a legal category in the Middle Ages and sodomy was in the purview of church courts. Even in these courts it seldom appeared.[70] Sexual abuse of young girls appears in a variety of city, royal, and ecclesiastical records. The city fathers did intervene in cases of sexual assault on young girls if they knew about them. In 1472 the mayor and aldermen concluded that John Jordan, who had been convicted of criminal assault (rape) of Margery Scoville, under fourteen years of age, should pay her £40, which was put into the hands of the chamberlain until she arrived at full age or married. John was put into prison, and when released, he was to leave the city within twenty days and pay a penalty of £200 or be returned to prison. He was deprived of his status as a citizen.[71] Another man who had criminally assaulted a girl younger than fourteen years old was to pay £40 to the chamberlain to keep it until she married or was of full age. He, too, was stripped of his citizenship and denied access to the city.[72]

Rape was a particularly difficult crime to define, but the laws, jurisprudential opinion, and the actual records make clear that the rape of virgins and young girls was particularly reprehensible compared to the rape of married women. In the case of rape, the girl or the woman had the right to appeal her case before the coroner and the justices. She had to show the coroner her torn clothing and blood indicating that she had resisted rape and had lost her virginity.[73] Rape was a hard case for a young girl to prosecute. She had to repeat the formula of the original appeal word for word as she made it initially to the coroner. The appeal was then made before a panel of justices, court officials, and male jurors. Failure to appear in court or any deviation from the original wording could end in a fine or imprisonment. By the fourteenth century, rape indictments could be brought by a jury rather than a personal appeal. Only a small number of cases ended in conviction, and these were of girls under fourteen and of virgins.[74]

Rape of young girls sometimes carried the implication that the parents were exploiting the allegation in order to extort money. In 1423 John Moleneux made a bond with Jerome Bragdini, a merchant of Venice, that neither his daughter, Agnes, nor he would bring further pleas against Bragdini on the pretext of "rape, trespass or injury done to her." Apparently, Moleneux owed Bragdini money and used the rape plea as a tool to avoid payment.[75] Sir Richard Roberd, a priest and bachelor of law, petitioned the lord chancellor that John Nele had brought a trespass charge against him for raping his daughter, aged five years, "too abhomynably to speak of" and had him put into prison. Nele wanted compensation for damages to his daughter.[76] Since this was a Chancery petition, we do not know the outcome, but it might be another case of pretense.

The alleged rape of eleven-year-old Joan, daughter of Eustace le Saddler by Reymond of Limoges, a wine merchant from Bordeaux, is the most graphically described in the court records, but again leaves the question of whether she was raped or was the victim of a father's exploitation for financial gain.[77] Three different versions of this rape survive—two by Joan and one by a court official, perhaps the coroner. The essential facts of the story are the same, it is in the details and dates that the accounts differ.

Joan was near her father's house at dusk when Reymond came and took her by the hand and led her to his rooms in a different parish and there forcibly raped her and inflicted wounds on her. In addition, Reymond of Limoges told the justices yet another story in which Joan's father and some of his friends had forced Joan to make the allegations in order to ruin Reymond's name. The stories differed in minor details, but the fact that Joan got the wrong date for the rape ultimately exculpated Reymond of Limoges.[78] Although Reymond pursued his case in court, it finally disappeared from the legal records. Joan may have been raped, but she did not win her case, and it could well be that her father made up the story for his own purposes.

Prostitutes, pimps, and keepers of bawdy houses were continually on the prowl for girls to sell to their customers.[79] Margaret Hathewyk was accused in 1439 of procuring a young girl named Isabel Lane for certain Lombards (general term for Italian traders) and other men unknown. Isabel was deflowered against her will in Margaret's house and prostituted elsewhere. Margaret also took her to the stews (bath houses or houses of prostitution) against her will on four occasions. In all cases, Margaret was the one receiving the profit.[80] Elizabeth Thebyn confessed that she was a prostitute and had lately taken to walking the streets of the city dressed in priest's clothing, "to the rebuke and reproach of the order of the priesthood." She and another woman procured a thirteen-year-old girl for a man who "committed the foul and detestable sin of lechery" with her. Another thirteen-year-old girl was put into prostitution by Elizabeth, the wife of John Knight. The court said that Elizabeth was bawd to a certain person who committed the "foul and detestable lechery in her house with a young girl... to the great displeasure of God and the perilous example of all other well-disposed people." Elizabeth was committed to Newgate and then led through the streets with basins and pans ringing. She had a B (for bawd) sewed to her dress on the right shoulder. After sitting in the pillory, she was exiled from the city forever.[81] The cases of forced prostitution of vulnerable young girls are repeatedly cited in the record sources, and the examples provide sufficient evidence of the problem of the economic exploitation of girls in the city.[82]

Family and friends, of course, could also be the ones to force the girls into sexual compromise. A girl, simply called Margaret, lived in lodgings with her mother, who sold her to a man called Roy Em, who deflowered her. Afterward, on the counsel of an old woman, her mother sold her to a certain Lombard, who fornicated with Margaret at the lodgings.[83] Actual cases of incest, however, were rarely reported.[84]

For many of the young women from the country who came to London hoping to find a service position, selling their bodies was the fastest way to make money. There was little that the city fathers could do except punish those who victimized them. They had no safe havens for these young women. For instance, when Emma, daughter of William le Wirdrawere of York, was found in the streets after curfew on the night of November 11, 1320, with only a bundle of clothes, the authorities could do nothing other than put her into the Tun (a prison) for the night.[85]

Anthropologists make much of the transition from adolescence to adulthood, a liminal stage that is marked in many societies by initiation ceremonies that may or may not coincide with physical puberty.[86] The evidence from London indicates that social puberty was much more important as a life demarcation than was physical puberty. Marriage was the marker of transition, not physical puberty. But even that distinction is lost in the case of child brides and grooms. The demarcation by marriage, however, was more important for young women than men. Males entering apprenticeship went through public ceremonies at their guilds and at Guildhall that included the enrolling of apprenticeship and oaths to abide by the city and guild rules, but we have no record of female participation in these ceremonies. When they completed apprenticeship, again males had public ceremonies of citizenship and guild membership. Girls could not join guilds and so did not go through such rites of passage. The rearing of boys and girls diverged as they approached adolescence. Girls were groomed for marriage, whether or not they would eventually marry. Girls' sexuality played a greater role in their economic value. They were exploitable for sex, but their value in the marriage market went up if they preserved their virginity.

≈3≈
Inheritance, Dowry, and Dower

The "Good Wife" poem advised that a mother should busy herself as soon as her daughters were born and "gather fast for their marriage, and give them spousing, as soon as they be of age."[1] Early marriage guarded against unacceptable romantic dalliances, but marriage usually required material wealth on the part of both the bride and groom. The training of young women, as we have seen, was more for marriage than for a craft, although not all young women married. As in most of northwestern Europe, London marriage contracts retained the dowry (the bridal gift at marriage) and dower (the husband's provision for his widow should he predecease her). Dowry and dower in London could be in the form of freehold real estate, leased property, money, and goods. London women could, as we have seen, inherit property and wealth in their own names and pass it on to heirs or heiresses.[2] Even among the poor, the presumption was that a girl should contribute a dowry to the economic partnership of marriage with some money and chattels or perhaps some supplemental trade.

Since the practice of inheritance, dowry, and dower varied across Europe, London must be compared to other European urban centers. These three means of wealth transfer were of major importance in the structure of urban society, having broad implications for the status of men, women, and children. London's law of female inheritance and the preference for giving dowry and dower in real estate gave women the custodianship and sometimes the control over large amounts of wealth in terms of real property and cash. Women also had guardianship of their children and often of their inheritance. The arrangement influenced the whole structure of London's marriage market and consequently of London society.

Inheritance

Women in London could inherit at sixteen if they married or at the usual age of majority, twenty-one, if they did not. Of the 193 female orphans for whom there is evidence for termination of wardship by inheritance, 159 married, or 82 percent.[3] None of the sons were described as receiving inheritance on marriage. The number married suggests that these women were twenty-one or younger. When the parents were still alive, as the historian Sylvia Thrupp found in her study of the merchant class, the age of marriage was seventeen or younger. The bride received the bulk of her claim to family property through a dowry.[4]

It is possible to trace the age of marriage in a few of the wardship cases, but the number is not large enough to draw firm conclusions about either the age of marriage or the age of female inheritance. Four women were married at nineteen, two each at ages sixteen to eighteen, and one at twenty. Only one married at twelve, and five at fourteen or fifteen. But to balance these out, one woman was "well over twenty-one," and two women married at twenty-seven and thirty, respectively.[5] Some, as we have seen, were married as children.[6]

The desire to marry a daughter at an earlier age seemed correlated with the amount of wealth that would comprise the dowry, but again, the sample size is small.[7] The practice in London follows that in other major cities. In Ghent, fifteen was the normal age of marriage for wealthy young women, whose person and estate could then be transferred to a husband.[8] In Italy, twelve was a common age of marriage, at least among the wealthy, but some fathers increased the dowry if the daughter waited until fifteen.[9]

The mayor of London retained some control over the age of marriage of orphans and their inheritance, so that when Dionisia, daughter of John de Hatfield, appeared in the Mayor's court to claim her inheritance, her husband was told that she could not inherit until she was sixteen.[10]

Fathers, in drawing up their wills or in the provisions made in the court of orphans, were very concerned about the marriages of their daughters. Beatrix, daughter of William Lynne, was made a ward in 1423 with her father's stipulation that she would inherit when she married; six years later she was married, and her husband came and claimed her patrimony.[11] The two boys and two girls who were orphans of Thomas Hawkyn were put in wardship together with the sum of £1,400. The agreement with the mayor was that the children could receive their portions "so soon as they come of age, or, being females, marry." In 1468, twelve years later, Johanna and her husband did collect her portion of the patrimony.[12] William Staundone made provision in his will that if his daughter lived beyond fourteen and married, she could have her portion. She, however, waited until she was twenty-one to claim the £200 owed to her.[13]

The girls with wealth who married young probably married men who were in their mid- to late twenties or older. Perhaps a large age difference between wife and husband also extended to craftsmen as well as merchants and wealthier Londoners by the fifteenth century.[14] With the age of apprenticeship rising from fourteen to as much as eighteen and with the terms of apprenticeship lengthening for young men, they would not be in a position to marry until they were at least in their twenties. If they were setting up a shop, they might wait longer. Women's training was considerably shorter, and as a result they may have married younger. Among the merchants and craftsmen, therefore, the age of first marriage might have resembled that of Italy.

But the small sample of early age of marriage and inheritance of the daughters of London merchants and craftsmen cannot be taken to represent all of London or trends in the country as a whole. The age of marriage for those women working as servants in London was probably higher, and they might have married men closer to their own age.[15] Servants would have had to establish themselves and set aside some money for a dowry. They might have preferred to return to their village or town of origin to marry. Many servants might have remained single all their lives. Because friends and family were contributing relatively little to these marriages, women and men probably had greater freedom in selecting their own partners. The argument is largely speculative, because evidence before 1350 is sparse and because no parish registers of births and marriages exist for the fourteenth and fifteenth centuries.[16] For sixteenth-century London, delayed marriage is better documented.[17] We are left, therefore, with incomplete information and speculation about the ages of couples when they married in medieval London and elsewhere.

Inheritance, of course, did not have to come with marriage in London. In the Archdeaconry court and Commissary court, many daughters seem to have been of age already. But a piebaker left property and his capital tenement to an unmarried, adult daughter. He left another daughter, who was still a minor, £10 to have when she married. And a carpenter, who left two minor daughters, provided for them to receive their bequest in equal shares when they came of age or married.[18]

Among the female orphans 16 percent inherited because they came of age. Only 5 percent of these were described as having completed an apprenticeship. William Fitzhugh left two children, a daughter aged seventeen and a son aged nine, in 1423. Four years later, when the daughter was twenty-one, she received her patrimony.[19] Likewise Johanna, daughter of William Whytheved of Weston, was sixteen when she became an orphan and collected her inheritance when she was just over twenty.[20] In general, the orphans' court simply speaks of the young woman as "being now full age."[21]

A scattering of cases indicates both earlier and later inheritance. Alice, daughter of Philip le taverner de Graschestret, was put into wardship in 1324 and in 1333 was given her inheritance at "sixteen years of age."[22] No mention is made of marriage. Emmota, daughter of Robert Foundour, was ten years old in 1362 when she became a ward. In 1371, when she would have been nineteen, she received her patrimony from the mayor "as she appeared to be capable."[23] Older ages of inheritance, increasingly common for young men, were possible for young women.[24] The only woman for whom there is such evidence is Agnes, daughter of Thomas Mountgomery, whose wardship lasted from 1427 to 1452. If she was an infant when she was orphaned, she would have been twenty-five when she inherited.[25] Although the cases are few, entry into a nunnery could prompt early inheritance. For instance, Isabel, daughter of Robert Westmelne, could decide at fourteen whether she would become a nun or marry.[26] Age of inheritance for females, therefore, varied from fourteen to twenty-one or older.

When real estate was transferred to an heiress, the presumption was that she would marry and that the progeny of the marriage would become heirs.[27] In the failure of surviving heirs, however, the property reverted to the next of kin. If the real estate came from the mother, then her next of kin inherited. Her husband could not take the property and leave it to his family. In other words, women enjoyed the same rights to lineal descent of property as did men. In northwestern Europe, the customs varied with the country, but for the most part, women kept their rights to inherited property.[28] Sixteenth-century Parisian law, for example, was similar to London in protecting the rights of female inheritance.[29] When Richard Jordan, a paternoster maker (prayer book maker), died in 1321, he gave his son one half of his tenement and Lucy, his daughter, the other half. If his son died before Lucy, she and her heirs were to have it. But if both children died without heirs, it would go to the next heir of his wife, Beatrix. The property was to pass through female inheritance, since it had come from Beatrix's family.[30] Women asserted their rights to pass on their real estate. Johanna de Standon, who was the widow of Ralph de Toudeby, was an heiress who resumed or kept her own name. Her will in 1359 stated that all her tenements were to pass to her daughter, and she specified that her brother be guardian.[31]

A particularly full description of the delivery of property to two married heiresses appears in English in the Mayor's court. William Myldenhale had enfeoffed (given temporary title of his freehold to) Rauf Barton with his tenement in Aldermanbury Parish in London in pledge for money that Rauf had lent to William. When William made his will and testament, he bequeathed this property to his daughters and to their heirs. "Jonet was weddyd to John Wotton draper in Dorchestre in the shire of dorset. . . . Eleyne was weddyd to William Chesse skinner of London." The daughters paid the money owed to Rauf Barton. Rauf met the daughters and their husbands before the door of the tenement and "there dede opynly rede the said testament be fore alle peple & after that the said Rauf took the saide Jonet & Elyne by the hondes delivering thaim bothe the rynge of the dore & saying these wordys, here y yeve & delyvere yow both seisyne & possession of this tenement to have & to holde jointly togedyr to yow & and to youre heires of yowre bodyes lawfully be goton after the wylle and affecte of the said testament."[32] The "livery of seizin" was essential to make the transfer valid, so we may presume that heirs and heiresses routinely went through the ceremony. The livery was done at the door if the property was a house, as in London, but if it was land, then the person receiving the land either stood on it or was in view of it when the land was given.[33]

Women experienced the same problems as men in defending their inherited real estate, but the right of women to inherit was never questioned. Usually, someone else had entered the property or had retained the deeds to the property. The two daughters of the late Richard Lacer brought suit against three different couples, including the widow and executrix of the man who was executor of their father, in order to obtain the deeds to property they inherited. The mayor and aldermen agreed that they should have possession of the deeds.[34] Ralph la Justice and his wife, Agnes, were not successful in an argument of intrusion against John Clerk. Agnes claimed that he had ejected her from a messuage belonging to her in Eastcheap. John denied forceful ejection, arguing that he had the right of entry from the prioress of St. Mary Clerkenwell. The prioress supported him by saying that the convent owned it and that she had given it by charter to Roger le Cordwaner and Avice, his wife. When Roger died, Avice returned it and the charter to the prioress. Agnes and her husband claimed that it had been given to Agnes on her first marriage and that she still had title. The inquiry proved that the prioress was right, and Agnes lost her claim.[35]

In English law a woman's inherited property passed to her husband for his life use by curtesy of England. Curtesy of England resembled the dower, in that it gave the surviving spouse the life use of inherited property from their marriage partner. But the dower of the widow was only a portion of her husband's property for life use. So curtesy of England was actually more generous to the surviving husband. No doubt, this additional benefit to the husband came because he had administered the land during their lifetime. He could not inherit it, but he had the use of it. Simon Barbur apparently took his wife's surname at the time of the marriage because she was Cecily, daughter and heir of Thomas Barbur. After her death he held her messuage worth 13 s. 4 d. yearly by curtesy of England. The property then went to her heir.[36] Edmund Cheyne enjoyed the life use of a variety of lucrative real estate and offices through his wife, Joan, daughter and heir of Stephen de Levelonde. Among these was the messuage of Fleet Prison and rents in London worth £10 yearly. Stephen de Levelonde had been in charge of keeping all the prisoners at Fleet as well as repairing Fleet Bridge, and this all passed to Cheyne when Joan died. Nor was this all. Cheyne also got the office of the bailiwick of the custody of the king's palace which involved provisioning the palace. For this office, he also had rents in Westminster to reimburse him for his efforts.[37]

Dowry

While a daughter's inheritance might be sufficient dowry, many girls received their dowries from living parents. The dowry might be equal to the girl's inheritance, or she might receive additional promises of inheritance on the death of the parents. Practice allowed for individual variation. Unlike the Continent, London did not have a tradition of notaries who recorded marriage contracts and kept a record of them, so that information on dowry is less systematic and is based on wills and court cases relating to dowries and dower.

For fathers with daughters, the habit of providing a daughter's dowry was deeply engrained in their minds. Mayor-elect Bat made a bad joke about a dowry for his daughter that caused him to lose his position. In 1240, after a period of revocation of London's privileges, Bat was admitted to the office and took his oath to the king. The bargain that the king had made was that he would restore to the mayor of London all honors and privileges, but not the £40 that previous mayors had received from the city. Mayor Bat had the bad sense to quip: "Alas! My Lord, out of all this I might have found a marriage portion to give to my daughter." The king accepted his resignation immediately.[38]

Among those who could afford it, real estate—inherited, purchased, or leased—was the preferred dowry. The property seems often to have belonged to the mother's dowry. Hugh Hirde de Borham and his wife, Matilda, former wife of Walter le Fotere, gave a tenement they jointly owned as a dowry to Richard Parent and his wife Margaret, presumably daughter of Matilda. The land is described as having been Matilda's dowry land and was situated next to a property that her former husband owned. The payment was a rose a year. Apparently, it was customary to pass on dowry property from mother to daughter, and the mark of inherited right was observed by a single rose a year to ensure the passage of title. Margery, widow of William Berkwey, "in pure widowhood," deeded property to William son of Andrew le Brocher as a free gift but with the stipulation that 3 s. a year be given to the secular clergy of London. She described her property as "dowry that came from Albreda my mother." In a complicated family transaction that established a dowry property, Robert de Esthall and his wife Johanna, as well as their daughter, Agnes de Esthall, endowed Thomas Romeyn and Juliane with real estate. The property included land and buildings in a free gift with a rose to be paid on the Nativity of St. John the Baptist. Agnes de Esthall, who described herself as having reached "full estate of 22 years and in my virginity," renounced her claim to her share of the property in exchange for a rose from Thomas on the same date. She described the property as coming from her mother.[39]

Other examples abound in the deeds of husbands and wives giving rents or property to couples for symbolic payment such as a rose or pepper corns, but many are less clearly identified as dowry than these early ones.[40] In the enrollment of deeds in the Husting court, the actual number of identifiable dowry transfers is small: in 1310–15 there were perhaps 9 dowry transfers out of 475 property transactions; in 1320–25, 15 out of 494; and in 1330–35, 9 out of 506. Many of the other property transactions, however, appear to have been dowry, since they are cases of a husband and wife transferring to a couple long-term leases or purchased freeholds.

The arrangements for the passage of property as dowry were often complicated and tried to accommodate the needs of all survivors, but also took into consideration the possibility of early death. Robert le Convers left his two sons real estate, but his daughter Katherine was to receive the dower tenement of Roysia, his wife, in the parish of St. Vedast. Katherine was also to have his tenement in the parish of St. Dunstan West, but his daughter Sybil had a lease of thirty years in that tenement. All the children received real estate.[41] A skinner, John Rote, who had a son and two daughters, managed to give tenements to all of them and the tools of his trade to his son. He left his two daughters tenements and gave, in addition, £20 toward each marriage. The evenhanded father gave each a piece of silver.[42]

The Inquisitions Post Mortem also show the use of real property as dowry in London. James Andreu, citizen of London, granted ownership of a great messuage with a shop, three small dwellings with three shops, and five other shops with solars to his daughter Katherine and her husband, John Dony, on their marriage.[43] John Normaund received a tenement from his in-laws on his marriage to Maud. When he died, she kept the property as well as the land they jointly purchased and took them into another marriage.[44] Henry le Gauger, a vintner, offered a dowry of two contiguous tenements for his daughter, Joan, on her marriage to John de Colcestre (Colchester), also a vintner.[45]

In making their assignment of dowry for their daughter, Robert de Esthall and his wife, Johanna, made it clear that they were giving up all claims to the property. They offered a warranty, that is, they guaranteed the title to the property by putting up another property of equal value. Johanna further made a *forisaffidatio*, that is, formally renounced her claim to dower in the property should she become a widow. People buying land were particularly concerned about the possibility that a widow could claim her right to the land after it was sold and for that reason wanted a formal renunciation of the widow's rights over it. In the "Twelve Points for Purchasers of Land to Look To," the first and second parts of this rhyme are:

Fyrst, se that the lande be cleere [clear],
And the tytle of the seller,
That it stond in no dawngeer [danger]
Of no womans doweere [dower].

The poem goes on to specify that the seller should be of age and the property warranted.[46] One senses that Esthall's new son-in-law had learned this poem by heart.

While not all testators and not all fathers made up a daughter's dowry with real property, there were advantages in doing so. The property ensured a daughter a place to live, often in a house or tenement close to the parental one. The deeds enrolled in the Husting court show that parents tried to get contiguous properties under their control.[47] Perhaps they liked the idea of having a daughter and son-in-law close to them to help out in business. Londoners also liked to acquire contiguous properties, as their wills show. Some parents realized that the dowry would be more secure and easier to trace if it was real property. Since real estate transactions were recorded in the Husting court, the parents and their daughter had a written record to appeal to in case of disputed ownership. The real property a woman brought as inheritance or dowry was subject to her husband's control in respect to his administration and any profit gathered. The husband of an heiress could administer her property but could sell it only with her consent, upheld in court.[48] Even the annual token gift of a rose indicated a continued interest on the part of the donors of the dowry.

If the dowry was given in movable goods or money, the husband administered it and could claim ownership of it. In the absence of notarial contracts or other preserved written agreements, it was easier for a husband to squander the money. Since provisions for dowry in movable goods often appeared in wills, which meant that church courts and not secular ones oversaw the disposition of such property, it was harder for family to keep track of movable property.[49] London's custom was that the widow would receive a third of the movables on her husband's death, but there is no indication that this included her dowry. London permitted women to keep their paraphernalia (personal belongings), including bedroom furniture, jewelry, and apparel, in addition to the dower.[50] Even if dowry was in cash and movables, the family could negotiate for their daughter to have rights in real estate by way of dower for her life use when they made the marriage agreement.

Some families preferred to make the dowry in cash and valuable goods or even convert real estate into cash. For the husbands, cash had a real advantage, because they could use the money in their trade or merchandising. John le Clerk left the daughter of his first wife £10 "to be paid to her as soon as she find an honest husband." John Ryvel, dying young in 1361, provided in his will that, if his wife was pregnant with a male child, the child was to have his hostel in London. If the child was female, he directed that the hostel be sold "for the said infant's marriage." Adam Brabason left his son his principal dwelling place, but he sold a tenement for his daughter's dowry and gave her £50, a silver cup, and a piece of silver with an image of St. Catherine on the bottom.[51] A wealthy money lender to the king, Bartholomew Castiloun, left his daughter, Alice, for her marriage two silver cups weighting 6 marks 9 s. 7 d.; a beaker with a silver cover weighing 3 marks 2 s. and 2 and one quarter d.; one silver bowl with a silver cover that did not fit it, weighing 23 s. 2 d.; six plain pieces of silver weighing 7 marks 2 s. 9 d.; two coconut cups with silver covers weighing 24 s.; twelve silver spoons weighing 20 s.; one mazer with a foot and a cover of mazer and two small mazers, value 20 s; one chapelet of pearls, valued at 40 s.; two salt-cellars of silver weighing 2 marks 5 s. 2 and one quarter d.; sum total 28 marks and 11 and one quarter d. 13 s. 11 d.[52]

Perhaps one of the reasons for giving silver and gold serving objects was their function as social capital. They added status to the new household that was very visible to visitors. In early modern Sweden, the furnishing of the house was important to both the bride and groom.[53] In Italy, while husbands wanted cash primarily, the families of the brides wanted to give fine clothing and jewels as well. Again, it was the social status of these gifts that marked the well-married woman.[54]

Fathers providing dowry in money could guarantee dower property for daughters by the contract that they made with prospective sons-in-law. The father of the groom or the groom would agree to provide real estate in exchange for money and movables. Consider the indentures drawn up by Thomas Sampson of Suffolk and the party representing the bride, Margaret, daughter of the late William Knightcote of London. The young man was given dowry toward the marriage in the total sum of £333 6 s. 8 d., including £100 in money and the remainder for the purchase of real estate, when an opportunity should occur, for the benefit of the couple and any progeny they might have.[55] Sir Hugh "Holes," who had been justice of the king, made an amicable arrangement before he died with John Godwyn, who was to marry his daughter, Isabella. He would give John £100 "as soon as he shall have acquired lands, tenements, and rents of that value and have settled the same upon his wife." Sir Hugh was making sure his daughter would eventually have real estate, but the dowry could be used by John to trade with in the meantime. Isabella died before the property was acquired, but the son-in-law was allowed to keep the £100.[56]

Those fathers and mothers recording their wills in the Archdeaconry and Commissary courts tended to provide dowry in movables. A bowyer (maker of bows for shooting) left 10 marks to his daughter for marriage in 1408, but another man was able to leave 100 marks to his.[57] A widow, a silkwoman by trade, had two sons and three daughters. One daughter was already married, but she left to one unmarried daughter twelve silver spoons with knobs of acorns, in addition to £40. The other unmarried daughter got £40. And the married daughter, who was executor along with her husband, was bequeathed a silver chest.[58]

Dowries in families with more than one daughter were not necessarily equal. One man gave his eldest daughter rents by way of dowry, the second daughter got 20 marks plus featherbeds, counterpanes, sheets, towels and other household items, and the third daughter got only 10 marks.[59]

Husbands, as well as parents of the bride, might have preferred to have dowry in real estate, because the transfer of real property was recorded in the city records. Movable goods were not officially recorded and were part of private transactions. John Abslon had been promised 300 marks for his marriage to Elizabeth, daughter of Robert Forster, but claimed that he got only £50, leaving him £250 short. Another man had made an arrangement with a father and son to marry the daughter. The father died, and he had not yet received the dowry from the surviving brother of the bride. In a complicated arrangement in which the collection of a debt was to be paid in installments of 10 marks a year by the debtor to the daughter of the creditor as dowry, no money was forthcoming.[60] John Uffenham even claimed to have witnesses to his dowry arrangement with the brother of his bride, Alice Dounham. Her brother had agreed to pay off a debt of £40 that she had incurred and give John £10 and access to her property, which should have paid him 10 marks a year. John married Alice but received nothing.[61]

Dowry was considered a necessary condition to an honorable marriage, even if the amount given was very small. One of the charitable bequests that a person could make to aid the poor was dowries for poor young women. Such bequests reinforced the general cultural presumption that marriage was the preferred state for young women. John Piken, a brewer, left money to be distributed to "poor maidens of good name and to lame and blind persons" toward their marriages.[62] The mercers, however, were among the most generous. Between 1400 and 1499 they and their widows left about £1,650 pounds toward maidens' marriages. One of the reasons for their generosity in providing dowries was that they employed a number of young women in their trade.[63]

The Dower or Jointure

Dower, as well as dowry, was a necessary condition for marriage between people with any property or movables in London. Dower gave widows a third of the husband's estate for life use if she had produced children and, after 1356, a half if she had not.[64] Family and friends of the bride and groom arranged the dowry and dower. The contracts were no doubt often written, but the oral tradition of reading the arrangements in front of witnesses was still the norm. Any private writings that recorded the agreement were not preserved beyond the immediate need, or they remained in private boxes of deeds that have not survived. We usually learn about these arrangements when powerful people had them recorded in the city records or when something went amiss and one of the parties appealed to the law. The lack of written evidence was a problem for these litigants as well as for the modern historian trying to reconstruct the exchange of dower and dowry.

The dower provisions were explicit in London law, so the prospective husbands and wives were not without a guideline in forming marriage contracts.

> Wives, on the death of their husbands, by the custom of the city shall have their freebench. That is to say, that after the death of her husband the wife shall have of the tenement in the said city, whereof her husband died seized in fee, and in which tenement the said husband and wife dwelt together at the time of the husband's death, the hall, the principal private chamber, the cellar wholly, and her use of the kitchen, stable, privy, and curtilage [a small piece of ground attached to the house] in common with the other necessaries appurtenant thereto, for the term of her life. And when she marries again, she shall lose the free bench and her dower therein, saving to her dower of the other tenements as the law requires.[65]

Freebench was the minimum. Thus Alice, widow of John de Harwe, applied to the city for the "widow's chamber": a portion of the tenement in which they dwelt including the hall, principal chamber, and cellar along with the use of kitchen, stable, garden, and privy. The mayor awarded her these even though her husband had died intestate.[66]

The real advantages of dower for women and the core of the wealth it provided lay in the last part: "saving to her [the widow's] dower of the other tenements as the law requires." The law states that the dower should be composed of tenements rather than movables (jewels, furniture, household goods) and that it should not be just the free bench should the husband be able to provide other real estate. Wills indicate that the London men honored their law. In inheritance, dowry, and dower, the emphasis was on ensuring a woman's future with real property, if this was economically feasible, and resorting to movables and cash only if tenements were not available.

The husband had several options for meeting and announcing the obligations of the dower in exchange for the dowry. The most secure way was to make a contract binding on the parties before the marriage. Properties that the groom already owned or rented would be promised to the bride at the time of the marriage. Robert Isham, son of Robert Isham, secured his dower with a bond that protected the land he acquired. When Robert married Margaret, orphaned daughter of William Radewell, an alderman, he made sure to get full title to a property worth £25 pounds a year. The property was described as being held outright and free of any other charges than the ancient rents and services due on the property. He and Margaret, along with their legitimate offspring, were to hold it, and failing heirs, he would receive it. "Further, he undertakes to make no alienation or demise of those lands whereby his wife's interest in them may be prejudiced." His wife's dower was secure.[67]

The other solution was to assign dower in a public ceremony. After the parties agreed to the contract, the groom announced the dower before witnesses at the parish church door (*ad ostium ecclesiae*) when they married.[68] The marriage might have taken place there as well. When a dispute arose later over the terms, witnesses would often refer to the exchange at the church door and recite the terms of the agreement made there. The advantage of a public announcement of dower was that the husband could not alienate the land assigned to dower, thereby securing the wife's portion. If the wife received the agreed dower when the husband died, she could not claim further dower. In the late thirteenth century, John de Flete, a capper, recited in his will his provision for his second wife: Casandra would have the life use of his capital messuage and the house adjacent with which he had endowed her "at the porch [of the church]" to hold as dower for her lifetime, with his eldest son inheriting at her death. His daughter was to have a dowry at her marriage of tenements, shops, and rents.[69]

Dower also could be provided by promising one-third or one-half of the husband's estate at the time of his death.[70] If the husband's fortunes increased over the period of marriage, this arrangement was a very good one, and the wife got more property and movables than she would have had at the time of the marriage. But the arrangement was risky, because the husband's business could fail, and the widow would be destitute. One thing the husband could not do was make his wife his heir to inherited real estate. When husbands tried this in wills, it was always disallowed. Thomas Pourte left a will giving his wife, Christiana, a messuage, but the court objected saying that the use and custom of the City of London did not permit the testator to devise to the heirs of his wife and her assigns. Christiana took a life interest in the property as her dower.[71] The law prohibited a wife from inheriting, because it would take the property out of the hands of the husband's heirs and would pass to her heirs.

Of the wills enrolled in the Husting court, 53 percent of the men made dower provisions. Adding the dower to a will was not necessary, since it had already been announced at the church door at the time of marriage and the right to dower was protected by London law, but it was a legal safeguard and a way of augmenting the dower. Real estate was the most common form of dower in the wills: 86 percent, compared with only 13 percent dower in goods and money alone and 1 percent dower with an annuity. Since men with real estate had to enroll their wills in the Husting Court, it is not surprising that the percentage was so high. Husbands sometimes added to the original dower by giving valuable chattels. It was customary to give the wife a third of the movables as well, but husbands could bequeath this as did Thomas de Wynton, who left his wife money, jewels, cups of silver and mazer, and other chattels "in lieu of dower of all his goods movable."[72] The husband could also give his surviving widow the choice of taking the dower agreed in the marriage contract or taking London's customary right to one-third of the property.[73]

The wills recorded in the Archdeaconry court are less detailed and more concerned with provisions for the testator's soul than the transfer of property. They also represented some of the poorer elements of the population and ordinary craftsmen of London.[74] Of the 116 men who made provisions for their widows, only 18 percent mention real estate, while 65 percent simply refer to the residue of their estate. Seventeen percent specify the dower, usually adding to it with specific sums of money or a portion of the residue.

The custom of giving wives real estate as their dower is perhaps why some fathers preferred to give sons, rather than daughters, property. Money and movables could make up the dowry, but for a son to make a really advantageous marriage, a substantial dower in real estate was necessary.

If the prospective husband did not have outright ownership of property that could be used for dower, jointure provided yet another way of securing a home and providing dower for the surviving wife and children.[75] At the time of the marriage, the husband's family could arrange to settle some of his inheritance on the new wife as a dower. In exchange, the bride's family offered money and movables. The husband and wife arranged in a deed that the property was in both their names and that it would pass to their heirs.[76] Thus the heirs of the marriage could inherit the property. If the husband predeceased the wife, the property was already in the wife's name so that she could keep the title to the property, take it into another marriage, and even pass it on to heirs. The amount of real estate was not set but depended on the marriage negotiations. The jointure became increasingly popular in the fourteenth century and explains part of the increase in endowing young women with movables and money rather than real estate. Johanna, widow of Robert Motun, contested his will, saying that they jointly acquired property to be held by the "longest liver" of them as well as their heirs and assigns.[77] Husbands seemed to forget these arrangements on their deathbeds. Richard Horn and his wife, Isabelle, contested the will of Peter le Hodere, who gave his widow, Isabelle, only seven years use of the property, although it had been a jointure in both their names and should pass directly to her.[78] Jointure, then, could be a real advantage to a widow, since she could have the property outright on the death of her husband and it was protected from any other liens on it.

Couples leased property together, even it if was not part of a jointure. If the property was leased by the couple, the wife would have the rest of the term of the lease should her husband predecease her. Joint leases are abundant in the Letter Books. For example, Walter, son of John le Maseliner, leased to William Crosh, fishmonger, and Alice, his wife, a brewery "to hold for their respective lives at an annual rent of 18s."[79] Alice may well have been a brewer setting up her own business. With the lease in both their names, her business would not be threatened by her husband's death. Leases tended to be long—ten to twenty years—so the survivor would have a good chance of holding the property after the decease of a spouse. Even small properties such as a stall were leased to husband and wife jointly.[80] The city also made their leases to couples. In an indenture of lease by the mayor and the city government, Robert Warner and Elianora, his wife, received a vacant piece of property on which to build a house. The term of the lease was sixty years.[81]

The many avenues to transfer permanent and temporary control of property to wives and widows indicates that Londoners wished to see their womenfolk secure for the future with real estate, if at all possible. Women were trained to deal with rents and property better than they were trained to undertake businesses or crafts.

The Broader Context of Female Inheritance and Dower

In order to appreciate the liberality of London laws regarding female inheritance, dowry, and dower, it is necessary to compare its laws and practice with others in England and on the Continent. Customs differed in England depending on which law covered a woman's social status and, consequently, her inheritance rights. In common law, the law of the nobility and freeborn, as opposed to borough law, inheritance by the first-born son (primogeniture) predominated, as was generally the case among the nobility of Europe. Primogeniture kept family land intact, rather than dividing it among all surviving children and then subdividing it again among their progeny. It kept families powerful and wealthy. If the first-born son died, subsequent sons would hold in succession. Failing a direct male line in England, all surviving daughters inherited equally. Among the nobility of late medieval England, 72 percent of the heirs of nobility were sons, and only 9 percent were daughters. Daughters were not excluded from family fortunes but would be given a dowry as their portion of the estate. Female heiresses tended to marry at an early age, a pattern similar to the daughters of the merchant class in London.[82] Dower in common law granted the widow a third of the estate for her life use.

Customary law in England, the law of the manors, had great variations in inheritance patterns. Much of the land was only rented by the peasantry, so that it was the right to rent that passed to heirs. Some areas had partible inheritance, as did London; some favored the eldest son and some the youngest son. But daughters inherited if they did not have a brother. In late medieval Bedfordshire wills, 14 percent of the men had daughters as heiress.[83] The wills also show complex family strategies to provide movables and purchased pieces of land or rents to all surviving children. In other words, peasant families, like those in London, followed the custom of providing for all children out of the family wealth.[84] In customary law, the widow might be provided the whole of the rental property in order to raise her family, but she might receive half, or simply a retirement settlement. Much depended on the age of the children and the mother and the supply of workers in the family.

In northwestern Europe, female inheritance laws, dowry, and dower were closer to those of borough law in England. The historian Mary Bateson speculated that borough law in England derived from earlier continental law.[85] In Paris and much of France, the noble custom of primogeniture was disregarded, and instead, the older system of dividing property equally among all surviving children was still practiced in the sixteenth century. Even daughters who had received the dowry (*dot*) could claim further benefits.[86] In Ghent, a similar situation of partible inheritance existed without regard to sex or age. Thus, as in London, women owned a considerable amount of real property, and this, in turn, put pressure on the male kindred to see women well married. In both London and Ghent, the families of the bride wanted to protect their property and make sure that rightful heirs received it after the woman died. Ghent, unlike London, had a well-established clan system that was perpetuated through the male line and led to the privileging of the father's family in determining wardship of children as well as their marriages.[87] Ghent's laws of partible inheritance were common in Flemish-speaking Flanders and much of the rest of the Low Countries. London did not have a clan system or even a strong patrilineal system, so that London's practices of inheritance, dowry, dower, and wardship led to strong horizontal ties with fellow Londoners and did not privilege patrimonial ones.

Not all of northern Europe, however, practiced partible inheritance. Douai, a town in the Low Countries, had a conjugal fund. That is, the couple entering marriage held their property together, and the survivor inherited the whole amount of the joint estate to dispose of as he or she pleased. Children received inheritances at the discretion of their parents or the surviving parent. Even a stepchild's property fell into the general conjugal pool. In practice, however, the Douaisans modified their customs to permit inheritance for the offspring of the marriage. Other parts of the southern Low Countries, however, did not place such emphasis on the conjugality of property but limited it in various ways to usufruct (life interest) of movables or a part of the property.[88] Borough law in England placed emphasis on the heirs, so that the conjugal couple had only lifetime interest in the property (either through curtesy of England or dower). If the couple did not have children, the property and movables would revert to next of kin.[89]

After about 1100 in southern Europe, the dowry replaced the system of "brideprice" (the gifts of the husband to the wife on marriage). The usual way to transfer a girl's family portion to her new husband was at her marriage rather than through inheritance. Although the shift in marital practice began among the elite, ordinary citizens also shifted their regime.[90] In Florence, inheritance laws disadvantaged a daughter. Even if she had no surviving brothers, her claim on the family estate was limited to one-quarter, and this could not include real property. Failing direct male heirs, the property would go to the agnates (male relatives on the father's side) within eight degrees of relationship, that is, the property was meant to remain in the male patriline through sons, grandsons, and so on. Even the male child of a daughter could not inherit.[91] In Venice, the law of *fraterna* divided the estate among all the sons in equal portions to be shared jointly. Women received their portion in a dowry, which was by law equal to that of her brothers.[92] When women left wills, they usually had more personal movables to distribute rather than real estate. In Venice, widows used wills to favor their natal families and their daughters.[93]

Just as inheritance systems for daughters differed substantially in northern and southern Europe, so, too, did the dotal (dowry) system. In Ghent, as in London, the couple was given cash, rents, perhaps land, and some furnishings as a dowry at the time of marriage. Daughters' inheritance also could become dowry.[94] In Douai, with its conjugal property, the *portement* was the properties each spouse brought to the marriage. The wife's *portement* included cash and household goods but listed immovables (real estate) and rents individually.[95] Both of these marriage customs included a dower in return for the dowry.

In Italy, the picture was much different, since only the dowry was given and not a dower. The dowry was a major investment on the part of the family; in Venice, the law decreed that it be an equal portion with that of brothers, and if the father was dead, the brothers were to pay.[96] Dowry inflation hit Italy in the fourteenth century. In Venice, the inflation from the mid–twelfth century to the early fifteenth century was about 40 percent. The inflation was so severe that the Senate tried to put a cap on it.[97] Florence likewise experienced dowry inflation. While in Venice the inflation seems to have been brought on by a desire to maintain social status in marriage or gain advantage of upward social mobility through marriage, in Florence the increasingly delayed marriage of men meant that fewer eligible bachelors were available for marriage (some died and others continued as bachelors). Fathers started arranging marriages for their daughters at increasingly young ages and offering bigger dowries as incentives. Even peasants in Tuscany experienced the dowry inflation.[98] It became so difficult for families to provide dowries that the state set up the *Monte Delle Doti*, which permitted fathers to deposit money for their daughters' dowries and receive a fixed increase in that sum after a set period of time.[99]

For daughters in London, inheritance and dowry were intimately con-nected, because the law assumed that the daughter would receive her part of the parental estate either by provision in a will, by London law, or by a settle-ment during the lifetime of the parents when she married. Not all daughters who survived to adulthood married, but the majority of those with property did. London's laws resembled the inheritance and dowry system of northern Europe in giving daughters and sons equal or nearly equal access to parental wealth. This acquisition of property through inheritance gave northwestern European women in the Middle Ages a very different relationship to their property and movables than the Mediterranean pattern. In Florence, the dowry stayed with the husband's family or reverted to the wife's natal family at widowhood. She would have to live with the husband's family or return to her own. Widows in Florence were less likely to remarry than northern European women. Over the next few chapters, we will explore how this relative independence in inheritance and dowry, with the addition of dower, influenced women's lives and the structure of medieval London society. If the Italian pattern favored male inheritance to perpetuate the patriline, how did London's more egalitarian division of property affect its social ties?

❦ 4 ❦

The Formation of Marriage

Marriage was both a contractual agreement and an emotional investment. For women, it was a defining moment in their lives. A woman ceased to be identified in the records and in daily life as "daughter of" and became the "wife of" her husband. On her husband's death, she was called "widow of" or "relict of." In a subsequent marriage, she would take the identity of her new husband, but if she had property from her first husband, she would be the relict of the former husband and the wife of the current husband.[1] Marriage usually meant a change of domicile for the woman. Unlike the Italian pattern, in which the bride moved into the husband's family household, she and her husband would usually have their own establishment. The English seemed to have a strong preference for conjugal family residences.

Marriage brought together material resources from two families or the savings of two individuals in the form of dowry and dower. It formed a new economic unit. For those with considerable wealth already, a good marriage could bring a much-needed infusion of capital. For craftsmen, a marriage partner could mean another worker in his shop, or someone to feed his apprentices or perhaps bring a useful skill or trade. For women, marriage could bring security of livelihood and a dower for widowhood, but it did not guarantee against poverty. It also meant responsibilities and perhaps child-rearing.

Many medieval marriages were arranged, but this did not mean that they were loveless, and love matches also occurred. Even wide age differences between the wives and husbands did not necessarily lead to unhappy marriages. Because marriage was so important, parents, family, business associates, masters, mistresses, and even matchmakers were constantly on the lookout for prospective brides and grooms. Individuals also looked for a good match. No doubt gossip and consultation with those in the same age group played as significant a role as it does today. The marriages were not between total strangers who met for the first time on their wedding day. A period of courtship might include supervised visits between the young people, the exchange of tokens (gifts of more or less value, depending on the wealth of the couple), letters among the literate, meetings in public places such as halls or taverns, agreements between couples to the marriage, and discussions with responsible parties.

Contracting for Marriage

The marriage contract was arranged, not usually by the bride and groom themselves, but with the help of family or "next best friends." Sometimes the master of a servant might arrange the match. The bride and groom might make their own agreements, but they usually had witnesses or go-betweens to ensure the agreement.[2] Although we do not have a large number of marriage contracts, a variety of other sources, including letters and petitions to the lord chancellor, speak about the marriage market.[3]

In addition to other factors, church strictures on marriage went into a consideration of appropriate marriage partners. Canon law (church law) regulated marriage because it was a sacrament. The Church established rules for a valid marriage, grounds for annulment, and even the canonically approved days for sex in marriage. One prohibition was against marrying those of too close a degree of kinship and affinity. Those related to the fourth degree could not marry—that is, people who were descended from the same great-great-grandfather were considered consanguineous. Affinity was also a ban to marriage, so a man could not marry the sister of a former wife, and vice versa. Even sexual relations outside marriage established affinity; if one had sexual relations with a fiancée's kinswoman, the marriage was invalid. The spiritual kinship from the baptismal ceremony meant that, for instance, a man could not marry a woman who was godmother to a child by his first wife. The rules were too restrictive and they could not be enforced, since they would have prohibited a number of marriages. People's memories did not necessarily stretch back to great-great-grandfathers. Instead, cases came into church courts if one of the parties brought charges of violation or the rules, or if the case was so egregious that it came to the attention of ecclesiastical authorities.[4]

The Church also required the consent of both partners to the marriage. The consensual theory of marriage implied that an individual had the final choice of marriage partner and that overriding control by the family, master, or next best friend was excluded. It was a short step from consensual theory to accepting private or clandestine marriages as valid. What was essential for the validity of a marriage was the "present consent" of the parties, that is, they said in the present tense that they took each other to be "my wedded husband" or "my wedded wife." The dangers of abuse were apparent, and sermons and synods spoke against secret marriages contracted against the wishes of responsible parties. The wisest course was to have witnesses present and to have the consent of a responsible person such as a father, guardian, or master. It was also possible to have a valid marriage by "future consent," that is, the parties said that they would marry, and then consummated the marriage.[5] If unconsummated, the marriage contract could be broken. In any case, canon law made the dissolution of a marriage or divorce difficult once the marriage occurred. It is tempting to say that the Church was leaving room for love in these matches, but the Church was more interested in preserving and defining the sacrament of marriage.

A modern reader would assume that love must be a criterion for marriage, but in the Middle Ages, love was not considered sufficient. The advice literature, including the poem of the "Good Wife" and others, was strongly against young couples forming their own love matches.[6] Medieval parents and sensible young people looked for an equal match of property and goods. It may seem unsentimental, but one should not project back into a former time the same importance of romantic love that is expected today.[7]

Some young Londoners did have a sense of romantic love. Anthony Pontisbury, an apprentice, was forbidden by his contract to marry until his term was fulfilled. In his appeal he explained that he had been bound as an apprentice at "a tender age" seven years earlier for a term of nine years. He had agreed, as his apprenticeship contract stipulated, that he would not marry during his term. He did marry, but defended himself by saying that the prohibition on marriage was "contrary to the laws of God and causeth much fornication and adultery to be within the said city." He went on to explain: "having an inward love to a young woman dwelling in the said city and the young women having the same unto him, intending that both were to love under the laws of God ... he has lately married and taken to wife the said young woman." His master had him arrested for trespass and imprisoned.[8]

The first step toward marriage was to identify an acceptable spouse. Networks of family and friends once again played a role, as they did in apprenticeships. We can imagine that gossip about the wealth of an orphan, the dowry provisions left to a young heiress in a will, and the elevation of a young man to the guild livery, as well as the news about the sudden death of a citizen and the availability of a young widow, made the rounds of streets, taverns, and dinner tables. A letter in the Stonor collection gives some idea of the way that contacts were made. Elizabeth Ryche Stonor had young daughters by her first marriage. She was visiting in London and wrote to her new husband that she was having dinner with her parents when one of the guests suggested a match for a child and her daughter. She replied that she would consider it and consult friends and family.[9]

Marriage arrangers saw their position as one of masculine power. As the historian Shannon McSheffrey has written, it was prestigious for men to use their influence to bring about marriages.[10] Alison Hanham observed in her book on the Cely family: "matchmaking was an enormously serious business for the parties and their relations, and a favorite sport for those less directly involved in the outcome."[11] The use of networks, gossip mills, courting expenses, and exchange of dower and dowry appear most coherently in the Cely and the Stonor letters. But cases in various courts and petitions to the lord chancellor indicate that their experiences were typical.

While the mayor had the responsibility of protecting orphans from misalliance, he had a self-interest as well. He could extract a fee for granting a license to marry an orphan as well as fines for the city. For the mayor, the power to oversee the marriages of orphans also meant that he could control the social, political, and economic benefits that accrued to the grooms from their marriages. The mayor could extract a heavy penalty not only on the abuser but also on the witnesses. When John Hurlebatie married Joan, daughter of Nicholas Aghton, an alderman, without a license from the mayor, those who had aided him in defying the mayor's right suffered severe financial punishment. The two witnesses, a merchant and a notary public, were committed to prison until they paid a fine to the mayor. The notary public pleaded ignorance, and his fine was commuted from £20 to 20s. But the merchant, who knew and had sworn to obey the city's laws, was fined the full amount and put out of his citizenship. Finally, the groom paid £40, which was considered to be the commission on the marriage.[12] The mayor made sure that he got his commission.

Like the mayor, matchmakers charged fees for arranging marriages. Women's roles in arranging marriages were informal, but male matchmakers appear in a number of petitions to the lord chancellor. These were private arrangements, probably largely unwritten, and seem to have fallen outside London law. For instance, Alexander Brounyng complained that John Lawley had asked him to "labor for his part in arranging a marriage with Elisabeth Rothwell, his aunt." If the marriage took place, he was to receive £40 for his "laboring." Alexander claimed that he had brought about the marriage, but John had refused to pay and was threatening him with a suit.[13] The nephew was trying to make money as a go-between for his aunt. Another man claimed that executors of the will of William Whetenale, a London grocer, had asked him to "labor to bring about the marriage of William's son and Margaret, daughter of William Hextall, esquire." He was to be paid £20 after the marriage occurred. The marriage took place, but the matchmaker claimed that he had not been paid.[14] In a more complicated case, John Lyonhyll, a goldsmith of London, claimed that three years earlier a clerk named John Alcok came to him and said he could arrange a marriage with the daughter of William Phelyppes, a goldsmith and chamberlain of London. The prospective groom was willing to pay. Alcok said that he had some plate that he wanted the goldsmith to buy from him that was worth £23 and more, but the plate was only worth £14. John Lyonhyll was to pay the full £23 to Alcok when the marriage took place. The father-in-law agreed to reimburse Lyonhyll for the matchmaker's fee. Meanwhile, the bride died, and the father-in-law refused to pay the rest of the agreed-on sum Alcok demanded for matchmaking (about £10).[15]

There were baser ways of finding a spouse—tricking a man or woman into sexual compromise or seductions with promises of marriage. In the case of seduction and fornication, the Church tended simply to hasten a marriage that had already been planned.[16] Neighbors and family might also act to force a marriage when a couple had been caught sexually compromised.[17] Even blackmail and prison could lead to marriages. William Gerardson, a beer brewer and a Dutchman (foreigners were distrusted, and since the Dutch introduced beer, a replacement for the traditional ale, he was very suspect), had spent twelve months and more in the house of John Evan. John had exhorted him to marry a young woman who was a servant in the house. William refused to marry her, and John was suing him for £20 pounds in damages for corrupting his servant. He either had to marry her or pay.[18]

In the advice poem "How the Wise Man Taught His Son," the young man was admonished not to look for wealth alone in choosing a wife; but rather, he was to look for one who was "meek, courteous, and prudent even though poor."[19] Although most fathers and men making marriage arrangements agreed that a woman should be suitably subservient, they would not consider these attributes, unaccompanied by wealth, as adequate.

Planning for marriage contracts among the propertied could begin early in life. We have seen at least one shrewd widow and widower who married each other and then married their two very young children without the mayor's permission. The motivation for such plotting comes out clearly in a letter preserved in the mayors' papers. Geoffrey Boner

> had three daughters, to wit, Isabel, Agnes, and Alice, and that in order to marry the said Isabel befittingly, the said Geoffrey had bought the ward and marriage of one John Hockele, who had lands and tenements in London to the value of 16 marks by the year from one Thomas of London, clerk, for which he paid 40 marks and a hanaper [box for keeping documents] of maser worth 13 s. 4 d., the said Isabel being at that time 16 years of age; and that the said John and Isabel were married and the said Geoffrey and Ellen [his wife] had given them goods and chattels to the value of £9 together with rents and tenements.

The family essentially purchased the groom and his dower and then provided very well for their daughter with cash, rents, and tenements as dowry. Isabel, "thus advanced," then wanted to deprive her sisters of an inheritance in London, but London custom forbade her to be so grasping. As the first married sister, she could have only her usual claim to the family fortune and could make no other claim unless the first had been a partial one.[20]

The terms of marriage contracts could be complicated when considerable property was involved. Sir John de Lovetot, Senior (a justice of common pleas), arranged for the marriage of his ward, Margaret, to a young Londoner. Probably both were minors. She was the heiress of her father, Thomas, son of Ralph de Normanville, and her uncle, Ralph. In addition to London tenements and rents, she received the advowson (right to appoint a clergyman) of a church in Kent. Her mother still had dower in part of the inheritance. The marriage contract arranged for the transfer of not only her land but also her wardship. The groom's father, Robert de Bassinge, paid £200 in installments to her guardian for this valuable young girl. The agreement, however, stipulated a 200-mark respite if Margaret survived to come of age in four years or if she died in that term but had a child by Robert's son. In turn, Robert allowed his son to promise a dower of lands and tenements that would produce 20 s. a year. She outlived her husband and received all the deeds ten years later.[21] This type of contract, complicated as is seems, might have been fairly standard, for a very similar case appears in an appeal to the lord chancellor in the fifteenth century.[22]

The actual process of negotiating a marriage contract appears more clearly in ecclesiastical court depositions than in the secular courts. Except for young orphans, particularly those abducted for their wealth, marriages were usually undertaken with due consultation with the prospective bride and groom. An intermediary, usually an older man who knew the correct forms for marriage and contract and had the respect of both parties, mediated the marriage. He acted as a go-between, talking to both parties, carrying gifts, inquiring of the interest of each party in a possible match. He made sure that neither of the parties had another commitment for marriage. McSheffrey gives a number of examples, but one suffices to create a sense of the ritual. In 1469 William Love, an embroiderer and parish clerk of St. Botolph, went at the request of Robert Pope to Lucy Bragge. He asked Lucy if she had promised to marry any other man, and if not, would she would be interested in Pope. She expressed interest and was willing to speak with Robert Pope and have a drink with him. Not long after the courtship, Love had them to Sunday dinner at his house, where, according to Love, they formally contracted marriage in front of himself and other witnesses.[23]

The canonical requirement of free consent and perhaps even the practicalities of arranging marriage contracts meant that some courtship and wooing would be involved after an initial contact had been made. Some of the matchmakers purchased the gifts for prospective brides and gave dinners and wine to parents to smooth the way. One matchmaker said that he was to get a

£20 commission, but that his costs had been 26 s. 8 d., so that he was now owed £30.[24] But couples exchanged gifts as well to show their earnestness about the arrangements and their regard for each other. Margaret Swan and Humphrey Charyet, an apprentice to a goldsmith, had made a marriage contract with the master's consent. "Humphrey at diverse times delivered to Margaret certain tokens," and she had given tokens to him as well. When Humphrey died, the master wanted the tokens back, claiming that they were worth £26, whereas Margaret said that they were not above 10 s. in value.[25] The tokens were usually jewelry, rings, and other such items. Depending on the wealth involved in the match, they were usually not of high value, and the term "token" was probably right, as Margaret said.[26] Sometimes the token was food that the prospective wife was to prepare for the suitor, a way to reinforce gender roles from the beginning of the relationship.[27]

Courtship, if no vows were exchanged, was a period in which the project of marriage could be abandoned, and so served as a period for the couple to get to know each other in a tavern or hall, where supervision was available. But it was also possible that agreement to the marriage came quickly, and the mediator would then undertake to supervise the couple in the exchange of vows that would make their engagement binding by using the vows of present consent. The couple was now married in the eyes of the Church, but a more formal, public ceremony would most likely follow. The process of marriage, in late medieval England, was an incremental one, with the possibility of dissolution up until the vows were repeated.[28]

Since marriage was such a significant business and legal transaction, it had to be publicly proclaimed by three readings of the banns at the parish church door on three successive Sundays. There were two reasons for these public recitations. First, in an oral society, one needed witnesses that the couple was about to make a major commitment to each other and that they intended to form an economic and sacramental union. Second, since legal marriage could be contracted clandestinely, the public reading was a way to prevent bigamy. Other claimants could come forward to voice their objections to the proposed marriage. In modern marriage ceremonies, we have a vestigial version in the phrase asking if anyone knows why this marriage should not take place. Not everyone had banns read, but it was a way of informing the public of a new household, and perhaps new landlords, and new business. Witnesses might be asked to testify to the reading of the banns years later.[29]

The next phase was the marriage ceremony, also often at the church door rather than in the church. While the Church wanted to encourage a marriage mass inside the actual building, the tradition was hard to establish, and the more public ritual at the doors was preferred. The marriage vows have a familiar ring, but the wife's vow is explicit about the sexual duty of marriage. In the legal parlance of both lay and ecclesiastical law, marital sex was given an economic term, the *marital debt*, and it was incumbent on both husband and wife to pay it.

> **Man:** *I take the N. to be my wedded wif, to hauve and to holde, fro this day forwarde, for better of for wors, for richer for pourer in sycknesse and in hele, tyl dethe us departe, if holy chyrche it woll ordeyne, and thereto y plyt the my trouthe.*

> **Woman:** *I take the N to be my wedded housbonde, to haue and to holde, fro this day forwarde, for better for wors, for richer for pourer in sicknesse and in hele. To be bonere and boxon, in bedde and ate bord, tyll dethe vs departe, if holy chyrche it wol ordeyne, and therto I plight the my trouthe.*

The priest blessed the rings, and the couple exchanged the words "with this ring I thee wed and with my body I thee honor."[30] By the late Middle Ages, the clergy hoped that the couple would have a nuptial mass as well, but, apparently, if one can judge by the clerical complaints, they did not.[31]

Like baptisms, marriages were festivals that both moralists and the London city fathers found objectionable. The moralists provide some clue to the problems that arose: "we enjoin that marriage be decently celebrated, with reverence, not with laughter and ribaldry, not in taverns or at public drinkings and feastings."[32] The city had other concerns. Rather like the city fathers of Florence, who deplored the poor imitating the rich in the question of dowries, those of London concluded that

> forasmuch as men of great estate had given large sums on the occasion of ... the marriage of their children, and others of less estate had followed their example to their own impoverishment, it is ordained that no one of the City shall give ... at a marriage of any one not being his own son or daughter, brother or sister or next of kin, more than half a mark [6 s. 4 d.], under penalty of 40 s. to the chamber.[33]

Advice books set the standards for the most socially prestigious marriage celebrations. They suggest the menu for the elaborate feast that would follow the wedding and instruct inexperienced servants and cooks who might be hired for the occasion.[34]

The celebration of marriages created considerable economic loss of capital to the couple or sponsors in the gifts and the entertainments. The problem was exacerbated by riotous behavior, indebtedness, and unpaid bills, or the city would have welcomed the revenue that weddings brought in terms of catering, wedding dresses, and gifts. The city fathers realized that it was fine for the rich to spend the money because they could pay the bills, but when the lesser people imitated them, they left honest merchants holding the debt, while the debtors went to prison. Conspicuous consumption was a problem in late medieval England, as parents of all social classes wanted their sons and daughters to have fine public displays.

One reason wedding feasts became boisterous was that they occurred in the flush seasons or during months of revelry. The most popular months in London, as well as Europe, were January (the saturnalia month of fertility rites) and October and November (the harvest and butchering feasts), the summer months when new crops were coming in, and mid summer day (St. John's Day), which was celebrated with bonfires. The Church prohibited marriages during Lent, Rogationtide, and Advent through Christmas.[35] This eliminated about eighteen to twenty weeks, or about a third of the year. Early sixteenth-century data show that both marriages and conceptions were less numerous during these weeks, indicating a fair degree of compliance.[36] If the ceremony and the feast ended with leading the couple to the marital bed, the London records remain coy about this final ritual of the consummation of marriage.

Contract Complications

Broken contracts were the stuff of courts, but in the case of marriage contracts, the emotions of the bride, the groom, the parents, and the "well-wishers" were at a fevered pitch. These were not simply financial arrangements; they represented the future of the young people and their families. Promises made at the church door were broken, or more was promised than actually existed. The complaints fall into the categories of forced marriages, thwarted marriages and breach of contract, and failure to pay the full dower or dowry. Sometimes other problems arose, such as a prior commitment to marry someone else. The cases are pathetic ones of the greedy, the dishonest, and the gullible.

The Church, as we have seen, hastened some marriages to move the couple from fornication to marriage, but most of the forced marriages that appear in civic, as opposed to church, court records involved the abduction of wards and minors along with their inheritances. John Spray, for instance, had been awarded the guardianship of Robert, son of William Huberd. In 1331, John came before the mayor and aldermen and complained that Master William de Rameseye, junior, and his wife Christiana, together with Rameseye's father, brother, other male relatives, and a chaplain, had forcefully abducted Robert and caused him to be married to Agnes, a daughter of William de Rameseye. The marriage meant that John lost 100 marks. William and Christiana appeared before the mayor and argued they were not guilty of abduction, "and as to the marriage, they said it had taken place with the assent of the infants." They obviously knew the requirement of free consent and made a point of mentioning it. They were acquitted of the abduction. The mayor then looked into the matter further and found that the marriage could not be annulled, so the mayor recommended that Robert decide if he wanted to continue living with John Spray or to live with William de Rameseye, his wife, and Robert's new bride. Robert chose to live with his new family.[37]

Breach of contract was a frequent grievance. James Helberd, a fuller, said that he had made a contract and faithfully promised to wed Joan Englefeld, a servant of John Broun of Winchester, and John had agreed to the marriage. Then John had taken action against him and put him in prison.[38] Breach of contract could be even more complicated. William Bumpsted, a mercer, complained that he had made a contract to marry Margaret Baker three years earlier. She was an orphan living in the house of Henry Bumpsted. Her father's executors took exception to the marriage plans. William acted rashly in coming and taking Margaret away and marrying her. The executors took her back and brought her to the archbishop of Canterbury's court to have the marriage annulled. The archbishop referred the case to Rome. William, meanwhile, was thrown into prison. Then the executors agitated with a third party over a debt that Henry Bumpsted owed, and William was afraid that Henry would be put into prison as well.[39]

Another problem that both husbands and wives faced was that the dower or dowry might not be available, even if it was promised. Widows were more likely to have to fight for dower than men were for dowry. In part, this was because the men received dowry immediately, whereas the widow had to make her case after the death of her husband. All sorts of things could go amiss with these contracts. John Johnson, a butcher of London, said that in order to arrange a marriage between his niece, Margaret, daughter of Richard Johnson, and Nicholas Okerford of London, a vintner, he granted her a dowry of £50 to be paid in three bonds, due on certain days at £20 each, with the last due in 1497. Then Nicholas demanded the whole amount at once.[40] And a disappointed groom, John Scarlet of London, a goldsmith, married the daughter of a widow from St. Albans. It was a classic contract. At the espousals, he settled a jointure of London property on her that yielded a yearly value of 10 marks. In exchange for this comfortable dower, the widow was to give him £20 in marks. He had not been paid despite frequent requests.[41]

Sometimes the contract specified that the father-in-law would provide not only a dowry but also support and contributions to setting up a household. One husband petitioned the lord chancellor for redress, saying that his father-in-law had promised him 20 marks of "lawful money of England" and his "finding" (support) for two years on his marriage to the daughter. He married the daughter but had seen nothing of the promised money, which his father-in-law utterly refused.[42] Even more modest amounts could lead to a petition. Richard Dryffeld, a clerk of London, married the daughter of a scrivener. He was to get 10 marks sterling at marriage and 100 marks for the household, but he had received only 6 marks and 26 s. for the household.[43]

Clandestine marriages could end in dispute about their validity.[44] The informal vows that appear in the church courts are similar to those of John Arnold and Mariana Fildors. John said, "May you nott fynd in your hert to love me as I may find in my heart to love you, on condition that you do the same to me?" After that, John gave his hand to Marrian and said, "I John take ye Marion to be my wyffe all others to forsake and thereto I plyte the my troth." After that the bride said, "I Marion take the John to my husband and thereto I plyghte the my trouth." Witnesses vouched that these words were said, and the court agreed.[45]

Even after the reading of the banns, prior contracts could lead to a threat of invalidation of marriage. Agnes Good stopped the marriage of her daughter, Joan Good, to Robert Nobylle, although the banns had already been announced. She said that another man had made a contract with Joan to have her as his wife.[46] Impediment of marriage cases averaged two and a half a year for the late fifteenth and early sixteenth century in an ecclesiastical court, but these cases did not end in resolution.[47]

Robert Baynet, an apprentice hailing from Royston in Cambridgeshire, had learned haberdashery from John King in London. He had made a marriage contract with a woman in Royston and had returned to London to buy goods he needed for his trade. A servant in John King's service claimed that Robert had made a contract of marriage with her already, and King took her side. Claiming damages to his servant, he had Robert put in prison. Robert's plea was a reasonable one. He argued to the lord chancellor that it would be to his material and spiritual disadvantage to marry the servant. If the servant had a claim of prior contract, she and King should take the matter to the church court.[48] He was a shrewd young man and had a good argument, but the petitions to the lord chancellor seldom tell the outcome.

In an extortion case, John Borell petitioned the Lord Chancellor in a tale of woe about the obstruction of his marriage plans, blackmail, and duplicity that he had experienced at the hands of an unscrupulous member of the clergy. John was a waxchandeler in London. He was planning to be married on a Saturday, and all the arrangements were made, and his friends were in London to celebrate the wedding. He complained that "Sir Thomas Jeffrey, priest and proctor of the Court of Arches and Maud Clerk, alias Bowys, now his alleged wife and 'a vicious woman,'" brought a false charge of prior contract of marriage the Wednesday before his wedding, "saying that I must appear in the Court of Canterbury where it was deposed before me that I had made a prior contract with the said Maud." John claimed that Maud had already brought a similar case against another man, one Bowys, saying she was contracted to him. He insisted that Sir Jeffrey and Maud bring written proof of prior contract to the court. They claimed that they had them. On the Saturday before he was to marry, John went to St. Paul's and met Thomas. He told him that there were no witnesses to the alleged prior contract and asked Sir Thomas "in good conscience not to stand in the way of [his] marriage." The priest responded that he would not prohibit the marriage if he was given a bribe of £20 or more. Since John could not pay that much immediately, he entered into two obligations (agreements to pay the amount asked) and gave him 40 s. John explained that "considering how much the postponement of the wedding would cost, I agreed to pay." The two went to the court and said that Maud had no witnesses.

Sir Thomas, however, knew that he could get more out of his victim. John went on in his plea to the chancellor, saying, "When I was in the church with my friends on the day of my wedding, Thomas came and said there was another woman who would come and stop the wedding unless she was recompensed with money." Thomas did not produce the woman but threatened to stop the wedding unless John gave him his ring. John did and, as he said: "And so I was married." All of this blackmail and extortion went on without the bride or his friends knowing about possible impediments.

John had gotten wiser, and his marriage must have been secure, because he took neighbors with him to confront Thomas when the first obligation was due. The priest, however, claimed that he had given the obligations to Maud and that John should settle with her. Maud wanted a further bribe because she said that Thomas had put them out to others and she would have to pay to get them back. John gave her 13 s. 4 d. to secure them. She never delivered the obligations.

When John threatened to sue, Thomas said that within the fortnight he would take the obligations into the Mayor's court. John, however, was able to bring the matter to the Chancery and arrange a mediation of the case with two arbiters. Each side put up £20 to abide by the arbitration. John claimed that he had abided by the agreement, but Thomas pursued the matter in the mayor's court and got a judgment. Thomas claimed that his attorney acted without his knowledge (the case is not recorded in the Mayor's court). John went to St. Paul's on Sunday to talk to the arbiters, who said that Thomas should withdraw if the attorney had acted without his knowledge. Thomas would not, so John went back to the chancellor to get the return of his obligations.[49] We do not know the end of John's tale, but we do learn from it that marriage contracts were a way for all sorts of unscrupulous people to make money on this lucrative exchange of wealth.

Letters of Love and Marriage

Court cases tend to show the negative side of marriage contracts, but fortunately two sets of letters give a more intimate and a more positive view of late medieval London marriage. The scramble for brides with good social connections and wealth appears in two collections of letters from the fifteenth century, those of the Stonor (covering 1290–1483) and the Cely (covering 1475–88) families.[50] These merchant families were as attuned to making a good deal in the marriage market as they were in the wool trade. The business side of the marriages comes through clearly in the letters, but they also show the network of friends and family that arranged for prospective grooms to meet young women, the courtship, and even the love and tenderness that developed between the couples. The Stonor letters preserve a series of letters from Thomas Betson relating to his long-anticipated marriage to Katherine Ryche, daughter of William Stonor's second wife.[51] Betson's letters point to a romantic and tender attraction to Katherine, a London orphan, who is too young to marry. George and Richard Cely, as their letters indicate, were interested in the financial rewards of a good marriage but also considered the attractiveness of the potential bride's appearance, her social connections, and her intelligence.[52] The two letter collections show us courtships leading to a first marriage, as well as the courtship and marriage of a wealthy London widow.

Both the Celys and Betson were merchants dealing in the wool staple. They bought wool from the suppliers in England and shipped it to the Low Countries to be turned into fine woolen cloth in Flanders. They were called merchants of the staple, or staplers. The term applied to the seal put on bales of wool or wool fells. Customs on wool was one of the chief sources of revenue from trade for the Crown. To collect the revenues, the Crown assigned ports—sometimes Calais, sometimes Bruges, sometimes Antwerp—as the point of unloading and taxing the wool; this central wool market was known as the *staple*. The location of the trade in one city meant that all the English wool merchants were well acquainted with each other and had a community both in England and on the Continent. The merchants of the staple were high-status persons in English society and sought out alliances in marriage within their circle or with the gentry in the countryside.

In 1375 Sir William Stonor, a country gentleman, married Elizabeth Ryche, the daughter of a London alderman and widow of a wealthy London merchant. Since the Stonors had sheep on their estates, the connection with London merchants of the staple was a natural alliance. Thomas Betson had been a business associate, perhaps an agent, of Elizabeth's husband and traded at the Staple in Calais. He acted as Elizabeth's agent in London and traded for Stonor until Elizabeth's death in 1479. Thomas was a good friend of Elizabeth and also of her mother and was engaged to marry Katherine Ryche, daughter of Elizabeth and her first husband and stepdaughter of William Stonor. Katherine was the oldest child of Elizabeth and a typical London orphan.[53] When her father died, her mother remarried, so she grew up with a stepfather. Her father, however, had apparently arranged for both her guardianship and her marriage before he died.

At twelve or thirteen, Katherine was too young to marry, but Betson was willing to wait for her.[54] Since Betson knew Elizabeth and her first husband in London, he would have known Katherine, as well, perhaps since birth. The Stonors had two houses in London, and Elizabeth seems to have spent much time in the city along with Katherine and her other children. Betson was so close to the family that he had his own chamber in the Stonor house, and Elizabeth refers to him in letters as "my son Betson."[55] Betson visited Elizabeth's mother, who was not a pleasant woman, took care of the younger children in London, escorted Elizabeth, and even remonstrated with her on her extravagant purchases.[56] The close personal bonds of Betson with Elizabeth and William Stonor meant that the arranged marriage had the blessings of important kin. Among the many matters of business preserved in the letters exchanged among these three are also tender love notes to Katherine.

We do not know the age disparity between Katherine and Thomas, but it was probably ten years, if not more. His kind and teasing letters to his young fiancée remind one of the housekeeping book that the "Ménagier of Paris" wrote for his young wife. The author, a wealthy member of the Parisian bourgeoisie at the end of the fourteenth century, married an orphan from the country, perhaps of higher birth than himself, and very much younger; he was probably in his sixties, and she was fifteen. He presumed that she would outlive him and remarry, and he wanted her to be a credit to her training. His book has an almost fatherly tone. Throughout the book he addressed her as "dear sister."[57] Betson's tone was more that of a man establishing himself in trade and anticipating a first marriage to a younger woman.

In Betson's first letter in the collection (April 1476 to William Stonor) he opens with greetings to Stonor and "to my worshipful mistress your wife, and if it please your mastership, to my mistress Katherine."[58] He calls her "cousin" throughout the correspondence, a term that was in general use in the fifteenth century for friends, not just blood relatives. The rest of the letter concerns the arrival of a shipment of wool.

From Calais on April 22, ten days later, he wrote to thank William Stonor "for your gentle cheer and faithful love, the which always ye bear and owe unto me." He wrote, as usual, of his good will toward his master and his household and sent with the letter-bearer a gift of pickled eels as well as a pipe of wine. But the postscript referred to his fiancée: "I beseech your mastership that this poor writing may have me lowly recommended to my right worshipful mistress your wife, and in like wise to my gentle cousin and kind mistress Katherine Ryche, to whom I beseech your mastership ever to be favorable and loving."[59]

At the beginning of June in 1476, Betson wrote a long letter to Katherine herself. The letter showed the affection that he had for her and his consideration of her age. He noted that he had received a letter about her health and that he was about to receive a token from her as well.[60] Betson continued his love letter, urging her to eat well so that she would grow up faster and become his bride.

And if ye would be a good eater of your meat always, that ye might wax and grow fast to be a woman ye should make me the gladdest man of the world, by my troth; for when I remember your favor and your sad loving dealing to me wards, for sooth ye make me even very glad and joyous in my heart; and on the other side again, when I remember your young youth, and see well that ye be none eater of your meat, the which should help you greatly in waxing, for sooth then ye make me very heavy again. And therefore I pray you, mine own sweet Cousin, even as you love me, to be merry and eat your meat like a woman. And if ye will so do for my love, look what ye will desire of me, whatsoever it be, and by my troth, I promise you by the help of our Lord to perform it in my power. I can no more say now, but on my coming home I will tell you much more between you and me and God before.[61]

Katherine had apparently communicated with him, probably through a messenger.

He returned her regards and asked her to give half to the others in the household but to keep the other half for herself. He then went on to discuss the affection that they shared for his horse.

I pray you greet well my horse and pray him to give you four of his years to help you withal; and I will at my coming home give him four of my years and four horse loaves till amends. Tell him that I prayed him so. And Cousin Katherine, I thank you for him, and my wife shall thank you for him later; for you do great cost upon him, as is told to me.[62]

The reference to the horse giving her four years and Betson giving the horse four years suggests a desire to lower the age gap between them. Betson's letter is full of reference to his impatience for her to grow up so that they can marry. The reference to "his wife" thanking the horse is again an anticipation of their marriage.

Katherine came to visit him in London, but they failed to meet. She apparently went to a tavern called Calais, but he was in Calais across the Channel. Signing the letter "your faithful Cousin and lover Thomas Betson," he adds "I send you this ring for a token." Even the address is full of tenderness. "To my faithful and heartily beloved cousin Katherine Rich at Stonor, this letter be delivered in haste."[63] Meanwhile, Katherine continued to grow. In December 1477 Betson wrote to Elizabeth that he was upset with Katherine because she had not written to him. He complained that he had written to her several times but received no response. "I wax weary; she might get a secretary, if she would and if she will not it shall put me to less labor to answer her letters again."[64] Apparently Katherine could write as well as dictate letters. In June 1478 he wrote to Elizabeth of his sorrow that Katherine was not in London when he arrived there from Calais. "My pain is the more; I must needs suffer as I have done in times past, and so will I do for God's sake and hers."[65]

By June 24, 1478, however, Katherine was fifteen, and Elizabeth charged Thomas to buy her trousseau. Apparently, she was unable to come to London at the time, and he was accustomed to make purchases for the family. He also had to ready his house for his bride. He understandably expressed some anxiety over this.

> I must beseech your ladyship to send me [your advice] how I shall be demeaned in such things as shall belong to my cousin Katherine, and how I shall provide for them. She must have girdles, three at the least, and how they shall be made I know not, and many other things she must have, ye know well what they be, in faith I know not.

It was apparently the task of the mother to shop for the trousseau, and Betson found himself ill equipped to do so. Even the offer to send Katherine to help was no comfort to him, because she did not have the experience herself to shop for a trousseau.[66]

The groom's preparation of his house was part of the tradition we have seen in arrangements for marriage. The social capital of the well-furnished house, with plate, tapestries, bedsteads, tables, and benches was part of the external show of a good marriage. Likewise, the well-outfitted bride with a valuable girdle and new gowns and coats displayed the status of the new couple.[67]

William Stonor as well as Elizabeth had given permission for the wedding to take place, and Betson wrote to William full of thanks and excitement: "Our vicar here, so God help me, will cry out upon her [read the banns] within this ten weeks and less, and by that time I shall be ready in every point, by God's grace, and so I would she were, forsooth ye may believe me of it." Stonor had invited Betson to come to the country to celebrate and meet with Katherine, but he had to decline because of the press of business.[68] The couple apparently married in August or September 1478.[69]

Katherine's marriage plunged her into adult life. In the first year of marriage, Betson suffered a serious illness. Katherine nursed him and carried on his business while pregnant with their first child, a son. In a letter from the end of September 1479, one of Stonor's agents described the scene at the house in Stebenhith. Betson was very ill but "made us good cheer as a sick man might," but "for good faith we saw by his demeanor that he might not prosper in this world." He fell asleep when they left his chamber.

Stonor was worried about his business, but his agent assured him that Betson's uncle and Katherine had everything under control. Betson had two books, one of expenditures and one of sales, and Katherine kept these in a chest "under lock and key." The choice of executors, in the event of Betson's death, was discussed, and the agent recommended that Katherine alone should be the executor. The agent suggested this move not because he had great confidence in Katherine but because he felt she could be manipulated by the family if the two honest merchants, who were customary as additional executors, were left out. On October 2 he wrote that a physician had put plasters on Thomas and that his health improved. Meanwhile, Katherine was in charge of everything and would communicate with her stepfather should Betson die. But on October 10, 1479, Betson's apprentice was able to write: "ye should understand that my master Thomas Betson is right well amended"; he no longer needed a physician.[70]

Thomas Betson lived nearly seven more years, dying in the spring of 1486. Katherine must have been about twenty-three at the time. He described himself in his will as a stockfishmonger and a merchant of the staple of Calais. He left his wife a place that he had lately purchased from Sir John Scott and a house in Holborn for her life use (dower). Since his children were minors, he appointed the warden and Fellowship of Stockfishmongers to be guardian of his children's goods, "to be charged with the finding of my said children." During their eight-year marriage, Thomas and Katherine had two sons and three daughters who were mentioned in the will. Following the pattern that was characteristic of many young widows with minor children, Katherine remarried. Her second husband was William Welbek, a haberdasher. She had another son and died in 1510 at the age of fifty or older.[71]

Richard and George Cely's search for wives appears in the Cely letters and is described by Alison Hanham in *The Celys and Their World: An English Merchant Family of the Fifteenth Century*.[72] Betson and the Celys interacted as members of the staple but were not close associates. Young men such as Thomas Betson and Richard and George Cely spent much time in Flanders, while their senior partners stayed in London or in their country houses, as did William Stonor and the father of the Celys. The Cely family included the father, Richard Cely, and three sons: Robert, perhaps the oldest, Richard, and George, the youngest. The father's letters show him to be a testy man of business trying to control his sons and his enterprise. Many letters concern wool purchases in the countryside, bringing them to London, shipping them to Calais for distribution, and tallying the resulting profits or losses. Richard Senior, the father, was semiretired in the country, having bought a place in Essex. Robert was a gambler and waster of money, and Richard had ambitions to become a country gentleman. He spent much of his time in the country, and his father encouraged these proclivities.[73] But the correspondence also dealt with personal matters including affairs, marriage, and court business.

The Celys appear in the letters as less pious and more men of the world than Thomas Betson. Remaining accounts indicate that George spent considerable money on his sartorial appearance.[74] While attending to his commercial activities in Calais, George had a couple of affairs with local women. His behavior was typical of men on foreign business assignments. A French admirer, Clare, wrote a love letter to him in 1479:

> Specially beloved, I recommend myself to you, George Cely. Know that I am very well, and I pray God it is the same with you. If it please you to know, I have loved you a long time, but I dared not tell you so. Know that I send you a token, and I pray you to have me in remembrance, and I pray you to send me a token of remembrance, just as I do to you, for love. And I let you know that my heart is set on no man but you, but I think your love is by no means on me.

She signed her letter "All Clare's heart is yours, George Cely; ever in my heart."[75] The affair blossomed, and George installed her in a house in Calais where he kept wool. A few notes George wrote on the back of a letter provide an idea of their intimacy (one presumes it is with Clare), showing them amusing themselves one evening. She undertook to teach him a song in French, which he wrote down in phonetic spelling. The lessons continued with useful phrases, coming to a phrase that suggested that what he is doing shamed her. The phrase was repeated. Presumably, the French lessons and singing moved on to more amorous matters.[76] It was not unusual for English and other foreign merchants to have mistresses and sometimes even wives in places that business took them frequently.

While George's affair was going on, his family in England was looking for a good marriage prospect for him. Richard used their social network of wool merchants for matchmaking. Heading north to buy wool, he met two close friends from the staple. One of them, Dalton, gave him a token to take to his mother. He delivered the token, and she invited him to come to breakfast the next day. George had already approached the lady, making a gift of knives to her sometime earlier. Richard and George had talked about the possibility of George marrying Dalton's sister. Richard met her at breakfast and described her as "goodly a young woman, as fair, as well-bodied and as sad [serious-minded] as I see any this seven year, and a good height." Richard Senior also approved the match, but nothing came of it.[77]

George, who was perhaps twenty-three, was not ready to settle down. While these talks were going on, George had a new paramour, a cook named Margery, with whom he had one child. Richard refers to the death of the child in a letter of 1481. He wrote to his brother that he had talked with their father in the orchard and he had inquired about how George was doing. "And I told him all that it was and he was right sorry for the death of the [illegitimate] child, And I told him … how I liked the young gentlewoman [Dalton's sister]."[78] In 1482 John Dalton, brother of the desirable bride, wrote to Richard that Margery was pregnant once again. This child also died shortly after birth. The young men trading in Calais did not think George's behavior out of the ordinary and even passed on a message that Margery needed a new gown for her churching.[79]

Robert, the eldest and wastrel of the family, had married young and unhappily. When his wife died, he made another marriage contract with Joan Hart in 1480, but they quarreled, and she sued in church court for dissolution of the marriage. Robert fled to Bruges. She demanded that all the gifts he had given her in courtship as well as all that she had given him would be hers. Finally, the Celys agreed that "she has all her own good that was brought to our brother's again, and all the good that our brother left with her save a girdle of gold with the buckle and pendant silver and gilt, and a little gold ring with a little diamond, and a tippet of damask." A priest arranged to have the contract annulled in the church court.[80]

Richard Senior died in January 1482. Not trusting Robert, he made Richard head of the family. The passing of wealth and power made Richard a very eligible bachelor in the mercantile community. As he wrote to George, while he was out buying wool in the countryside, he was greeted by a fellow stapler who asked him if he "were in any way of marriage." His friend said that a local gentleman named Lemeryke, a justice of peace in the county, had a daughter whose mother had left her £40 a year. His friend suggested that if Richard waited until Sunday, he could look at her, and named a man who could be an intermediary to her family. Having received permission from her father, Richard attended matins so that he could see the young woman, Elizabeth, and her stepmother. He described the scene to George.

> And to matins the same day come the young gentlewoman and her mother-in-law [stepmother], and I and William Bretten were saying matins when they come into church. And when matins was done they went to a kinswoman of the young gentlewoman, and I sent to them a pottle [1/2 gallon] of white romaney [wine]. And they took it thankfully, for they had come a mile a'foot that morning. And when mass was done I come and welcomed them, and kissed them, and they thanked me for the wine, and prayed me to come to dinner with them. And I excused me and they made me promise them to drink with them after dinner. And I sent them to dinner a gallon wine, and they sent me a her-onceau roast [a roasted young heron]. And after dinner I come and drank with them, and took William Bretten with me. And we had right good communication, and the person pleased me well, as by the first communication [on first impressions]. She is young, little, and very well-favored and witty [intelligent], and the country speaks much good of her.

The letter ends with the agreement that a betrothal would all rest on negotiations when her father was in London. Nothing came of the arrangement.[81] But the letter is very instructive, once again, of the role of men as matchmakers and women as those who facilitate the meeting of the prospective couple. The gifts of drink are similar to the gifts of food in other evidence.

Everyone thought that the time was ripe for Richard's marriage, and the matchmakers were buzzing with ideas. One business associate urged him "to go and see Rawson's daughter." Rawson was a wealthy alderman, and his daughter would be an excellent match. Richard apparently also thought that he should marry, but, in a worried letter to George, he wrote that a woman called "Em" was pregnant and that he was the obvious father. Em is not mentioned again, but it seems that he was worried that the pregnancy would interfere with his matrimonial prospects. Richard did go to see Rawson's daughter, Anne, and her dower of 500 marks as well as her person were attractive. They were married, and in January 1483 Agnes, Richard's mother, completed her part of the marriage contract in her will. She directed that "according to her promise made to Richard Rawson ... and to Isabel his wife, before and at the time of marriage of the said Richard Cely and Anne," that they should have the house in London on Mark Lane as well as the household goods. As the wills and deeds showed, dower land and dowry could pass to the newly married couple. The marriage was advantageous for Richard because Anne brought a very large infusion of capital into the Celys' trading business. After Richard's death, Anne petitioned to receive her dower of 500 marks back with interest, as well as a portion of Richard's trade profits, arguing that her money helped to build the business.[82]

With Richard married, it was George's turn to think seriously about finding a wife to add further capital to their business. Like his brother, he was looking for a wife among the staplers or the merchant community of London. At a dinner in 1484, George's business employee (factor) in Calais sounded out the possibility of a marriage, without revealing his own identity. The mercer, father or friend of the prospective bride, said that he was well disposed to George, but that there was another man interested in her as well. George lost out to his rival in the short time that his factor began his letter.[83]

The marriage market moved swiftly. Richard had written in 1482 that a wealthy merchant had been buried on March 27, but his widow became a vowess (she vowed not to remarry in a church ceremony) the next day, and so she was out of the market. Since her husband had left her 1,800 marks as a dower, there must have been many a disappointed suitor. But George was successful in his wooing of a young widow, Margery Rygon. It happened so fast that news reached Calais before George's factor completed his letter inquiring about the arrangements.

> Item, sir, William Salford [a maternal relative of Margery] is come. And I spake with him and welcomed him. And he told me how that your mastership and the other gentlewoman [Margery] were at point [concluded] in that matter. Of the which I was right glad, and so he said he was. But he spered [asked] me none other questions, not yet. And, sir, it is said here by many persons here how that ye be sure [contracted] to her. With the which, sir, I am well content and right glad thereof. And sir, all those here that knowth you, both merchants and soldiers, commend you greatly saying "if that gentlewoman should be worth double that she is you were worthy to have her." And as for any making of search of your dealings here, I trow there is no man that maketh any. If

they do, they need go no farther than the books in the treasury, where they may find that your sales made within less that the year amounts above £2,000 stg., where that the person that labored for to 'afore you, he and his brother had not in this town this twelve months the one half of that.

Margery had been the second wife of Edmund Rygon and was young and childless. Rygon, a draper and stapler of London, had considerable property in Calais as well as in the English countryside. Margery was his chief executor and received the bulk of his estate.[84] She was a prize catch, indeed. As the factor's letter suggests, there were other suitors, but a search of the treasury books would show the considerable profits that George was making. The implication is that those negotiating this marriage made a thorough investigation of George's business prospects.

Wooing such a widow was expensive. Because other men wanted to marry her, George had to provide lavish courtship gifts as well as a dower. While Richard's mother bequeathed a dower property in London for Anne, George had to provide property out of the money he inherited. Anne later claimed in a petition to Chancery that George had spent all of his joint inheritance with Richard on "jewels, diverse and many rich gifts and pleasures given to one Margery Rygon, then widow, and other her friends, time of his wooing, expenses of his marriage and household, and in lands [bought] to have th'expedition of his said marriage. The purchase of land and property amounted to £483 13 s. 4 d." He did buy property during this period, as his accounts indicate, but probably not as much as Anne had alleged. His own accounts show that he spent 53 s. 6 d. on the fine gold for a wedding ring. He also bought plate and jewels, including a ruby that had belonged to King Richard, which alone was worth £100.[85]

The wedding party lasted ten days (May 13–22, 1485). The actual wedding probably took place on May 18. The cost of the festivities might have totaled around £12 16 s. The purchases were all detailed in accounts and included various fish, poultry, meats, and butter. Spices and some herbs and vegetables were not included in the accounts. Expenses were born by the groom, as was customary. The quantities seem vast, as they do at many of the medieval feasts, and Hanham estimates that the grocery bills would amount to six months of ordinary household expenditure. In addition to rabbit meat, the feast included three live rabbits to release at the feast, perhaps as a fertility symbol.[86]

In June 1484 the newlyweds went to visit Richard and Anne at the Essex estate. By September, George was off again to Calais, leaving Margery in London. Margery wrote him a letter in what may be her own hand. Hanham has a lovely speculation that the little holes in it may indicate that George carried it around on his person, perhaps sewed to a garment. Margery writes as a wife ought to do to her husband and inquires after his welfare and asks that he write to her. She was lonely in a new house with new servants.

> Sir, letting you wit I sent you a heart of gold to a token by Nicklay Kerkebe. And ye shall receive in this letter a fetterlock of gold with a rib there in. And I pray you, sir, to take it in worth at this time, for I knew not who should carry the letter, and therefore I sent none other thing with this letter. No more unto you at this time, but Jesu have you in his keeping.

Margery was pregnant when she wrote, the live rabbits at their wedding feast apparently having worked.

Her separation anxieties increased with George's absence and the expectation of her first child. A family friend and fellow stapler wrote at the end of September that she was afraid of being in the house at night alone and had "delivered Thomas her man [young boy servant] away unto his mother, and therefore she prayed you that ye would deliver you of another lad 'that side of the sea,' for to be in his stead." Margery also asked the friend to inquire about the little fetterlock of gold and to urge George to come home when business was done. Such a little lock was found in a horde of money and jewelry and is now in the British Museum.[87]

Margery was living at the time in a house on Mark Lane that had belonged to Richard Cely Senior. She was in a new house, afraid of the dark, without her familiar servants, and expecting her first child. Her letter and that of the Celys' friend give a glimpse into arranged marriages. The affection was strong, pregnancy occurred early, and the wife had to adjust to new surroundings. But Margery soon had children and devoted servants to keep her occupied while George was away on business.

When George died in June 1489, his five-year marriage to Margery had produced four children and a fifth in the womb. In his will, George left Margery the property promised to her in her jointure and left his children £50 each. The four sons were also to have land in the country and in London, and the child in the womb was to have other properties.

Margery was sole executor and was to be guardian and take the profits from the property. Still young and very wealthy, she married a third time. Richard died in 1492, leaving his wife and three daughters. Anne, as we have seen, sued in Chancery for a larger share in the estate of George and Richard. She, too, remarried.[88]

A letter from Elizabeth Ryche Stonor gives an idea of life going on after the death of the first husband. Elizabeth spent a part of her first year of marriage to Stonor in London and wrote to him asking him to send two basins and ewers of silver, the silver candlesticks, and the monstrans and the little silver basin to set it in.[89] She wanted these items to commemorate the first anniversary of Thomas Ryche's death. The whole exchange indicates an acceptance of both the old and the new husband as part of her life.[90]

Court cases distort the picture of human nature, giving the worst side full play. They also miss some of the stages of the process of contracting a marriage. The letters balance the picture, and in the case of the Celys and Stonors, we are fortunate to have such evidence. They show the process of negotiation and the satisfaction, or lack thereof, with the marriage contracts. We can assume that most marriage contracts were honorable and were adhered to and that many of the marriage partnerships were successful. Marriage was a pooling of considerable wealth —vast for those of the upper ranks of society—and was also important for the laborers and servants. But money alone was not enough; the Celys and Thomas Betson wanted wives who could manage their households and businesses, who were attractive, and who came from their own social class. They trusted their wives with business when they were ill or away, and they made their wives their executors. While both partners contributed to the capital formation at marriage with dowry and dower, the husband was the dominant partner in the management of it. But with the death of a husband, the widow was left with the problem of obtaining dower, raising their children, and deciding whether or not to remarry.

✵ 5 ✵
Recovery of Dower and Widows' Remarriage

A Venetian writing of his visit to England around 1500 observed the concentration of wealth and property in women's hands. He accurately reported that London law divided a testator's property three ways, allowing a third to the wife for her life use, a third for immediate inheritance of the heirs, and a third for burial and the benefit of the testator's soul. But he also commented that the wife managed during her lifetime to secret away some extra wealth. The widow took into a second marriage, as well as her portion, the inheritance of minor children, for the new husband's use, if not ownership. The children, he claimed, never received the full value of their father's estate.[1] The Italian visitor observed that in London, unlike

Venice, long patrilineages did not exist, and he blamed this on the division of property when the head of the family died. The twentieth-century scholar of London Sylvia Thrupp argued that the reason that strong patrilineages did not develop in London was that as soon as merchant families acquired wealth, usually in two generations, they married into the gentry families or bought estates in the country and were absorbed into the gentry.[2] But the Italian visitor might also have been correct about the reason that London seemed to have more horizontal social ties than the vertical ones that were common in Venice, Florence, and Ghent. London's laws were generous with daughters, wives, and widows, with the result that a significant amount of London's real estate and liquid wealth passed through the hands of women.

This chapter explores the success of widows in recovery of their dower and the high rate of remarriage among women who went to London's courts to plead for dower or to arrange for the wardship of their children. The considerable wealth of these women in property and movables contributed to the capital formation of London's merchant class in the late Middle Ages. The case of the Celys and Betson suggest the importance of this infusion of wealth through marriage to London girls or widows. For London men, finding a suitable mate with accumulated wealth and social status and connections outweighed the importance of establishing a patriline. A widow with a dowry, dower, and perhaps minor children whose property a new husband could manage was a very attractive marriage prospect. London men favored this recirculation of the wealth through remarriage of widows to men of a similar social status, sometimes even within the same guild. The result was that London developed horizontal ties among the social elites rather than male bloodlines. These bonds of intermarriage, in turn, made the guilds and the elite very powerful in London and its politics in the late fourteenth and fifteenth century.

Widowhood must have been a common experience in London, as it was in all European urban centers. At least among elites, the relatively late age of marriage for men and early age of marriage for women in European cities, perhaps also in London, meant that many women experienced early widowhood. Though we do not have full statistics, historians would like to know how many women became widows in a year and what their ages and conditions were. In spite of the dangers associated with childbirth, women in the Middle Ages seem to have outlived their husbands on the average. In the London wills, 53 percent of men's wills mention a surviving wife.[3] In Tuscan cities in the fifteenth century about a quarter of the women were widows.[4] What happened to these women's property, therefore, is of major importance.

Recovery of Dower

We know that brides received dower at the church door, through a will, by contract, or by the custom of London, but did the women actually acquire the money and property due to them?[5] Promises of dower could not be sustained if the husband did not have clear title to it. The relatives or next best friends of the bride could ask to see the deeds and could even consult the records, but slips occurred, and deeds were disputed. Although the husband was not supposed to alienate dower property without his wife's permission, he might have done so surreptitiously. In the matter of recovery of dower, as in provisions for orphans, London patriarchs kept a watchful eye on widows' property and provided them with a venue for their cases. The Husting court heard common pleas including cases involving recovery of dower, and a separate roll of common pleas was kept.[6] The concern of the magistrates and patriarchs of London, however, was only partly motivated by a consideration for the welfare of a fellow citizen's widow and family. They were also interested in preserving clear title to property and maintaining the inheritance of orphans. Their interest did not extend to preserving lineages, as was the case in Italy or Ghent. The "self-interested patriarchy" played a role in dower disputes.

Tracing property ownership, however, was not the only motivation for patriarchal concern about widows. A recurrent theme of medieval prescriptive literature and sermons was protection of widows and their inheritance and condemnation of those who cheated them. Among others, William Langland in *Piers Plowman* referred to the superior holiness of the poor widow who gave her two mites (roughly 1/24 d.), which was her sole support, compared to others who gave only a part of their abundant wealth. He was, of course, calling upon the poignant parable recorded in the gospels of Luke and Mark.[7] Government had laws protecting the widow's portion. King Henry III, for instance, confirmed that widows of London are "freely absolved from all kinds of tallages, redemptions, and all kinds of contributions" because he was unwilling to infringe on their liberties and customs "but rather being willing to protect them and their liberties." He further ordered the city officials not to molest widows and to make amends without delay so that he would hear "no more clamor thereupon."[8] Apparently, women were protesting, or their second husbands were.

The widows we can observe in the records were seeking control over considerably more than a "mite." They were, for the most part, widows of comfortable London craftsmen or wealthy merchants. Although not the stereotypical poor, defenseless widow of medieval literature, the widows studied here had to sue to receive their full dower from other parties who had a claim to it.

Widows who felt that they had not received their full dower initiated their cases in the Husting court of common pleas.[9] London law was, as usual, explicit about the way to pursue a writ of dower (*Unde nihil habet*).[10] The records of this court are continuous, with a few interruptions, from the late thirteenth into the fifteenth century. The dower cases sampled in this study span over a century (1301–1433).[11] These court records have not been studied, so that the evidence presented here is a suggestion of the possibilities of this court for studying dower. The cases show the length of time it took to get a resolution, the use of attorneys, widows' success rate, their remarriage, and a variety of other information about the circumstances that led to success or failure of the widows' cases.

The total number of cases (299) decreased from 96 in 1301–6 to 6 in 1427–33. The decrease in the number of cases can be explained partly by a diminished population after the plague of 1348 and its subsequent visitations and also by the drop in popularity of the Husting court of common pleas.[12] The number of cases drops steadily, perhaps indicating that the families and couples were keeping more written records of contracts. Unfortunately, no source records the percentage of distressed widows forced to sue for their dower, but one to sixteen cases per year in London's common pleas seems a small number.[13] One would hope that dower provisions were so clear that this small number represents the full picture, but that is unlikely. Many disputes might have been settled out of court, by reference to written evidence, or simply abandoned by less aggressive or legally informed widows.

The competence of widows in bringing suits for recovery of dower, as well as their appearance in the court of orphans, suggests that women were comfortable in public life and well informed about London laws; they were knowledgeable about their legal rights and court procedures.[14] Most did not use attorneys or rely on second husbands to initiate their cases. No doubt they had help of male kin, guild brothers, or attorneys. But it is also plausible that their legal information passed through women who had been through the procedure before or that women accompanied other women to court and learned the system by observation. These cases permit us to see women in action in complicated legal cases.

A widow could expect a lengthy court process that would take eleven months on the average. Some cases could take years.[15] Widows initiated the proceedings for recovery of dower by procuring the writ of dower, *Unde nihil habet*, and presenting it in the Husting court of common pleas. The process was mechanical up until the parties viewed the disputed property or the heirs were requested to warrant the possession (seisin) of the husband's property. Few widows employed attorneys until that stage. Although the percentages fluctuated somewhat, about 52 percent of the widows eventually called on attorneys at this point, while only 32 percent of the defendants did.[16] Over 58 percent of the single widows used attorneys before the plague of 1348; after that the percentage went down to about 20 percent. The number of remarried widows hiring attorneys varied, but averaged 47 percent.[17] Among defendants, the number of widows who used attorneys was under a quarter. In general, therefore, widows were more likely to use attorneys than defendants.

Hiring an attorney did not force the cases into lengthier legal battles, nor did it increase the chances of winning the case. Written records, the warranty of heirs, or reliable witnesses were decisive. The attorneys must have been used for court appearances during the waiting periods and for searching and copying records.

The chief contenders for the widow's dower were people ("tenants" by the legal formulation)[18] who claimed title to the land, buildings, shops, taverns, wharves, and so on that the widow said were part of her dower. When a widow started the proceedings to gain control over her dower, the stalling process of defendants began. The tenants were summoned three times and allowed an essoin (an excuse not to attend court) the fourth time. In practice, this formula was almost always followed. Since the court met every two weeks with several vacation periods, the process automatically extended for two months. During this time, the litigants might have resolved the dispute out of court, or one of the parties might have died (neither of these events was necessarily mentioned in the court rolls). The tenants then inspected the property (a view) and after that they were allowed one more essoin. This would add another month. They could have a view even if the widow's claim to the property through the husband was clear.

If the former husband's claim was in dispute, the tenants could call the heirs to warrant ownership. It could take months for the correct people to testify, because they might be in outlying counties and have to wait until a royal circuit justice could interview them. In about three-quarters of the contested cases, the defendants called one or more parties to war-rant. The defendants that Sibilla, widow of Roger Loveday, sued called to warrant his son by a former marriage, who vouched that his father did not legally hold the property on November 4, 1302, when Sibilla and Loveday married.[19]

For the most part, the widows faced men as defendants (two-thirds to three-fourths) or couples (49 percent in 1301–6 but dropping to about 15 percent thereafter) who were tenants on the property that the plain-tiff's former husband had promised in dower. Because widows might have been dowered with a number of different properties, they often had sev-eral concurrent cases going on at the same time. The average number of defendants was two to three.[20] The general assumption based on the royal court of common pleas has been that the husband's brother or a son by an earlier marriage would be the most likely to gain by defrauding the widow of her dower.[21] In London, only about 10 percent of the cases involved someone related to the widow, usually a son or the husband's brother.[22] But the third most likely kinship relation was a sister-in-law, either married to the husband's brother or a sister of the husband. These disputes were often over the way that the initial patrimony was divided, as was the complaint of Anne Cely.

The disputed dower followed the same pattern as bequests made in wills. For the most part, widows sought rights over real estate (about 90 percent or more of the cases) and only occasionally over money in addi-tion to real property. The most common dower plea was over a messuage that would have given the widow a home and a yard area as well. Shops, gardens, and wharves also appeared. Some of the disputed dowers were sizable—examples include one with ten shops and four solars; one with twenty messuages along with shops, cellars, and solars; one with sixteen messuages and twenty-four shops. Even if the dower was worth only 20 s. or a third share of 44 s., widows and their new husbands pursued the mat-ter in court.

Once the case came into court, a number of actions were possible. The parties could settle out of court, or the widow might have died so no resolution appeared in court. During the fourteenth century, 56 to 83 per-cent of the cases reached resolution.[23] By the fifteenth century, there were too few cases to be statistically significant, but only a third of the cases came to resolution.

If the parties pursued the suit in court, the various stages set forth in the *Liber Albus* came into play. Views of the property or scrutiny of deeds and wills enrolled in the Husting court were common and could be decisive. Other actions might be the removal of the plea to another court (usually to the king's court under a writ of *melius*) or a delay of the case through an agreement to delay the case proceedings. In the first instance, the widow might have property outside London that would make it easier for her to take her case to the king's court, or she might perceive that she stood a better chance there. In the second, the parties might decide to delay the court case either because one of the parties was too ill or too busy to pursue the matter, or was out of the country, or was trying to arrange an agreement. In London, such a delay was called a "love day."

The defendants had a variety of arguments that they used to dispute the widow's right to dower. The most common one, in 70 percent of the cases, was that the husband did not have title to the property at the time of the marriage.[24] When Matilda, widow of Thomas de Lincoln, complained that she had been given one tenement for life and that Adam Pykemann, fishmonger, retained it, he was able to prove that Thomas was not seised at the time of her marriage. Likewise Agnes, widow of Gilbert Trippe, found that the jury would not support her claim because her husband did not have legal possession and could not have endowed her at the time of her marriage.[25]

Although this sad commentary on the honesty of husbands was the most common objection that defendants cited, in other cases they claimed that the widow had renounced her dower.[26] Agnes, widow of William le Marschal, lost her claim against John de Langton, clerk. He used a variety of arguments, first saying that she had remarried Francisco de Villers and therefore lost her rights. This argument apparently was not clear enough, so he appealed to William le Marschal's will. In it she was to relinquish her right to a messuage in exchange for 10 s. 1 d. per year for her life. John was able to prove that she and her coheirs had consigned the property to him. Johanna, widow of Simon Corp, won her case against a couple who claimed that she had agreed to accept goods in lieu of dower. She successfully argued that the goods were in the capital tenement and the will did not exclude her right to the tenement, which she would have automatically under London customary law. She was able to point to the clear statement in the will that she would have the real estate and one-half of the household goods in lieu of dower.[27]

The widow sometimes cited the wrong property in her suit and then either had to drop the case or begin again.[28] Or she might have remarried and had to begin the process with a new writ including the name of her new husband. Other technicalities led to defective writs. When Emma, widow of Robert Burdeyn, brought a writ against William de Thorntoft, he claimed that he held the land with his brother, Hugh, who was not mentioned in the original writ. The widow had to start the process again with both William and Hugh mentioned in the writ.[29] Thomas de Pakyngho and Christina, former wife of John de Braghwyng, had to start their case again because they spelled the defendant's name wrong. It was Edelena, not Elena.[30]

In a few cases the defendants claimed that the marriage was not valid and, therefore, the widow had no claim to the property. Maria, widow of Simon le Bole, sued Simon atte Gate, butcher, and John de Stafford, cordwainer, for her dower. Simon used the argument that her husband was never seised of the land, but John said that Maria had relinquished her claim to one-third of 13 s. 4 d. eight and a half years earlier when she had committed adultery with John de Thorp. She did not deny the adultery but claimed that she had been reconciled with Simon before he died. She did not win.[31] The most complex of these cases involved Isabella Pledour, who claimed to be married to Richard Lyons and demanded 3,000 marks from his estate. The executor claimed that their marriage had been annulled "on account of certain impediments" and that she had no claim. She had sued in the Husting court of common pleas to get certain property and had been rebuffed because she was not legally married. Finally, the court appealed to the bishop, who affirmed that the couple had been legally married but that, at the request of Richard Lyons, the marriage was annulled.[32]

Widows were not always innocent victims of husbands' deceits or tenants' rapaciousness. The widow and sometimes her new husband contrived to lay claim to property that the widow had legally sold or rented. John del Mauntes, Johanna, his wife, and Simon de Merworth were able to produce a charter with the seal of Alinora, widow of Adam Russel, that clearly showed that she had alienated the property to them. Alinora and her attorney could not deny that it was her seal.[33] Some widows were aggressive about keeping more than their share of a former husband's property. John Cope, son and heir of Adam Cope, and Ivo, son and heir of Ivo de Fulham, both took their mothers to court to regain their inheritance.[34]

The rights of the husband to devise (sell) the property assigned to the wife as dower was a thorny problem in borough law. Some boroughs would only allow it in extreme poverty, and if all other property had been sold, but others gave husbands the right to sell.[35] In London, the enrollment of the land transactions and deeds in the Husting court indicated a final concord when a husband and wife jointly alienated property. The court examined the wife in private, separate from her husband. If she voluntarily renounced title, she could not make a later claim for dower.[36] Thus when the parties could produce evidence of the woman's signature or seal, she lost the case. But some purchasers had to pay twice for their property if they did not have a clear record. First, they paid the husband and wife for the property, and after his death, they had to secure title again from the widow for her dower.

Of the cases that came to a resolution of some sort, the widows had good success; 53 percent of them recovered all or part of their dower. Widows won in 72 percent of their cases where a kinship relation is mentioned. In a dispute with another widow, who had not remarried, the plaintiff won in only 42 percent of the cases. Widows won in only 25 percent of their cases against the clergy. Clergy probably had more sense of written evidence or had better access to the terms of men's wills than other adversaries.

Widows could win their cases in a number of ways.[37] The most common was through the defendant's default. If the defendant did not essoin or have a love day to delay proceedings, then the mayor instructed the sheriff to take a third of the property into his hands. If the defendant continued to default, the widow recovered her dower. For instance, Matilda, widow of Robert de Worsted, mercer, claimed property from Randulph de Branghinge of London and Robert de Dodgard and Elena his wife. They did not come to court, and the land was taken into the hands of the city. After they were summoned to and failed to appear at two more sessions of the court, Matilda regained her dower.[38]

The second most common resolution in favor of the widow was for the defendants to voluntarily surrender the dower to her. For instance, Cecilia de Morton, sister-in-law to Lenota, widow of Richard de Morton, claimed that she had received a shop from her father, but in the end she surrendered one-third of it to her brother's widow. Richard, son of Robert Morton, surrendered dower to his stepmother and her new husband, and the guardian of a minor son surrendered the property to his widowed mother. Many of the voluntary surrenders were among kin.[39]

Rather than an outright surrender, the parties might reach a concord. Emma, widow of Godefried de Essex, agreed with Richard de Refham that, out of the £100 in question, she would get 43 s. 6 d. In another case the defendant was *non compos mentis*, and his attorney agreed to an out-of-court settlement.[40]

In 47 percent of the cases, however, the widow did not win her suit. She might have tried to pursue the matter out of court or in another court.

The Mayor's court had a scattering of widows' pleas for recovery of dower, but they are not as systematic as those in the Husting court of common pleas. Of those women losing their cases, fifty-four did not present a writ or retracted the writ before the case came to trial, and in another nine cases, the widow defaulted. In these cases of default or deficiency in regard to the writ, we cannot know if the widow tried legal action again, if she gave up, or if she reached an acceptable out-of-court settlement. Widows lost outright in twenty-four cases. Of the cases that came to a resolution, therefore, widows lost outright in only 13 percent of them. If legal action did not guarantee the dower recovery, at least the odds were worth the relatively small fee for pursuing the case.

Widows in the Marriage Market

A widow had a unique status in both borough and common law. She was not under the legal guardianship (*mund*) of either her father or her husband. While the moral literature perpetuated the image of widows as poor and devout women, another image of widows was also prevalent in Christian literature. Widows could be potentially independent, powerful individuals, and sexually aggressive. Chaucer portrayed such a widow in "The Wife of Bath." A widow could enter into contracts alone, sue for debt, run her business or till her land, and marry off her children. She could also choose her own husband the second time around. If she gained this economic and legal freedom of action, moralists worried, would she also exercise sexual freedom? Remarriage seemed a convenient solution to curb widows' freedoms and distribute their wealth to other males.

Widows had the choice of remarriage as an option for spending their remaining days. These days might be short if they were widowed in plague times or if they were already over forty. But widows might also be looking at a long widowhood if they were healthy and twenty. If they had minor children, they had needs that those women without children would not face. If their marriage had been unpleasant or childbirth painful, they might not want to remarry. On the other hand, they might not have children yet and hope to by remarrying. While they had legal freedom to continue a craft or business, they may have found the prospect daunting and preferred to have a new husband handle affairs. Other widows might respond with relish to their new independence, carrying on their husbands' businesses or seeking to live a single, pious life as a vowess (a woman who vowed not to marry but remained in the world rather than entering a nunnery).

In addition to individual preferences, all widows faced external pressures, such as suitors' designs on their property and moral standards imposed by the Church, the community, and folk wisdom. Freedom in the Middle Ages always came at a price, and for widows, the price could determine the limits on their freedom of choice to remain single.

Medieval lay and ecclesiastical thinkers imbibed the concerns of St. Paul and St. Jerome that women's sexual appetites were voracious, particularly if they had already known sexual intercourse. St. Paul favored remarriage as a solution.[41] Most lay men's concerns were with the material assets the widow had available, but the moralistic literature seemed much more obsessed with her sexual resources. Sex did, indeed, have a practical side, since the heirs of a widow's body could ensure inheritances and continuation of economic benefits, but the physical use, enjoyment, and disposal of her body was the main preoccupation of the moralists.

Neighbors and friends expected the widow to wail and lament her loss, since failure to do so would indicate a hard heart. But the widow was not supposed to make an excessive show of mourning because that made others uncomfortable. She was expected to bury her husband, see that his will was executed, and prepare to live a chaste life while rearing children and looking after her household. Somber clothing was recommended:

> hit falleth to wedowes for to use symple and comune clothinge of
> mene colour and noght gay ne starynge, ne of queynte and sotil
> schap, and take ensample of the holy wedowe Judith, of whom
> holy writ maketh mynde, that anone when hir housbonde was
> deed sche lefte all hir gay attyre and apparaile.

Some moralists, however, could readily observe that black became the complexions of young widows, showing off the delicate tones of their skin and hair. Such vanity posed a threat to their chastity.[42] Preservation of chastity came foremost in the minds of the moral advisers to widows. Now that her husband was gone, she would have to preserve her own good reputation. The advice followed the usual lines for women: keep to your house and surround yourself with honorable female servants.

The moralists were particularly worried that these free women would dress well and wander about to tempt men and themselves with lust. One moralist concluded: "Of this St. Paul complains": They go wandering about from house to house, and are not only idle but tattlers also and busybodies, speaking things which they ought not." He offered the solution that a neighbor gave a man whose cat strayed: "Shorten her tail, cut her ears, and singe her fur; then she will stay at home." So, too, he concluded, should immodest widows be treated, so that "they will not then be so much desired of folk."[43]

Moralists had mixed views about widows' remarriage. Marriage in itself was a sad necessity for procreation, and widowhood could not restore virginity in any case. For older widows, the moralists recommended against remarriage. They were to educate their children and generously share their wealth with the church and charities. But the younger widow, one whose traditional black garments set off the vermilion and white of her complexion, was a special problem. Since she would have more temptation to sin, her passions still being strong and she attractive, she should remarry. If she did not have children, she should remarry soon.[44]

Widows with wealth found themselves under pressure from friends, family, and suitors to remarry.[45] As seen in the negotiations for George Cely's marriage, the market for widows was very aggressive. Two sources give us an insight into the remarriage of widows: suits for recovery of dower and widows appearing in the orphan's court. While neither of these is a complete record of the remarriage, they show surprisingly high percentages of women who appeared in court with a second husbands. Parish registers from the sixteenth century provide a better basis for such a calculation than do medieval records. They indicate that 25 to 30 percent of widows remarried; for widowers it was higher. Remarriage was fairly rapid, with almost half of those remarrying doing so within the year. These figures come mostly from villages.[46] Over 50 percent of the peeresses in fifteenth-century England remarried once, and younger widows remarried even more frequently.[47] Canon law required no mourning period during which a widow or widower could not remarry, so that remarriage could occur soon after the death of a husband or wife. Neither the Church nor society seemed to have a sense of "unseemly haste" when a widow or widower remarried quickly.[48]

Only 3 percent of husbands whose wills are recorded in the London Husting court expressed an objection to their wives' remarriage. A husband might even feel more comfortable about both his wife and his business if she remarried. In 1403, a skinner left his business and apprentices to his wife along with her dower, specifying that she either continue the business or marry someone in the trade within three years.[49] Other men left their wives certain leases for life or until they remarried, presuming that the widow would do so.[50]

Of the widows taking their dower cases to the Husting court of common pleas, an average of 34 percent had remarried in the period of 1301–1433, either before they brought their suit or shortly thereafter. Disputed dower cases were initiated fairly quickly after the death of the husband and the probate of the will, as can be observed by comparing wills with the initiation of dower cases. In this short time, roughly one-third of the widows had remarried and brought the case with their new husband. The percentage of widows who remarried was 25 percent before the Black Death but increased to 50 percent and higher in the decades following the plague of 1348–49. The percentage then dropped to 38 percent in the fifteenth century.[51]

The other source of information about remarriage of widows is the Mayor's court of orphans. As with the suits for recovery of dower, the widows remarried very swiftly because the children would have to appear in court just after the probate of the father's will. Between 1309 and 1458, 57 percent of the widows with minor children had remarried. Perhaps the greater demand for women with children, rather than women with disputed dower, reflects the added incentive for the new husband of having use of the minors' property. What is interesting is that the pattern of remarriage is similar in dower cases and court of orphans data: a lower percentage of marriage in the preplague period and an increase after the Black Death. In the period 1309–48, 34 percent of the widows with children remarried. Widows might have preferred the security of marriage during the famine years of the early fourteenth century, when the price of grain was very high and people were literally dying from starvation in the streets of London. The period from 1349 to 1398 was a time of recurrent visitations of plague and a variety of other diseases, so the population continued low, but 55 percent of the widows with children remarried. In the period of 1399–1458, 68 percent of the widows with minor children chose to remarry. The decrease in remarriages in the dower cases may be an artifact of the decreasing popularity of the Husting court of common pleas.[52]

The figures from neither of these courts can be taken as a reliable indicator of the overall rate of remarriage. Statistics derived from medieval sources require caveats. In both the dower cases and in the widows' appearances as guardians of their children, the women involved are mostly widows of London citizens who pursued crafts or were merchants. The statistics only show those women who appeared in court as remarried very soon after the deaths of their husbands. Widows who had neither minor children nor a disputed dower do not appear. The evidence, incomplete as it is, does show that men and women in London were not refraining from remarriage, thus keeping fertility low. Rather, the marriage market was very active, and the figures available represent underreporting rather than exaggeration. That the population did not recover in London is most probably the result of elevated infant mortality. The shortfall of females, as seen in the orphans' court, might have increased the desirability of widows as marriage partners, since there were fewer females in the population of wealthy women of marriageable age. But the very small size of those families coming into orphans' court also indicates that, even with second marriages, survival of children had not increased.[53]

The presence of minor children did not seem to impede remarriage of a widow or the first marriage of a man. One might think that while the widowed mother of minor children would find it advantageous to turn the management of a craft or business over to a new husband, her prospective husbands might prefer a younger, unencumbered woman. But widows had property, and so did their children; a new husband could manage the wards' property to his advantage until they came of age. Although over 57 percent of the widows remarried, the number of children did not appear to make a significant difference in the decision: 60 percent of the widows with one child remarried, 66 percent with two children, 55 percent with three, and 51 percent with four or more.[54]

Crass economic factors must have motivated the new husbands and account for the upswing in remarriage among urban women at the end of the fourteenth century and in the fifteenth century. As we have seen, the value of orphans' property increased steadily in the fourteenth and fifteenth centuries so that marrying a widow with minor children was extremely advantageous. Combining the third from dower with the third bequeathed to the children could provide a substantial influx of capital. A fifteenth-century grocer married a widow with a dower of £764 and was then appointed guardian of her six children with permission to trade with their patrimony (an equal amount) until they came of age. Thus he was able to use two-thirds of a profitable business for his own purposes.[55]

Changes in London's economy and society following the Black Death may have played a significant role in the remarriage of city widows. London was beginning to play a major role in international trade, not simply in raw wool but also in woolen cloth. London was also the center for redistribution of goods, a manufacturer of crafts, and a center of consumption.[56] For London merchants to fully participate in these larger markets, they needed an influx of capital. A further factor was that guilds became increasingly important in the regulation of London society and government following the Black Death. These horizontal lines of trade and craft brotherhoods strengthened in the society as well, determining social interactions. As we have seen, men increasingly turned to members of their own guild or one closely related to be one of the guardians of their orphans. Since the value of property put into both the widows' dowers and children's bequests had increased substantially by 1368, one can understand that guild brothers would want to keep the wealth among themselves. While few husbands took the precaution of insisting that their wives marry within their profession, guild brothers might have had an implicit understanding about the matter. If one may judge from the numerous and valuable bequests that widows left to their husbands' guilds, the loyalty must have extended to wives as well. The recirculation of widows and their wealth within the guild was another type of protectionism in a period when guilds were becoming increasingly protectionist about their political and economic roles. Trade secrets would not leak out if the widow remained within the brotherhood.[57]

Such evidence as we have suggests that in the selection of a new husband, London women increasingly turned to the same or a related craft or business. Thrupp, in *The Merchant Class of Medieval London*, found that the mayor and aldermen, who had control over the marriages as well as the wardships of orphans, arranged for 84 percent of merchants' daughters to marry merchants. When widows remarried, the proportion was even higher. In thirty-seven cases from the fifteenth century, thirty-four widows chose husbands from the merchant class, twenty-two of whom were from the same company as their former husbands.[58] The same pattern may be observed for the crafts. The historian Steve Rappaport was able to demonstrate that by the sixteenth century, widows insisted on suitors joining their guild as a condition of marriage. In 1592, Mr. Wilks appealed to the Merchant Taylors because Helen Hudson, a vintner's widow, would not marry him unless he transferred to her company. The Merchant Taylors responded by sending a delegation to the widow Hudson to see if she would join them. But she declared that she "will by no means assent to leave her trade." Finally, Wilks was allowed to leave the Merchant Taylors and become a vintner.[59] We have already seen that Thomas Betson and Richard and George Cely married wealthy women associated with their own trade.

The pursuit of well-situated widows was very competitive. Widows would rely on family and friends, as did women in first marriages, but they could also make up their own minds about a husband. Nicholas Boylle, a draper of London, claimed that he ran into John Walsale in Lombard Street, who told him that he knew of a widow who was worth 200 marks and more. He offered to arrange a marriage and said that he would charge a commission of £20 if he succeeded. Nicholas said in his petition to the lord chancellor that the woman wanted to know if Nicholas had the good will of his father and wanted assurances in front of his father that he would leave all his goods and livelihood to her and his son by their marriage. He delivered jewels to her as part of his courtship. But in the end she married someone else. John wanted the £20 commission, but Nicholas refused because no marriage had resulted.[60]

Independent widows, negotiating on their own, occasioned a number of petitions to Chancery. All parties had one complaint or another. There were the disappointed prospective husbands. Roger Radnore of Worcester, a chapman, complained that he had made a contract of marriage twelve months earlier with Alice George, a London widow, and she had sworn in church to the contract and had delivered goods to him. But a rival, William Whetehall, appeared and "subtelly labored with Alice," and she made another contract and married him. When Roger came to London to buy goods according to his occupation, Alice and William had him arrested for the goods she gave him when they were engaged.[61] Elizabeth Baxter, widow of John Croke, said that she married John Being, and they both consented to the marriage. They had lived together as man and wife, but then another woman appeared and claimed she had contracted to marry John. When the church court upheld her, John took Elizabeth's goods, beat her, and imprisoned her.[62]

The widow's ambiguous position as an independent agent also muddled marital arrangements among family members. While family and friends might assume that they exercised control over the widows, their legal rights were not clear. William Yong claimed that Elizabeth Kesten, "widow and well willer and lover" to him, would have married him, but her brother interfered and had him put in prison. On the other hand, Margaret Wodevyld of London said that her brother-in-law was trying to marry her off to a country bumpkin and she would not have him. The brother-in-law had her arrested and jailed. Parents-in-law, who stood to lose control over the dower, also complained bitterly about the legally independent widow. Richard Rous of Cornwall complained that his widowed daughter-in-law was abducted and married while she was in the governance and rule of her uncle in London. He stood to lose the property he had given in dower at his son's marriage. She, of course, could take the dower with her to the new marriage and keep it for her lifetime.[63]

Modern sympathies, like medieval ones, assume that widows would remarry because of a need for male companionship and economic security. But women as well as men could accumulate wealth through marriage. A widow could serially remarry, accumulating dowers as she outlived husbands. Although there are many cases that indicate the high status of a woman with property, that of Thomasine Bonaventure is perhaps the most dramatic. She was born into a gentry family in Cornwall in the 1450s and had a brother who was a priest in Kent with connections in London. She probably moved to London as a high-class servant, most likely in a merchant tailor's household. She married Henry Galle, and when he died in 1467 she received not only a dower of half his property (she was a widow with no children) but also a bequest of £100 in cloth from his shop, the terms of his apprentices, and £100 in cash. It appears that she planned to take over the business. Soon, however, she married another tailor, Thomas Barnaby, and the business passed to him. Barnaby died less than a year later. Again Tomasine was left without children and an additional dower. She then married John Percyvale, another tailor. He eventually became mayor of London. When he died in 1503, she apparently assumed the tailoring business of her last husband, including the training of apprentices. She was so wealthy that she fell victim to one of Henry VII's money-raising schemes. He pardoned her for a trumped up offense in exchange for a payment of £1,000. In her will, she founded a grammar school in her birthplace in Cornwall.[64]

For the widow who remained single, keeping an honest reputation was also somewhat problematic. Jane Burton, a London widow, claimed that she was of good name and fame but that people of malice and evil will, without cause, accused her of having a house of misrule. They had her put in jail and forced her to leave her house. Another widow claimed that in a dispute over rent, her opponent brought a charge against her, calling her a "common woman" (whore). She said that they came while she was at high mass at St. Bride and right after the Passion pulled her out of her pew, and took her off to prison. She indignantly argued that she had been "a pure maiden and wife in the same parish for 14 years." Both women took their case to Chancery.[65]

The remarriages also made complications for the children of first and second marriages. They had to wait until their stepmother died and, unless there was a careful record, they could lose their inheritance during the long wait. The issue of the second wife's right to have a half of her husband's property came up in a case in 1368–69. "Lucy, widow of Henry Bretforde, to have a moity [half] of her late husband's goods, not withstanding his having left children by a former wife and none by the claimant." Her claim was upheld as being the custom of the city, but this right eroded in the sixteenth century.[66]

London Compared to the Continent

As William Caxton observed, only two in ten London families managed to perpetuate themselves. Caxton, who had lived in Flanders for thirty years before returning to London to establish a printing business, was struck by the absence of long lineages among the merchant elite. He commented in the preface to his edition of Cato the Elder that the children of London citizens had inherited great wealth from their fathers but failed to carry on the family name or perpetuate family fortunes. On the Continent he had observed that family lineages lasted for generations, indeed, for centuries. He was convinced that the problem was a moral one. London youth lacked proper values, and if they were raised on the lessons of Cato, they would amend their ways.[67] The Italian visitor also found the lack of patrilineages odd, but he shrewdly observed that the conveyance of property tended to favor women. The London situation was contrary to that on the Continent, although closer to that of northern Europe than of southern Europe.

A study of property and marriage law and practice in sixteenth-century Paris and Dauphiné shows a pattern similar to that of London. Parisian widows had the right of return of lineage (inherited) property in addition to half of the community property, the other half to be divided among the husband's nearest heirs. In statutory law regions, the wife received the return of dowry and the portion allotted to her in the marriage contract. The wife was given control over the inheritance as well as guardianship of the children. It was even possible, with the consent of family, for the widow to remain guardian of the children if she remarried. Patrilineage was not endangered in Paris, because familial councils controlled inherited property and wardship arrangements. Furthermore, a tendency to endogamy among the ruling oligarchy in Paris kept property and inheritances in the family. The data, of course, is from the sixteenth century rather than earlier. Increasingly, however, the husband's will determined the amount the widow received, and eroded the generous provisions of earlier law.[68]

A study of late medieval Ghent showed that the transmission of property favored the remarriage of widows, but not the weakening of patriline. Ghent had generous dower provisions similar to those of London, so that widows were very desirable marriage partners. But the widow did not have control over the wardship of her children or their inheritance.[69] Instead, the father's family took in the orphans and their inheritance and thereby ensured strong patrilines, which have even been called clans. A widow's remarriage tied up a portion of the inheritance for her lifetime, but it did not undermine the patrilineage.[70]

In *The Marriage Exchange*, the historian Martha Howell has shown, in her examination of the customs of Douai and late medieval Flanders, that there was a considerable shift in legal status of marital property in the Low Countries. In this region of southwestern Belgium and northern France, custom favored the conjugal unit at the expense of both lineage and family. Property brought together in marriage belonged to the couple and, at the death of one of them, passed to the survivor. Usually children of the marriage received portions of the property, but in Douai this was not strictly necessary. A surviving wife or husband could dispose of it as she or he wished. Yet custom shifted in the region, giving the husband greater control over conjugal property, even if he predeceased his wife. By the mid–sixteenth century, the wife lost the position of manager of her property and that of her former husband at his death. Her legal and practical status approximated that of other regions in northern Europe. The change in custom was implemented with the greater use of wills and contracts that limited the woman's ability to control conjugal property. Patriarchy and patrilineage became governing ideologies behind the legal change.[71]

In Leiden, the law of 1599 allowed widows to receive communal property, with the provision that any children of the marriage would receive their portions. Brothers and sisters inherited both movable and immovable property equally. Later wills tended not to remove these rights but to reinforce them. Widows could become guardians of their children and were left with a house, if the couple had sufficient wealth. A widow could take this wealth into a second marriage as well. In practice, widows who remarried were mostly those who were left craft shops. Very rich widows and very poor ones tended not to remarry.[72]

The historian Christiane Klapisch-Zuber has shown that in Florence in the late fourteenth and fifteenth centuries, the young age of the brides and the importance of dowry, along with the absence of dower, encouraged the development of vertical patrilineages. Because the husband was much older than the wife, widowhood was very common in Florence. A struggle over the dowry and the widow ensued on the husband's death. The wife's natal family wished to regain the dowry and marry the widow into another household. The former husband's family tried every inducement to keep her, including promises of a comfortable and secure widowhood. While the widow could leave with her dowry, her children remained with the family. Children, therefore, were deprived of inheritance of the dowry if she left. Among the young widows of the elite class between the ages of twenty and twenty-nine, two-thirds remarried, but the number decreased as the widows aged. Florence, therefore, had a situation in which patrilineage was the dominant ideology and could be preserved through keeping the children within the father's family. The dowry remained there as well, if the former daughter-in-law could be persuaded to stay.[73] While women in Florence had no access to their dowry, widows in Venice did. Widow's wills indicate the leeway they had in disposing goods to the benefit of female relatives.[74]

Why did Londoners prefer the horizontal social structure to the patrilines that other cities favored? In part, I argue, London law and London men felt strongly about the survival of their truncated conjugal families. They made generous provisions for their wives and children, gave widows easy access to the city courts to recover dower, and protected orphans from unscrupulous relatives. Their system for passing on real property through women guaranteed the financial stability of their families. While most women found it difficult to carry on their husbands' trade, they could deal freely in real estate, so that these assets were a safer investment to entrust to women. Tanners, for instance, left real estate or other property to wives, but the business to sons or apprentices.[75] The law protected women who rented property or bought and sold property just as it protected men who did so.

A second reason for favoring the transmission of property through women was the increasing importance of the guild system in London in the late fourteenth and fifteenth centuries. As these horizontal lines of trade and craft "brotherhoods" grew stronger and as the wealth became more concentrated in the hands of surviving widows and heirs, it is understandable that guild brothers would want to keep the wealth among themselves. It was not just the widow's wealth that was attractive but also that she might have a fully equipped shop with apprentices, clients, and trade secrets, as was the case with Thomasine Bonaventura. Marriage to a widow of high social status also could help a young man enter London society at a higher status than he could acquire otherwise. The evidence that we have suggests that women, like Thomasine, did turn to the same or a related business in selecting their marriage partners and that this was routine by the sixteenth century.[76]

The fourteenth- and fifteenth-century London evidence shows that as long as the men of London found the city's laws and customs of passing property through women to be beneficial to their own desire for capital, social prestige, and the preservation of their children, they felt no need to create strong patrilines and change the laws. The provision for London's women helped to determine the horizontal nature of London's society at the expense of the vertical, patriarchal lineages that were more typical of the Continent. While Caxton thought it was a moral failure that could be corrected by reading Cato, the Venetian was closer to the mark in blaming London's laws.

❧6❧
For Better or Worse: The Marital Experience

The marital relationship is so sensitive and so culturally specific that it is difficult to form an opinion of medieval marriage separate from our own conceptions of successful or unsuccessful marriages. For instance, corporal punishment of wives, children, and servants was acceptable in the Middle Ages, but what degree of physical correction was allowed by the standards of the time? Many other problems could arise in London families. Did the presence of young male apprentices corrupt masters' wives and did the nubile servant girls lead to sexual indiscretions that were a constant irritant for wives? Working side by side in a shop or participating in joint ventures could produce cooperation, but also accusations of laziness, cheating, and indebtedness. While men's wills show concern and respect for their wives through bequests, granting of guardianship of the children to mothers, and trust in making wives their executors, they do not speak of everyday life together. From the marriage contract on through life together, a husband and wife entered into a partnership, but not necessarily an equal one. A London wife took her husband's name, came under the law of coverture (became the legal responsibility of the husband), and placed her dowry under her husband's administration.

Both the household economy and moral and religious teaching defined gender roles in marriage. Wives were responsible for the smooth running of the household, servants (if present), and children. They might also work with their husbands at a trade or act as their attorneys when they were abroad trading. While they might have other occupations that brought in money and real property, they were usually not the chief breadwinners, nor did they have absolute control of the dowry and the property reserved for dower. Laws put limits on husbands' exploitation of marital wealth, but the men were in the shop or the marketplace and could manipulate household revenues. We do not know the extent of discussion between couples over economic decision-making; to some extent it must have been an individual matter, depending on the age and competence of the wife and the sensibility of the husband.

The well-defined gender roles of males and females in medieval society could have reduced conflict in marriages. Social scientists have developed the "resource theory" to describe gender balance in marriage.[1] This theory suggests that if the couple lives within socially accepted gender roles in terms of economic contributions, they will have little conflict. But if that balance is lost, then discord can occur. In the medieval household economy, the contributions of both husband and wife were of major importance to the survival of the household unit.[2] Although the husband's role was given higher social and economic status than that of the wife, there was little competition over who performed which tasks. It was, perhaps, because of the well-defined marital economic relationship that accord, not to be confused with marital bliss, was normal. If marriage worked as a viable partnership, it was a good one; but partnerships could turn sour.

Sources for assessing marital function or dysfunction are limited for the Middle Ages. Ecclesiastical courts handled the establishment of legitimate marriages and the dissolution of marriages. While economic differences may have been at the root of some of the cases of petitions for separation or divorce, the Church would not probe this matter. Sometimes the dissatisfactions with the partnership appear in the Husting court, but often it is appeals to the lord chancellor that reveal economic dissatisfactions.

The law of coverture made a normal suit in court almost impossible, outside of dower and inheritance violations. Since the husband and wife became one at marriage and a single economic unit, it was impossible for one party to bring suit against another. Coverture bound men as well as women. The court of recourse, therefore, was the equity court of Chancery.[3]

Marital Expectations

Marriage vows presumed a commitment for life: "for better or worse, for richer or poorer in sickness and in hele, to tyl dethe do us departe." The carnal nature of marriage was also spelled out in the vows that the woman took: "to be bonere and boxom, in bedde and atte bord." Both women and men were expected to be sexually available to their partners. It was expressed in economic terms: to pay the marital debt.[4] Cultural expectations about marriage, however, went beyond sex. Sermons, stories, advice literature, parables, and popular carols emphasized respect between the partners but also the subservience of the wife.[5] The husband was to show forbearance toward his wife and those in his household. On the parish level, clergy were supposed to offer advice on successful marriage. Myrc's *Instructions for a Parish Priest* suggests that the priest ask husbands in confession if they helped their wives and "meyne" (family or household) when they needed it and refrained from causing strife.[6] Wives, like maidens, were to preserve their virtue as honorable extensions of their husbands and were supposed to show obedience to them. Marriage was a rich topic for sermons.[7] Since medieval preaching relied on popular stories and folklore in order to illustrate sermons, they are an excellent guide to folk wisdom about domestic relations.[8] Both the husband and the wife were instructed in expected behavior and in the calamities that could befall them if they departed from normative domestic roles. The stories are, for the most part, humorous.

The wife is cautioned against adultery, disobedience, scolding, drunkenness, and speaking out against her husband. An amusing parable is that of the woman who complained to a fortuneteller about her husband. The fortuneteller instructs her to go to a certain forest. Once there, she is to repeat her complaints about her husband in English verse. A voice (that of the concealed fortuneteller) tells her to hold her tongue.[9]

A popular sermon on wifely obedience was the one in which three merchants, on their way home from a fair, are discussing wifely obedience. Each claims that his wife is the most obedient. They agree on a bet of a penny each to the winner and the trial of commanding each wife to step into a basin full of water. The first two women refuse to step into the basin without an explanation of the reason for doing so. Each is beaten by her husband. At the third house, the three merchants sit down to a meal of eggs, but there is no salt on the table. The husband asks his wife "sele [salt] sus table," but she mistakes this for "seyle [jump] sus table." She jumps on the table and knocks off the dishes and drinking cups. The husband is angry, but she meekly explains that she heard him command that she jump on the table and she did so out of obedience. The two guests agree that she was the most obedient and so, in merriment, they all agree that the host has won the wager.[10] Many of the sermons speak not only of obedience but also wifely devotion in life-threatening situations.[11]

Fewer sermons dwelt on the desirable and undesirable qualities in a husband. Husbands are admonished to remain faithful and not ask the impossible of a wife.[12] They are warned of falsely accusing their wives of adultery and of moving too swiftly to punishment. The most amusing of these stories tells of a knightly husband who suspects his wife of adultery. He dresses up as a priest so that he can hear his wife's confession. Recognizing her husband in priest's clothing, she confesses that she first loved a shield-bearing youth, then a soldier, then a fool, and finally a priest.[13]

Some of the sermons offer parables on the disasters that can follow quick anger. A man who suspected his wife of adultery with his steward has the steward's head cut off and presented to his wife. A holy man visits the husband and commands the head to speak; it declares the wife's innocence.[14] A husband murders his saintly wife and makes it appear as if she hanged herself. She is buried in a swamp, as is fitting for a suicide. But a blind man, washing his face in the water, regains his sight, and others are cured as well. Her husband confesses his crime, and her corpse is brought to the church.[15] Murdering wives are also held up as negative examples. A woman whose husband has ignored her sexual desires and has not played the husband's role tries to seduce his brother. When the brother-in-law repulses her, she kills him. She tells her husband that he was the real murderer, because he would not be a true husband to her.[16]

Lay advice literature likewise emphasized the desirability of marital harmony. In "How the Wise Man Taught His Son," the father advises his son to find a meek and wise woman rather than a wealthy one: "If you find such a woman, you should cherish and not burden her, for it is better to eat homely fare in peace than have a hundred fine dishes served with strife." Likewise, a husband should not anger his wife or call her bad names but correct her faults with fairness and gentleness. He should take his wife's side when she has a complaint, but not until he has examined the matter, for if he acts too swiftly, they may both regret it. The companion piece, "How the Good Wife Taught Her Daughter," echoes this advice. The key to a happy marriage is to love and honor one's husband above all earthly things and meet his moods with "fair" and "meek" words. Beyond these basics, the good wife recommends being cheerful, faithful, respectable in public, and capable of managing the household tasks and servants with good order and firmness.[17] If the wife was to manage a household, prudence was indeed an essential quality. The couple was to put on a public face, even to servants, of a well-ordered marriage. The husband should not undermine his wife by correcting her in front of the household.

Theological writers emphasized the persuasive powers of women in correcting their husbands. Within the growing business world of the early thirteenth century, wives could encourage husbands to avoid usury and give alms. In the partnership of marriage, the wife was seen to have the moral force of persuasion to do honest business.[18]

Economic and Business Partnerships

Husbands and wives did cooperate in business ventures, and men put considerable trust in the judgment and business acumen of their wives. As we have seen, men trusted their wives as guardians of their minor children, and 83 percent of the men leaving wills in the Husting court named their wives as executors. In the Archdeaconry court, which recorded craftsmen and the poor rather than the substantial property-holders, 82 percent made their wives executors.

Making a wife an executor indicated a husband's high level of trust in her knowledge of his business and her honesty. To settle a will, the executors had to know who owed money to the husband and to whom he owed money. The wife had to know the business factors who were handling merchandise, what merchandise was abroad or in the country, who owed craftsmen payment, and what the craftsman might owe for raw materials. Men seemed to feel that their wives were well equipped to handle these matters, perhaps indicating a confidence that arose from a joint discussion of debts and deals. Husbands who were out of the country or in the provinces left their wives in charge of their affairs, including the training of apprentices. Some men even assumed that their wives would be able to take over their businesses in the event of their deaths. The partnership that was established in the marriage contract with the exchange of property also carried into the business partnership in many men's wills. An added reward for the wife acting as executor was that she got the residue of the estate for her efforts, as we saw in the case of the widow who married George Cely.

Margaret Croke, mother of Elizabeth Ryche Stonor, is one of the best documented widows acting as executor for her father and then for her husband. Her father had been mayor of London, and her husband had moved from being a skinner to a wool merchant. She spent much of her widowhood settling his debts and pursuing suits in order to collect debts owed to him. She and the other executors employed an attorney to settle matters in both London and Calais. Among the items she was trying to secure were three thousand woolfells that she claimed were her own but had been arrested in Calais. In addition to merchandise, there were outstanding claims on real estate.[19] No doubt other widows were as competent as Margaret Croke.

The Stonor and Cely letters present a more intimate idea of marital and business relations than do court cases. The letters mix business with family matters and intimacy. Elizabeth Ryche Stonor addresses her husband, William Stonor, as "Gentylle Coussen" or "enteirly best belovyd Cosyn" and at other times as "right interly and best belovyd husband."[20] Her letters deal mostly with business that involved both of them, as well as the important contacts that she made in the city. Obviously, he relied on her knowledge of the business world in London to serve her in looking after his investments in wool and her dower property.[21] Her letters often say that she has "read and [does] right well understand" the contents. Other matters in the letters relate to family affairs, the welfare of the children, and the marriage of her daughter, Katherine, to Thomas Betson.

Elizabeth's letters show great concern for her husband. She writes that she has received word that he is getting better, but she is very concerned that William's brother, who is staying at Stonor, has the pox, which she knows is highly contagious. She begs her husband to come to London, but if he does not, she asks that he let her hire some horses to go to Stonor, for "in trouth I can finde it in my heart to put myself in jeopardy there as ye be, and shall do whilst my life endureth to the pleasure of God and yours." She writes that she anticipates his arrival the next night and explains, several times, that she has not been merry without him.[22] He also writes that he has missed her and wishes she were there.[23] She thanks him for sending a ring, but the stone fell out in transit, so she suggests sending only gold rings in the future. He also frequently sends her game, which she shares with her father. She purchases for him some powdered nutmeg, which he is to drink before going to bed for its wholesome qualities.[24] She prays "her gentile and loving husband" to take his ease.[25]

An example of Elizabeth's letters to her husband show the mixture of business, personal matters, and affection between them.

> Right entirely and my most special beloved husband, I recommend me to you in the most hearty wise, desiring to hear of your welfare, etc. thanking you for your letter and of your partridges. And for Robert Warner, he is come to town: diverse of your servants and mine have spoken with him: he sayeth that he can receive no money as yet, notwithstanding he intendith to speak with me or he depart, and will content me if he may. I pray God that he may so do. I pray you to send me a answer of the matter that I wrote to you for the Lombard. And if hit might please you to take the labor to ride over, then ye may answer to the matter yourself, which will be to me great hearts ease and pleasure; for I think it right long since I spoke with you, Sir, I trust to Jesu to see you here in short time. No more to you at this time, but Jesus preserve you in his keeping. Written at London the Friday before St. Bartholomew's Day.
> By your own wife Elizabeth Stonor.[26]

The Lombard referred to in the letter was an Italian merchant dealing in wool and wool fells. The money that was to be collected was for the sale of wool from the Stonor estates.

The one letter we have from Margery Cely to George uses terms of address similar to Elizabeth's, but there is a sort of desperate urgency in desiring him to return. She uses the usual phrases: "It is a long season since ye departed from me" and "I wot well I shall never be merry to see you again." But she added a frantic note asking him to send her word in haste of the time he will be home.[27] Elizabeth was older than Margery and more experienced in business, indicating that not every widow could run a business and deal with contracts and employees.

The custom of leaving the wife at home to manage affairs was strongly ingrained in London merchants and craftsmen. Many of these men, such as Ryche, Croke, Stonor, and the Celys, had business factors who routinely handled their trade, but often the best expedient was to put the wife in charge of matters in London. Wives had direct access to accounts and knew the general family business deals. They could also assume legal responsibility, if need be. Elizabeth Ryche Stonor worked closely with Thomas Betson but handled some of the transactions on her own. To many men, such as Stonor, trusting his wife to carry on the business was a matter of routine. Thus Joan, "wife and attorney of John Olney, woolmonger," sued to recover a debt owed to him, but the man she was suing was going abroad on the king's service and had a writ of protection from such actions. A wife might also use a husband's writ of protection, as did Ellen, wife of Nicholas Mate, in a suit of debt brought by Elizabeth atte Hawe. He had sought protection while overseas on the king's business.[28]

A wife left to handle her husband's affairs while he was away on business had to be very shrewd in her arrangements, or she could end up being duped or bullied. In court cases, the women who could not cope appear with regularity. Managing apprentices was difficult for women who were not really in the trade. Thus an apprentice to John Morem claimed that his master was in prison and his mistress was unable to train him. Another apprentice complained that his master was imprisoned for eight weeks in Calais and that the mistress could teach him nothing.[29] But far worse problems arose for women left alone to manage businesses. William Martyn and his wife had hired a brew house on Fleet Street from John Colman. The assumption seemed to have been that Maude, William's wife, would manage it while he was away. John was supposed to roof the house but did not, so William and Maude sued him. They were losing money because no guests would "lie in beds through [because of] rain." While William Martyn was away, John Colman and two servants went to his house, where Maude lived with two servants. They threatened the servants so that they would not work and repeated their assault several weeks later. In her husband's absence, Maude "requested that the defendant find surety of peace against [her] and her servants, because the said William is abroad in the service of the Prince, and in his absence the said Maude has no aid."[30] Another woman, Robinet, wife of Thomas Dyrel, complained that a brewer harassed her about suits of debt while her husband was in the service of the king on the Isle of Guernsey. She had been promised immunity from such claims and wanted the lord chancellor to protect her.[31] An absent husband, in these women's experience, provided the opportunity for men to take advantage of them.

The unsettled political conditions between France and England during the Hundred Years' War meant that the wife might be called on to organize her husband's rescue from imprisonment. The fourteenth and fifteenth centuries saw the many phases of the Hundred Years' War, in which merchants might be arbitrarily imprisoned by belligerents who expected ransom, and all merchants feared pirates as much as they feared shipwreck. Ransoms were a common means of earning extra money in this period, and it was often the wife who had to raise the sums to release her husband. Joan, wife of John Pound, a citizen of London, sought the help of the mayor of London in getting her husband released. The mayor sent letters to the officials of Ghent, Bruges, and Ypres explaining that John Pound had freighted a ship to Sluys with goods valued at £50, which he had bought at the fair of Antwerp. On the voyage home, Joan claimed, Arnold Jonesson, captain of the castle of Saftinge on the Scheldt, captured the ship and "carried the said John and the goods to the castle, where he still detained them." Beatrice, wife of Reginald Fuller, a tailor, paid William Knott, also a tailor, 8 marks in the presence of London's recorder and an alderman. She asked him to obtain the release of her husband and John Goldesmore, a fuller, who had been captured by Frenchmen and were in prison in Boulogne. Reginald had already been liberated by John de Burer of Boulogne, so he could raise 20 marks to pay the ransom. The ransom had been reduced to 8 marks, so Reginald was free, but William Knott was to secure the release of John Goldesmore or return the money.[32]

Communication between wife and husband when he was abroad was often by messages passed by word of mouth or, less frequently, by personal letters. Other merchants and seamen would bring back word of a husband's whereabouts and how he was doing, as we have seen in the Cely and Stonor letters. But messages often went astray, and the wife did not always know where her husband was or if he was alive. When one apprentice complained that his master had left the kingdom a long time ago, his wife told the mayor that she had heard nothing about where he was.[33] Matilda Blankett, wife of John Blankett, had been married eighteen years when he disappeared. She asked the church court to ascertain if he was alive. They found that he had died on London Bridge during an uprising.[34]

It is easier to trace the cooperation of husband and wife among merchants than it is in crafts. The historian Judith Bennett, who devotes a chapter to brewers and brewsters working together, could not accurately determine, even with the brewers' guild records, how the tasks were divided in the household. Women (widows, wives, and single women) did have membership in the guild. She speculated that women did most of the brewing and that men had the public face in the marketplace. Many of the men, while becoming members of the guild, actually followed a different profession.[35] Husbands and wives ran inns and taverns together. Wives and daughters certainly worked with their husbands in the textile industry and in many other crafts as well. These family members are not mentioned, although they appear as widows inheriting shops.[36] Among tanners, men did the tanning, but women often had a seld or stall where they sold the products.[37] The records do not discuss the disposal of profits within the household. All collections of urban wills in England and many from northern Europe indicate that men left their craft shops, tools, and apprentices to their widows with confidence that they would carry on the trade or remarry men who could.[38]

Marital Fidelity

When a husband's trade, merchant activity, military service, or even pilgrimage took him away from home, both the husband and wife feared not only loss of life but also infidelity. Marital infidelity was one of the constant themes of literature, appearing in fabliaux, Chaucer, Boccacio, and romances. Infidelities could occur when the couple was living in the same town, as we have seen with Richard Cely and other men with two families in London, or the temptation could come when the husband was far away from London.

Separations of husband and wife were fraught with uncertainty, and the anxieties over them often centered on conjugal faithfulness. A beautiful, younger wife was perceived as being particularly vulnerable. During a prolonged separation, however, a wife might not wait for her husband to return before remarrying. Harry Peterson, one of the workmen of the king's "gonnes" [guns], complained that about fifteen years earlier he had married a woman of Brabant, had brought her to London, where they lived together as man and wife for four years and more, and had a child with her. After that he was away for ten years in the wars of the "king of the Romans [German emperor]." He had left his wife behind in the charge of her brother. While he was gone she took another husband, "but now he has come home and wanted to take up their marriage again." She refused, preferring to stay with her new husband. The church court took her side, so Harry petitioned the lord chancellor to intervene because he was "weary and impoverished over the matter."[39]

The wife might, however, receive false word that her husband was dead and decide to remarry. John Ketyng went off to Ireland with a servant, William. Time passed, and servant William returned wearing the gown, doublet, and hose that John Ketyng had worn when he left London. He told John's wife and neighbors that John was dead. On this evidence the ecclesiastical authorities stepped in, and the summoner asked the wife to come before the Commissary court to probate John's will. She was then declared a widow, and all her neighbors viewed her as such. A suitor soon appeared, John Talbot, who asked her to marry him. She accepted, and the banns were read on three "solemn days." No one came forward to claim a prior contract, so they married. He moved into John Ketyng's house with her. But John Ketyng was *not* dead, and he entered his house and took away his goods as well as those belonging to Talbot amounting to £30. He also brought an action against Talbot and had him put in jail.[40] Often enough, of course, the husband really was dead. Alice, widow of William Rolf, a shipman, took a letter from the mayor of London around to ports where her husband traded, asking "for love's sake to give up the goods and chattels" of Rolf, since he was lately drowned at sea.[41]

Other women took lovers while their husbands were away. Richard, son of John le Mareschall of Smithfield, was charged with abducting the wife of Stephen Hereford. The neighbors all knew about the affair because Richard had been at the house frequently. When Stephen was away at Winchester Fair, Richard was at his house all the time, and friends and neighbors of Stephen determined to put a stop to it. They searched the house for Richard but could not find him. Finally, they directed the adulterous wife to open a chest closed with iron, and therein they found Richard. Richard left London for Waltham and did not see the wife again. When she learned that her husband was returning, the wife left home with some goods. Finally, she got the ecclesiastical court to force Stephen to reconcile with her.[42] Katherine, wife of John Middleton Junior, took advantage of her husband's absence and, "led by various rotten people," took jewels and treasure worth £400 and went to live in Shrewsbury. She refused reconciliation and sought a divorce, but he had died.[43]

Wives, too, worried about the fidelity of their husbands. When husbands were home, servant girls, who were present in many households, could prove too tempting to resist;[44] and when traveling, husbands might establish more permanent relationships, as George Cely did. Such relationships were fraught with problems for wives. Elizabeth, wife of Thomas Montague of London, complained that her husband continued in an adulterous relationship with a woman of Stratford atte Bow at the manor of Oldford, and that the affair was imperiling his soul and also destroying the livelihood of Elizabeth because he was spending all their money on the mistress. Should a bastard be the result of one of these unions, inheritances were endangered. Roger Thorney, a London mercer, was acting for a fellow merchant who died intestate on board ship. The deceased merchant's goods were duly sequestered when the ship docked, but matters got complicated when "one Edward, an evil disposed person being a bastard and a Fleming born at Bruges in Flanders, which calleth himself bastard son" of the late John Pykering, claimed a debt against the estate.[45] Wills are full of evidence of these far-flung families. Geoffrey Bonere, a paternoster maker, left bequests to his illegitimate daughter in Flanders. Thomas Gippyng (alias Lincoln) was a draper from London who spent considerable time in Lincolnshire on business. He had a legitimate wife in London, but he left the residue of his estate to his two bastard daughters and his bedding to Juliana Pleydon of Lincoln, who was, presumably, their mother.[46]

In the fabliaux and stories based on them, usually we hear of how the clever wife managed to deceive her husband and pursue adulterous sex. But there is also a genre of women's narratives about separation that speaks about sexual honor, the constancy of love, the cleverness of women in preserving their chastity, and their own skills in household management. The oldest of these is a sixth-century Sanskrit version. The formula is a simple one in which the wife is left alone but the husband has a token that shows his wife's fidelity, such as a shirt that never gets dirty or a flower that never wilts. There is a fifteenth-century English version called *The Wright's Caste Wife*.[47]

The story is one not only of the wife's preservation of her honor but also of women's work (spinning flax), her space in her house, and her economic success in exploiting the situation of her husband's absence. A wright [carpenter] is hired to work on a lord's castle. He is newly married and worried about his wife's faithfulness when he is gone. So he builds a tower for their bedroom and puts a trap door in the middle that leads to a pit. A mere touch will send a person into this pit. Her only dowry is a garland that will not fade as long as she is faithful. Taking the garland with him, he goes to honor his contract. The lord of the castle inquires about the garland and goes to try his luck with the wright's wife. She at first refuses, but then says she will go to bed with him. She asks for money in advance and has him go first into the bedroom. He falls through the trap door and into the pit. When he begs to be let out, she points out that she has nothing to fear from him as long as he is there. He finally begs for food and drink, but she says that he has to work for his food. She sets him to beating flax to separate the fibers. The steward, missing his lord, asks the wright where his lord went and then notices the garland. He goes to try his luck and meets the same fate. In order to eat, he must sit on a bench and pull the fibers through a swingel. Finally, the proctor of the church notices the garland and goes to seduce the wife. He meets the same fate and agrees to take a spindle to make linen thread in order to eat. So far she has collected considerable money from the three men and has set them to do what is women's work—turning flax into linen thread.[48] Her final triumph is when the lord's wife and the wright appear and inquire about what is going on in the pit. The lord's wife enjoys a laugh at her husband's expense and tells the wright's wife to keep all the money the men gave her, as well as the profits she will make from selling the linen thread. She has humiliated the men by a sex role inversion, kept her honor, and profited from the attempts to seduce her.

Unhappy Marriages and Domestic Violence

While wills give a generally optimistic picture of conjugal life, individual cases show the unpleasant side of marriage. Couples entered into marriage knowing that it was a permanent commitment. Divorce or annulment of a marriage had to be taken to the church courts, and the church was more interested in keeping the marriages together than dissolving the union.[49] Writers who have analyzed the late medieval church court records remark on the scarcity of divorce litigation cases.[50] In London in the late fifteenth and sixteenth centuries, the court had only about fifteen cases a year, and few ended in divorce.[51] The bond of matrimony was not easy to break, and for the most part, people entering into marriage seemed to accept that.

A study of the church courts in York has shown that in the fourteenth century, women were plaintiffs in three out of four cases brought to the ecclesiastical court. They were successful in their cases, but not as successful as men. What is interesting is that they sought to preserve their marriages, whereas men sought dissolution of marriage. Women seemed to find economic security in marriage, but men only sued for preservation of a marriage when they could be the financial gainers. By the fifteenth century, the pattern changes, with more women seeking to dissolve their marriages. Perhaps the changing economic circumstances gave women more security outside marriage, but the evidence is not persuasive, since the number of cases is so small.[52]

Only six grounds for dissolution of marriage appear in the English ecclesiastical court records. The church permitted divorce or annulment if one member of the couple was forced into the marriage and did not consent to it. Divorce was also possible if one of the couple lived in fear of his or her spouse—a rare plea. Most common among the royalty and nobility was the plea of consanguinity and affinity, and they were often closely related. A man and woman who lived adulterously while one or both had a living spouse could not marry, and if they did so, the church divorced them. Infidelity alone, however, was not a ground for divorce. Likewise, the argument for annulment based on impotency was rare. The possibility of bigamy and precontract for marriage with another man or woman, when consent was the only requirement for a valid marriage, led to considerable confusion and was the most common grounds for divorce or annulment.[53]

Ecclesiastical courts investigated precontract and bigamy carefully, because the opportunities for collusion were obvious.[54] Richard Kelly was accused of having two wives, Alice Kelly in Ireland and Elizabeth Clifford in London, and Robert Close fornicated with Joan Lacy and contracted a marriage with her and also with Mariona Bryght.[55] A pathetic case appears in an appeal to the lord chancellor. Elizabeth Baxter, late wife of John Croke, gentleman, says that she contracted marriage with John Being, who "of his own free will and liberty lawfully contracted matrimony" with her, and "at his own cost caused the matrimony to be solemnized in a book before the Archdeacon and before many people." At the marriage he swore on the book and before the archdeacon that he was free of all earthly women except for Elizabeth. Elizabeth Baxter said in her petition that "they lived together for half a year after that with love and charity as husband and wife." To improve her case, Baxter was citing the culturally expected behavior of a successful marriage. Elisabeth Cotton then appeared and claimed a prior contract. The ecclesiastical court agreed, and John took the goods that Elizabeth had brought to the marriage as well as those he had given her in marriage. He beat Elizabeth about the head and body "as she can here demonstrate" and then sued her and her parents for a debt. He then had Elizabeth and her mother jailed.[56] As in all these Chancery petitions, we do not know the outcome or if the allegations were true.

On occasion, the church court did have sympathy with a difficult situation. Joan Alpe complained that her husband, William, refused to live with her. William Alpe did not dispute this but said that his wife was insane and that he refused to live with her for fear of his life. He was, however, giving her 10s. a year for food and clothing. William's story was believed, and he made a formal agreement to continue providing for her upkeep. Neither husband nor wife could remarry while one was alive. Likewise, Andrew Peerson confessed that he had exchanged marriage vows with Agnes Wilson but that he refused to have the marriage solemnized because she was a "great scold," and even her ward had indicted her on this complaint. Again, the court allowed a divorce, but with the provision that neither could remarry while the other was alive.[57]

An unusual ground for divorce was that of impotence. If the parties could not consummate the marriage within three years, one of the couple could bring suit. Because of the possibility of deceit, the court might require a physical examination of the woman by "honest women" to see if she was a virgin. For a man, seven "honest women" were instructed to test the man in the suit. The practice in York and Canterbury was explicitly described. In a warm room, one witness "exposed her naked breast, with her hands warmed at the same fire, she held and rubbed the penis and testicles." She embraced and kissed him in an attempt to arouse him and admonished him that he should prove himself a man, but he did not.[58]

In a London case, the husband apparently did successfully undergo the test. William Sharpyng, vintner, was summoned to answer Walter Southous in a plea of debt for £100 in 1370. Walter Southous was the guardian of Joan, who had married William Sharpyng. The marriage had apparently gone unconsummated. With a £100 bond, the husband had agreed with the guardian not to hinder but to assist his wife, Joan, daughter of Richard de Coutenhale, to secure a divorce by ecclesiastical law on the grounds of his impotency. He agreed to submit to examination before a judge of his virility (*virillia sua monstrando*). In other words, he would undergo some proof, perhaps that described above, of his virility. Meanwhile, he was to allow his wife to come and go freely. Both sides agreed to the plan, and Walter made a bond for £100 to William that, if William passed the test, he would cancel William's bond and pay the full amount of Joan's dowry. William passed and asked that the bond be nullified. Walter claimed that William had broken his promise and that when Joan was on her way to consult her counsel, William and six other men lay in wait for her and assaulted her so she could not get to her counsel. William said that he had found his wife in the vintry and had returned her to his house, but she had gone with him willingly. He said that this incident occurred before the bonds were entered into and that afterward he had not molested his wife. He won his case, and, one presumes, he got his dowry and his wife. Fortunately, William was not damaged by this early scandal and was able to go on and become a worthy among vintners.[59]

Marital discord did not necessarily lead to a plea in the church courts, since the divorce plea was so difficult. Some wives left voluntarily. Joanna, wife of Andrew Stevyns of London, feared for her life and sought refuge with her sister and brother-in-law. But she moved on when he threatened them as well. They claimed that they did not know where she was, but Andrew sued them for the goods she had carried away.[60] John de Walkern, a citizen of London, complained to the mayor that while he was journeying on a pilgrimage to Rome, his wife, Lucy, had removed his goods and chattels from the city. When he returned he went "from county court to county court and from town to town until he discovered a portion of the goods at Lynn." No trace of Lucy is mentioned.[61] John Reffaw said that his wife had left him ten years before and "has been out of his minding for that long." But someone brought an action of debt against him in her name, and he could not afford to pay it.[62] John Fisshe brought a bill of complaint alleging that John Haliwell, his journeyman, on Sunday after the Feast of All Saints (November 1, 1365) had run off with the plaintiff's wife, Elizabeth, taking with him cloth, linen, wool, and other goods and chattels worth £200. The journeyman and Elizabeth both admitted that they had sexual contact, but not that they had taken the goods. Still, the journeyman paid 40 marks in damages.[63] Some of these wife-stealers were repeat offenders. William Skynnere entered into a bond of £10 with Richard Palmere not to carry away his wife again.[64]

Not all cases of desertion or even abduction were the result of force or even of leaving with a lover. The "consensual abductions" that appear in royal courts seem to have been cases in which a woman departed with her goods and her husband sued to get the goods back, not his wife. The wife had left voluntarily. The abductor might not even be a lover but a family member helping the woman leave.[65] Chancery petitions show that while lovers might have helped unhappy wives leave a marriage, family members, including fathers, siblings, and children of a first marriage, also offered aid. Again, since the Chancery was a royal court, the husband was suing not for restitution of the marriage but the property the wife took.[66]

Since secular law had no provision for division of property at divorce, arrangements had to be made in ecclesiastical court, privately, or not at all. Ecclesiastical courts, when they allowed separation, did make provision for the support of a spouse, as they did in the case of William Alpe's insane wife. But Hugo Manton and William Rydley both expelled their wives from their houses and refused to provide livings for them.[67] Petitions to Chancery indicate that private property settlements were made when the couple mutually agreed to quit bed and board. Like marriage contracts, these are not preserved. But when they failed, a petition to Chancery was one of the only solutions. A London husband who refused to support his abandoned wife was brought to Chancery by a priest who wanted to force the support.[68]

Sometimes it was an outside instigator who caused problems between spouses. Another Richard Palmer brought a bill against the two men who were trying to defraud him of money. In order to stir up further discord, they had "several times come to the plaintiff, speaking evil of his wife, Margery, and other times to the said Margery speaking against [Richard] for which the plaintiff was several times on the point of killing his wife and his servants who were around him."[69]

Richard Palmer's case raises the question of how much evidence we have of domestic violence in medieval England and London in particular. A popular image in our own folklore is that domestic violence was prevalent in the Middle Ages, as were many other evil things. But the charge needs investigation. The supposed "rule of thumb," that a man could beat his wife with a stick no bigger than his thumb, is not a medieval precept. In the *Oxford English Dictionary* and in dictionaries of proverbs, the phrase is simply explained as a rule for practical decisions for the measurement of cloth or for weights.[70]

In general, early modern studies of domestic violence both in Germany and England have shown a considerable increase in incidences of domestic violence and in the overall reporting of sexual offenses after around 1600 or later, suggesting a shift in sexual attitudes and gender roles.[71] In both Protestant and Catholic areas, the role of the patriarch in families was elevated and made more oppressive. The close connection between the position of the *paterfamilias* and that of the king, state, or commonwealth gave further empowerment to heads of households and considerable sympathy to their corrective role in both ecclesiastical and lay courts that tried cases of domestic violence.[72] The studies of early modern Europe cannot be read back into the Middle Ages to explain what was happening in the fourteenth and fifteenth centuries, or even earlier.[73] Changes in religion, in concepts of states, and even in attitudes toward marriage and morality evolved during the late sixteenth and seventeenth centuries. While we have observed the corrective role given to the *paterfamilias* in medieval England, the evidence of widespread abuse is absent.

One might assume from the Statute of Treason of 1352 that men lived in fear of their subordinates—servants and wives. A clause covering familial homicide was added to those that defined treasonous acts related to the person of the king and the realm of England.

> And in addition there is another kind of treason, that is to say when a servant kills his master, a woman kills her husband ["*un femme qu tue son baron*"], [and] when a secular man or a man in religious orders kills his prelate, to whom he owes faith and obedience.[74]

In declaring these actions treasonous, the law meant that a woman who killed her husband, a servant who killed his master, and a monk who killed his abbot would be punished as a traitor. A woman would be burned, and a man drawn, hanged, and quartered. No new law was needed, as this had long been the practice. But the curious addition of private, familial violence to a statute dealing with state treason tells us much about the shoring up of patriarchal authority in the period following the Black Death.

The members of Parliament were wrong about the threat of domestic insurrection. Only 2 percent of all homicide indictments tried in the royal courts were for intrafamilial murders, as were 6 percent of the cases reported in coroners' inquests in rural counties and in London. In manorial courts, which tried misdemeanors (assaults, trespasses, and debts), only 2 percent of the cases involved family.[75] In ecclesiastical courts, only 0.02 percent of the litigants used the argument of cruelty, even though it was grounds for separation.[76] As in modern domestic violence, the husband was the aggressor against the wife in all court records, but brother against brother predominated over spousal cases in the manorial courts.[77] Perhaps members of Parliament, like legislators today, were reacting to a particular, notorious case of a wife killing her husband.[78] They did not, of course, have crime statistics, since such systematic records had not yet been compiled, but they all had served as jurors or county and city officials and knew how few cases of intrafamilial violence were tried.[79]

The London evidence is sparse. Joan Gade charged William Beneyt, a fuller, with having killed their illegitimate son and having threatened her, although he had previously promised to marry her. William produced the son alive in court, and they were each asked to provide sureties for good behavior. Her reputation was so bad that she was unable to find anyone to stand surety.[80] Some idea of the types of argument that led to homicide can be found in the case of the death of Alice, wife of John Ryvet, in his shop. They had gone to bed and were awakened at midnight by a fire caused by a lighted candle. It was the custom of women to put out the candle, so, when they managed to leave the burning shop, John blamed Alice for the fire and pushed her back into the shop.[81] He fled. Alice was badly burnt and, although she managed to escape, she died of burns a week later.[82]

A family feud led to the death of Alice, the second wife of Richard de Portsmouth. There had been an argument at curfew between Alice and her stepson, Robert, son of Richard. The jurors said that young Robert hit her with his hand while her husband hit her with a staff on the neck, causing her to fall down the stairs of the solar where they lived and to break her neck.[83]

A pair of cases shows the typical complexity of domestic violence. A servant and his master were arguing over the terms of a contract when the servant stabbed his master in the heart. Because the master's wife was there and did not raise the hue and cry, she was suspected of collusion.[84] In another case, the husband and wife were arguing in the solar when the servant came up the stairs to intervene. The servant was carrying a knife, but the husband grabbed a staff and killed the servant.[85]

As for the much-dreaded husband-murderesses that the Statute of Treason wanted punished, these, as the statistics showed, were very few in number. A short entry in the Eyre of 1276 says that Emma, wife of John le Maxon, took sanctuary in the church of St. Martin and confessed that she killed her husband.[86]

Figures on domestic violence are notorious for underreporting, and one might raise legitimate questions about the reliability of the medieval figures. The homicide figures, however, are consistent with what others have found for medieval Europe and are also compatible with comparative anthropological data.[87] The general descriptive quality of the term "domestic violence," as opposed to outright intrafamilial homicide, is culturally rooted. Medieval Europeans favored physical correction as a valuable tool in educating students, novices, and apprentices, in training servants, and in castigating wives and children.[88] But the medieval use of castigation and correction did not imply "violence," a term that historians have used too loosely.[89] It would be inaccurate to apply our own, very recent definitions of domestic abuse back onto situations in the Middle Ages. One must also leave aside the more modern types of domestic violence, including marital rape and mental cruelty, since these were not medieval categories. Medieval norms prescribed what I have called a "culturally restrained patriarchy"; that is, late medieval English social norms accorded to the head of the household considerable privileges, including the responsibility for correcting household members, but it did not condone excessive violence.

While we cannot know how many marriage partnerships worked in a mutually agreeable manner, we can find evidence of both trust and distrust between husband and wife. It is easy to be drawn to the examples of failed marriages, but the evidence points to a general acceptance of the cultural norms that marriage was a lifetime commitment, a mutual agreement, and a presumption of an effort at a working partnership, even if the wife was the subordinate partner. The evidence of wills and guardianship of children gives strong statistical testimony for success rather than failure of marriages.

❧ 7 ❧
Standard of Living
and Women as Consumers

The standard of living of women in various status groups in urban centers and the consumer products they bought were essential to all urban
economies, including that of London. From the high end of the economy
to the low, women were major participants in the day-to-day commerce of
London. While not major producers of wealth in terms of crafts or large
entrepreneurial activities, they were among the important consumers. They
owned, bought, and rented houses, rooms, and shops, and they were often in
charge of the upkeep on these establishments. They received as dowry and

gifts clothing, jewelry, and household goods. They bought food for themselves and their households, and they purchased clothing and such luxury items as they could afford. To understand women's standard of living, we must look at the spaces women frequented, the housing they occupied, the goods they possessed, and the things—both material and spiritual—they bought. The living conditions of women from the highest status to the lowest offer an intimate understanding of their lives.[1]

Women's Space

When William Fitzstephen wrote of his beloved city of London in the late twelfth century, he commented on the inhabitants as well as the environment. The men were all barons, rather than merely citizens, and "the women of London were very Sabines." His allusion to the Sabine women who were carried off to provide wives for the womanless followers of Romulus in Rome is curious, but fits with the rest of his description of London. His London does not have women; it has schoolboys engaged in intellectual contests, laborers looking for work, peasants coming to market, youths displaying their fighting talents, jockeys racing horses, and old men enjoying the games of boys. Women are not even shopping or preparing food; instead, the men of the city could buy their food from cook shops and vendors.[2]

Later travelers to England found the streets surprisingly populated with women. In 1562, Alessandro Magno, a young Italian merchant, wrote that "the Englishwomen have great freedom to go out of the house without menfolk; the husbands do not spend their time in household jobs, but the women themselves carry the goods if they are poor, or make their maids do so if they have them, and they are free to buy whatever is needed." He goes on to observe that women serve in shops and that "young women gather outside Moorgate and play with young lads, even though they do not know them." One was a game in which the women were thrown to the ground and the men would not let them up until they got a kiss.[3]

By 1575, a Dutch traveler in England wrote that English women are not kept strictly shut up in houses, as in Spain. Instead, they go to markets to shop, "sit before their doors, decked out in fine clothes, in order to see and be seen by passers-by," go to banquets, visit neighbors, attend church, and take part in the festivities of childbirths and churchings.[4]

To observers of London, the very presence of women and the space that they occupied was a matter of the prejudices that the natives and foreigners brought to their observances of the city and its inhabitants. Fitzstephen, a clerk writing an introduction to the life of the twelfth-century martyr Thomas Becket, was establishing the environment in which a male saint grew up. His is a very masculine, clerical reading of the London landscape. Italian and Dutch travelers, writing much later, were struck by the presence of women in the public space of London compared to Italy or Spain. The women had freedom to move about, but they also had freedom to be consumers and to display what they bought on their persons in public. Had times changed that much? It is a hard question to answer, with just biased, individual observations.

We have only scattered references to women's space in London and their environment. As we shall see from these bits and pieces, much depended on women's social class and economic opportunities. One crude assessment is based on the places where women died from homicides or accidents. Of the 267 preserved coroner's inquests into accidental and homicidal deaths in London in the late thirteenth and first half of the fourteenth century, only 30 women appear as victims. One conclusion is that women's lives were generally more sheltered from both accidents and homicides. Even with such a small sample, much can be gathered about the places men and women were at the time of their sudden deaths. Men were mostly outside in streets, lanes, and the river rather than indoors when they met a violent death. Women's violent deaths, on the other hand, were more likely to be in the home; but roughly a quarter of them occurred in streets.[5] To the degree that these figures represent the frequency of places where violent social interactions occurred or fatal accidents happened, women appear to have been spending most of their time at home or in streets probably near to their homes.[6]

Housing and the Urban Environment

Housing varied immensely for both women and men. Only the wealthy and the relatively well-off could afford a freehold house (free tenure of property with the right to pass it on to heirs) or shop. Rentals were common. Those who could afford to do so gave dowry and dower in real estate. Widows, with only free bench, might be left with access to the family hearth, a bed chamber, and garden. Servants and apprentices often lived in the employer's house, sometimes sleeping in the kitchen or on the shop floor. Retirement arrangements varied greatly, and many did not retire but worked until they died, sometimes as beggars. The homeless sought shelter in church doors, under bridges, and other places that afforded some protection from the elements.

Bishops, secular lords, and wealthy merchants built the largest houses in London. The plans of these houses indicate a courtyard layout. The hall and main dwelling unit lay at the back of the yard. A range of buildings included shops with tenements above them faced the street and could be rented for profit, while ensuring the privacy of the courtyard house behind.[7] Medium-sized properties that were long and narrow were usually built in an L-shape. The frontage was similar to that of the courtyard properties, but the hall and other residential rooms would extend back along one side of the property. A smaller courtyard abutted the other property line. The smallest properties included street frontage with a shop, room behind, and a kitchen in the courtyard. Sometimes the property was too small for a courtyard.[8]

By the end of the fourteenth century, ranges of houses with shops, cellars, and living quarters could be three to four stories high and could include a hall, pantry, parlor, buttery, and courtyard behind the houses.[9] Smaller houses had only two stories. Wattle and daub (woven sticks covered over with clay) filled the spaces between the timbers in the framing, but by the fifteenth century, brick replaced the less substantial filling. The appearance was a typical "half-timbered" style, but in the finer houses a facade of stone added a continental elegance.[10]

Gentry and noble women usually had a place in town where they and their family could attend to shopping, business, legal matters, and social contacts at court. They acquired houses or rental property as dower for their life use, or they received them as dowries when they married. For instance, Maude, widow of John Lovell, knight, allowed her son to use a house in Paternoster Lane when he came to London, but it was quite clear that this was her property and the son had no claim to it.[11] Elsa, widow of Richard Seymour, knight, arranged with her son that, if she wished to reside in London, she should have a messuage there at her pleasure as part of her dower. Her son could stay there when she was not in residence.[12] When John de Montagu, Earl of Salisbury, died, his property included a tenement in London called Romaynstrent that he held by the right of his wife, Maud, for a rent of thirteen roses.[13]

London women rented properties for themselves. The Bridge House Rentals from 1460 to 1484 permit a systematic look at women in the rental market. London Bridge was one of London's most important assets, because it connected Southwark with London proper. Like many medieval bridges, it was built up with shops and some dwellings. London citizens, appreciating the convenience of the bridge, left property toward its upkeep. The bridge masters kept a careful account of these properties, listing the renters, the price paid, and the tenements they rented. Of the ten years of rentals preserved in that period, an average of nineteen properties, or 7.4 percent of the renters, were women. The number remained fairly consistent, varying between 5 percent and 8 percent. The value of the property was also quite consistent, at an average of £38 a year, or 6.4 percent of the annual profits of the Bridge Estates. Of the 189 women renting in their own names, 21 percent were listed as widows. The rest may have been single women or possibly women acting as *femmes soles* who inherited leases or who had their own businesses and leased shops. Most of the women rented tenements or cabins (shops) either in the middle of the bridge (the most expensive part), or in other locations on both sides of the river. The value of rented property varied. Margaret Butman, for instance, rented a place for 6 s. 8 d., a typical rent, but Alice Comerton rented a place for £7. While most of the renters appeared only once in the rentals (48 percent), 6 percent appeared more than once, including Joan Watson, a widow, who kept her tenement and garden in Southwark for thirteen years (1460–73), and Isabel Barnaby, who kept her bridge middle property at a rent of £1 per annum for nineteen years. Thirty-one percent leased from two to five years, and 14 percent from six to nine years. Because of gaps in the records, the figures are sketchy and would tend to make the longevity of lease holding appear shorter. Still, the majority of leases to single women were probably short, either because of the death of a dowager or single woman or the marriage of a leaseholder, so that the husband's name would appear along with hers.[14]

Other rental properties show considerable range. The church wardens' accounts record the rents on properties bequeathed to them. The annual rents varied from 8 s. to £4 in the late fifteenth century, and the residences ranged from one or two rooms to eighteen rooms. Two widows rented a house together for 8 s. a year.[15] The mayor and aldermen leased to Laurence de Bliseworth and his wife a house adjoining Bishops Gate and a small cabin within the walls for an annual rent of 4 marks for their lives.[16]

Rent of a room, since it did not contain a kitchen, often included board as well. In the mid–fourteenth century, a landlord complained that a man and his wife had "lived at his table" for three months and owed him 34 s., or about 11 s. a month, for room and board. In a fifteenth-century suit, a woman paid 6 d. a week for room and board, and a husbandman made arrangements for a kinswoman at the same rate.[17] Another single woman contracted for bed and board for 16 d. a week. She did not pay and left after eighteen weeks, owing 16 s. She had left a girdle for security, and her land-lord had claimed it, but she was trying to get it back.[18] Cheap housing, of course, had disadvantages. Julia of Camberwell and another woman rented a solar that was so dilapidated it fell on Julia and killed her.[19]

Some very low-rent places existed in the city. Margaret Kind, who occupied a bench at St. Andrew Hubbard, paid 2 s. a year to the church war-dens for the privilege.[20] She must have given the church wardens part of her take as a beggar. Alice de Goldenlant, a pauper and beggar, had a lean-to by the wall of a chapel and died of disability in this makeshift abode.[21]

By the fifteenth century, the fortunate poor found shelter in alms houses, but most of these establishments were for decrepit members of guilds or their widows.[22] Hospitals occasionally took in the poor, but on the whole they provided for poor gentry and clergy rather than those of the labor-ing classes, and they accepted more men than women.[23] St. Bartholomew's church and priory made arrangements with some couples and widows to take care of them in their old age and in sickness. These women made a corody (an agreement for maintenance and care) with the hospital either by an agreed-on fixed payment or by quitclaiming property (giving title to a prop-erty) to the hospital. These were essentially retirement contracts or pensions in which the type of care was specified and the amount of food, quality of clothing and bedding, heating, housing, and other matters were arranged. The person might stay in the hospital or in property near the hospital.[24] A man who appeared frequently in the St. Bartholomew's Hospital in property transactions gave a substantial property from himself and his wife three years before he died in return for a tenement that they could rent for a penny a year. Some widows made corodies to ensure a place to stay and food. Not all of the contracts were permanent. Some were renewable, and some were made on the condition that the hospital would care for the donor should the need arise.[25]

The hospital performed other functions for widows as well. They over-saw property transactions and helped those with financial difficulties through temporary crises. For instance, Margaret, the widow of John Godefrey, a car-penter, quitclaimed a house and one-third of a yard to a clerk. In return, the clerk granted her a shop for life at a token rent of a rose a year. Since she no longer had to pay 10 s. annual rent due on the bigger property, she could live more easily on her own. Sometimes the arrangements were temporary. The hospital would take a widow's property until she could pay off debts, or remarry and let her new husband pay the debts.[26]

A hospital's oversight was perhaps a good alternative for some widows and elderly, because family could not always be trusted. Maude, widow of Simon atte Grene, had dower in two messuages producing 100 s. a year. John of Donyngton, a nephew, had taken her in, but another relative complained that Maude was "now very aged and had little sense or discretion to look after herself" and John was not taking adequate care of her or maintaining her according to her station. The solution of the mayor and aldermen was to put Maude in the care of a couple whose wife was a kinswoman of Maude. Since this couple would not inherit, whereas the nephew and the other complainant could, they were more reliable caretakers.[27] In many respects, the care of this aged widow was much like the care for an orphan.

The records also give a sense of people finding housing where they could. We might call this "crashing for the night." Two young women were accused of adultery in the church court because they lodged with two men, only one of whom was related to them.[28] Lucy Faukes customarily slept on the shop floor of a couple.[29] Squatters were also a problem, breaking into unoccupied property and staying there against the will of the owner.[30]

Women arrested on suspicion of having committed felonies were held in Newgate jail. They had a separate room, but in 1406 they complained to the mayor and aldermen that they were uncomfortably housed in a small chamber in the jail and that "when they wished to relieve nature, they were obliged to pass through a certain house of the said gaol called 'Bordardo,' where a great number of men were confined to their great shame and hurt." The women pointed out that there was a house with a solar belonging to the city that stood near Newgate and that the city might build a tower there. The city agreed to build the tower with the provision that it be put to no other purpose but to house female prisoners.[31]

Inns provided temporary housing for travelers to London or for people planning a short stay. When the aldermen inspected the inns and hostels in 1282 and again in 1384, they listed 197 inns. Although they were scattered through the city, most were located just outside the walls. Accommodation varied from a single room to a suite of rooms and stables for horses. Some shared rooms went for as little as half a penny a night.[32]

Not only wealth but the stage of a woman's life cycle determined her housing. Some women lived very well as married women but suffered reduced circumstances as widows. Other women found their housing enhanced either by remarriage or inheritance. But many women, particularly widows, experienced increased poverty, in spite of their best efforts or because of misfortune. Widows, as we have seen, could be extremely wealthy, but the death of the husband could bring financial disaster, as the widow lost her husband's income and might only have one-third of the property.[33] Medieval London had few safety nets for housing the very poor.[34]

If Londoners could not guarantee housing, they were picky about maintaining clean streets and also keeping their privacy. To prevent disagreements between neighbors over waste water, latrines, and windows overlooking one another's property, Mayor Fitzalyne established regulations, called the Assize of Nuisance, that permitted the city to investigate breaches of building codes.[35] Through an appeal to the Assize of Nuisance, individuals could control the behavior of their neighbors regarding violations of building codes. Householders had a number of concerns that involved encroachment on their property or quality of life. Latrines and windows were two frequent complaints. While the city had ordinances regarding the placement of latrines and required that they be lined with stone, often the privies were too close to wells or the smell was a nuisance to neighbors. Usually they were located in yards or in the cellars of houses. But more elaborate ones were located off solars, with wooden shunts (called pipes) connecting them to the cesspit. Some of the privies were cleaned with runoff water from roofs. Alice Wade, for instance, had an illegal arrangement in which she connected a privy in her solar to a gutter that ran under the house of a neighbor, who complained about the stench.[36] Privies could rot out and cause users to plunge to their deaths. Richard le Rakiere (his surname indicates that he made his living pushing muck in London's streets) was sitting on a latrine in his house when the planks, being rotten, gave way, and he fell in and drowned.[37]

The city provided public privies. Mayor Richard Whittington of storybook fame made a generous bequest in his will for two rows of sixty-four seats each, one for men and one for women. The latrines were located where they would be flushed out by the tide.[38] For the most part, the urban cleaning seemed to work well through the first half of the fourteenth century, but after the Black Death of 1348, standards appeared to have slipped. It was hard to control the rats, mice, bacteria, and other dangers of the filth.[39] In a wardmoot (a meeting of the inhabitants of a city ward to complain about offenses to the alderman) in 1422, the people in Farringdon Without complained that "the common privy of Ludgate is defective and perilous and the ordure thereof rotteth the stone walls and makes a horrible stench and a foul sight, to the great discomfort and nuisance of all folk dwelling thereabout, and a disgrace to all the city."[40]

Privacy was important to Londoners. When some of their neighbors removed parts of the roof of a shared privy, Andrew de Aubrey and his wife complained that the extremities of those seated on the privy could now be seen, "a thing which is abominable and altogether intolerable."[41] Windows overlooking property or into windows of neighbors were also an invasion of privacy. Isabel, widow of John Luter, made a series of complaints about neighbors having windows overlooking her various properties. Most grievous was a leaden tower that John Le Leche put on the wall of his tenement adjoining hers "upon which he and his household stand daily, watching the private affairs of the plaintiff and her servants."[42]

The cramped living spaces, both outdoors and in, led the population to spend much of their time in the streets and to use them for all sorts of purposes. Housewives and maids threw kitchen waste, slops from chamber pots, and dirty rushes from the floors into the streets. Drunks urinated from upper stories onto the streets. Rowdy young men created problems of noise and fighting. Dung from horses and other domestic animals as well as human feces were common. The streets were public spaces for all kinds of activities, and each in turn needed regulation so as not to become offensive.

To keep these public concourses clean, the city went to lengths to collect filth. Muck rakers regularly cleaned the streets, and the city provided carts and "gong boats" to remove the refuse. Although people commonly relieved themselves in the streets, the citizens did not regard such behavior as acceptable. In 1299 two citizens reprimanded a groom of the prince for relieving himself in a lane rather than going to a public privy, which, they argued, would have been "more decent."[43]

As much as possible, London tried to make individual householders responsible for keeping their properties clean. When in 1318 the city granted to Philip le Turnour and Alice, his wife, a small house outside Aldgate, it was with the agreement that they would pay 4s. a year and that they would live in the house and keep the road under the gate clean as "tenants of the house had been accustomed to do in times past." But by 1320 the house had changed hands, and the tenant had to be reminded of his duty. Landlords also wrote into their contracts that the tenants were responsible for keeping the property clean of dust and rubbish.[44] Those who offended were brought to the wardmoot. William Emery, a poulterer of Farringdon Within, was charged with throwing goose, heron, and horse dung into the streets. In another charge, he was accused of laying dung in the highway and "for casting out horse piss that had stood under his horse a month or six weeks" so that all passers-by were offended.[45]

Foul odors and infections were not the only threats to Londoners. Streets were scenes of commercial and pleasant social intercourse and also of violence. To suppress rowdiness and crime at night, London imposed a curfew and mandated that the wards establish a street patrol to see that it was enforced. Curfew was rung on the bells of St. Mary-le-Bow, All Hallows Barking, St. Bride in Fleet Street, and St. Giles Cripplegate at perhaps nine or ten o'clock in the evening. For women, venturing into the street at night was dangerous. Consider again the case of Joan, the eleven-year-old daughter of Eustace le Seler, who was outside her father's house at curfew when she was abducted and carried to another ward, where she was raped.[46]

People of all ranks lived side by side in London streets, houses, and neighborhoods. The Italian wrote that the population of London included those of low degree as well as merchants and nobles, artificers from all over the island, and people from Flanders and other places.[47] They became accustomed to the smells of the city, but they wanted their privacy. They cooperated with each other, protected each other, and became irritants in each other's lives.

Standards of Living

London records of various types permit us to form an intimate picture of the material lives of London's women. London's taxes, for instance, excluded some material goods that were regarded as necessary for the maintenance and dignity of people. London law allowed "all folk, foreigners as well as denizens, to be quit of payment at the...quay for trunk, fardel, pannier, or wallet which a man may carry under his arm for his necessaries for his back [clothing] and a bed." Citizens were given an additional privilege of being quit of all manner of warfage fees for one man.[48] When a prospective servant girl or apprentice came into town, she would not be taxed for her small personal possessions, just as a man would not be. When the king and Parliament imposed a subsidy tax in 1332 (a tax on the movable goods of the laity valued at over 10 s.), they exempted from assessment "a dress for the man, and one for the woman, and a bed for both, a ring and a chain of gold or silver, and a girdle of silk that they use every day; and also a goblet of silver or mazer from which they drink."[49] After 1334, Londoners persuaded Edward III to tax them on the same basis as the counties rather than boroughs. This privilege gave them the additional exemption of taxation of armor and riding horses, all jewels and dresses of the husband and wife, and all vessels of gold and silver. The tax legislation obviously covered a range of people, from the poor immigrant, carrying only what she or he needed for a change of clothes and a bed, to the wealthy, who already had sufficient goods to be taxed but who needed some expensive luxuries in order to maintain their comfort and social status.

The lay subsidies of 1332 in London show who was wealthy (although tax evaders, of course, managed not to be counted) and where the prestigious quarters of town were. The lay subsidies were a tax on movable goods (not real property), and those whose total wealth was under 10 s. were not taxed. Sixteen London taxpayers were assessed over £60, 172 people were taxed from £15 to £60, 141 paid from £7 10 s. to £15, and 253 paid £3 15 s. to £7 10 s. The vast majority of Londoners paying taxes were assessed at £1 to £3 15 s. (502) or 10 s. to £1 (543). An estimated 50 percent or more of Londoners were so poor that they paid no tax.[50] Only 3 percent (fifty-six) of the taxpayers were women, and of those, only four fell into the category of owing £15, and only two owed £7 10s. The others fell into the lower taxpaying brackets. While some of these women were listed as widows, others were listed only by their own names. The lay subsidy roll of 1411–12 shows that the number of taxable women had increased to 12 percent.[51]

Wealth was concentrated along the river front at the wharves and quays. The Vintry was important for wine, and the fishmongers congregated in Billingsgate and Queenhithe. The Cheap, of course, housed merchants purveying a variety of luxury goods and thus a concentration of wealth. In the 1332 lay subsidies, the poorer areas were toward the east, including Cornhill, Portsoken, Aldgate, and Limestreet.[52]

In an autobiographical section of *Piers Plowman*, William Langland described Cornhill, where he lived in the late fourteenth century with his wife, Kit.[53] He knew the poor of the area well. The prostitute Clarice of Cock's Lane, Hick the hackney-man, pickpockets, a rat-catcher and a street sweeper, Rose the dish-seller, and "a heap of secondhand salesmen" all met in the house of Betty Brewer.[54] The gender mix in such a brew house is the essence of London.

The poor and laboring classes, however, were not isolated in certain areas of the city. While in modern urban areas the rich tend to live spatially separated from the poor, London housing generally did not permit such clear divisions, since poorer people rented solars, shops, and rooms from more wealthy landlords who owned the whole house. A surviving wardmoot indicates the mix of neighbors within a ward. Aldermen, wealthy and respected inhabitants, lived side by side with craftsmen and prostitutes. Lymestrete wardmoot reported on January 10, 1423:

> Mawde Sheppyster keeps open shop, retails and is not a freewoman; also she is a strumpet to more than one and a bawd also.
> Thomas Brid is a forestaller and regrater of victuals coming to

the market. John Cool is a sustainer of them in his shop. Anneys Edward, Gass Furneys, Cateryn Sprynger and Julian Blyndale are regraters of poultry and wildfowl.

The prior of Wenlock rubbed shoulders with these small-time offenders and added his own nuisance by extending his garden three feet into the highway, an action that stopped the dung and water from flowing into the gutter. In Cripplegate Without, a brothel in Grub Street was attracting a noisy clientele, including priests and their concubines. Among the general nuisances to the neighborhood was the smell from the private privies of grocers and goldsmiths.[55]

When the tax assessors entered a house to determine the value of the chattels in it, they followed a systematic pattern. They first visited the treasure chest and then the rest of the house, moving on to the kitchen, larder, granary, craft or brewing facilities, and stables.[56] The other systematic evaluation of goods came when a person died and an inventory was taken to evaluate the contents of the house in order to settle the estate. These assessments are more intimate, for they actually name the items, and we can walk through the house with the assessors and imagine the people living in them. Only a few of these survive for late medieval London, but they can give us a valuable picture of the physical environment that women (and men) traversed daily in their rounds of duty and pleasure.[57]

The house and effects of Sir Matthew Philip, an alderman and a goldsmith, whose inventory dates from 1476, represents the most elite of our sample. He was married twice; his first wife died in 1470, and his second wife, the widow of a grocer, outlived him. The evaluators of his property started in the hall, which was the public room of the house. Its furnishings were lavish, since this was the room for business, pleasure, and dining. Sir Matthew's hall had valuable tapestries worth £6 and lesser ones worth 10s. The benches along the walls were made comfortable with twelve cushions. To facilitate business, conversation, and repasts, there were six light stools, two low stools, a folding table and a long table with a tapestry cover, two joined tables, and two cupboards, presumably with plate and cups for offering visitors a drink. The high status of the owner is shown by the furniture, including a folding table and joined furniture—a new luxury of the fifteenth century. Smaller items such as candlesticks, hearth tools, and so on added to the comfort of the hall. But it remained a formal room compared to the rest of the house, because of its large size and high ceiling of oak and plaster, which increased its imposing formality.

But wealthy Londoners and even those who lived in more modest circumstances had found that a parlor (a word derived from *parler*, French for "talk") provided a more private, intimate setting. In the Philip home, visitors would have known the difference between being invited into the hall as opposed to the parlor. In this more intimate room, four benches around the sides were covered with green silk and two matching cushions of green silk. Fifteen other cushions and a carpet added elegance. Several windows are mentioned, and the room had a great round looking-glass. The fancy joined furniture in the room included tables, chairs, stools, a form, and two cupboards. To enliven and make the room even homier, it included a birdcage and an English book, the *Chronicles of London*. Here was a room that the family could live in and that honored guests would be invited into as esteemed visitors. The Ménagier of Paris recommended dogs as well as birds to keep his young wife company in such a room.[58]

A sense of the hospitality that the household could provide comes from the inventory of the buttery. The important ritual of washing hands before dining was easily accomplished in Mathew Philip's household, because the buttery had ten basins and six ewers of latten (brass or brass-like alloy) and several other ewers and basins in reserve. Three chafing dishes provided for quick meals or keeping a meal warm. At least sixteen candlesticks of latten could light the room. In addition, there were a number of pots and pottles, a bread chest, a little ship chest, and a chest for candles. Knives and linen cloths for the table were available.

Luxury did not cease in the chief chamber for the master and mistress of the house. This room was brightly colored with tapestries on the wall, green window curtains, and a chest covered with red worsted and cushions embroidered with roses. The bed had a tapestry tester (a square canopy over the bed), a feather bed, and a pair of sheets. It also had a small bed that could go underneath the main bed. The lady of the house had a great round looking-glass. Furniture was as fine as that in the parlor, and the room had a number of chests and a clothes press. Completing the comfort was a holy water container, a fireplace, and a white chamber pot.

The furnishing of Sir Matthew's bedchamber is reminiscent of the famous "Portrait of Giovanni Arnolfini and His Wife" (1434) by Jan van Eyck. The marriage scene is in the bedroom, with the bride and groom holding hands. A mirror is in the background, and the marital bed is prominent to the right. For women, the bedchamber had an important significance similar to that implied in the picture. The bed symbolized the consummation of the marriage both physically and materially. The household effects that a woman brought as dowry might include the bedding, clothing, a mirror, and so on. The bedchamber was also the locus for conception, birth, and child-rearing. Children of the marriage perpetuated the descent of property and wealth of both sides of the family to the next generation.[59] Finally, as a dowager, the widow had the use of the principal bedchamber, along with several others in the house, as her "freebench," or the very minimum that a widow could expect for her upkeep.[60] The many chests in Phillip's chief chamber and others around the house had a special significance for the mistress of the house, because she was the keeper of the keys to chests.

A second bedroom in the alderman's house was not as elaborate but did have red silk hangings, a tester, and cushions as well as turned and joined chairs, a cupboard, chests, and so on. It, too, had a fireplace. A drying chamber and a press chamber contained further blankets, bolsters, cloth, sheets, beds, and so on. Clearly, Sir Matthew Philip and his two successive wives had lived in very comfortable and colorful surroundings.[61]

The appointments in all the houses surveyed in the surviving probate inventories of the late fifteenth-century showed considerable comfort in fabric, furniture, kitchen utensils, and silver and gilt objects for serving. We have seen that Elizabeth Ryche Stonor had some of her silver and gilt objects transferred between her country and city residences. Some wealthy merchant houses had a number of rooms, including garrets for storage and various work areas. One house had a garden on the river and a white boat. These wealthy men and their wives lived a life of luxury and comfort.[62]

Some of the inventories tell the contents of the servants' rooms as well, so we can form an idea of how the help lived in these wealthy establishments. Richard Bele, a butcher, had "in the maydyns chamber" a bed with a worn mattress, coverlets and blankets, and sheets of rough linen. The value was only 5 s. His estate was valued at £154 3 s. 4 d., so he had the means to do better by the maid. But his provisions were similar to others. Some people housed the servants in their garrets rather than providing separate chambers. A draper provided for his household help more comfortably. The cook had a chamber near the kitchen. This prized servant, usually a man, had a curtained bed with a tester, a coverlet with embroidery, a feather bed, and chests all valued at 24 s. 8 d. The maiden's chamber was likewise well outfitted, including a chamber pot. This house also included a man's chamber, with the furnishings coming to 5 s. 14 d.[63] Male and female servants had separate chambers, indicating a sense of both respect for privacy and good sense in household management.

Servants and mistresses, however, might live together in equal discomfort. Elena Scot, a servant of Margaret de Sandwich, descended from a solar she shared with her mistress and another woman to seek embers to start a fire in December 1321. Her foot slipped, and she fell to her death.[64]

Not all housing was as grand as the ones in the inventories. Some contained basic furniture and perhaps even the necessities of a trade such as brewing.[65] A woman or a husband and wife who rented a property would have had to bring furniture (a luxury), chests, pots and pans for regular cooking, wall hangings, and so on to make the place comfortable. If the wife planned to do brewing or another craft, she would need the items and utensils for the trade. The goods taken from the house of Catherine, widow of William atte Wode show the remaining elegance of a widow. She had a fur, two pairs of beads and one pair of knives, two purses, a double cloak, four smocks, four kerchiefs, three coffers and three great chests, a bed with tapestry work, a pillow, a table cloth and towel, a pair of andirons, and two women's saddles.[66] The house would have contained other amenities, but these were her private possessions.

Moving to a less respectable social scale, that of a concubine and her lover, who murdered a man, and fled to a church for sanctuary. Their goods, according to the coroners' jurors, included one canvas, a carpet, several coverlets and old blankets, one table cloth and three towels, two chemises and a gown of green cloth worth 5 s. and a gown of blue cloth worth 4 s., a trunk of little things, an ear-cushion, woolen thread, several brass pots and pans, a dish and ewer, and one andiron. Their total worth was 32 s.[67]

A silkwoman, however, was able to leave to her surviving minor children, a boy and a girl (three boys had died under age), silver cups, spoons, a power box, a vessel for serving Rhenish wine, and various silver pieces valued at £16 2 s. 6 d. In addition, she left her daughter a black furred gown, a black hood, and other clothing.[68] This would be in addition to real estate that they received from their father. Like many widows, she used a cleric, the master of the House of St. Thomas of Acon (or Acre), to secure these bequests.

Wills provide insights into the possessions of the wealthy and even those of the poor. Two sets of wills, those of the London Archdeaconry court and the Commissary court, are particularly helpful in forming an idea of the economic circumstances of ordinary craftsmen, laborers, and even paupers.[69] As we have observed, these courts tried to provide all Christians with the opportunity to make a will and in the process managed to collect bequests to the Church, even from the poor. The Husting court wills, on the other hand, dealt with those who had real estate and so tend to represent a more comfortable level in the social scale.

Since only widows, single women, and married women who had the explicit permission of their husbands could make a will, our knowledge of women's possessions is limited. For the most part, real estate had been settled by prior arrangement in the granting of dowry to a daughter, by rules of inheritance, or by a dower granted to a widow. Widow's wills tend to dwell lovingly on clothing, household effects, plate, silk girdles, and such items.[70] But widows enrolling their wills in the Husting court had property to leave as well as movables. Margaret, widow of John de la Tonk, left her niece and her servant two mansion houses for their life use, and Alice, widow of Robert Lyndiwyk, instructed that a tenement be sold and some of the money go to her two goddaughters.[71] A wife making her will with the consent of her husband confirmed the provision of a former husband's will that his son would have real estate (her dower) until he got an ecclesiastical benefice of greater value than the profits of the real estate. Then it was to go to the daughter of the former husband.[72]

The craftsmen's wills in the Archdeaconry court represented a variety of trades, including tilers, brewers, an embroiderer, a fishmonger, a grocer, spicers, saddlers, a minstrel, and so on. Their estates were, for the most part, modest and often simply provide the wife with her dower or the residue of the estate without specifying what this would be. Among female testators the Commissary court lists five silkwomen, six single women, an anchoress, a fishmonger, and a servant. The silkwomen, a group of women who produced silk thread and ribbon, were charitable in giving to the prisoners, hospitals, parish churches, the poor, and religious fraternities. Other than these monetary gifts, their estates included clothing, bedding and linen, furniture, silver spoons, and other household items. The wealthiest of these women, the widow Beatrice Filer, had five children for whom she provided £140 as well as silver spoons and other objects. Her estate probably also represented part of her dowry and dower from her husband. She also made lavish gifts to various churches.[73]

The two courts record the wills of beggars and paupers. In the Archdeaconry court, 16 of the 228 wills were those of testators described as paupers, of whom seven were women and eight were men. The Commissary court has a much fuller set of wills and an index of occupations but only lists one beggar and one pauper. Most of the poor were residents of a parish, and some had former occupations but died with little wealth. In other words, they were not strangers to their neighbors or the parish priests. One had a house and garden that she left to a couple with contents worth 14 s. 4 d. Another widow had some money and household goods that she left to her daughter. A son of one of these poor women got the residue of her estate. The widow of a minstrel left the residue of her meager estate to another minstrel and asked to be buried next to her husband. Many of these widows had a few household luxuries such as linen, brass pots, silver spoons, a bed, and clothing. These Londoners had a minimum of luxuries worth mentioning in a will and, as we shall see, most left them to the parish church or the clergy for the saving of their souls in the afterlife.[74]

Even poorer than the beggars, who appear in wills, were those who eked out a day-by-day existence. The London coroners reported that on July 3, 1322, a "great multitude of poor people was assembled at the gate of the Friars Preachers seeking alms" in the ward of Farndone. At daybreak the people surged forward for alms, crushing those already at the door. "Robert Fynel, Simon, Robert and William his sons and 22 other male persons, names unknown and Matilda, daughter of Robert le Carpenter, Beatrix Cole, Johanna 'le Peyntures,' Alice la Norice and 22 other women, names unknown," were among the dead.[75] The event occurred during a famine year when food was scarce throughout England and both denizen poor and outsiders came to London hoping for aid. Others are described in coroner's inquests as dying of hunger in their rooms or on the streets.[76] Londoners were not indifferent to these poor people. In one of the worst famine years of the early fourteenth century, 1318, Robert de Lincoln left a bequest of 1 d. for each of the two thousand poor people.[77] A penny would buy a loaf of bread, so this generous bequest would keep body and soul together for a day at least.

The actual cost of living appears in several court cases. These reflect the needs of women and men with modest incomes rather than the very wealthy, who presumably successfully lived on credit or paid their creditors. Matilda, wife of Robert Aleyn, a knight, stayed with two servants at the hospital of the Blessed Mary outside Bishopsgate. Her bill came to £15 6s. 8d. for bread, beer, fish, meat, and other victuals. Expenses included 18s. for two loaves, two gallons of beer, and two dishes of cookery every day from July 11 to August 22, 1378. For fifty weeks from August 22, 1378, she paid 40d. a week for victuals and had a bill of £8 6s. 8d. From August 5, 1379, she had bill for forty-two weeks at a charge of 40d. a week, amounting to £7. She refused to pay her bills, and her husband said that goods she had left in a forcer (strong box) would cover the expenses. Matilda had the key to the forcer, and when it was brought to her, it contained little of value, including six small buttons made from pennies. Judgment was that she would have to pay.[78] Living less lavishly were Bernard de Gascoigne and Johanna, his wife, who absconded owing Gilbert de Meldebourne 34 s. for room and board for ninety-four days.[79]

Food played a large role in London life. All travelers were a bit awed by the quantity of food available. Alessandro Magno commented on the quantity of fish, poultry, and meat, particularly beef and mutton, available every day. He also mentions the great contribution of the English to cuisine—whole roasted joints.[80] The Venetian visiting in 1500 also noted that the English took great pleasure in a "quantity of excellent victuals." He observed that they remained long at the table, but were parsimonious about the amount of wine they served because they had to import it. On the other hand, they had quantities of beer and ale, but they did not force this on visiting Italians. It was just as well, since Magno described it as "cloudy like horses' urine [with] husks on top."[81]

As Langland observed, the brew house and tavern were popular places to meet, and women as well as men drank considerable amounts of ale. The "Good Wife" cautions her daughter that she should not spend all the money she makes selling her cloth in the city on taverns because "they that taverns haunt / From thrift soon come to want." Not only is this empty consumerism, but young women who overindulge are likely to get drunk and lose their market value for marriage.[82] Even married women who frequented taverns came under censure. In one tavern song, the gossips—Elinore, Joan, Margery, Margaret, Alice, and Cecily—come together at a place where they can get the best wine and strong ale. They bring cold dishes to enjoy with their drink. They get drunk and complain about their husbands, particularly those who beat their wives.[83]

In addition to food and drink, clothing was important to Londoners of all social classes. All aspects of cloth making required intensive labor, including weaving, finishing, dying, and tailoring. Clothing was expensive. One can understand the importance of clothing from a coroner's inquest in 1322. Lucy Faukes, who was staying with Richard le Sherman and Christina, came in one night at curfew "clad in good clothes." Richard and Christina quarreled with her, hoping to start an argument and have a reason to kill her for her clothes. Finally Richard took a "Balstaf" and hit her on her head and killed her. Christina stripped Lucy's clothes, and the couple fled.[84]

The probate inventories and wills describe colorful clothing lined with furs and silks. Outer garments such as gowns, hats, and hoods were of violets, greens, scarlet, crimson, russet, red, murrey, blues, and mixed colors. The alderman Sir Matthew Philip had the most elaborate wardrobe of gowns, but he would have needed these as part of his official dress. Doublets were of tawny or black. Women were also well dressed. For instance, Margery, relict of Thomas Broun, bequeathed to her daughter a mantle dyed with *murre* in grain furred with *Gris* (back of squirrel) and all her clothes to match. Two other women got good gowns furred with *putes* (weasel or wild cat), a mantle of violet furred with *Gris,* and a hood of the same. Margaret, widow of John de la Tonk, also left colorful gowns and robes furred with miniver (fur from the belly of squirrel during winter).[85]

The sumptuary legislation of the fourteenth and fifteenth centuries tried to regulate the clothing that people wore and the food they ate according to their social class and income. Servants and day laborers were to have meat and fish once a day and wear clothing that did not exceed 2 marks for the whole cloth it was made of. Yeomen and craftsmen were to have clothing worth no more than 40 s. Knights could wear clothing worth 4 marks and a half but not cloth-of-gold, silver, or furs. Wives and children in each social class were to live within their social status. Only when merchants had goods worth £500 could they wear clothing similar to gentlemen with income of £100 a year. The legislation was an attempt to keep the people of England within social class lines; the discrimination against the upstart burgesses and merchants is quite clear.[86]

Enforcing this legislation proved impossible. In London, a thriving trade in frippery (secondhand clothes, shoes, and furniture) took place in evening markets in Cornhill and Cheapside. The merchants, women among them, came under suspicion because they sold at dusk and because they were suspected of selling stolen property. Richard and Christina could have taken Lucy's clothing there and sold it. In any case, those of an inappropriate social class could always acquire secondhand finery from a fripperer.[87] Furthermore, pious Londoners left bequests of their clothing to their servants and the poor, which would certainly have been clothing above their station. John de Worstede, a mercer, left his wife all the goods of their chamber except his clothing, which was to be distributed among the poor.[88]

Fine clothing was only part of the wealth of Londoners. If even a beggar and a woman with a modest income had silver spoons, the wealthy had most impressive plate for setting their tables and jewelry for adorning their persons. The probate inventories showed butteries full of silver saltcellars, silver drinking cups, covered bowels of silver, coconut cups (polished coconut shells) mounted in silver, and beautiful mazer (fine maple) bowels decorated with silver. The widow Margaret Tonk left several silver cups of Paris work, silver girdles, and various beautifully embroidered bedspreads, testers, and other fine fabrics.[89]

Women as Consumers

We must assume that the men of the household did not purchase all of the contents of their home, clothing for the family, or even food and other provisions. We have already seen that poor befuddled Thomas Betson wrote to Elizabeth Ryche Stonor asking for advice on buying a trousseau for his young bride, since he had no experience in doing so. He claimed to have little knowledge of what she would need. But he had filled all sorts of orders for Elizabeth in London and abroad. In addition to the consumption of material goods, women and men alike were great consumers of spiritual benefits to be derived from gifts of charity, support of chantry clerics, parish guilds, local churches, hospitals, and masses for the salvation of their souls and those of departed relatives.

Isabella Whitney, a woman writing in 1573, described the best places for shopping in a poem, "The Manner of her Will and What she left to London and to All Those in it, at her Departing."[90] The streets and districts she describes were still those that were characteristic of medieval London. Watling Street and Canwick Street offered woolen cloth, while linen could be bought in Friday Street. Foremost among the shopping streets was Cheapside. This wide market street was a place of public gatherings and also of luxury shopping. It was there that Isabella Whitney directed men and women who would buy fine mercery and silk. The Goldsmiths also plied their wears, including

> jewels such
> As are for ladies meet.
> And plate for furnish cupboards with
> Full brave there shall you find,
> With purl of silver and of gold
> to satisfy your mind;
> With hoods, bongraces [shades for bonnets], hats or caps
> Such store are in that street.

Also in that area were items of lawn (thin linen or cotton fabric) such as gorgets and sleeves, as well as purses, knives, combs, and mirrors. To shop for women's footwear, she recommended Birchin Lane and St. Martin's Lane, where artisans sold boots and shoes and pantables, or overshoes for walking in the dirty streets of London. She also directed women where to find the best tailors, saying that they could be found on Bow street, but that every lane had a tailor who would do "indifferent well."[91]

The opportunity to shop, as Isabella Whitney says, was one of the most appealing aspects of London. Shops were often built in rows and included both retail and work areas. The shops usually had a chimney and a privy. A typical goldsmith's shop had a board that closed up the shop at night and could be lowered to form a counter during the day. Gold and silver items were displayed in an openwork cupboard on the wall that could be locked. A woman who shopped pointed to the item she wanted, and it was brought down for her inspection. Other shops had a similar layout. The back of the shop had the hearth, furnace, anvils, and other tools of the trade, and there apprentices and the master made new objects or refashioned old ones.[92] Selds, also popular for retailing, were much more rudimentary, being basically weather-proof stalls or arcade areas built on the fronts of buildings. They resembled a bazaar in which various dealers could display their goods for sale. Selds offered women a place with cheap rent to retail products of family industry or goods for some wholesaler.[93] They were also places where women could shop. In addition to shops, the pavements were a place to display grain and other items for sale, and street vendors (many of whom were women) conducted their business in the streets.

We have some idea of the shopping that women did in the elite shops. Margery Randolf bought from Walter Adryan "a circlet, a hanap [handled cup] of silver with a foot, a fermail [buckle] of gold, a girdle of silver, 12 silver spoons, a nut [polished cup of cocoanut] on a foot, and silver covercle, a silver cup and covercle, a hanap of mazer, with an impression of St. Thomas of Lancaster thereon, and with a covercle, hanap of mazer with an impression of a head, 2 caplets of pearls and of prayer beads, a table cloth of 5 and a half ells, and 4 linen sheets." She paid 10 marks sterling in the mid–fourteenth century.[94] This was a large purchase, but wealthy widows could buy more; for example, Etheldrede Bolsore ordered a bracelet wrought in gold and set with rubies.[95]

Women with comfortable amounts of spending money certainly enjoyed shopping sprees, but husbands and moralists tried to impose some limits. The Ménagier of Paris had suggested the reasonable limits that a good bourgeois wife might spend. He wanted his wife to be careful about the resources of his purse, as well as the need to maintain their social status. She was a young woman, but he did not want her to introduce too many new fashions. He wanted her neatly dressed with her collar straight, and her petticoat, frock, and coat aligned.[96] The Ménagier was simply reflecting the criticisms of the times on the excesses of women's dress.[97]

The supply of goods to and from London can be traced in the Stonor letters. The factors in London, including Thomas Betson, provided wine, salt fish, fine clothing, spices, canvas, and silver plate. Elizabeth Stonor often commissioned Betson to buy things for her. Betson, like the Ménagier of Paris, warned her and her husband about too much expense.[98] A portion of her account book even remains to indicate the type of shopping that was done either by her or for her in London.[99] The supplying of grand houses in London and the countryside with suitable clothing, drink, candles, luxuries for the table, and decorating was a major contribution to the economy of London, and much of the ordering was done by women.

Ordinary woman shopped for daily food from street vendors who purveyed fruits and vegetables, cooked items, ale, and wine. Some people, as we have seen, took their meals where they rented. Others bought prepared food because they did not have access to fires for cooking.[100] London in the late twelfth century, as William Fitzstephen pointed out, had excellent cook-shops where everything from peas porridge to a swan could be purchased. Women with larger households might send their cook out to make the necessary purchases, or if they went themselves, they were accompanied by their servants. One imagines that the opportunity to be in the midst of a number of acquaintances and friends while shopping was a further inducement for women to do their own shopping.

In addition to goods, women also bought services. They were responsible for the employment of household servants, workmen for the upkeep of their large property holdings, and horses and vehicles for the conveyance of their goods. They had need of lawyers for their numerous legal suits, and they had recourse to apothecaries, doctors, and priests. Some of these service expenses are discussed in later chapters, but the comfort of a bath deserves notice here.

While "stews" have a bad name associated with the baths in Southwark that catered to prostitution, men and women could pay for an honest bath that the poorer homes could not provide.[101] The stews in London required surveillance to be sure that they were reputable. In 1428, a man who ran one of the stews for men in London was reminded that no "washer-women" were to enter the stew and that it was to be kept "for stewing of good and respectable men." The owners entered into a bond with the city to that effect.[102] Stews for women, likewise, came under scrutiny. The stews for women had similar injunctions against "washer-women" or allowing men in. Only "good and honest women to be [were] stewed there at times appointed and not otherwise." The period in which the mayor and aldermen seemed to have taken particular note of these amenities was 1427–28. "Stew Lane" was in the parish of St. Mary Somerset, but stews for women were also licensed in

St. Michael Queenhithe. The bond, £20, was high for keeping these baths honest.[103]

Physical comfort and luxury were not the only concerns of London women. Charity, fraternities, parish churches, spiritual comfort, and salvation were all part of women's consumer spending.[104] Men were equally generous, but the women's gifts are the concern here. Some of the largest bequests were for chantry priests to say prayers for the donor and her or his family and also for the general welfare of a parish church or a parish guild. Alice, widow of Thomas Juvenal, died in 1318 and left tenements to the church of St. Agnes within Aldersgate.

> After the publication of the statute of Mortmain, by her will proved, proclaimed and enrolled in the Husting of London... she bequeathed, for the maintenance of a chaplain to celebrate at the altar of St. Nicholas in the church of St. Agnes aforesaid for her soul and the souls of all faithful departed, 6 marks yearly quit-rent from the premises, which were to be held by her executors for their lives in survivorship for the maintenance of the said chaplain. She also bequeathed the last-named tenement except the cellar, to Nicholas of Leicester, chaplain, one of her executors, for life; and after his death she willed that two chaplains should be provided by her other executor, if surviving from the said tenement and the others bequeathed above to celebrate forever as above in the said church.

Alice's careful preparations for the benefit of chaplains at St. Agnes and her soul went awry. One of the sheriffs of London occupied her property and then one of the chamberlains, but in the last years of the reign of Edward III, the rector and parishioners of the church wrested the property from the chamberlain and once again appointed a chaplain to fulfill her will.[105]

There were other cases in which women left considerable property or money for masses and prayers and the parish churches had to go to court to retrieve the money. Sabina Yerdele had set apart £100 for a chaplain to celebrate mass in All Hallows the Great "for her well being in life and her soul after death." She had appointed a chaplain at an annual salary of 10 marks and placed the money in the hands of a man for whom she felt "trust and affection." When the chaplain was not paid after her death, her executor brought the man to court. He claimed that she had exonerated him in her will from payment should he fall into poverty. The will proved that he was right, and as a compromise, he paid the chaplain back salary and an installment for the next year.[106]

Pious giving was not limited to wealthy women. Those described as paupers in the Archdeaconry court were as generous as they could afford to be. Both men and women left goods to the church. A woman with an estate of 6 s. 6 d., a silver spoon, and other goods left it all to the clergy.[107] Other women also specified goods, such as the widow Alice, a beggar, who gave 29 s. to the parish church and 6 s. 8 d. to the chaplain. She gave an additional 6 s. 8 d. for the poor and the residue of the estate to the chaplain to say prayers for all the faithful. Another woman, a minstrel's widow, left money to pray for the souls of herself and her husband.[108] One female pauper had the amenities of linen table cloths and napkins and left them to her parish church.[109] A common pattern among male testators with no relatives was to reserve 2 s. 6 d. for burial services and leave the remainder to a member of the clergy, who also acted as executor.[110] Both wealthy and poor women tended to be more directive in the use of their gifts, instructing the exact use of items in the church.[111]

Women were also active in parish fundraising. They mended and laundered altar cloths, banners, and other fabrics, raised funds for specific building improvements, such as windows, and organized themselves into female guilds of maidens and married women for fundraising.[112] The Hocktide festival (celebrated on the second Monday and Tuesday after Easter) was a fundraiser for the church. On Hock-Monday, the women captured and tied up the parish men and released them, for a fee to be given to the church, and on Tuesday the men did the same to the women. On the whole, the women were more successful at fundraising than the men during Hocktide. But the whole holiday came under censure as a disorderly event, and the mayor of London issued injunctions against it between 1406 and 1419.[113] Women also purchased more seats in parish churches than did men. In St. Margaret's Westminister between 1460 and 1530, women bought two times as many seats as did men.[114]

In addition to the same-sex guilds, parishioners organized into parish guilds to support their church, provide candles and religious ceremonies, offer some aid to poor parishioners, and hold an annual convivial feast.[115] Membership was open to couples as well as to single women and men.[116] London had a number of these guilds that attracted donations in wills.[117] For instance, William Catesby, a brewer in London, and his wife, Sarah, bequeathed a tenement to the fraternity of All Saints, on the condition that the "whole profit and rent thereof" be used to support a chaplain of the said fraternity and for masses for their souls.[118] As with craft and merchant guilds, it was the men, not the women, who acted as wardens of these guilds and of parish churches.[119]

Women's gifts went beyond the parish level to various hospitals, religious houses, and the city of London.[120] In many respects, the gifts of wealthy women helped to establish their position in society during and after their deaths. Alice, widow of William de Chabham, gave a parcel of land twenty-four feet square "to serve as a fountain head to the Conduit of London," and Margery, daughter of John de Lyndeseye, gave a shop and brew house for the maintenance of London Bridge.[121] Tomasine Percyvale (née Bonaventure) shared with her husband an interest in education, and she established a grammar school in Cornwall.[122] Lady Joan Bradbury, like Tomasine Percyvale, was married to a mayor of London. She was left a wealthy widow by her two marriages, one to a tailor and one to a mercer. In her twenty years as a widow, she made substantial real estate purchases in her own name in London and in the countryside. She established a chantry in St. Stephen's Coleman Street and gave the Mercers' company the use and eventual ownership of her mansion house in London. Her real estate bequest made the Mercers a very wealthy company. She also made substantial gifts to the church and town of Saffron Walden, where she grew up. Her will included numerous charities and a large amount set aside for her funeral and prayers for her soul.[123]

Women in London appeared in all aspects of London's consumer economy. They owned or rented residences, be it only bed and board. They violated the city's nuisance laws and made complaints about violations. They shopped in the markets or directed their servants and business factors to do so. They did not sit passively in their houses but rather were very much a presence in London, be it in markets, houses, streets, or churches. William Fitzstephen in his twelfth-century description of London depicted a city in which women were not visible. Women appeared only as Sabines, presumably in a captive, reproductive environment and not on the streets. The foreign observers of later centuries seemed to have been more aware of women than the clerical Fitzstephen.

❧8❧

Women as Entrepreneurs

Women's economic activities included entrepreneurship and work in various occupations. Women's work was essential for the medieval economy in both the rural and urban areas, but it was not highly paid, and in urban centers women might move through a variety of jobs, including service, vending, and crafts. Despite London's law permitting married wives to trade as *femmes soles* and widows to take over a husbands' businesses, few women became entrepreneurs. Necessary as female labor was, it had less of an economic impact on London's capital formation than the money and property that passed through women in the form of inheritance, dowry, dower, and their role in the consumer economy. If women did not contribute to London's capital formation as entrepreneurs, their labor was essential for the functioning of the city, if they were helping in their husbands' shops, spinning, or working in service positions. Women were also important to the economy as mothers, household managers, trainers of servants, and caregivers. This unpaid labor was basic for a functioning society and economy. This chapter, however, looks at women in the real estate market, their management of property, and their business ventures.

The number of women who participated in either the market economy or the workforce is impossible to know because of the poor population statistics and inadequate registration of women's work. Part of the problem of assessing the market role of women in medieval London and in England in general is that the records are not systematic. Unlike some of the Flemish cities, England does not have registers of citizens, runs of records of market taxes and stall holders, membership in guilds, bank records, and so on. In addition, unlike many continental cities, notarial records do not exist, and it is not clear that written records of marriages and other business transactions were systematically used in England. Bonds and deeds are mentioned, but usually when they become a subject of contention. As a consequence, historians of England are often left with lame terms such as "many women must have been engaged in the credit market."

A "Golden Age" for Women?

Several scholars have posited a "golden age" for women in this period in England. But what constitutes a "golden age?" Early twentieth-century historians of women looked for productive roles for women in the economy and mostly found them within the household. Looking back at the period before the Industrial Revolution and the exploitation of women in factories, they argued that men and women each contributed to the household economy and were on a more equal footing. Even single women enjoyed more economic opportunities in the expanding economy of the late Middle Ages.[1] In the late twentieth century, the "golden age" meant free entry into the workforce, equal pay, and opportunities to enter into a business. Both views ignore the real economic and social context of women in fourteenth and fifteenth century England.

The most recent version of the "golden age," presented by the historians Caroline M. Barron and P. J. P. Goldberg, places the emphasis on demography. The depopulation of England following the Black Death in the mid–fourteenth century and the continued low population in the fifteenth century, the argument says, opened opportunities for women in businesses and in employment in jobs that were previously only open to men. The arguments are based on laws that seem to treat women's employment as equal to men's, a few examples of widows who successfully continued their husbands' businesses, silkwomen in London who practiced their craft and sold their goods, and a scattering of other women who had businesses or well-paid jobs.[2] An additional argument is that young, single women did so well in employment that they delayed marriage and many did not marry at all.[3] Demographic shortfall alone, however, could not open employment to women, and patriarchy put limits on women's access to business.[4]

Scholars of early modern history have illustrated a decline in women's economic position in the sixteenth century but have not called the fourteenth and fifteenth centuries a "golden age."[5] Changes in city and guild regulations set work hours and restricted employment of women to only members of husbands' families. The erosion of the household as the primary unit of crafts and the increased location of the means of production to capital investors and larger industries led to a decline in the status of women's work.[6] New technologies disadvantaged women as well as men in the sixteenth century because the number of small production units decreased in favor of larger ones.[7] The most recent study of women in the late medieval and early modern economy, that of the historian Marjorie Keniston McIntosh, has shown that for all of England, a number of factors led to a worsening of women's economic opportunities in the sixteenth century, and certainly by the 1590s.[8]

A constant factor in looking at women in independent economic activities is that their own reproductive cycle had a profound influence on their opportunities. Women had few opportunities for formal training, marginal positions even for skilled labor, marital status that dictated their work patterns, interrupted employment, and multiple trades.[9] Some years ago, the historian Olwen Hufton described women's work as an "economy of makeshift."[10] For most it was.

None of the arguments stray far from the central issue of patriarchy. To what extent did it limit women's participation in the economy and to what extent could women manipulate patriarchy to their own advantage? Did the depression of population in the late fourteenth and fifteenth centuries aid women in gaining higher status employment, starting businesses, and overcoming limitations put on them? The "self-limiting" nature of patriarchy in regard to the inheritance, wardship of citizens' orphaned children, and the dower of the widow might have worked for family members, but did these patriarchal limitations apply when women entered the marketplace on their own or when they were employees rather than family?

Women's Participation in the Real Estate Market

Since women acquired real estate through inheritance of freehold and rentals, through dowry or dower, and through purchases made with their husbands or on their own as widows and single women, the immediate question arises about the role they played in the property market. While widows could not alienate their dower, they could sell leases hold rights that would be valid for their lifetime, when the property reverted to heirs. Women's inherited property could be leased, sold, and passed on to heirs through a will. Property bought jointly with a husband could also be leased. If the property came from a jointure, the person who lived longest acquired the use of the property. Single women could rent property in their own names, as could married women under London's law covering the rights of a married woman trading *femme sole* (a married woman came under the protective law of the husband as *femme coverte de baron*, but London permitted a married woman to act as though she was a single woman). Under these circumstances, a married woman could rent a house or shop, but she had to pay the rent herself and could be impleaded or sued as if she were single. She could also go into debt to cover the expenses.[11]

In order to give a context to specific examples, I took a series of five-year samples of the Husting court deeds to track women's participation in the selling, leasing, and subletting of properties.[12] Anecdotal evidence plucked from the records to show that women did act on their own is adequate only as examples; the statistical information puts them in context. Women's participation in the real estate market fluctuated over time and in the end declined considerably (see table 8.1).

The information does not contain the value of the property but only the deeds recorded in the years surveyed. Males, husbands and wives, wives acting on their own, widows, and single females are all noted.

The number of deeds enrolled increased steadily in the fourteenth century from 304 to reach a high point of 841 in 1370–74. The plague of 1349 and its subsequent visitations were, of course, responsible for some of the rise, but the market was already increasing before that date (601 properties in 1340–44). It was not until 1420–24 that the numbers decreased

TABLE 8.1. Sellers or Leasers and Buyers of Property by Sex and Marital Status, Based on Deeds Enrolled in the London Husting Court

YEAR	MALE		HUSBAND/WIFE		WIFE		WIDOW		SINGLE FEMALE		TOTAL
	S	B	S	B	S	B	S	B	S	B	
1300–1304	46%	63%	41%	32%			7%	3%	6%	2%	304
1310–1314	46%	65%	35%	25%	(1)*		9%	3%	10%	6%	475
1320–1324	45%	62%	41%	30%		(4)	6%	4%	7%	4%	494
1330–1334	61%	65%	24%	29%	(2)	(1)	8%	3%	6%	2%	506
1340–1344	62%	66%	26%	27%	(1)		8%	4%	4%	2%	601
1350–1354	62%	65%	27%	31%			7%	2%	4%	3%	655
1360–1364	57%	66%	29%	27%			9%	5%	5%	2%	716
1370–1374	61%	66%	31%	29%	(5)	(3)	6%	3%	2%	2%	841
1380–1384	62%	68%	31%	27%		(2)	5%	2%	2%	3%	644
1390–1394	70%	77%	23%	19%		(5)	6%	3%	1%	(3)	736
1400–1404	69%	69%	24%	24%		(1)	7%	5%	(4)	2%	498
1410–1414	68%	79%	28%	16%		(1)	4%	4%	(1)	3%	409
1420–1424	73%	79%	19%	15%			7%	5%	1%	4%	315
1430–1434	69%	81%	25%	15%		(1)	5%	4%	1%	(1)	314
1440–1444	65%	81%	25%	16%	(2)*	(1)	7%	2%	3%	1%	268
1450–1454	65%	78%	30%	17%		(1)	5%	4%		(1)	144
1460–1464	62%	76%	36%	17%			2%	5%		2%	139
1470–1474	42%	77%	54%	12%		(3)	4%	6%		2%	129

S = SELLER   B = BUYER   ( )* Numbers are shown rather than percent since these were so small.

Corporation of London Record Office, Husting Court Wills and Deeds. The five-year samples were taken from the nineteenth-century handwritten calendar of the rolls compiled by W. T. Alchin and taken over by Reginald Sharpe, records clerk, and his assistants. This compilation is contained in reels 28 and 29 of the microfilm edition, *The Husting Rolls of Deeds and Wills*, 1252-1485 (Cambridge: Chadwyck-Healy, 1990).

substantially, reaching a low point of 129 in 1470–74. The recording of deeds shows a similar decrease to that found in other records in London.[13]

Over the whole period, the number of wives buying and selling real estate on their own was so minuscule that the numbers are not even converted to percents. Women were not taking advantage of their *femme sole* status. Perhaps the very low numbers also indicate that husbands were not pressuring their wives into selling dowry property. Widows were the sellers of property in 6 percent of the cases over the whole period, with a slightly more active engagement up to 1364 (8 percent), but the percentage dropped after that date. Overall the number of widows buying property was 3 percent, but by the beginning of the fifteenth century, widows increased their buying of deeds to 4 percent of the total transactions. Perhaps real estate was a good investment for widows with extra capital.[14] Single women were never large participants in the real estate market. In the first half of the fourteenth century (until 1364), they comprised 6 percent of the sellers, but this percentage had dropped steadily by 1450. Single women were buyers in 3 percent of the transactions overall. Probably women with some property were very attractive marriage partners, so that those who appear as single may represent those not yet married or those who chose not to marry. It is also possible that inheritance patterns were changing and that daughters were given movables rather than real estate.

Women acting on their own, therefore, represented only a small share of either the buyers or sellers of property, but husbands and wives acting jointly were sellers in about a third of the transactions in the deeds. While there was a dip in the late fourteenth century, they resumed their role in the fifteenth century. As buyers, however, their market activity dropped steadily from 32 percent in 1300 to 12 percent through 1474.

The gainers in market activity were males acting alone. Until 1374, they were enrolled as purchasers in 65 percent of the deeds. In 1380, their share of the buyers' market increased, rising to 85 percent over the period to 1474. Explanations for the increasing domination of men in the market remain speculative. The increased value of widows in the marriage market in the fifteenth century may have led men like George Cely to acquire more property in order to compete. Since the number of widows remarrying increased, demand for dower property might also have increased.

Another source of information about women in the real estate market is London's possessory assizes.[15] Since all land in London was held in burgage tenure, that is, it could be bought and sold freely without any feudal interference, suits over ownership arose frequently. London's possessory assizes contain 273 cases from the fourteenth and fifteenth centuries. Of the 1,395 litigants appearing in court, women comprised 20 percent. Their participation dropped in the fifteenth century. Their roles varied. Their suits could be over dower properties, rentals, inheritance, and jointures. Sometimes they brought their own case or were the sole defendant, but mostly they acted with a husband or attorney. Of the women involved, thirty-five can be clearly identified as widows, nine of whom had remarried. An additional twenty-nine were not identified as widows and could have been single. Of the widows, fourteen were defendants, and thirteen were plaintiffs. The widows, acting alone as plaintiffs, won their cases 61 percent of the time.[16]

Deeds and court cases, however, do not tell the whole picture of women as participants in the real estate market. As executor of a husband's will, a widow was often instructed to sell various properties to pay for his debts, for funeral expenses, and for various charities and gifts to parishes, religious houses, and chantries. Her name might not appear in the deeds, although she was the vendor of the property.

Individual cases of couples and women acting in the property transactions appear regularly in the Letter Books and elsewhere. These cases are helpful in understanding the type of property actions in which women engaged. We have already seen that some of the joint purchases were made by a couple or by a widow to provide a dowry for a daughter. One disappointed husband, William Nightengale, a draper, complained to the lord chancellor that Jane Dawebeney, a widow, had agreed on a dowry for her daughter to be given after marriage. It included £100, a gold ring, a horse, and the lease of Dawebeney's Quay in St. Dunsten's to hold for thirty-four years. He had gotten nothing.[17]

Women leased inherited, dowry, dower, and purchased property. In doing so, they were protected by the same laws as men were. A landlord could collect rent through confiscation of chattels left on the property if the tenant defaulted on the rent for two years or left the property. Both landlords and tenants were expected to give adequate notice of termination of the rental agreement.[18] Alice, wife of Robert Motun, leased lands inherited from her father to another party for fourteen years, and Katherine, daughter of Matilda and Walter de Kyngstone, leased her inheritance for seven years.[19] Many of the other leases were of dower property. Richard de Wodeford, fishmonger, and his wife, Agnes rented part of Agnes's dower property to William de Croydon, fishmonger, and Christina, his wife, stipulating that it was for the lifetime of Agnes only.[20] Thomas Pipere, a pouch maker, and Johanna, a widow of a mercer, jointly leased her interest in property held by her former husband.[21] Another source of rental income came from the property of wards, which could be leased until they came of age.[22]

Some of the property transactions were clearly for commercial ventures. They varied from stalls and shops to taverns and wharves. Sometimes these commercial properties must have been sites of a former husband's business, as was the case of Johanna, a widow, who rented out a shop in the parish of St. Nicholas Shambles.[23] Isabella, widow of Thomas de Neville, a woolmonger, leased a brew house, garden, and wharf for fifteen years from John, son of John Dode, and Agnes, his wife, daughter of John Larwence.[24] Perhaps she was planning to brew herself, or she would sublet it. Robert de Lenne, "jeweler," and his wife rented a movable stall beneath Ludgate for a term of ten years at an annual rent of 40 s. They must have hoped to profit from a heavy volume of traffic.[25] A husband and wife, who were fripperers, leased an extra seld to another fripperer for an annual rent of 10 marks.[26] We have already shown that women were active in renting properties on the Bridge Estates, and such buying and selling of leases for shops appears elsewhere in the records.[27]

Elizabeth Fraunceys, widow of John Godman, who bought land for her life use with the help of the goldsmiths' guild, may have been planning her retirement. She made provision that the land would go to another goldsmith and his wife after her death.[28]

Both women and men used property to pay off debts. One man arranged to cancel a debt owed to a couple by allowing them to rent a brew house at the price of a rose a year for four years and after that time to pay annually 7 marks. This canceled a bond that the couple had entered into with the grantor. Some of the agreements, however, may represent mortgages on which a balance was due.[29] A single woman, Isabella, daughter of Ralph, and her mother, Margery, agreed to let to Nicholas Clark, an armorer, tenements in Westcheap until a loan of £13 8 s. 9 d. was paid off.[30]

Women, as we have seen in the recovery of dower cases in the Husting court of common pleas, were adept at defending their property. They knew the value of the written document as well as oral testimony. When a man sued John Yakeslee, a cornmonger, and could not collect because London officials could not find him, the court ordered that his rents be sequestered. Whereupon Margery, his widow, came and was able to show that the rents were part of her dower land and would pass to her son. She described her self as *femme sole* and succeeded in her argument.[31] When a man claimed that a shop and dwelling place belonged to him, Joan Grene of London, a widow, asserted that she had possession for a term of fourteen years "by virtue of a legacy from Thomas Hay, goldsmith, enrolled in the Husting pleas of land" (1408). She was given her full claim, and the other claimant had to wait.[32] Another widow produced written proof that she owned a moiety (half) of a ship, and the court upheld her.[33]

Where did these women's proofs of leases come from? Many of the records refer to "forcers," or chests, in which the documents and deeds were kept. Going back to Anglo-Saxon times, women were buried with a ring of keys to symbolize their status, and keys also appear on effigies of women in the later medieval times. Alice, widow of William Spicer of Devizes, whose will was proved in London in 1379, left her "forcer with deeds and other contents" to her executor.[34] Agnes de Braghyng was the guardian of a son and daughter of James de St. Edmund. In her will she provided that her executors bring two black coffers to Guildhall containing the muniments that belonged to their father's estate and their inheritance.[35] But other widows had to go to court to get the box of deeds. Floria, widow of Andrew Shadefore, sued for the detinue (retention) of her "box of deeds," one of which provided her with a dower of a life interest in a tenement in Walbrook. John Pyle, accused of keeping the box, produced it in court with the said document. All parties agreed that the box should be returned to Alice, and no other claims were made against her.[36] Women had other chests and uses for which their ring of keys were important in the business of London.

In addition to forcers to protect written records, women had their own seals to authenticate agreements. Andrew Blund, son of Robert Blund, late citizen of London, made a complex arrangement to provide for his two sons and Helen, his wife, and mother of the boys. His property holdings were extensive, with rented messuages, shops, and many tenements. The agreement was that the two sons, Hugh and Henry, were to have it all at the payment of 6 d. annually to the grantor and £30 per annum to Helen. Helen was to have the right of reentry and taking pledges if the rent was in arrears. She was also to have her lodging (*hospitium*) in the chief messuage during her lifetime. Her sons were not to alienate the quitrents and thereby deprive her of her annual rent. Both parties signed a chirograph "of which one was delivered to the grantees [the sons] and the other to the said Helen." Both were sealed and witnessed.[37] This arrangement suggests an uneasy family relationship in which trust was not presumed among family members. A chirograph was a deed written on one sheet of paper or parchment with a copy on each end signed and sealed by the parties involved. Then some word, perhaps a religious one, or even "chirograph," was written across the blank space. A jagged cut was made across this lettering and each party got one half. Legitimacy could be established by matching the two halves. Women also had seals that they used on their contracts and written documents.[38]

Widows and heiresses appeared in the Assize of Nuisance administering their property with competence. The Assize covered a number of disputes between neighbors over open gutters and runoff water, cesspits, building and the dilapidation of walls, boundaries to land, and windows that overlooked property. As in the property transactions, men alone and couples predominated, but women acting on their own appear as both plaintiffs and defendants. The cases are not numerous enough to quantify, but a smattering of examples indicate the nature of their activities. Amice Horn complained that her neighbor's house was ruinous and overhung her land so that she could not build on it. Her neighbor counterclaimed that a turret on her house was the reason for the dilapidation of his. She won.[39] Likewise, Alice at Stakes, who complained that a cesspit of a neighboring couple's privy undermined her wall and that the plaintiffs also stacked wood that broke down her wall, prevailed.[40] Women, of course, were responsible for their tenements and the tenants. Thus Thomas Whitcherch complained that Maud Frembaud had a window opening on his yard and "that her tenants constantly came out of it into his gutter," where they threw excrement and other refuse so that the water could not run down and damaged his property. Furthermore, another of her rents adjoining his tenement had a broken-down plaster wall that the tenants used to enter and exit his house and through which they could see "his private business." She was ordered to repair it.[41]

Shifts were taking place in late fifteenth-century London, however, that eroded some of London's laws regarding women. Mothers were no longer assured of assuming guardianship of the children of a marriage, as citizen fathers increasingly relied on men as guardians for their orphans. The increasing male dominance of the property market may indicate a weakening of the legal and customary rights of London's women. Sixteenth-century English law emphasized giving real estate inheritances to sons and movables to daughters. Furthermore, wives were more likely to be put under *coverte de baron* so that their property became more subject to their husband's control.[42] The sixteenth-century information does not include London, but it is possible that daughters inherited more movables than real estate. The borough customs regarding the dower, however, persisted into the eighteenth century in London.[43]

Women in Business

London's law permitted married women to run their own businesses separate from that of a husband and to be responsible for their own credit and debts if they registered as *femme sole* merchants with the mayor.[44] This was an unusual privilege that London women enjoyed, and only a few other boroughs adopted it. Widows and single women could become freewomen of the city and run their own businesses by inheritance, completing apprenticeship, and, probably most usual, by marrying a citizen. Freedom of the city gave women the right to trade, be they single, widowed, or married. They might have a business that they established with capital from their husbands, as we have seen with husbands buying taverns or inns for their wives, or their trade might be related to that of the husband, for example, a woman who did silkmaking while her husband was in mercery.

A case from 1384 relates a woman's clear statement of her rights as a freewoman of the city. Matilda, widow of Hugh Holbech and executrix of his will, was summoned to answer a plaintiff, William Croydon, on a plea of detinue (retention of goods) worth £10 5s. 10d. The plaintiff claimed that he had put a number of items, mostly brewing equipment, in the custody of Hugh and that when he died, Matilda refused to return the items. She, however, "denied having received the goods...and offered to defend her law as a free woman of the city." The plaintiff assented, and on May 26, 1384, she "made her law with six other women according to the custom of the city." On the appointed day, she had the women present and the plaintiff, and the women swore that she did not have the goods. William was fined for making a false claim.[45] Other cases also show that women could prove their innocence of charges by defending themselves as a "freewoman of the city" and be examined under oath.[46]

The advantages of London's legal economic freedom, however, can be overemphasized.[47] Women could, for instance, inherit public offices but could not practice them. Thus while John Sench could designate his daughter as heir to his position as keeper of Fleet Prison, she could only reap the financial benefits thereof, not be the real keeper.[48] When an assayer of oysters, John of Ely, farmed out inspection of oysters to women, he was severely reprimanded, since "women, who know not [how to do it]; nor is it in the worship of this city that women should have things to do with governance."[49] Women could not hold official positions in London, and even the assaying of oysters was considered an office.

While the entrepreneurial activities of women in the marketplace, as opposed to real estate, are more difficult to measure, some idea can be gleaned from a statistical analysis of the original bills for the Mayor's court.[50] These bills are not published, and they may or may not have appeared in court. Women comprised 5 percent of the plaintiffs and 6 percent of defendants. In other words, women played a small role in the overall business covered in the original bills.

If we look at the marital status of the female plaintiffs (fifty-one total), 39 percent were widows, 26 percent were single (as indicated by name), and 26 percent were married couples pleading jointly. The rest were unknown or were groups including wife, husband, and daughter or an unrelated man and woman. Only one woman brought a bill charging a man with breaking into her house while she was trading *femme sole*, to her damage of £100.[51] Of the defendants (fifty-eight total), 26 percent were widows, 14 percent were single, 40 percent were couples named jointly, and the rest were a scattering. Eleven women were cited along with their husbands, as London law required, as trading *femme sole*.[52]

The largest percentage of actions in the original bills for the Mayor's court (83 percent) involved debt cases and a few cases involving relations between master and servant or apprentice, property, breaches of contract, and use of force. The numbers become too small to be significant when broken down by female plaintiffs and defendants, but they tend to concentrate in debt cases and inheritance.

As in the real estate transactions, individual cases help to make the picture of women in business clearer. The status of *femme sole*, as individual cases show, was very ambiguous. The line between the wife's trade and the household economy was often unclear. John Davell, citizen and draper of London, was confined to prison because he had outstanding debts and had not paid them. He had left his wife, Anne, to cope as best she could. In her petition to the lord chancellor, she said that she tried to survive "by the labor of her hands trying to maintain her self-respect and honor." She had to provide her husband with meat and drink in prison and also had "two children on her hands at her daily biding and charge." In this dire situation, a single woman sued her for a debt, saying that she was trading as *femme sole* and should pay the money owed to the plaintiff. Anne argued that she was *coverte de baron*, a married woman who was not responsible for her debts, but since her husband was in prison he could not pay.[53] A husband, however, could involve his wife in debt arrangements that she felt forced to accept. Catherine, wife of John Peris, a salter, appealed to the lord chancellor, saying that her husband bought certain goods worth 40 s., but he caused her to be bound to the creditor and "she might not say nay" to her husband. Afterward he left town, and though he had sufficient wealth to pay the debt, Catherine, as the signator of the debt, was in prison.[54]

Married women who acted as *femmes sole merchants* were cited, if infrequently, in court because of their business.[55] The case of Isabelle, wife of

John Yerdele, helps us to understand problems of unraveling the household economy. John Yerdele sued William of Grenyngham over a debt for thirteen woolen cloths valued at 102 marks. William explained that Isabella, wife of the plaintiff, was a "common maker of woolen cloths." She had delivered the cloths to a fuller and ordered the fuller to take them to William. The fuller did so. William pleaded "that by the custom of the city contracts made by married women engaged in mercantile art were as effectual as contracts made by their husbands, that Isabella had used the art of making woolen cloths and sold the same as *femme sole*." On May 20, 1374, she went to William's house and told him that she had sold the cloth to customers for 102 marks and he was to deliver the cloth to them, taking a bond from them for 204 marks as security of payment. She came to him because he was "an officer of the city and better able to enforce payment than either Isabella or her husband." William had no profit from the sale. John Yerdele claimed that he had no knowledge of the city law of *femme sole* and claimed that he had made his own contract with the defendant. Since John did not appear in court, the defendant was exonerated, and John was fined.[56] His subterfuge to get the money failed, but we do not know if Isabella was able to keep her money separate from the household money. John might have been working under a patriarchal assumption that profits from his wife's business were his profits.[57]

While Isabella was known to trade *sole*, many of the cases of women acting *femmes soles* show that all parties—husbands, the women themselves, and creditors—manipulated the law. A frequent ploy was to try to get the husband involved in repayment of the wife's debt or at least to guarantee it. A mercer brought a bill of complaint about an agreement between himself and a carpenter concerning a debt of £22 that the latter's wife, a goods supplier, incurred with him. The mercer pressured the carpenter into agreeing to help get the money paid, and the carpenter agreed to pay £10 down and to get his wife to pay the whole should they still be husband and wife. No money was paid, and the husband did not force the wife to pay. Indeed, he pointed out in court that the bond had been tampered with, including erasure of dates and other alterations in a different hand. This clever carpenter with his paleographic skills failed to produce his part of the indenture, which he should have possessed, and did not deny that he had entered into such an arrangement.[58] The household must have paid.

While it was expected in London law for a husband to be named along with his wife who was trading *femme sole* in the collection of debt, the payment should have come only from the wife's trade. But one wonders if the husband ultimately agreed to pay all or part of the sum, or if some of these cases, as illustrated above, were subterfuges by husbands and wives. In the Mayor's court original bills, a number of these cases are ambiguous. For instance, John Donsel, grocer, sued William Elyas and his wife Sara for detinue (withholding of goods), for 20 marks. Sara, trading as *femme sole*, had given her gage to Agnes Franceys in a coffer and had not released it. One wonders why John Donsel was suing rather than Agnes. Had they recently married? Was William Elyas trying to make good on the loan or to force his wife into releasing the coffer?[59]

The case of Elisabeth, a woman trading *femme sole*, shows that marriage might be a way out of a failed business. She contracted with Thomas Wandesford, a mercer, in May 1441 for lodging, meat, and drink for herself and her servant for £10 a year. The record does not tell her trade. Three years later she married, owing the mercer £30, which her husband paid.[60]

A woman who had been trading *femme sole* might continue to do so after the death of her husband. Two men, who were fishmongers, came before the mayor and aldermen in Guildhall in 1440 and said "under oath that Margaret Salisbury, widow of John Salisbury, was and had been for a long time merchant *femme sole* within the city." She responded that "she had been and was a merchant *femme sole* and prayed that in future she might enjoy the benefit of the custom relating to the same."[61]

Women were active in the debt/credit market, and even foreign women participated in the London market.[62] Women trading *femmes soles* won debt cases,[63] although one woman who recovered a debt had to agree to return the money if she were slanderous.[64] Mariota Convers, apparently a pawnbroker, had a jewel of John, Count de Harcourt, but sold the pawn to a Lombard, who pawned it to a Florentine for less money. She landed in prison because she did not return the full value.[65] In another case, Joan Cok, jeweler of London, pleaded against John Russell, "who at one time out of affection for her gave her counsel and persuaded her to give him her signet." He made three false obligations in her name, and then the people holding the papers came with the bonds for £24, £100, and 200 marks. The perils of love or friendship forced her to petition the lord chancellor for redress.[66]

The mechanisms of credit and debt are crucial to understanding the success of women acting on their own in business. The *femme sole* cases indicate that women procured goods, such as silk or malt, on credit and delayed payment until after they had sold the goods. Often women in business had to acquire the initial start-up credit from their husbands, but women could get credit on their own if their reputation for skill and hard work was sufficient.

Widows might have inherited a business or used their cash to start a business. Much of the credit was informal arrangements with running accounts and even tallies (sticks of wood with notches that showed the amount due), but when a large transaction was involved, as in the case of Isabelle, wife of John Yerdele, women and men took the precaution of having an official make a bond for the sale. Isabelle had it made out at twice the value of the cloth (204 marks). Her action was not uncommon and was used to ensure the repayment of the original debt.[67]

Another major group of women who traded regularly on their own were widows. Widowhood placed a woman immediately in the position of acting as her own agent. While many remarried, a large percent acted as executors of their former husbands' wills and continued responsibility for settling their debts. Most of the arrangements must have gone smoothly, because relatively few cases appeared in the Mayor's court.[68] Cristina, widow of John Patyn, fletcher, acted as executor for her husband's estate. In trying to collect a debt for £40 8 d. from two men who bought sixteen hundred sheaves of arrows from her husband, she ran into difficulty because the purchaser failed to seal the obligation. Appearing in court six months later with her new husband, she was able to show that her late husband had devised the money for their two orphaned boys. She won her case.[69] In another case, the widow and her fellow executors were sued for a bond of £86 13 s. 4 d. She and the others argued that they had already settled the estate the same day that the claim came in. The plaintiff asked them to swear on the Gospels that they had done so. They did, and he dropped the complaint.[70] Most of the cases involved debts of the former husband, but real estate could also be involved. One widow was trying to convey a deed to a shop when two men snatched it from her and her coexecutor, ripping it. They were found guilty.[71]

Widows are found in a variety of trades, including victualing, innkeeping, silk making, embroidery, dressmaking, and so on, that they may have pursued when their husbands were still alive.[72] The poll tax of 1381 for Southwark showed 137 female-headed households; most of the women were in victualing, textile work, or apparel production.[73] One London woman successfully supported her four children as a dressmaker and was able to give them £20 to be divided among them when she died.[74] Those who inherited their husbands' trades could continue to run their shops, hire apprentices and servants, and market the products. Chandler's widows seem to have done very well, and Agnes Brightwell, a widow, used her son-in-law as a factor for trading overseas.[75]

Women could be successful in pawnbrokering and credit.[76] Amy, widow of John Donat, carried on the business of her husband. The Donat family were Italian but had deep ties in London as well as Italy and France.[77] They dealt in high-end pawn, credit, and merchandise. Amy secured custody of jewels worth 1,000 franks belonging to the Duke de Berry, who owed John's brother 1,430 franks. Amy brought the jewels to court and after consideration of the terms of the bond and the fact that the duke had not paid for the pawn, the jewels were returned to her. The first case was in 1392, but Amy Donat was still carrying on her husband's pawn business in 1394, when she held a bond for delivery of pearls, jewels, cloth, and other goods. John Billyng, esquire, and Elizabeth Beauchamp claimed that she had detained a bond that they made with Philip Vannoche of Siena. Philip also sued. Amy asked that they settle the matter between them about the goods and said that she would, depending on the outcome, return the bond. Amy again came through unscathed and handed over the bond, but Philip went to prison and paid a fine. She appeared in court again in a debt case involving John Donat and another trading partner. This time she had to pay damages worth £22 and ended up in prison.[78]

Widows usually did not continue in businesses that were dirty or required physical strength. We have seen that tanners did not leave their businesses to their widows, and skinners usually did not either.[79] One successful skinner's widow, Matilda Penne, has been traced. She either learned her skills from her husband or learned them as an apprentice. As a widow, she was able to train and maintain apprentices and perhaps also used some men as factors to help her buy skins in the market. She was connected to the skinners' guild, at least in a social way, and left them money, as did her former husband. She left her business to a male skinner.[80] Two widows of bell founders who left their trademarks on bells also appear in London records.[81] While these women had good relations with their apprentices, they are balanced in the cases by those who faced disasters when acting *femme sole*.

The number of widows who remarried, sold out, or retired must have been great. While we know something about those who remarried, we do not know the failure rate of the others. The problems that widows faced acting in their own businesses are clear, even in anecdotal records. A cordwainer was summoned to answer John de Wynslowe and Alice, his wife, executrix of Henry Sket, a cordwainer, on a large bill for leather that he received from her when she was trading *femme sole*. He was to trade on her behalf and render an account to her, which he refused to do. Immediately after the death of her first husband, he purchased ox hides and cow hides from Alice to the value of £29. He claimed that he paid but did not appear and was not punished.[82] Isabel Donton, a widow, claimed that Richard Weste, a sergeant of London, had put a false seal on an obligation for her to pay 40 s.[83]

Complaints and suits against widows inheriting their husbands' businesses often came from apprentices who were not trained. When the ironmonger Richard Gosselyn died, Beatrice, his widow, "who by law and custom of the city and the will of the deceased ought to have kept up his household and instructed his apprentices," did not. Instead, even her own brother testified that she had sold everything belonging to the business and dismissed John Haccher, an apprentice, so that he was "falling into destruction and desolation." Haccher was allowed to be admitted to the freedom of the city, and another apprentice was given to an ironmonger to complete his training.[84] William Skydmore, son of a gentleman, was apprenticed to a mercer but found himself in a similar plight and appealed to the Mayor's court.[85]

When widows did undertake to train their apprentices, the apprentices often became rebellious. The fullest account that we have is that of Edward Bowden, who violently and suddenly beat his mistress. He reviled her and tried to strangle her. The goldsmiths were outraged and called "worshipful men" to decide what to do about Bowden. They concluded that he would only get worse if they sent him to prison. Instead, they had him stripped and beaten in the kitchen of the goldsmiths' hall until his blood flowed, demonstrating the authority of masters and mistresses over rebellious apprentices in a very graphic way.[86] Roger, son of Richard Grosse of Thame, was an apprentice of Emma, widow of William Hatfeld, a chandler. She finally had to have him committed to Newgate "for being rebellious, refusing to serve her and unwilling to be punished by her as was fitting and proper he should be."[87] More successful were the widows who continued to train in the trades they had followed during their lives—weaving, silk making, and other female crafts.[88]

It is difficult, however, to find a balance in anecdotal evidence. Men also had considerable problems with rebellious apprentices, and both men and women enjoyed lifelong affections and relationships with them. Likewise, both sexes were exploitative of their apprentices.[89] Thomas Bunny, for instance, thought that he had bound himself to learn the craft of sheath maker for knives. He found that his master sold his indenture to Joan Hunt, who kept stews at the far side of London Bridge, in Southwark, a center of brewing and prostitution. He complained that he did "grievous work, such as carrying water in tynes [large tubs]," and that he fell and was permanently injured. To make matters worse, "she incited a certain Bernard, who was then her paramour, to beat and ill-treat him" so that he fell sick, and she turned him out. Fortunately, the Mayor's court exonerated him, and Joan was to have nothing further to do with him.[90]

Failing reliable statistical evidence, we cannot know if women enjoyed a period of increased entrepreneurship following the Black Death than they did previously. The small number of women appearing in court trading *femme sole* and the scattering of widows successfully taking over their husbands' businesses suggests that they were not generally running their own businesses or, if they were, they were not in trades with high prestige. We can say that widows remarried in greater numbers, which may mean that they inherited trades as well as real estate, but preferred to pass the trade on to their new husbands. In two areas, however, the historical argument has been that women did have a strong presence—silk weaving and brewing.

Silkwomen, Brewsters, and Guilds

The silkwomen of London enjoyed the most independence and wealth in their trades of all women either acting *femmes soles* or as wives.[91] They produced thrown silk to make a heavier silk yarn that they wove into ribbons, laces, hairpieces, girdles, cords, and other goods.[92] Even Thomas Betson realized that a silk girdle was an essential part of the trousseau of his new wife.

Although the silkwomen in London never formed a guild as did silk-women in Paris, Rouen, and Cologne, they did engage in cooperative work actions.[93] Because England was too cold to grow silkworms, the women relied on imported silk thread and raw silk. The profit of their products depended on the price of these imports. When Nicholas Sarduche of Lombardy got complete control of all of the silk thread in London, he was able, in the space of two weeks, to raise the price from 14s. to 18s. He managed this coup by buying silk from other foreign merchants before it went on the markets (forestalling). Those merchants who did not sell to him were also able to get higher prices for their silk. He cheated further, in that he weighed his silk on his own scale rather than on the king's small beam, contrary to a statute of Henry III that required all foreign merchants to use the official beams. By using his own scale, he was able to avoid paying duty on the silk.

Seeing their profits decrease, the silkwomen delivered a complaint against Sarduche to the mayor on November 29, 1368, requesting immediate remedy. They argued that the high cost of raw silk was detrimental to their trade and to the whole realm. If the mayor could not help, then they would go elsewhere. The mayor responded quickly, summoning Sarduche to appear. When he did not, his goods were confiscated, and he appeared on December 1. He offered as an excuse that he had been directed by his master and partners abroad to raise the price of raw silk because there was a rumor of a shortage. With his goods confiscated, he could not post bond and was sent to prison.

The silkwomen pressed on with their cause, petitioning Edward III for redress as well. They informed the king that they had

> no other means of livelihood than their craft, that a certain Nicholas Sarduche for a long time past had been in the habit of forestalling and regrating all the crude and colored silk and other kinds of merchandise brought by aliens, thus grievously enhancing the price ... to the great damage of the King, the commonality of the land and the petitioners.

They asked the king for remedy. Since the king and the mayor were customers for the silk, redress came quickly. On January 25, 1369, the king requested that the records on Sarduche be delivered to him. Sarduche remained in prison until he appeared before the king on June 16, 1369. He was found guilty and paid a fine of £200.[94]

The silkwomen of London became prominent in the fourteenth century (a century after the silkwomen of Paris), and the industry spread to all of England, so that by 1455 and 1482 they were mentioned as a group in the Rolls of Parliament. Like other craftspersons, they had an apprentice system, and some of the contracts or the breaking of them are preserved. The members of the craft came from "good and notable householders" in the city. While the women who did silk work and traded on a large scale certainly fit that category, these women also employed other women to work for them as apprentices and sometimes as servants.[95]

Alice Claver, who died in 1489, provides a rare insight into the world of an elite silkwoman. She was probably apprenticed to a silkwoman and must have been a very good craftswoman. She married a mercer, as was common among silkwomen, since the trades were complementary, but she traded as *femme sole* in her business. Her circle of friends included other women who traded as *femmes soles* in silk products, apprentices, mercers, and her fellow parishioners. She and some of her friends were extremely successful, filling orders for the Crown and taking apprentices and servants. They acted as godmothers for each other's children and mentioned them in wills. Alice even acted as sole executor for one of the women. It is no wonder that these women were able to act in concert against the Italian price fixers; they were a tight network already.[96]

But if silkwomen are to be the best case scenario for women trading *femme sole*, what are we to make of the dispute between two men that appeared before the lord chancellor and involved the testimony of a number of silkwomen? William Lovel of London, a vintner, complained against William Hull of a debt that his deceased wife, Agnes, owed to Elaine, William's wife. Lovel wanted the return of silks that Agnes had from his wife or else payment of £22 6s. Elizabeth, wife of the mercer, John Stokton,[97] testified that Agnes had been accustomed to buy and sell silk and that she bought silk from Elizabeth valued at £45, of which Hull paid £22. Elizabeth also sold silk that Agnes supplied. Another silkwoman, Margaret Durant, married to William Durant, swore that Agnes had been the wife of Hull and was in the silk trade, and traded especially with Elaine, wife of William Lovel. The gossip was strong among these women, and Elaine asked Margaret how well Agnes paid for the silk, and Margaret answered "full evilly." Emma, also involved in the trade, was the wife of a waterman, and she swore that she knew for certain that Agnes had been the wife of William Hull and sold and bargained for silk during her lifetime and especially with Elaine Lovel because Agnes told her so. As Agnes lay on her deathbed, William Lovel sent his apprentice to Emma and told her to save 2 and a half pounds of silk she had from Agnes and keep it for William.

After citing all this expert testimony, Lovel added his interpretation of London's law, which must have reflected not only his idea of the household economy but also a more general view of the role of women's income in relation to other income sources for the household. He does not use the term *femme sole*, so perhaps his statement is a more general one.

> Whereas the common use within the said city is and for some time past hath been that the wives of men of worship and thrift enfranchised in the same city have by the sufferance of their husbands in the absence of them used to buy and sell all manner of merchandise toward the increase and living of them and their household, the duties of all which bargains coming or growth has always been contente by such wives or for nowne payment of them by their husbande.

His eloquent statement of the intention of London that women's earnings are supposed to augment the household economy goes on to specifics. He was absent, but by his sufferance, his wife had contracted with Agnes and sold Agnes, late wife of William Hull, a mason, an amount of silk at the agreed-on value of £22. Before payment, however, Agnes died. William Hull was "subtilly intending to utterly destroy your said orator and his wife plainly denyth to pay any penny thereof." Not only that, he urged the other silkwomen not to trade with Elaine. Lovel claimed that he had paid Agnes's debts in the past, but now refused, thereby sending Elaine to prison.

Perhaps a scrivener wrote this description of how a wife's income was to relate to the household economy and how husband and wife entered into these craft arrangements with a mutuality about the assumption of debts within the household. The case offers a snapshot of the household economy and a man who could articulately summarize it. Hull denied that he knew of such a London law and said that he pleaded in common law.[98]

The case is a remarkable glimpse into the network of silkwomen, some of whom also traded with Alice Claver's friends. It shows a positive side of the household economy, with an industrious wife and a supportive husband, but perhaps it also illustrates a cheating wife and an avaricious husband. Sources are deceiving when they tell beautiful and engaging stories, as this one does, but even if it is not a representative case, it shows, as do other cases, that the *femme sole* laws written in the *Liber Albus* were not completely clear in practice and may not even have been well known. The husband and wife, as well as their creditors, seem to have thought in terms of a marital or household unit of debt and credit rather than women being solely responsible for their debts.

The long-term employment of women in silk and linen production and related trades—for example, seamstress, embroiderers, cappers, and girdlers—showed a general decline. In the thirteenth century, women participated in a variety of trades related to mercery. Wives, daughters, female apprentices, and skilled servants did most of the crafting of products for adornment, while their husbands sold these items in shops or by peddling them. But in the period of depopulation in the late fourteenth and fifteenth centuries, many men took over the crafts. It was perhaps even the men in the mercers' guild who wrote up the petition to the king about Sarduche and price of silk. Women in mercery were gradually being eased out of positions of responsibility, and men were moving in to take over both selling the product and the craft involved.[99]

Like the silkwomen, London brewsters have been studied in depth. The term "brewster" is the female form of "brewer," and its frequent usage in the fourteenth and fifteenth centuries indicated that women were doing most of the brewing. The trade in both the countryside and in London was largely a female enterprise before the Black Death, but gradually changed to a male-dominated industry by the sixteenth century. Brewing became more commercialized and therefore involved more capital for equipment and more credit/debt arrangements.[100] As with other crafts, single women were at a disadvantage because they could not get the credit needed to invest in large-scale brewing. Widows, unless they had the capital, had a well-established business, or inherited a brewery, also had problems maintaining their craft. Rising cost of grain was another factor in undercutting women's ability to get credit. While the decreased population following the Black Death might have caused a decline in all brewing because there were fewer consumers, the surviving population more than made up for the loss by increasing consumption. But the pattern of consumption changed with more ale and beer sold in taverns, and these were increasingly owned by males.

The brewers' guild of London, incorporated in 1438, permits an insight into the participation of women in brewing. Women constituted about a third of the guild members as single women, widows, and wives in 1418–25, and roughly 10 percent of the business was run by women. But the unmarried women did not maintain a membership beyond two years. The brewers were unique among guilds in London for having female members at all. Many of the married brewsters worked separately from their husbands, who were in another trade, but the couple registered jointly. While the women in the commercial trade might do very well, they did not have a governance role in the guild, and very few of them wore the livery. Further, the husbands are listed as the creditors and debtors, much as was the case in other crafts, even when the woman was declared to be *femme sole*.[101]

The switch from ale to beer confirmed the gender change in brewing. Ale, made with malt, water, and yeast, was unstable and could go bad quickly. Women could be competitive in the ale trade because of the constant demand for new batches and the possibility of making these batches in smaller quantities. The addition of hops, adopted from the Continent, acted as a preservative for the new beverage, beer. The continental brewers who came to England employed few women. When the Englishmen started brewing beer, they followed the same pattern. The longer lasting beer permitted greater capitalization and commercialization of the industry.[102]

The historian Judith Bennett argues that brewsters never had a "golden age." Instead, she sees a continuity of the low-paying craft through the great changes of the fifteenth and sixteenth centuries in the industry. Women were not as directly involved in brewing as they were in the fourteenth century, but they moved into service positions in taverns.[103]

Innkeeping was closely related to brewing and taverns, and a few women ran them successfully on their own. Inns and taverns were, in some respects, extensions of the domestic and work spaces of women, in that they involved providing sleeping space, victuals, and drink. They were a temporary home for travelers and a place to eat and spend time for Londoners who lived in close quarters. Inns, however, were rarely run by single females or even *femmes soles*. In 1384, only 10 women were listed as innkeepers, compared to 183 men.[104] The official tallies of inn and tavern keepers, however, must underrepresent women's actual participation in the lodging and victualing business.

Some female innkeepers do appear in the records.[105] One woman was cited for having faulty pavement in front of her door, another as having received life interest in "The Peynted Tavern"; and another woman took a three-year lease on a tavern.[106] But some of these women were engaged in shady business. Isabella de Topesham, "hostelere," was found guilty of detaining 80 florins entrusted to her by Nicholas de Trougbrugge at her hostel.[107] Another was horse-trading, and her apprentice robbed her of the money; and another harassed a former guest and had him put into prison.[108]

The small number of women recorded as taverners and innkeepers must underestimate the number of women providing beer, wine, rooms, and food in London.[109] Taking in lodgers and boarders has been a time-honored by-occupation for women. In medieval London, the frequency of such arrangements might well have been greater than it is today. Two factors contributed to both the supply and the demand for lodging. Many London widows had rooms to rent and needed the extra income.[110] On the demand side, London did not replace its own population but relied on immigrants from the countryside, and as a major trading and administrative center, the city also had to house a number of foreign merchants, fortune seekers, suitors at court, and delegations to the Crown and royal courts. Widows had a ready market for their rooms and meals, but they were not registered as innkeepers.

Conclusions about women in entrepreneurial and trades activities are difficult, since the evidence is deficient.[111] Much of the evidence is based on anecdotal information, and the quantifiable data available from court rolls, taxation, and guild records all point to a very small role in business and trades. Independent women, widows, and particularly single women played a small role in the real estate markets, and wives acting as *femmes soles* in crafts or trade had a negligible role. When women did appear in court cases acting as *femmes soles*, the creditor was often trying to get the husband to pay her debt, or she was having trouble collecting debts owed to her.

While London's provision that a married woman could act as *femme sole* would appear to be a golden opportunity, perhaps women did not want to take the risks involved in starting businesses on their own, including being liable for their losses and debts. Getting credit to start a trade hindered single women, married women, and widows. On the other hand, a husband whose wife had an unsuccessful business might want his wife to register *femme sole*, so that he would not be liable if she went bankrupt. A wife's choice was to take the risks of *femme sole* or operate as *femme coverte* and be under the domination of a husband.[112] *Femme coverte* might have appeared to be a more sure solution.

Modern historians are perhaps too eager to look for the independent, entrepreneurial women. William Lovel's statement seems to indicate a general opinion, if not law, in London that what a woman produced by her own business or wages belonged to the household economy. Many women as well as men must have shared this view and would not have thought of seeking *femme sole* status. Patriarchy was the dominant culture of the time, and the patriarch was head of his household. Perhaps the question to raise is what made the women who chose *femme sole* status so different? Not all silkwomen had this status, and brewsters did not seek the status. Did some women take this initiative because of the distrust of a husband or because of the cooperation of a husband?

The evidence in this chapter does not point to a "golden age." It suggests that a few more women were in business in the first quarter of the fifteenth century, but these were not high-status positions, and they did not translate into official power. Only a tiny minority of women had the training or the capital to move into entrepreneurial positions. Studies of women on the Continent and in England suggest that women were increasingly squeezed out of the few business opportunities that they had in the sixteenth century.[113] The same change seems to be occurring in the late fifteenth century in the real estate market in London as well. The business world was becoming increasingly male. Guild prohibitions on women's participation occurred not only on the Continent but also in London.

New technologies did make a difference in women's employment. The heavy loom in the Low Countries put women in a disadvantageous position, as did commercial brewing in England. Power went where the capital was and where the access to the new technologies was; it was in the hands of men rather than women. Women, through marriage, provided much of that capital, but they did not directly control much, even in real estate. Even if we assume that women had little voice in household economic matters (and that might not be true), when they moved to men's territory in the guild and the market, they moved into a patriarchal culture that would not recognize them other than as wives or widows.

⁂9⁂
Servants, Casual Labor, and Vendors

The number of women who held prestigious entrepreneurial roles, either in trade or real estate, was limited, but those in small businesses, service jobs, wage labor, and illegal activities for economic gain was much larger. Women in medieval cities did much of the day-to-day retail trade. The numbers and the marital status of these women are impossible to determine statistically in London. Those historians who have seen the demographic slump of the late Middle Ages as a "golden age" permitting women to enter entrepreneurial activities extend the glow to working women, seeing new opportunities for women in wage labor. But others have taken a more reserved view, seeing their position as marginal or little changed from the past. London evidence for these women is mostly anecdotal, as is much of the evidence in other studies. The historian Marjorie Keniston McIntosh has produced the best study of women and work in England from the thirteenth through the early seventeenth centuries.[1] Women were most numerous as servants with few skills, but some women found more skilled trades and made a living at them, particularly in the luxury items. Other women made their way as hucksters, selling beer, wine, and prepared foods in the streets. Women did not generally enjoy continuity of work but changed their occupations and work as the needs arose. These women's lives tended to be determined by opportunities that came and went and were combined with domestic responsibilities for family, their own health, and their old age. When all else failed, women sold their bodies, not as a glamorized "sex workers" but in casual encounters to tide them over. One cannot romanticize the lives of the working women, most of whom lacked stable employment situations.

The women entering trades or wage labor in London could be natives of the city, but the majority were migrants from the countryside, as in other cities in England. Perhaps many of these were single women, but the evidence is not unequivocal.[2] Because female immigrants and servants in general could be an ephemeral population, we do not know how long they stayed in employment. They might well have regarded service in town as a life-cycle option in which they could make enough money to return to the countryside and marry, or they could have married fellow servants in the city. Some must have become skilled laborers and worked for decent wages. And, given the constant need for more immigrants to replenish urban populations, many must have died. The figures on age are few and come from cases in ecclesiastical courts, but they indicate that young women tended to be in their late teens or early twenties.[3] The young immigrants, as examples in this chapter will show, were a mobile group, who would not necessarily stay in one place but might move on as opportunity for employment or unemployment dictated.[4]

Servants

The most common employment for young people coming to London was in service or perhaps as laborers. Not all servants were young. Some women remained in service or returned to service as widows.[5] The generic term "servant" connoted a number of different levels of skill and responsibility. Households with the conjugal couple, perhaps children, and servants were known in medieval records as *familia* or *menie*. The name implied a close relationship between the master and mistress and the other residents or workers in the house. The terms used for servants in the records varied greatly: *serviens*, *famulus* or *famula*, *ancilla* (maiden or female servant).[6] Servants could live with the family or, if they were laborers, they might have their own rented rooms. The terms *paterfamilias* or *materfamilias*, when they appeared in London records, applied to innkeepers, perhaps because of their official peace-keeping function.[7]

Servants varied in status, depending on age and skill. A servant could be as lowly as a water carrier or scullery maid, or an educated man who acted as a clerk or business factor for his master, or a woman who acted essentially as a female companion to the lady of the house and did household management for a very young bride or widow. Some stayed in a household for years. Some, like Thomasine Bonaventura, came from country gentry and eventually married the master of the house. But many were hired for short-term work and moved on after a year or two. Some servants may have learned valuable skills while working in a household and could find employment in a skilled trade or take the skill into an advantageous marriage.

Servants could be easier to manage than apprentices, since their contracts were for a year or less and they usually did not have as much parental or familial oversight as did the apprentices. Apprenticeship was an elite training, requiring a contract about behavior, the nature and length of the training, and guarantees of monetary payment by both master and apprentice. Guilds, mayors, family, and friends all kept close watch over apprentices and protested bad treatment. Ordinary servants, on the other hand, could be isolated far from family, and their relatives could not travel to the city to rescue them. Some may have long ago severed ties with their family and village or had no living relatives.

As with all quasi-familial bonds, the relationship between master/mistress and servant could be good or it could be horrendous. When it worked well, close friendships formed. Servants might even take the names of their masters or mistresses and might even risk their lives in their defense. With such close ties, masters and mistresses might appear in courts defending their servants and making generous bequests to them in wills. But part of the familial relationship also implied discipline exercised by the master and mistress, which certainly meant corporal punishment. If the normal behavior was that parents should discipline their children by not sparing the rod, apprentices and servants could expect to receive the same treatment or worse. Another implication of the master/servant relationship was a sexual one. As head of the household, the master might take sexual liberties with the female servants who were part of his *familia*. As with apprenticeships, only female sexual imposition is recorded, not male-on-male relationships. We have seen in previous chapters that masters might provide for their female servants and their offspring in their wills. In a further example, John de Prestone, a corder of London, left £40 to Robert, son of Johanna de Wandlesworth, who was a servant of John. The money was later used for an apprenticeship for Robert.[8]

The number of servants in London is impossible to determine. Figures from the fourteenth-century poll tax returns from Worcester do provide some information on servants in that town, as do those from York and several other towns. Two-person households predominated, mostly consisting of a married couple. Those described as servants/sons comprised 11–17 percent, while servants/daughters made up 10–15 percent. A comparison with other cities shows that those in service varied from 17 percent to 30 percent.[9] In medieval Southwark, a city more comparable to London, servants comprised 18 percent of those taxed, of which 7 percent were females. Only 10 percent of the households had servants.[10] The poll taxes reported taxpayers over the age of fourteen. We know that the servants often evaded the tax collectors, so the number might have been greater.

Not all households in London could afford servants, either for domestic work or for help as laborers in a trade, but many did employ them. Servants added to the prestige of the master and mistress. Women and men who were high status, or aspired to it, preferred to appear in the streets with a servant.[11]

Service contracts were normally made for a year, although they could be longer or shorter. The servant made an agreement or a covenant with the master or mistress. The service agreement could include room and board, clothing, and wages for a live-in servant. Those who did not live in would have a wage. Work of ordinary servants included running errands, buying provisions, cleaning the house, and attending to the needs of the master and mistress. Some may have helped with the shop or the craft.[12]

Age of entry into household service might have been younger than the usual age of fourteen for apprentices, but London's cultural ideas put some limits on how young a servant girl could be. In one case, a girl's mother, Juliana Chaumberlayn, went to the Mayor's court and complained that the plaintiff had taken her daughter at the age of seven into service and she had served in his house for seven years. The Mayor's court returned the child to her mother "out of charity because she is too young."[13] In one pathetic case, Joan Style, a "may [maiden] child of age of seven years," is described in a petition to the lord chancellor as a victim of a dispute. Several people claimed that they had a contract with her for a service position and in their fight over her, she was put into prison for eight days. Finally, a widow took pity on her and took her side in the dispute. The widow was then imprisoned and had to pay a fine of 4 marks for enticing her out of service of another man. The basis of the suit was a violation of the Statute of Laborers of 1351, which limited wages to those of the pre–Black Death level and punished those who accepted higher wages or agreed to pay them. Joan and her new mistress got caught in personal grudges that ended up with both of them being punished.[14] One imagines that parents were willing to put their female as well as male children into service at a rather young age because, as was not the case with apprenticeship, they did not have to pay a lot of money to secure the position and the child would learn household service. The master would have a malleable youngster to train up for service.

Selection of servants was very similar to selection of apprentices. Because many servants would live in the household with the master and mistress, it was important to find compatible young people. Kin were the most reliable source of servants. Younger sons and daughters of brothers and sisters in the countryside, country cousins, and business contacts all produced recommendations for young people for service.[15] If the arrangement worked well, and it often did, the young person could end up as heir.[16]

Parents of London children might make the service arrangements, and sometimes orphaned children were put into service with a guardian. Constance, late servant to William Vyne, a woolmonger, had been put into service before her father died and perhaps by her father. Her master left her 10 marks as a legacy. The court of orphans protected the 10-mark legacy she received.[17] Acts of charity dictated some of the arrangements. Sir John Percy, a priest from Canterbury, said that a female servant, a stranger to the country, came to him poor and destitute and asked his aid in finding a post. He inquired around and found an employer who contracted to give her meat and shelter in exchange for work.[18]

It was a risk to recommend servants. Sir John, for instance, faced a suit under the Statute of Laborers from someone who claimed to be the former master of the young woman. John Twigge, a haberdasher of London, brought Agnes Copley to serve Wolfram Cook, a physician of London in 1483. She served three weeks and left his service. Cook later hired her back without Twigge's knowledge, and she robbed him. Twigge argued that he had not provided the reference for Agnes's reemployment and was not liable to be sued.[19]

Some of the contacts ended problematically for servant girls. One young country woman, Joan Rawlins, from Aldenham in Hertfordshire, planned to go to the city to seek a position as a servant. John Barton, a tailor, offered to take Joan to London and find her "good and honest service." Joan "put her trust in him." When they arrived, Barton went to a waterman's house in Southwark near the stews and asked her to wait for him. He went to find a bawd (a man or woman who would sell her into prostitution) with whom to place her. Joan apparently knew that Southwark was the center of prostitution. As soon as he left, she "begged the waterman's wife on her knees that she should be delivered and conveyed to the city." The waterman's wife arranged for the mayor and the alderman to interview Joan. They knew that John Barton had previous convictions for selling girls into prostitution, and he was sentenced to imprisonment in Newgate. He was then paraded about town holding a horse's tail and wearing a paper on his head explaining his crime. This proclamation was to be read at various places so that young women and others would know about him. He was then put into a pillory for public display. After that he was expelled from the city with no permission to return.[20]

Servants also sought their own positions. Robert Mascall, a malt-man of Aldenham, explained that Joan Smyth had come to his house in Aldenham "in poor and simple array and almost perished for default of sustenance." She told Robert that she "was clearly discharged of all manner of bonds to any man's service" and preyed him "on God's mercy" to help her. He claimed that "having pity out of alms more than any other reason he took her in." After she worked for three years in exchange for meat, board, and wages, someone turned up and claimed her under the Statute of Laborers.[21]

With general depopulation of the late fourteenth and fifteenth century, servants were hard to find and hard to keep. Enticing and outright raiding of servants appear in the records. We have already seen a girl of seven who was put in employment against the wishes of her mother and another girl of the same age who ended up in prison. Agnes Wombe and John de Sloghteford were attached to answer a charge of having enticed away the female servant of Thomas de Shene "by flattering speeches."[22] In one case, even lending out a skilled servant, an embroiderer, did not guarantee her return. Margaret la Garnystere brought an action of trespass against Agnes, widow of Thomas Bagge of Southampton, for detaining her servant, an embroiderer. The plaintiff had borrowed a half mark and loaned the servant's labor to her to pay off the debt. The plaintiff thought the agreement was for about a month, while the defendant claimed that the skilled servant was lent for a year. But Agnes agreed to give the servant back and received the repayment of her loan.[23]

Half a mark for a skilled female laborer for a month was very good pay.[24] Unskilled domestics earned considerably less. One man sued for the return of his daughter with three years' wages, which came to only 12 s., or 4 s. a year.[25] Servants were free to make complaints against their masters in the Mayor's court and in petitions to the lord chancellor. Emma atte Grene complained that she was to sell ale at 5 s. a barrel, and each barrel contained thirty gallons. But her master insisted that she pay 6 d. extra for a barrel and had detained 8 s. due from her wages. The master had witnesses to the contract; Emma got her 8 s., but she owed him 16 s., for which she had given a tally.[26] Many female servants or their husbands took the liberty of complaining about nonpayment of wages.[27]

The suit of Isabel, servant to Walter Salman, permits a glimpse of the relative wealth of an ordinary female servant before and after her service period. When she entered service, she had given into Salman's custody for safekeeping three pairs of sheets, one quilt, one mattress, one bedcover, one coverlet, one blanket, one broad cloth of eight yards, two lambskins, and other goods and merchandise worth 47 s. 10 d. She contracted for seven years of service, covering the years 1372–79, probably receiving as compensation room and board and 1 mark a year, so that she was owed 7 marks. Salman refused to pay this sum or to return the goods, and Isabel sued.[28]

Living arrangements varied. We have seen in the inventories of big houses that a servant sometimes had a separate room or might sleep in the same room as the master or mistress, in the shop, or in the kitchen. The housing of servants must have depended on the status and wealth of their employer. Recall the living arrangements of Elena Scot, a servant of Margaret de Sandwich, who in December 1321 descended from the solar in which she and her mistress lived. She was going to seek a start for a fire but slipped on the top step and fell to her death.[29] Sometimes, however, the record indicates that the wife and husband lived in separate households but that the wife's occupation was temporary and it was assumed that she would return to her husband's household after her term of service. One man sued for the sum of 2 marks and a bed as back wages for his wife, who had acted as a nurse for four years in an employer's house.[30] Some married servants lived together in the household. William Demon and May, his wife, sued the executors of their former mistress for an annuity of 40s. a year, to be taken from her lands outside Bishopsgate. She had promised the annuity in return for their long and faithful service, but they did not have anything in writing.[31]

Because of the ambiguous relationship of the master to his *familia*, complex legal cases involving servants, including sexual exploitation, appear in the records. As governor of his household, a master was responsible for the welfare of his servants as well as for their behavior. Damages to a servant, while under contract, were considered damages to the master. The close living quarters and the power of the master over female servants raised a number of legal and moral issues. The problems of the relationship appear in a number of cases, one of which was outright slavery; others were impressments of servants beyond their terms or nonpayment of wages; and a number were sexual exploitation.

An example highlights the complexity of the master–female servant relationship. John Langrake, a citizen and barber of London, found himself in trouble for taking pity on Joan, the servant of William West, rent gatherer to the Master of St. Thomas of Acres. She was only twelve, and even Langrake described her as "of right wanton disposition," running away from service several times "for God knows what reason." He was returning home when he found her at eight o'clock in the evening, sitting at his neighbor's stall right next to his door. She was quaking and shivering with cold. Langrake asked her who she was, where she lived, and why she sat there. She said that she lived in Smithfield, that her mistress had beaten her and driven her out of the house, and she had nowhere to go. John consulted with his wife and, with her consent, brought the girl into his shop and gave her supper with the other servants. He allowed her to sleep in the shop. The next morning, he again asked her whom she served and, receiving an answer, took her by the hand to William West's house. He turned her over to William's wife, who took her and said, "See what comes of thee for thy remiss to thy master." Langrake went away, believing he had done a good deed. Ten days later, West sent a neighbor to Langrake telling him that West was suing him for sexually abusing Joan in his shop. Langrake said that the whole time Joan was there, his wife, his *menie*, and three of his neighbors were present, and he would not pay the damages that West was claiming.[32]

With the voices of Langrake, the Wests, and Joan each telling a different version of this story, which one is telling the truth? West was claiming damages to his servant and wanted a monetary settlement. Langrake was claiming that West was not a good governor of his *menie*, because he let his servant wander out at night. Joan's story of physical and sexual abuse might have been made up to gain sympathy from Langrake and then of the Wests, or elements of it may have been true. All three narratives were plausible in the context of the relationship of female servants and masters in medieval London.

West's story of a servant as an extension of his household economy highlights the ambiguous position of the female (and male) servant and the master's control over her. While the master was bound by his patriarchal position to protect female servants and see that they were not damaged, his power over them through the service contract could lead to an assumption of sexual license. After all, biblical and folkloric traditions upheld the sexual privileges for a master among his maidservants as a cock among hens. Even the sermon *exempla* talk of the master who forsook his beautiful wife for the maidservant who was ugly because she was kinder than his wife, and of a dying woman who did not want her lusty husband to remarry and was assured by her maid, who loved her husband, "If he gets hot, I shall blow upon him until he cools down."[33] Servant women were a sexual temptation in the household, and the traditional patriarch's roles of protection and "possession" could become blurred.

Societal norms dictated that it was a public disgrace to demonstrate a lack of good governance. When William Rotheley denied room to his maidservant, the goldsmiths not only fined him but also reprimanded him "because he ... against all humanity sent his maid out of his house and suffered her to lie out two nights so she was fain to borrow money to lie at the Pewter Pot [an inn] to the dishonor of the fellowship." Not only was he disgraced by his failure at governance, but the guild was chagrined by his failure to rule his house with dignity.[34] Other men sued for damages over the violation of their maidservants because these women were in these men's governance. Robert Hunteston sued Richard Carpenter in 1367 because Carpenter entered his house against his will and lay with his servant, Alice Grenerman, and impregnated her. The servant bore Carpenter a daughter, and he absconded with her and the child along with goods worth £20. The story might not be true, as it was not prosecuted, but, again, it is believable. A text writer complained that a servant of a vintner ravished and defiled his servant for three days, when he and his wife were at mass, "against his love and his leave," and he was going to sue for damages.[35] Other cases tell of girls taken involuntarily from service for the purposes of sex. A case that reached the king in 1436 appears in a writ from the Chancery to the mayor. Richard Peryn and his wife, Margaret, were committed to prison for enticing Isabella Potenam, a maiden, from the service of her master and carrying her to a house in All Hallows Berkyng and causing her to be debauched against her will. The pair were arrested.[36]

While in the best of circumstances liaisons with masters might become marriages, many young women complained of losing their honor and their savings to unscrupulous, exploitative masters.[37] For instance, Joan Norman, a single woman of London, said that she was a victim of a plot between her former master and John Haliday, a London hosteler. Her former master accused her of breaking into his chest and stealing 40 s. She said that she had trusted her master and had given him a girdle worth 40 s. for indemnity. He had her arrested and put into prison. She said that she was poor and had no property but the girdle and could live only by her own hard work. Begging her former master to return her property had done no good; she had "sought him in the name of the Virgin Mary, protector of all women, to be her good master." But he was willing to let Haliday pay the 40 s. in exchange for Joan—to "have his way with her."[38]

The church court records of the late fifteenth and early sixteenth century are replete with accusations, not proof, of sexual liaisons with female servants. One of the accusations was that Robert Frannceys had eight women with child in his house in the space of seven years and that Joan, his servant, was pregnant when she went away within this six weeks.[39]

The allegations of sexual imposition appear in cases related to taverns and inns or hostelries.[40] Adding to the "familial" relationship of master and servant was the ambiguity of the space in the tavern or inns. It was both a place of business and a domestic space to which outsiders resorted to find the comforts of home: drink, food, and lodging. Was it male or female space? Couples usually ran the space, with the wife overseeing the domestic end and the female servants. But women could run taverns alone.

The taverner or innkeeper (male or female) was empowered by statute law and London ordinances to act as *paterfamilias* or *materfamilias* over both the household and the guests (they were part of the *familia*). He or she was thereby required to assume legal responsibility for the good and honest behavior of guests, employees, and kin. The position was both quasi-legal and quasi-familial, in that it required both discipline and nurturing protection.

Despite the confidence that the London government put in the hosts and hostesses of taverns and inns, they continued to have a bad reputation.

Every female role associated with taverns and inns turned the domestic nature of the association on end and implied tainted womanhood. The disparaging term "ale-wife" was not the only insult directed at women associated with brewing and drink.[41] For a *materfamilias* of a tavern, the titles of "procurer" or "bawd" were ready to the tongue and, for the tapster, the association with prostitution was all too much of a stereotype. In a mid-fourteenth-century London ordinance, brewsters were lumped with nurses, other servants, and "women of disreputable character" in a prohibition against adorning themselves with hoods trimmed with finer furs "after the manner of reputable women."[42]

Women who worked in the service occupations in taverns, particularly tapsters, were at risk of being pimped by their masters and mistresses for the sexual satisfaction of male customers. Thus Thomesina Newton was said, in the London Commissary court, to have worked for William Basseloy, the *paterfamilias* of a tavern who acted as her pimp. The owner of the Busche tavern was accused of pimping for his two servants, Mandeleyn and Alice. Others were accused of adultery with members of their establishment, as was the proprietor of the Lodyn Proche with his tapster, Mariota, and William le Hostler of Le Crown, who was said to be the father of the child born by his servant, Matrosa.[43] The *materfamilias* was no better than her male counterpart. One who kept "le tavern near the church" was accused of adultery with her servant, and the one running Le Schippe procured her tapster as a prostitute.[44]

Added to the sexual vulnerability of servants were impositions of longer terms and problems of collecting pay. At least one case involving a female servant seemed to imply slavery. A petition to the chancellor regarding a foreign servant, probably a slave, implied selling her person. Maria Moriana said that she had served Philip Syne of Venice for twenty years, taking from him only meat and drink. Philip had fallen into great poverty and could not fend for himself, his wife, or Maria except by alms of well-disposed people. Philip proposed to sell Maria for £20 to Dominic, a merchant of Genoa, but Maria was "utterly opposed" to this. Nonetheless, Philip made a bond with Dominic in Maria's name for £20. Philip told Maria that he would give her all the debts owed to him in recompense for service she had provided if she would sign the bond at the notary's house. "She being innocent and not able to speak or understand English was easily persuaded to put her seal to the agreement." Philip then had her arrested for debt and put into prison. The only way she could get out was by selling her person to Dominic for the debt. It would not be unusual for

Italian families to travel with a slave, since female slaves were common in Italy.[45] Since she could not speak English, someone must have taken pity on her and written to the chancellor on her behalf.

The story of being duped into signing a bond was not at all unusual, and both male and female servants complained about it. Elizabeth Pycely of London, a single woman, petitioned the chancellor that she had been a servant to Richard Fote, a draper, for her full term and should have had £4 for her wages. When she told him that she would depart and wanted the money owed her, he claimed that she owed him £4. He kept her prisoner in the house for five days and forged an obligation made out to himself in her name for £4. He forced her to put her seal to the obligation and then sued her. Some of the disputes over wages appear to be have been an effort to keep the women as servants when there was such a scarcity of good help, but it did limit women's options of leaving because it was harder for them to run from the situation than it was for men.[46]

Female servants, however, could be predators as well as victims. Women who worked about the house often had a keen sense of the value of goods in it and had access to keys to locked chests. John Hilton, a pewterer and citizen, complained that his servant, Agnes, had represented herself as unmarried. While he was away at St. Ives's Fair, she broke open his chest and stole goods that she took back to her husband in Dublin. Another brazen servant duped a priest from Warmington, in Cambridgeshire. Elizabeth Grey, servant to Thomas Walkot, took goods from him and left them on deposit with a priest. She saw the priest on a trip to London and asked him to bring the goods the next time they met. This he did, and Elizabeth ran away from service, taking the goods with her. A customer of a shearman left an old gown worth 28 s. to be sheared, but a servant stole it and departed.[47]

The poem "How the Good Wife Taught Her Daughter" includes a passage on how to manage servants:

> And wisely govern thy house, and serving maids and men,
> Be thou not too bitter or too debonaire with them;
> But look well what most needs to be done,
> And set the people at it both rathely [quickly] and soon.

The mistress was to be particularly careful when her husband was away from home to maintain discipline, punishing those who did nothing while rewarding those who worked hard. The mother also tells her daughter not to be above hard work, but to pitch in like a "housewife" when there is much to do, both to get the tasks finished sooner and to serve as an example for the servants. The "Wise Man" has less to say to his son about servants. The son is to maintain a balanced perspective and to referee fights between the mistress and servants.[48]

The "Good Wife" was also concerned about the amount of trust one could put in a servant. Urging her daughter to treat them fairly and even generously, she suggests that they will, therefore, be less likely to gossip about their mistress. As we have seen, she wisely cautions her daughter not to give them her keys and not to be seduced into trusting them through their flattery. To keep their tongues from wagging, servants should be paid on their term day, whether they are continuing or ending their contract. The mistress should also give them goods in kind, and "then they shall say well of thee, both the young and the old."[49]

The advice was good, of course, but women had problems managing servants. Margaret Pounce, a widow, and her servant, John Hochum, filed counter-complaints with the lord chancellor. She complained that she had hired Hochum, a glazier, for a year term twelve years earlier and that he had only worked ten weeks for her. She also claimed that he owed her 50 s. for a loan she had made to him. His petition to the chancellor claimed that he had worked for her faithfully, but she was in debt for 20 s. and would not pay. She sued him for trespass under the Statute of Laborers when he tried to collect, claiming that he was suing her out of malice for 20 s.[50] Obviously, the discontent between mistress and servant could be a long-running one.

One housewife tried to apply the techniques of good management of servants. William Elwold, a London baker, claimed that he had returned tired from a pilgrimage. He "commanded his wife to set his servants to supper and departed to his bed." But one of the servants, John Baker, who received 20 d. weekly as well as meat, drink, and lodging, used unfitting language about his master at supper in such a loud voice that his master overheard his outrage. The good wife rebuked him for using such language against a master who paid him as well as gave him meat, drink, and housing. The mistress did not succeed, and the master rose from his bed and told John to eat his supper or he would chastise him. But John assaulted his master. The other servants intervened, or there might have been more trouble. Then John sued William and enlisted others to make a case against him, so William counter-complained to the lord chancellor.[51] The good wife had not prevailed against the angry undercurrents of the household.

But the service arrangements were not all sour or exploitative. Devoted service did not go unrewarded. Of those recording their wills in the Husting court, 2.4 percent left bequests to their servants. The bequests were usually made in the form of money or household goods and clothing. Some were annuities from 20 s. to 40 s. One man, a widower, left his shops to his female servant.[52] When Isabel, Lady Bouchers, died, she left a bequest of a 40 s. annuity to William Demon and his wife, May, "for their long and faithful services."[53] Because some of these servants were also relatives, the bequests kept wealth within the family.

Hucksters, Victualers, and Women in Transient Trades

Women participated in a number of small businesses, many involving food preparation, vending of ale or victuals, or selling sex. These occupations tended to be transient and sometimes coincided with a husband's business. These women often appear in the records because they were on the fringe of legal and illegal trade.[54]

Hucksters, women who did not sell goods from their homes but hucked or haggled goods in the street, were often associated with the selling of ale and also fell under the taint of women associated with inns, taverns, and brewing. Sometimes they were called "tranteres" or "regraters." They bought goods such as grain, malt, salt fish, bread, beer, wine, and some preserved goods (salt fish) and prepared foods and resold them in neighborhoods.[55] Sometimes they had stalls or shops, or they simply spread out their goods on the street. In the busy lives of Londoners, hucksters played an important role, since they could supply quick meals and drink, making it unnecessary to go to a shop or prepare food.

Many regulations governed hucksters, both male and female. Bakers, for instance, were to sell hucksters thirteen loaves at the price of a dozen (a baker's dozen) so that poor people were not defrauded.[56] Brewers and brewsters, cooks, and pie bakers were not to buy ale to sell again to "hucksteres," because many of these women had withdrawn to Westminster, Southwark, and elsewhere and sold ale brewed in London.[57] Those who sold ale, including hucksters, were to use the legal measure.[58] Those selling fish were confined to certain streets.[59] Sunday selling was always a problem, but it was prosecuted more vigorously under Mayor Catworth, who wished to keep the day holy. Butchers, fishmongers, poultrers, and taverners were not to sell fish, flesh, or fowl, and bakers could not begin their trade until after seven o'clock in the morning. Included in this ordinance of 1444 was the provision "also that noone herb wife, milk wife ne seller of Boowis [boughs], Flouris [flowers], Briddez [birds] ne none other bringe none to selle upon Sonday on the peyne aforesaid, but that these and all other kepe theire mercate [market] here upon the Saturday."[60] Likewise, the regulation of the "Evynchepyng," or evening market for frippery (old clothes), affected both men and women. No one was to sell these on Cornhill after the bell that hangs on the Tun had been sounded at sunset.[61] Hucksters were not to buy oysters and mussels before nine o'clock on pain of forfeiture.[62]

Enforcement of city ordinances of these petty economic offenses was difficult. Many of the trades were transient ones, and, like modern, nonlicensed street vendors, the hucksters could pick up and leave at a whisper of official presence. The report of the aldermen to the mayor on wardmoot business was not systematically preserved, but it is in the records of this very local court, at the ward level, that the researcher can at least know what the local people thought worth reporting to the aldermen, who then passed on the information to the mayor. The wardmoot records for various wards for the years 1421–23 report 480 offenses. Of these, 30 percent of those indicted were men, 20 percent were women, and 6 percent were married couples. The rest were complaints about disrepair of rents and problems with inns. The offenses in the latter cases were nuisances that mostly involved infractions of building codes, intrusions on streets, and piles of muck and dung. The cases involving men, women, and married couples were misdemeanors, of which 15 percent were for committing multiple offenses. Hucksters were often accused of being forestallers, that is, buyers of goods before they reached the market so as to sell them at a higher price, or of being regraters, that is, buyers of provisions in order to sell them at higher prices than they would get on the open market. In seventeen cases, the items women sold illegally were victuals, such as poultry, eggs, butter, and other goods, and forty-eight women were charged with being illegal hucksters who sold ale without using the proper measure. A scattering of women were charged with scolding, prostitution, or being foreign [not native to London] but acting as if free of the city. Men also committed the above misdemeanors, but added extortion to their repertoire of community offenses. Married couples were accused of the full range of offenses.[63] Males appear most frequently in these records, but women hold their own in the misdemeanors that involve these petty economic offenses.

A few examples clarify these types of misdemeanor. Alice, wife of Robert de Caustone, was condemned to the pillory for women called "la thew" (a special pillory for women in which they were allowed to sit rather than stand) for thickening the bottom of a quart measure with pitch.[64] Alice le Strengere, who resided in New Temple, and other women who were widows or wives of chandlers were selling wax candles of false weight in December, not only a dark month of winter but also one in which candles played a large role in religious festivities. They were excused, provided that they did not offend again.[65] A number of men and women were accused of the same offense, and their candles were returned, with the understanding that they would not do so again.[66] John Wastelle, a poultrer, was charged with selling snipe, thrushes, and a woodcock that were spoiled. But John Smyth declared under oath that he had bought the birds elsewhere and that he had given them to the first man's wife to pluck. John Wastelle was sentenced to stand at the pillory with the birds burnt under his nose, because it was determined that he owned them. John Smyth acknowledged that he was suborned by Wastelle's wife to "bear false witness on the promise of a pair of hose." He was committed to prison but soon released.[67]

Forestalling and regrating were common accusations for both men and women. These illegal hucksters were often found guilty. One inquisition elucidates the scheme: "Elene Steer, Katherine Lylye, wife of Henry Racheford, Margarete Bury, Luce Clerk, Jonet Wodham, Katherine Wylde and all their fellows are regraters of fish, eggs, chickens, and capons." According to the record, "they rise in the morning and wait in the evening, when such victual or butter or cheese come, and go into the boat and buy it up privily, thus making a dearth of such victuals and hindering common people of the city."[68] William Bullok and Juliana de Donecastre, both of Gracechurch Street, were accused of forestalling hay. She confessed, was put in prison, and paid a fine of 20 d.[69]

Women in these small businesses were often the victims of cheating. Agatha, wife of John Freman of Maldon, suffered 20 s. damage to straw she was carrying for sale when two smiths set it alight.[70] Other women sued for debts unpaid, as did Agnes Pepul, a poultrer, but the case goes on to say that while the debt was indeed owed, it was confiscated by the king because her husband had committed murder.[71]

The enforcement of restrictions on hucksters was not always honest. William Gelde, a former servant to one of the sergeants of the late mayor, was committed to prison because he visited the houses of diverse hucksters and pretended that he was appointed to confiscate the ale he found in their houses. He went to their houses with tablets in his hand that he said he would inscribe with their names as being "huckesters" and present them to the mayor. The women knew that he was servant to the former mayor and thought that he still was, so they offered bribes and diverse gifts. One offered 12 d. and another 6 d. in order not to have their ale confiscated and their businesses closed down. He was discovered and punished by standing at the pillory for an hour and having his offense announced to the community.[72]

Some women fought back. Eva la Callestere was attached to answer a plea of trespass. An official went to seize a false grain measure, and she bit his finger. He claimed 100 s. in damages, but she contended that he falsely entered her house and wanted to lie with her. She lost, but only paid 12 d. in damages.[73] Benedict de Shorn and Agnes Greilong, along with other fish-mongers, were accused of setting up shops and stalls on London Bridge to sell wholesale and retail, but this was forbidden by London law. Benedict fought the case but ultimately lost.[74]

These examples make clear that women were numerous in the small business activities of London. While they lagged somewhat behind men, they were nonetheless very important. Their numbers in court cases may underrepresent their presence because, as in criminal indictments, officials may have been more lenient in citing them than men. While not numerous among the entrepreneurs, their contribution to the day-to-day supply of neighborhoods was of major importance.

The number of debt cases appearing in the Mayor's court involving women is minor compared to those involving men. Women seem to have been more comfortable suing for debt in the church courts, since they were more liberal. On the other hand, the Commissary court did not have much legal clout in getting the money back. Few judgments were actually rendered, and most cases were dropped, presumably in out-of-court settlements. By 1500 these courts lost favor, and a court of Requests in London handled most of the business.[75] In the Commissary court for 1485, eleven women were charged with debt, all by men, and twenty-four men were charged, twenty by men and four by women.[76] By the beginning of the sixteenth century, London set up its own courts for dealing with small debts, since they had grown so numerous and the church courts were not satisfactory.[77]

Prostitution was another source of income for women, most of whom were not professionals but entered into it out of desperation, out of coercion, or as a supplemental income. Prostitution held an ambiguous place in the Middle Ages. It was morally condemned, and prostitutes were scorned; but they were regulated and tolerated. London was no different from other cities but, unlike some continental cities, did not have city-regulated brothels.[78] London ordinances tried to limit prostitutes to Coklane or to export their problems to the stews of Southwark, but never gained complete control over prostitution.[79] Prostitution was seldom a trade, as silkmaking or embroidery were, but rather was more closely akin to huckstering. It was part of the makeshift economy of women. The image that the cases bring to mind is not of women making a profession of selling their bodies but rather of sexual liaisons that were casual street and alley affairs. One finds accusations of sex in houses, in fields, in an alley angle of Broadstreet, in ecclesiastical establishments, outside a mud wall.[80] Some women had rooms, and some bawds provided places for sexual contact, and taverns and inns lived up to their reputations as meeting places for illicit sex.

Economically and socially, taverns were ideally suited to provide sexual services, since their clientele were largely traveling men who might have expected the *paterfamilias* or *materfamilias* to provide for their sexual needs. A 1516 case demonstrates the role of the taverner or innkeeper as a go-between. Elizabeth Tomlins was in an alehouse next to the Bell Inn and sent for the hostler inquiring if Gregory Kyton, a priest, was there. The innkeeper told Kyton that there was a woman waiting for him. It was arranged that the priest would have her in his chamber, and the innkeeper then suggested that the priest go to the George Tavern in Lombard Street and that Elizabeth would meet him there. The hostler took her into a chamber at the George, and the priest came and joined them. The hostler's pay was a meal shared with them at the priest's expense.[81]

Taverns also provided opportunities for pimps and prostitutes that apparently went unregulated by the proprietors. The tapsters acquired neighborhood reputations. Elizabeth Machyn, tapster of the Red Lyon, was accused of adultery and of doing the same at "Le Cok" in Woodstreet, while Mariona, who was a sometime tapster at the Vine in the parish of St. Helen and at the Choker in the high street, was accused of being "a common scandalizer, especially with Thomas, one of the deacons of St. Paul."[82]

John Mande and his wife pimped his sister at a tavern.[83] The Pye in Queenhithe had a reputation as a place "which is a good shadowing for thieves and many evil bargains have been made there, and many strumpets and pimps have their covert there, and leisure to make their false covenants." The neighbors wanted it closed at night.[84]

Although the historian Ruth Mazo Karras has traced a few women and one man who seemed to have made a profession of prostitution, the modern term "sex worker" seems out of place in late medieval London. Some of the women seem to have done fairly well, perhaps as procuresses rather than prostitutes.[85]

Karras's best example is actually of a man, John Rykener, who posed as a woman. His case is remarkable, of course, because he dressed as a woman and prostituted himself as a woman. What is unremarkable about his case is that it demonstrates the way prostitutes moved in and out of that role, traveled around, and combined it with other trades. Calling himself Eleanor, he was arrested having sex with another man in a stall, but he apparently performed sexual acts as if a woman. In his testimony, he said that he had spent five weeks in Oxford doing embroidery but fornicating with students as well. Then he went on to Burford for six weeks and was a tapster in an inn, as well as taking clients from traveling merchants and clergy. Dressed as a woman, he probably learned embroidery from a woman who trained others in the craft and also had the reputation of putting her servants out to prostitution.[86]

Since the concern of this section is the marginal occupations of London, a full discussion of prostitution and punishments is unnecessary. An overview of life on the margins, not only of prostitution but also of the general economy of makeshift that William Langland described in *Piers Plowman*, comes from the late fifteenth-century London ward of Portsoken. It was close to the Tower and was, as the name suggests, a port area. The wardmoots cover fourteen years between 1465 and 1483.[87] The Portsoken records give 423 cases, including 431 individuals or married couples. Fifty-one cases, or 12 percent, involved problems with property and offenses against the Assize of Nuisances. Of the individuals accused, 44 percent (189) were male, 29 percent (124) female, and 27 percent (118) married couples.

What were the alleged offenses? With multiple charges made against these people and with a small sample size, sorting out the people and their offenses is not particularly statistically significant. As was typical of the marginal economy, a variety of misdemeanors accumulated in the charges. Women appearing in these records were mostly accused of sexual offenses. Seventy-one, or 57 percent, of the women were accused of being strumpets or whores; thirteen, or 11 percent, were accused of being bawds (pimps). The accusation for being a scold involved eighteen women, or 15 percent. The rest were accused of a scattering of other offenses, including huckstering without being free of the city. Male offenses included being a bawd and harlot monger, 14 percent; not being free of the city, 44 percent;

suspicious behavior, 6 percent; and begging, 5 percent. Married couples had the same range of misbehavior as did individual women and men, including procuring, trading as if free of the city, suspicious behavior, and acting as false beggars. But some of the charges were of men pimping their wives.

These records permit us to trace the number of repeat offenders, which was 107 (66 percent men, 23 percent women, and 10 percent married couples). Apparently, these by-occupations of a marginal nature were so profitable, or at least sufficiently remunerative, that the parties had managed to keep starvation at bay and to stay alive during the interval between complaints long enough to offend again.

The Portsoken population that was charged as being offensive to neighbors in the wardmoot were single men and women. Women were most often listed by their own names rather than as "wife of" someone. Most of the people appeared to be English in origin, and few were listed with permanent occupations.

The prevalence of prostitution in these late wardmoots is mirrored in the records of the London Commissary court from 1471 to 1515 (with missing years), which show that 377 women were charged with prostitution and only ten admitted guilt.[88] Pimping, likewise, appears frequently. Of the 1,030 suspects, only seven pimps were convicted.[89] Pimps or bawds could be both male and female, as we have seen in the Portsoken wardmoot.[90] If the court records come even close to a true picture of pimping, it is a very sordid one. Mothers and fathers pimped their daughters, husbands their wives, mistresses their servants, neighbors women in the neighborhood.

Some women seem to have been more routine offenders as prostitutes, and officials referred to them by their street names: Little Nan, Little Margery, Little Kate, Long Alice, Great Molle, Johanna Greatbelly, Pale Besse, Pusse le cat, Bouncing Bess, Katherine Sawners alias Flying Kate, and Joan Havyer alias Puppy. Mariona Wood appeared with such regularity that the allegations of her prostitution can be followed in both the church courts and wardmoot. Mariona was first cited in Portsoken in 1479 for being a harlot. Her name appeared regularly in the Commissary court between 1482 and the 1490s. The charges included fornication, adultery, prostitution, and pimping. She had a series of aliases: "longa mariona wode alias Birde alias taler" [long Mariona Wode, alias Birdie, alias taler, perhaps tale teller]. The city courts did not punish her, and the church court excommunicated her but could not enforce the punishment.[91]

The evidence of financial reward for prostitution is meager. Joan lived in the house of Spanish Nelle, a pimp. She allegedly received 4 d. for the first night with a man and a beer and an article of dress the second night.[92] But other cases show that the pimp, at least, was making a profit. A husband and wife pimping women allegedly got 20 d., 21 d., 40 d., and one time 44 s. One pimp got £4 40 s. for pimping a woman, but this may be over a period of time. Another got 40s. We have some idea of the arrangement in the case of Alexander Elwold, who kept two whores. One, Magistra Elena, paid him 2 s. a week from her earnings.[93] In another case, Margery went to the house of Joan Wakelyn, and together they went to the house of an important Lombard. Joan got 12 d. "for her wicked and unlawful behavior, and gave Margery 4 d.[94] Pay for women selling themselves could be as low as a sheaf of wheat.[95]

If prostitutes offered special services, it is difficult to tell from the records. One was accused of specializing in clergy.[96] A frequent term of insult was "Lombard whore," but if it indicated a special service, it is impossible to know. The names attached are not necessarily Italian, so it seemed to carry a particular meaning of defamation.

In addition to illegal huckstering and prostitution, a range of criminal activities could provide some extra income. Forgery was one possibility. Johanna Coghenho and William Sutton were indicted in 1423 with "fraudulently and deceptively" fabricating "a certain false and fictitious writing in the similitude of a sealed obligation that bound a skinner to pay the sum of £100." She was found guilty, but because she was too feeble and infirm to undergo the usual punishment at the pillory, she was to stand for an hour there with the false obligation around her neck and "the cause of her standing there be openly published and proclaimed." She faced criminal charges, for she was accused of having been part of a "covin" that was involved in such counterfeits.[97]

Another woman became involved in a complicated extortion plot. John Westowe complained that Richard Rede, who was prosecuting him in the Sheriff's court, offered Elene Faux a cloth for a gown if she would be a bawd between Richard's wife, Catherine, and John. Elene Faux offered Catherine 20 s. if she would lie with John. John also approached a priest saying that he would give him a noble (gold coin equal to 6 s. 8 d.) if he would record before a judge that he saw John and Catherine together. The scheme failed. Catherine and the priest were willing to testify.[98]

Since women were keepers of the keys to chests, they often safeguarded goods held in pledge for debt or simply held for safekeeping. Elizabeth Fyfeld, wife of Richard Fyfeld, was accused of retaining money, pepper, and other goods. Another woman was sent to prison for detaining a gold and diamond ring in her chest.[99]

If the Sheriff's court records had been preserved more abundantly for London, more cases of thievery and women's involvement as compared to men would likely appear in greater clarity. But again, individual cases must suffice. Some of the records of women caught with stolen goods do survive, and London, like other franchises of royal justice, had the right to hang these people. A few women belonged to groups who stole. Maude de Oxford, Roesia de Burton, and Geoffrey de Wynchecombe were attached for having stolen goods in their possession, including five cups of mazer taken from St. Lawrence Lane in 1329. The ringleader, Geoffrey, was a cleric and was released to the bishop, but Maud was found guilty and hanged, and Roesia was acquitted.[100] Another woman was taken for having a brass pot worth 5 s. that she feloniously stole. She was found not guilty.[101] Other women fenced (bought and sold) stolen goods.[102] But these few cases indicate that we are seeing the tip of an iceberg for women committing petty to serious crimes involving property.

The employment picture for women in low-paying trades, service, and labor, be they single or married, is not good. The court records show the negative side of both women's and men's opportunities and do not have much evidence of a positive side to transient labor and service. The depopulation that occurred in the century and a half after the Black Death increased the number of positions available, but these were not necessarily prestigious positions for women. The evidence indicates that the dearth of population, if it benefited women, only did so in the first quarter of the fifteenth century. By the end of the century, women were being edged out of positions that they had even earlier enjoyed. New regulations regarding women's employment in guilds and increased population erased and ultimately worsened women's position in small trades and the labor market.[103]

It is hard to apply modern concepts of wage employment or even modern ideas of "sweatshops" to medieval workers. In some respects, the medieval urban laborers and servants had less of an opportunity than modern ones to organize collectively and act against employers. We do not even know much about their chances of success in suing a master. Female employees were often isolated within households and often on their own in the city, lodging with masters and mistresses or seeking lodging where they could. They were often sexually compromised. Urban women who were not married to either successful merchants or craftsmen, highly skilled in their own crafts, or in high-level service fit into the interstices of the economy as best they could. They did not enjoy secure lives, and probably not long ones. The difficulties they experienced, while in part imposed by patriarchy, as in the case of servants, paled by comparison to the experiences of both males and females of the poorer ranks of society. It was a "catch as catch can" existence.

Conclusion

London women played a major role in London's economy in the fourteenth and fifteenth centuries. Marriage was presumed to be the basis of the household economy in London, as was typical throughout Europe. It was the conjugal couple that formed the stable elements needed to make a functioning and well-ordered society work. London wives pursued their traditional roles, managing the households, apprentices, and servants and adding to the general well-being of the urban economy by practicing some crafts and by helping out husbands in finishing goods or in retailing various wares. Married and single women carried on much of the small retail trade in necessary commodities such as beer, ale, food, and other goods. All these occupations were essential to the city's economy, but the major contribution women made to London's growing international status in the late fourteenth and fifteenth centuries was as conduits of capital through their marriages. The exchange of dowry and dower formed the new household.

London women acquired their wealth for dowries through a variety of means. London law permitted daughters to inherit equally with their brothers, and that inheritance went toward their marriages. Or the parents could make a settlement of a dowry for a daughter while they were alive, and the daughter contracted marriage. Some women worked in various trades or as servants until they acquired sufficient money and goods to offer in exchange for dower. Widows also had dowries, but the real advantage of marrying a widow was that she could take the dower of the former husband into subsequent marriages. The city laws made mothers guardians of their orphaned children and their inheritances so that a man marrying a widow got not only the dower for as long the woman lived but also the use of her children's property until they reached the age of majority. The dowry and the matching dower from the husband made London women a source of liquid capital. Women were so important to the well-being of the city that special laws protected their rights and courts willingly heard their pleas in their own voices or through attorneys. Men's wills, even those of noncitizens, and court cases show that Londoners followed the customs of the city in regard to women's property and dower.

London's laws and customs have raised a number of questions about the status and position of women in London society. This book has investigated the treatment of girls compared to boys from birth, their education and training, the legal provisions made for girls and women, the exchange of dowry and dower in marriage contracts, the marriage partnership, and the success of widows in actually claiming their dower. The prospects of women as entrepreneurs and as employed persons have also been explored. The major emphasis has been on the wealth that women accumulated through London's generous laws toward women. But how much control did women have over this wealth, even if it was a small amount? Did becoming *femme couverte* on marriage limit a woman's options to control her property or pursue an independent trade? The ceding of so much wealth to women led foreign observers to question the type of society that London men envisioned in their laws. Since they delayed inheritance of their male heirs through dower for their widows and allowed daughters to inherit equally with sons, they obviously did not think in the same fashion as the clans of Flanders or the citizens of Florence and Venice. They did not even follow the common law of England in emphasizing descent of property and title from father to son. Men in London did not seem to value patriarchical descent of title and prestige through the male line. Rather than emphasizing the establishment of a patrilineal, vertical descent, London patriarchs preferred to keep capital and real estate liquid. Their means of doing so was to manipulate the longstanding laws and customs for protection of women and children by passing wealth through women to men of their own social status. London, as a consequence, developed strong horizontal ties that passed wealth through women to other men rather than passing it directly to male heirs. In late medieval London, the expansion of personal capital and the growing power of guilds were more important than the extension of a male kinship system.

Women were valued not only because of their wealth but also because there were perhaps few eligible brides in London. All sources indicate that there were 10 percent fewer female than male children. The early childhood years seemed to have been particularly risky for girls. In families with only one child, that child was usually male. The girls who did survive, however, often outlived their brother or brothers, and, given London law, they then came into the full value of the inheritance. Following the depopulation of the Black Death in the mid–fourteenth century and the continued low population in the fifteenth century, these survivors became increasingly wealthy, with real property, valuable jewels and plate, and money accumulating in their inheritances as other family members died. They were very sought after as marriage partners and probably, if they had a good dowry, married in their mid- to late teens.

From birth, London girls were schooled in the lessons of their gender. They were given female names and assumed their fathers' identities. The general attitude of the Londoners, both male and female, was that girls should be reared to marry. The records present little evidence that female children were educated or apprenticed equally with males, although city ordinances and parliamentary statutes suggested that they could be. When they were apprenticed, their contracts tended to be for a shorter period. Men were apprenticed for seven years or longer, but women were often released from apprenticeship earlier. While London women could take apprentices, the few surviving contracts and law cases indicate that girls were apprenticed to the husband of the family while the wife actually did the training in her own trade, such as silk thread making, embroidery, and related trades.

A daughter's inheritance was usually described as her dowry or "toward her marriage," although the daughter could also marry and receive her portion while her parents were alive. London parents provided the best financial arrangement they could afford. Often the dowry was in real estate. The dowry property often descended from mother to daughter. Or the dowry would be part of the joint real estate that the parents owned or rented, which they gave to their daughter and husband at the time of marriage. In the fifteenth century, a preference seemed to be to provide dowry in movable goods and money rather than real estate. The liquidity of the dowry was important to the growing capital economy of London.

Fathers and mothers with sons had to provide for apprenticeships and the problems of setting sons up in business or employment. Since the apprenticeships for men was long, London men delayed marriage. They were often in their late twenties or older when they married. A groom contracted to provide a dower that would match the value of the dowry.

Dower was usually in the form of real estate, so that wills show an increase in real property left to sons by the late fifteenth century. Men who made their fortunes as merchants sometimes had to buy property to form the dower. The Cely brothers were a case in point. The son who became senior partner got the father's residence after the death of his mother, who had it in dower. The younger son spent much of his inheritance buying property in London to provide dower for his wife, a widow who was already well situated.

Marriages were, for the most part, negotiated. While some young people married for love and without responsible parties to arrange the contracts for them, the usual pattern was for their elders make arrangements. Parents, relatives, or respected men might seek out reliable marriage partners, matchmakers made deals to bring together couples, and some couples found their own partners and entrusted the financial negotiations to reliable parties. The contract—few of them are preserved—could be complicated, indicating, for instance, that the groom would receive a certain amount of capital but would turn some of this into real estate that would become the dower for the wife. A husband might make a jointure with his wife in which the couple would take title to the property together and the "longest liver" would get the property and pass it on to his or her heirs. Sometimes the exchange of dower and dowry was a simple monetary transaction. Many of the contracts were not written, or if they were, they were kept as private papers and have not survived. At the very least, dower guaranteed the widow her free bench, or the right to rooms in the house that she and her husband had occupied before he died. But dowers were usually much larger and could include shops, gardens, rented tenements, and wharves.

The dower and dowry were announced in front of witnesses "at the church door." Sometimes when a widow went to court to plead for the dower, she could bring witnesses who had been at the church door and who could testify that the property ought to be hers. Widows won their suits of dower in 53 percent of the cases. The high success rate is testimony to the fairness of the legal process and the openness of the court to hearing widows' complaints about disputed dower property.

About one-third of the widows who disputed their dower provisions had remarried when they brought their cases to court or had married while the cases were proceeding. The number or remarriages rose sharply in the period following the plague. Remarriage of widows appearing with young children in the court of orphans was even higher, with two-thirds remarrying between 1309 and 1458. The percentage of remarrying widows increased substantially in the late fourteenth and fifteenth centuries, as widows and heirs became increasingly wealthy. Men marrying widows with young children received a third of the former husband's estate as long as his new wife lived (the dower) and two-thirds if she had minor children. He could invest this money, with a fair return to the estate, until the orphans reached the age of majority. Widows were much in demand for remarriage, and some remarried frequently, taking their dowers into subsequent marriages. The flow of capital and real estate through widows contributed to the wealth of London men, merchants, and tradesmen alike. Tradesmen marrying the widow in the same trade could gain apprentices, shop tools, customers, and trade secrets. A merchant gained not only real capital but also social capital by marrying a high-status widow. For the widows, remarriage had a number of advantages. Instead of living on a third of the former estate and without the husband's income, they could augment their standard of living by remarriage. Furthermore, they did not have the worries of keeping up a business and training apprentices. Widows who did not want to remarry could become vowesses—that is, they took a vow of chastity but did not become nuns. And some widows preferred widowhood to remarriage and fended off suitors.

To our modern thinking, arranged marriages are inconceivable and marriages for property rather than love are out of the question. Even in arranged marriages, there was time for courtship, and ecclesiastical law did not permit couples to be forced into a marriage they did not want. Marriage by consent of the parties was encouraged and happened in most cases. A period of courtship, exchange of gifts, and shared meals in the company of others permitted the couple to become acquainted if they had not met before. Marriage was based on the assumption that it would be a partnership, starting with the initial marriage contract and continuing with the division of tasks in the household. The partnership was not equal, because the woman became *femme couverte* on marriage—that is, her husband became responsible for her finances and her behavior. But the husband could not alienate her inheritance, nor could he sell property promised in dower without his wife's permission. Were the marriages happy? Probably most marriage brought satisfaction to the couple, and some were very loving, as we know from a few letters, bequests in wills, and directions to be buried next to a spouse. A good helpmate was very desirable, as is shown by the number of women and men who remarried.

But could women function independently in London society? Women were certainly some of the major consumers in London's economy. London women did not rely on men to go out in public for shopping or court appearances. They went themselves or with servants, if they could afford them. They had to provide food, bedding, and drink for their households, and they bought clothing, jewels, plate, furniture, and other goods for the comfort of themselves and their families. They were consumers of charity at hospitals and at church doors. But they were also consumers of the spiritual and social benefits that could be derived from association with their parish churches. They bought more pews in the churches than did men, and they contributed to the upkeep of the parish churches and to various charities. If we think of London streets, they were not devoid of women. Women went out to do their shopping, went to church, and visited in streets, taverns, and each others' homes. Many women were the street vendors who sold items to other women and to men.

With the large amount of real estate that passed through women's hands and the capital that they accumulated, they had the possibility of becoming entrepreneurs as well as consumers. London did not bar women from trading on their own as single women or as widows, and even had a law that allowed married women to register with the mayor and trade as *femmes soles*. A woman trading *sole* could carry on her own business and be responsible for her own profits and debts. The records of deeds, however, show that few women—married, widowed, or single—participated in the real estate market. Husbands and wives bought and sold property, but, increasingly, men were the major players in the real estate market. Perhaps the shift by the middle of the fifteenth century coincides with the tendency of men to purchase dower properties, but it might also indicate a more general trend of men assuming economic dominance. Although married women could trade *femmes soles*, few appear in the records, and those who do are usually cited for debt along with their husbands. Some women were successful on their own as brewsters, silk workers, and innkeepers, but most wives preferred to work under *coverture* and contribute to the general household economy. Since women were not reared in apprenticeships that would lead to lucrative trades, the work within the household economy was a more obvious role. A scattering of widows did successfully pursue trades, taking up the businesses they inherited from their husbands. But most women found remarriage or retirement a more comfortable option.

The usual approach to women and their economic contributions in medieval England and in Europe has been an analysis of women's success in their own businesses and as workers in various crafts. Many European cities, particularly in the later Middle Ages, have excellent records to do such studies, but England does not have comparable information for a statistical study. Many young women and men migrated to urban centers in England, and most of them left no trace in the records. The urban environment was a harsh one, and many young people died of disease before they could leave a mark in city records, or they moved on in search of employment elsewhere. We can say of late medieval London that there was a continual influx of some skilled and mostly unskilled workers. Many of the young women were servants. Some were of high rank, more in the category of ladies' companions, but most were of a lower status. They encountered many problems, including sexual exploitation, difficulty in getting wages, and sometimes contracts that were extended without their consent. Some did learn valuable skills such as weaving and silk making, but they were not highly paid. Some did domestic tasks such as nursing. Servants could fit well with the families they lived with, and many may have been poorer country relatives who came to serve in the city. Valued servants were rewarded with bequests in wills.

For women without skills, a variety of retail trades offered some opportunity as hucksters. These women would buy beer, wine, fish, prepared foods, grain, and so on and then resell them in the streets. In the busy, crowded city of London, having a local vendor was as important as take-out food is for us today. But the women who engaged in these retailing businesses were always regarded with suspicion and often arrested. They lived on the margins of the economy. They were valuable, useful additions to London's economy, but their trade was often illegal. When all else failed, women on the margins of London's economy sold their bodies. These were not glamorous "sex trade" workers but desperate women trying to avoid starvation.

Two general questions regarding women's history are raised in this book. One is the role of patriarchy in determining women's lives. Patriarchy dominated London, as it did elsewhere in Europe, but the city developed its own peculiar patriarchal culture. It was a self-limiting form of patriarchy, in that it protected wives and children of citizens, rich or poor, from other unscrupulous males who might take advantage of them, but it also allowed temporary use of widows' and orphans' wealth to other men of their social class, with the presumption that the father's heirs would eventually get their full inheritance along with an augmentation mandated by the city. Foreigners wondered if the heirs ever saw the inheritances, or if women managed to secret away part of it. For the most part, the system seemed to work, and through the fifteenth century no attempt was made to curtail the wealth of daughters and widows. Their inheritances, dowries, and dowers were too valuable to London's economy. Women, as well, learned to manipulate the patriarchy to make their lives as comfortable and profitable as possible. Some did better at this than others, of course, but they were raised with an understanding of the law, their rights, and the use of courts. They appear with great frequency in London's courts, pleading their cases in their own voice, that of a second husband, or that of an attorney.

The other issue that has been addressed in this book is continuity and change in women's lives. Much of the book has spoken of long traditions of women being reared with the values of patriarchal society and schooled to take up the role of wives when they came of age. They were not educated as well as their brothers, and they were not put to learn crafts for careers in trade. The continuity of women's rearing and the expected roles for them in society does not diminish the position they occupied. The basic unit of economy in preindustrial Europe was the household. But women did not simply marry and lose their identities to patriarchy. That would be a naïve underselling of women's ingenuity. Women learned to work within the web of the dominant culture and to make their own way, if they were clever and able to do so.

The major events that swept through London and Europe also affected them. In the famine years of the first half of the fourteenth century, women suffered as much or more than men. More female children than males probably died. The plague opened up some opportunities for survivors, including women. The accumulated wealth of heirs, heiresses, and widows increased substantially in the decades following the Black Death, and these women became important for the flow of capital in London through their marriages and remarriages. While some historians have spoken of the late fourteenth and fifteenth centuries as a "golden age" of employment and entrepreneurial success of women, the records do not sustain this argument. Perhaps a few women did well, but those who married well did better. Those who married several times did even better, as they accumulated dower after dower. Does marriage and remarriage mean a "golden age"? That is a question that is unanswerable. But there were always those on the bottom who did not survive or barely survived. By the end of the fifteenth century, London had an overabundance of labor and the guilds began to change to the merchant companies. London's men took more control over their property, heirs, and inheritance into their own hands. Like much of the rest of Europe, England included, women seemed to be losing status in London. The will was the most convenient means of manipulating the conveyance of wealth. Men could make wills, but married women could make wills only with the husbands' consent, and widows had only their inheritances or their household goods to give to friends and relatives. Wealth came to follow men more than women by the late fifteenth and sixteenth centuries.

Glossary

Archdeaconry Court Wills Archdeaconry of London provided poorer people to make wills and record them in their records. The wills are mostly of craftspeople and the poor.

Borough Town with a charter from the king permitting municipal corporation and rights of self-government.

Borough law Laws specific to boroughs as opposed to the king's law (common law); London's borough law was the model for most other towns in England.

Calendar A list of documents with summaries of their contents.

Citizen of London Citizenship of London could be acquired by inheritance, by completing an apprenticeship in London and becoming free of the city, and by redemption (buying or being awarded the rights of citizenship); women became free of the city by marrying citizens.

Common Law Law administered by the king's courts.

Consistory Court Court of the bishop of London. Testimony was transcribed in deposition books.

Glossary

Commissary Court Ecclesiastical court that heard cases much like a modern-day magistrate's court. The cases tried were for correction of delinquents of ecclesiastical laws. The court also provided wills.

Corody An allowance of food, drink, and shelter in return for property or payment.

Coverture Legal doctrine that a husband covered his wife's legal identity during their marriage. She had none of the legal rights normally allowed to men or to widows.

Curtesy of England Husband's right upon his wife's death to a life use of the estate that she owned during their marriage, providing that the couple has a child who was born alive.

Currency 1 d. = 1 penny, 1 s. = 12 d., £1 = 20 s. 13 s. 4 d. = 1 mark

Customary law Law of various regions and manors of England; cases tried in manorial courts.

Dower Wife's right upon her husband's death to a life use of a portion of his estate; in London it was one-third to one-half of the estate, depending the presence of heirs of the marriage.

Dowry Money, goods, or property that a woman brings to her husband on marriage.

Fee simple *or* **freehold** Real property that included the rights of alienation and inheritance until the death of the holder; it then descended to the holder's heirs.

Enfeoffment Transfer of possession of an estate in land.

Essoin Excuse for not appearing in court as ordered.

Femme couverte Married woman who was subsumed under the husband's legal and economic protection.

Femme sole Woman who had never married or was a widow. In London, a married woman could get permission from the mayor to trade on her own account, or *femme sole*.

Forestalling Buying goods for resale before they came on the market.

Forisaffidatio A woman's formal renunciation of her claim to the property in her dower should she be widowed.

Glossary

Frankpledge *or* **tithing group**   System by which males over the age of twelve were grouped in tithings (groups of ten) and were responsible for the good behavior of their members.

Freedom of London   Rights of London citizens to trade in the city, participate in its government, and enjoy protection of its laws.

Girdle   Narrow band that encircles the waist; often made of silk, with gold, silver, and precious ornaments.

Guild   Corporation of merchants or craftsmen inside a borough.

Inquisition Post Mortem   Inquest held on the death of a tenant of the king to discover land that the tenant held in fee, to find the heirs, and to discover any rights such as wardships or offices that belonged to the king.

Inter vivos   Settlement of wealth or real estate made during the life of the donor.

Jointure   A woman's freehold right for life in an estate made in lieu of dower; in London this sometimes made her heir to the property

Messuage   Dwelling house with yard and outbuildings; *capital messuage* is the house of the husband and wife.

Orphan   In London, a citizen's child was considered an orphan if the parent, usually the father, died and had left the child his heir; the city, through the court of orphans, was responsible for guaranteeing the wardship of the child and the inheritance.

Partible inheritance   Equal division of parents' goods and real estate among all surviving children of the marriage.

Petitions to Chancery   When cases fell outside the normal judgment of courts, individuals petitioned for an equity decision from the lord chancellor; the process began in the late fourteenth and fifteenth centuries.

Quitclaim   Title to the property given in exchange for a contractual agreement for specified services and housing.

Regrater   Person who sells at a higher than market price.

Seisin   To be seized of; in possession of land.

Solar   Attic room.

Glossary

Surety   Person who is liable for payment of another's debt or obligation.

Wardmoot   Local pleas made against the offenders for misdemeanors and property offenses for one city ward.

Warranty   A guarantee a property by putting another property of equal value as insurance.

Notes

Abbreviations

CCorR	R. R. Sharpe, ed., *Calendar of Coroners' Rolls of the City of London, 1300–1378* (London, 1913).
CIPM	*Calendar of Inquisitions Post Mortem*, 14 vols. (London, 1904–1954).
CEMCR	A. H. Thomas, ed., *Calendar of Early Mayor's Court Rolls of the City of London, 1298–1307* (London, 1924).
CIPM	*Calendar of Inquisitions Post Mortem*, 14 vols. (London, 1904–54).
CLMC	R. R. Sharpe, ed., *Calendar of Letters from the Mayor and Corporation of the City of London* (London, 1885).
CLRO	Corporation of London Record Office
CPMR	A. H. Thomas (vols. 1–4) and P. E. Jones (vols. 5–6), eds., *Calendar of Plea and Memoranda Rolls of the City of London, 1323–1482* (Cambridge, 1926–61).
EETS	Early English Text Society
GL	Guildhall Library Archives
HW	R. R. Sharpe, ed., *Calendar of Wills Proved and Enrolled in the Court of Husting, London, A.D. 1258–A.D. 1688*, 2 vols. (London, 1890).

LBA–LBK	R. R. Sharpe, *Calendar of Letter Books of the City of London, A–K (1275–1497)*, 11 vols. (London, 1899–1912).
Liber Albus	Henry Thomas Riley, ed., *Liber Albus: The White Book of the City of London* (London, 1861).
LRS	London Record Society
SS	Selden Society
TNA: PRO	The National Archives: Public Record Office

Introduction

1. B. M. S. Campbell, J. A. Galloway, D. Keen, and M. Murphy, *A Medieval Capital and Its Grain Supply: Agrarian Production and Distribution in the London Region c. 1300* (Belfast, 1993), p. 172.

2. TNA: PRO Just 2/94A, ms. 2, 3, 5. CC*or*R, p. 61.

3. Jens Röhrkasten, "Trends in Mortality in Late Medieval London 1348–1400," *Nottingham Medieval Studies* 45 (2001), pp. 172–209.

4. Caroline M. Barron, "'The Golden Age' of Women in Medieval London," *Reading Medieval Studies* 15 (1989), pp. 35–58, and P. J. P. Goldberg, *Women, Work and Life Cycle in a Medieval Economy: Women in York and Yorkshire c. 1300–1520* (Oxford, 1992), pp. 345–361, are modern proponents of the expanded opportunities for women in urban centers. Chapter 8 has a more detailed discussion of the history of the proponents of this view.

5. Judith M. Bennett, "History Stands Still: Women's Work in the European Past," *Feminist Studies* 19 (1988), pp. 269–283. "Medieval Women, Modern Women: Across the Great Divide," in *Culture and History, 1350–1600: Essays on English Communities, Identities and Writing*, ed. David Aers (Detroit, 1992), pp. 147–176. "Confronting Continuity," *Journal of Women's History* 9 (1997), pp. 73–94. For a collection of her essays see *History Matters: Patriarchy and the Challenge of Feminism* (Philadelphia, 2006). Marjorie Keniston McIntosh, *Working Women in English Society* (Cambridge, 2005), pp. 28–36, has a very good discussion of the positions of historians writing on women in the economy in England.

6. Kim M. Phillips, *Medieval Maidens: Young Women and Gender in England, 1270–1540* (Manchester, 2003), has a complete discussion of the preparation of young women for marriage in medieval England.

7. Amy Louise Erickson, "The Marital Economy in Comparative Perspective," in *The Marital Economy in Scandinavia and Britain, 1400–1900*, ed. Maria Ågren and Amy Louise Erickson (Aldershot, 2005), pp. 3–4.

8. Judith M. Bennett, *Ale, Beer, and Brewsters in England* (New York, 1996).

9. J. B. Crotch, ed., *The Prologues and Epilogues of William Caxton*, EETS, o.s., vol. 176 (London, 1928), p. 77.

10. Charlotte Augusta Sneyd, trans., *A Relation or Rather a True Account of the Island of England; With Sundry Particulars of the Customs of Those People, and of the Royal*

Revenues under King Henry the Seventh, about the Year 1500, Camden Society, series 1, no. 37 (1846), pp. 26–27.

11.   For a complete discussion of London government structures see Caroline M. Barron, *London in the Later Middle Ages: Government and People, 1200–1500* (Oxford, 2004).

12.   Martha C. Howell, *The Marriage Exchange: Property, Social Place, and Gender in Cities of the Low Countrire, 1300–1550* (Chicago, 1998). She has a very good overview of marriage contracts and the changes in them for the northern Europe. The pattern I describe differs somewhat from that of northern Europe, but the privileging of the wife is more or less consistent in the northern European marital property arrangement.

13.   The differences in marriage regimes between northern and southern Europe is covered more fully in chapter 5. The important article describing the shift in southern Europe is Diane Owen Hughes, "From Brideprice to Dowry in Mediterranean Europe," *Journal of Family History* 3 (1978), pp. 262–296.

14.   Barbara A. Hanawalt, *The Ties That Bound: Peasant Families in Medieval England* (New York, 1986), pp. 205–219. The concept has recently been extended in a collection of essays edited by Maria Ågren and Amy Louise Erickson, *The Marital Economy in Scandinavia and Britain, 1400–1900* (Aldershot, 2005).

15.   Alison Hanham, *The Celys and Their World: An English Merchant Family of the Fifteenth Century* (Cambridge, 1985).

16.   For a discussion of the ecclesiastical courts, see Richard M. Wunderli, *London Church Courts and Society on the Eve of the Reformation* (Boston, 1981). In the current book, the wills in the Archdeaconry court have been used in full, and those in the Commissary court have been sampled. The Commissary court heard pleas that involved debt (broken contracts) and a number of petty moral offenses such as defamation, sexual crimes, and so on. These were used for examples.

17.   The various sources for London are well summarized in Barron, *London in the Later Middle Ages*, pp. 2–4. See also McIntosh, *Working Women in England*, dealing with London sources. Abbreviations of sources used in the notes appear in a list at the head of the notes section.

Chapter 1

1.   Ffiona Swabey, *Medieval Gentlewoman: Life in a Gentry Household in the Later Middle Ages* (New York, 1999), pp. 34–41, provides some family background.

2.   *CIPM 1399–1405*, vol. 18, p. 101.

3.   Henry Littlehales, ed., *The Medieval Records of a London City Church*, EETS, o.s., vols. 125–128 (London, 1905), p. 1. One couple was brought into the church court for undergoing the purification ritual at home with a Friar officiating rather than in the parish church. William H. Hale, *A Series of Precedents and Proceedings in Criminal Causes Extracted from the Year 1475 to 1640. Extracted from the Act Books of Ecclesiastical Courts in the Diocese of London, Illustrative of the Discipline of the Church of England* (London, 1847),

p. 14. For a discussion of early modern practice see David Cressy, *Birth, Marriage and Death: Ritual, Religion, and the Life-Cycle in Tudor and Stuart England* (Oxford, 1997), pp. 55–79. Few cases mention either midwives or wet nurses in London, but both must have been common. In Florence, men kept records of the amount paid to wet nurses, but no such accounts exist in England. Christiane Klapisch-Zuber, *Women, Family, and Ritual in Renaissance Italy*, trans. Lydia Cochrane (Chicago, 1985). Her essay "Blood Parents and Milk Parents: Wet Nursing in Florence, 1300–1530," pp. 132–164, explores the extensive use of nurses among middle-class Florentines. See also Louis Haas, *The Renaissance Man and His Children: Childbirth and Early Childhood in Florence, 1300–1600* (New York, 1998), chaps. 4 and 5. See also Leah L. Otis, "Municipal Wet Nurses in Fifteenth-Century Montpellier," in *Women and Work in Preindustrial Europe*, ed. Barbara A. Hanawalt (Bloomington, Ind., 1986), pp. 83–93. Again, London had no such municipal service for the poor.

4. CIPM *1391–99*, vol. 17, p. 514. One vicar had to be released from debtor's prison in order to perform the baptism.

5. CIPM *1399–1405*, vol. 18, p. 101. Another father had four men CIPM *1391–99*, vol. 17, p. 514. Yet another baptismal party had six men holding torches at the baptism of a knight's child in London. CIPM *1405–13*, vol. 19, p. 223.

6. Joseph H. Lynch, *Godparents and Kinship in Early Medieval Europe* (Princeton, 1986), chaps. 7 and 12.

7. Barbara A. Hanawalt, *The Ties That Bound: Peasant Families in Medieval England* (New York, 1986), pp. 173–175. The information comes from a register of freemen at York who were required to give the names of their godparents in order to prove that they were English and not Scots. The father selected the most prestigious man or woman to lift the child from the font.

8. In London Husting court wills between 1300 and 1350, 29 percent of sons had the same name as their father, and 26 percent of daughters had their mother's name. The common names for daughters were Johanna (Joan), Isabella, Alice, Matilda, and Agnes. See Barbara A. Hanawalt, *Growing Up in Medieval London: The Experience of Childhood in History* (New York, 1993), pp. 46–47.

9. CIPM *1413–18*, vol. 20, p. 267.

10. CIPM *1383–1405*, vol. 16, p. 123.

11. CIPM *1399–1405*, vol. 18, p. 320.

12. CIPM *1399–1405*, vol. 18, p. 320, CIPM *1413–18*, vol. 20, p. 48.

13. CIPM *1352–61*, vol. 10, pp. 111–113.

14. CIPM *1352–61*, vol. 10, pp. 111–113.

15. CIPM *1352–61*, vol. 10, pp. 111–113.

16. CIPM *1399–1405*, vol. 18, p. 320.

17. LBH *1375–99*, p. 183.

18. Lynch, *Godparents and Kinship*. See chaps. 10 and 11 for the development of the liturgy and the actual ceremony of baptism.

19. GL, Ms. 9051/1; HW, vol. 2.

20. See Hanawalt, *Growing Up in Medieval London*, p. 46, for the number mentioning godchildren in the Husting court wills. *HW*, vol. 2, pp. 359, 455 (1431); GL, Ms. 9171/1, fol. 98.

21. GL, Ms. 9171/1, fols. 60, 87, 98, 108, 187v; GL, Ms. 9051/1, fols. 2v–3, 5v, 98v, 201, 203, 208. The terms for godchildren vary: "spiritual children" and *filiolo* sometimes replace "godchild." See for instance *LBE 1314–37*, p. 72 (1316), in which Hawisa de Mymes bequeathed 40 s. to Hawisa, her goddaughter (*filiole*), and *LBF 1337–52*, p. 92 (1343), in which a godson is referred to as *filiolo*.

22. *HW*, vol. 2, p. 282. For currency equivalencies, see the glossary under *Currency*.

23. GL, Ms. 9171/5, fol. 193.

24. Lynch, *Godparents and Kinship*, pp. 179–181, discusses Germanic practice, as opposed to Christian sponsorship.

25. *LBE 1314–37*, pp. 24–25 (1314). The great majority of these surnames reflect an East Midlands or West Midlands origin. Eilert Ekwall, *Studies on the Population of Medieval London* (Stockholm, 1956.)

26. GL, Ms. 9064/1, fols. 40v, 37v, 51.

27. Amy Louise Erickson, "The Marital Economy in Comparative Perspective," in *The Marital Economy in Scandinavia and Britain, 1400–1900*, ed. Maria Ågren and Amy Louise Erickson (Aldershot, 2005), p. 8, observes that in that Sweden-Finland, in urban areas only, followed the law of sons and daughters inheriting equally.

28. Mary Bateson, ed., *Borough Customs*, SS, vol. 21 (London, 1904), vol. 2, p. xciv.

29. In *CPMR 1364–81*, vol. 2, pp. xxvii–lxiv, A. H. Thomas discusses citizenship. He concludes that fewer than one-seventh of citizens were recruited from citizen stock (p. xxx) and that for every freeman in London from 1300 to 1537, there were three non-infranchised adult men (p. lxii). In *LBD 1309–14*, pp. i–viii, xiv–xvi, R. R. Sharpe gives a brief discussion of citizenship and of the terms of wardship. See also Gwyn A. Williams, *Medieval London: From Commune to Capital* (London, 1963), pp. 44–49, and for citizenship, Steve Rappaport, *Worlds within Worlds: Structure of Life in Sixteenth-Century London* (Cambridge, 1989), pp. 23–60. On p. 53 he concludes that in the sixteenth century, about three-quarters of the adult male population, or slightly more than one-fifth of the total population, were citizens.

30. Barbara Megson, "Life Expectations of the Widows and Orphans of Freemen in London, 1375–1399," *Local Population Studies* (1996), p. 21, has shown the full range of crafts of freemen leaving orphans and their wealth.

31. Hanawalt, *Growing Up in Medieval London*, p. 91.

32. *CPMR 1413–37*, vol. 4, p. 6.

33. *LBC 1291–1309*, p. 205 (1307).

34. *Liber Albus*, pp. 95–96. When a man abducted and failed to register a ten-year-old girl who was a citizen's daughter, the mayor had him arrested; *LBI 1400–1422*, p. 111 (1412). *LBI 1400–1422*, pp. 220–221, restates the law in settling one case.

Elaine Clark, "City Orphans and Custody Laws in Medieval England," *American Journal of Legal History* 34 (1990), pp. 168–187, has discussed these laws and their application for London and Bristol. Caroline M. Barron, *London in the Later Middle Ages: Government and People, 1200–1500* (Oxford, 2004), pp. 268–273, has a brief discussion of the laws governing orphans and their administration.

35. David Nicholas, *The Domestic Life of a Medieval City: Women, Children, and the Family in Fourteenth-Century Ghent* (Lincoln, Neb., 1985), pp. 109–129. The laws and practice of placing orphans in Ghent have similarities and differences with those of London. As in London, the city government took over the care of the inheritances of children and assured their welfare. But, unlike London, the father's clan was more important than the mother's claim to rearing the children. No such tender care for the fate of the inheriting child appears with allowing an older brother to take charge of the child and its inheritance. On the other hand, the clan was an expansive unit that permitted the mother to take care of the child and also welcomed the husbands of daughters into the clan structure. As in London, the Ghent city fathers punished abuses of wardship and made payments to the guardians out of the ward's estate for its upbringing. In Florence, on the other hand, the care of children who lost a father went exclusively to the father's family. The widow, should she leave the former husband's household, relinquished her children. Klapisch-Zuber, *Women, Family, and Ritual in Renaissance Italy*, pp. 117–131.

36. *LBG 1352–74*, pp. 229–230.

37. *CEMCR 1298–1307*, p. 77.

38. *LBG 1352–74*, pp. 229, 239–240.

39. Barron, *London in the Later Middle Ages*, pp. 189–190.

40. In *LBD 1309–14*, pp. iv, xiv, Sharpe discusses the wardship procedures. *LBG 1352–74*, p. 79, mentions the name of one of the common pleaders. For a general discussion, see Charles Carlton, *The Court of Orphans* (Leicester, 1974), chap. 1, on the medieval foundation, and the rest of the book for a discussion of the Tudor-Stuart period.

41. *LBG 1352–74*, p. 91.

42. *LBG 1352–74*, pp. 230–231.

43. *LBK 1422–61*, p. 26.

44. *HW*, vol. 1, p. 377 (1332).

45. The kin included uncles or aunts of the child, grandparents, elder sons, and a nephew.

46. *LBF 1337–52*, pp. 103–104.

47. See in Hanawalt, *Growing Up in Medieval London*, p. 225, table 6.

48. David Herlihy and Christiane Klapisch-Zuber, *Tuscans and Their Families: A Study of the Florentine Catasto of 1427* (New Haven, 1985), p. 217, found that almost all the men remarried.

49. Hanawalt, *Growing Up in Medieval London*, p. 105.

50. *LBA 1275–98*, p. 4 (1275); *LBC 1291–1309*, p. 5; *LBE 1314–37*, p. 82 (1318); *LBF 1337–52*, p. 60 (1340); *LBH 1375–99*, pp. 52, 141, 216 (1380s).

51. *CPMR 1381–1412*, vol. 3, pp. 15–16.

52. *LBH 1375–99*, p. 82.

53. See Hanawalt, *Growing Up in Medieval London*, p. 224.

54. Through 1368, only about one-third of the cases in the Corporation of London Letter Books recorded the value of inheritance. Until 1438, 40 to 50 percent of the cases register the bequests. After that, almost 100 percent of the cases record the amounts.

55. Jens Röhrkasten, "Trends in Mortality in Late Medieval London (1348–1400)," *Nottingham Medieval Studies* 45 (2001), pp. 172–209.

56. Hanawalt, *Growing Up in Medieval London*, p. 100. The total number of families of orphans appearing between 1309 and 1428 was 495.

57. *CPMR 1381–1412*, vol. 3, p. 99 (1384).

58. *LBD 1309–14*, pp. 180–181. For further discussion and examples, see Hanawalt, *Growing Up in Medieval London*, pp. 100–104.

59. *CPMR 1323–64*, vol. 1, p. 242. For other cases see *CPMR 1381–1412*, vol. 3, pp. 72–73; *LBE 1314–37*, pp. 19, 301–302; *CPMR 1323–64*, vol. 1, pp. 138–139, 226; *CPMR 1364–81*, vol. 2, pp. 50, 168; *LBG 1352–74*, p. 315; *LBH 1375–99*, pp. 52–53, 84. Some guardians were put into prison until they found a way to pay, *CPMR 1364–81*, vol. 2, p. 39. *CEMCR 1298–1307*, pp. 110–111, tells of a couple who got a writ through a ruse that gave them a house belonging to a ward of the city to her damage of 10 s.

60. *LBG 1352–74*, pp. 55–56. For other cases see *LBI 1400–1422*, p. 111; *LBG 1352–74*, p. 122; *LBE 1314–37*, pp. 293–295.

61. *CCorR*, pp. 114–116.

62. *LBK 1422–61*, p. 93 (1428); *LBC 1291–1309*, pp. 81–82; *LBE 1314–37*, p. 121.

63. *CPMR 1323–64*, vol. 1, p. 205.

64. *LBE 1314–37*, p. 47. *LBI 1400–1422*, pp. 141–142, recounts the case John Hurlebatte, who married Johanna, the orphaned daughter of Nicholas Aghton, late an alderman, without license from the mayor and aldermen. Hurlebatte said that he had contracted the marriage before two witnesses, but that the marriage was not yet solemnized. The court, however, found that he was married, and he and the two witnesses were put into prison until they all paid a fine to the mayor of £40.

65. The case is a long one, in which Margaret made several involved complaints. She claimed that when John Bryan found he could not pay his apprentice, John Fraunceys, the sums that he owed him, he conspired to marry him to Alison so that her 110 marks would cover the debt. These espousals, Margaret claimed, were illegal because they were done without the permission of the mayor and chamberlain (CLRO MC 1/1/62). Although Margaret referred to the enrollment of John Rayner's will, it does not appear in *HW*. The other parties likewise do not appear. Fraunceys was a common name, but Richard Fraunceys does not appear. *LBH 1375–99*, pp. 10–12, indicates that Rayner's executors had quickly paid off Margaret's inheritance for 41 s. 4 d. Most likely, Bryan was eager to eliminate her influence. In 1380, five years after Alison's father died, Bryan came to court and got permission for Alison's marriage, paying the chamberlain 20 s. for permission. The Letter Book does not say that it was for a marriage to Fraunceys. Obviously Margaret retained some contact with her daughter, but she had no power to control her marriage.

66. CPMR 1437–57, vol. 5, pp. 51–52.

67. TNA: PRO C1/16/307.

68. CLRO, CP, 26 10d. CPMR 1413–37, vol. 4, pp. 242–243 (1429). The young man was supposed to inherit property at the decease of his grandmother but had suffered many delays. The mayor and aldermen intervened.

69. LBK 1422–61, p. 237.

70. LBE 1314–37, pp. 29–30.

71. See Hanawalt, Growing Up in Medieval London, p. 223, for table with the numbers. Of the total number of orphans recorded, 780 were female and 951 were males. Megson's study "Life Expectations of Widows and Orphans" from 1375 to 1399 also shows that the disparity decreased during the postplague period, p. 25.

72. Herlihy and Klapisch-Zuber, Tuscans and Their Families, pp. 132–134. The imbalance was marked through most of the ages of men and women in Florence. Male children outnumber female in most human populations; the sex ratio at birth is 105 males to 100 females. Because males do not survive as well as females, it evens out as children grow older, creating a 50/50 ratio.

73. J. A. Burrow, The Ages of Man: A Study in Medieval Writing and Thought (Oxford, 1988), pp. 12–26.

74. Mary Dove, The Perfect Age of Man's Life (Cambridge, 1986), pp. 20–25.

75. Joan Cadden, Meanings of Sex Difference in the Middle Ages (Cambridge, 1993), chap. 4. Women's heads were smaller than men's heads, they did not fully grow bodily hair, and their very reproductive organs were inverted and internal compared to men's. Reasoning, because of the smaller brain capacity, was less developed in women and men. Medical literature also advised on how to conceive a male fetus (pp. 253–254).

76. LBK 1422–61, p. 391 (1464).

77. GL, Ms. 9051/1, fol. 10. The Archdeaconry court contains 228 wills. For a full description of the church courts of London see Richard Wunderli, London Church Courts and Society on the Eve of the Reformation (Cambridge, Mass, 1981).

78. GL, Ms. 9051/1, fols. 21v and 96A.

79. HW for the years 1309–23, 1355–68, 1409–21, 1455–68. The sample included 390 lay men's wills that record 467 sons, of whom 282 got some form of real estate, compared to 159 of the 360 daughters.

80. HW, vol. 1, p. 697.

81. Elaine Clark, "City Orphans and Custody Laws," pp. 168–187. See Hanawalt, Growing Up in Medieval London, p. 224, for statistical tables. There were 229 individuals for whom an age can be determined. Joel T. Rosenthal has studied the ages at which sons and daughters of the nobility became heirs (although not necessarily entering into their property). He found that for the late fourteenth and early fifteenth century, 22 percent were heiresses, and 78 percent were heirs. Their ages when their fathers died show a clustering around the age of twenty-one: 24 percent of the boys were under ten, while 20 percent of the females were; 32 percent of boys were aged eleven to twenty, and 26 percent of the girls. At ages twenty-one to twenty-nine, 29 percent of the young men became heirs, and

34 percent of the heiresses. The nobility, therefore, seem to have lost fathers at a later age. The hazards of life in London could account for earlier death of fathers, or it could be that the age of marriage for men in London was later than it was for wealthy young knights and earls who had to perpetuate a family line. Joel T. Rosenthal, *Old Age in Late Medieval England* (Philadelphia, 1996), p. 20.

82. Hanawalt, *Growing Up in Medieval London*, chapter 8.

83. In total, there were 572 families for whom the number of surviving children can be identified.

84. Evidence comes from Letter Books covering the years 1309–1497. The figures are 164 females and 253 males, with a total of 417 only children. For two children of the same sex in the family, forty-five had two females, and sixty-eight had two males. But for three to five same-sex children in the family, twenty-four (57 percent) had all females, and eighteen had all males.

85. Megson, "Local Population Studies," p. 25, found the average size in 1375–99 was 1.5 children.

86. See Hanawalt, *Growing Up in Medieval London*, p. 57, for figures. For 631 orphans, it is possible to identify those who survived to maturity and those who died as minors (199, or 31 percent.) The most likely explanation is the increase in a number of diseases, not simply plague, in the fifteenth century.

87. *CPMR 1381–1412*, vol. 3, pp. 208–216 (1393), *LBH 1375–99*, pp. 404, 446–447.

88. TNA: PRO Just 2/94A. Cases of children one, seven, and nine days old appear in the coroners' inquests in 1339, but their deaths are attributed to natural causes (*CCorR*, pp. 22, 254, 260).

89. GL, Ms. 9064/2, fols. 168v, 99.

90. Richard H. Helmholtz, "Infanticide in England in the Later Middle Ages," *History of Childhood Quarterly* 1 (1974–1975), pp. 282–340, discusses the penance expected in the event of overlaying and the infrequency of the occurrence.

91. William H. Hale, *Series of Precedents and Proceedings in Criminal Causes*, pp. 41, 52.

92. For a more complete discussion of the English evidence, see Barbara A. Hanawalt, "Childrearing among the Lower Classes in Late Medieval England," *Journal of Interdisciplinary History* 8 (1977), pp. 1–22. Further discussion is in Hanawalt, *The Ties That Bound*, pp. 101–103. For information on cases of infanticide from jail delivery rolls (three cases of infanticide out of four thousand cases of homicide), see Barbara A. Hanawalt, *Crime and Conflict in English Communities, 1300–1348* (Cambridge, 1979), pp. 154–157. For the number of cases coming into ecclesiastical jurisdiction and the rather mild punishment for those that did, see Richard H. Helmholtz, "Infanticide in England in the Later Middle Ages." Infanticide was not made a criminal offense until the middle of the seventeenth century. See Naomi D. Hurnard, *The King's Pardon for Homicide before 1307* (Oxford, 1969), p. 169.

93. Jean-Claude Schmidt, *Holy Greyhound: Guinefort, Healer of Children since the Thirteenth Century*, trans. Martin Thom, Cambridge Studies in Oral and Literate Culture 6 (Cambridge, 1983).

94. *LBG 1352–74*, pp. 2–3.
95. Charles Pendrill, *London Life in the Fourteenth Century* (London, 1925; reprint, Port Washington, N. Y., 1977), p. 183.
96. GL, Ms. 9064/2, fol. 168.
97. *LBK 1422–61*, p. 89. A case sent to the king and his council stated that "citizens of London ... might leave freeholds by will in the same manner as chattels." But Thomas de Petresfeld claimed that the recipient was a bastard and therefore could not inherit. Inquisition established that he was not a bastard and therefore could inherit the freehold.
98. Wunderli, *London Church Courts and Society*, pp. 76–80. Terms of slander tended to be sexual, rather than referring to illegitimacy.
99. Helena M. Chew, ed., *London Possessory Assizes: A Calendar*, LRS, vol. 1 (London, 1965), pp. 42, 47–48.
100. *CIPM 1361–65*, vol. 11, pp. 214–215.
101. *CIPM 1365–70*, vol. 12, p. 131.
102. *CIPM 1391–99*, vol. 17, p. 508.
103. Derek Keene, "Tanners' Widows, 1300–1350," in *Medieval London Widows, 1300–1500*, ed. Caroline M. Barron and Anne F. Sutton (London, 1994), p. 17.
104. Sylvia Thrupp, *The Merchant Class of Medieval London* (Ann Arbor, 1948), p. 343.
105. *LBH 1375–99*, p. 387 (1392).
106. *LBG 1352–74*, pp. 261, 303. In *LBI 1400–1422*, p. 40, the guardianship of Alice, legitimate daughter of John Hardwiyk, haberdasher, and of Isabella, his bastard daughter, was committed to John Frensshe, goldsmith, who married the widow of John.
107. *LBE 1314–37*, p. 250.
108. GL, Ms. 9064/1, fol. 34v. See also fols. 15, 619, 76, 93v, 139v.
109. Klapisch-Zuber, *Women, Family, and Ritual in Renaissance Italy*, p. 135. Haas, *Renaissance Man and His Children*, chaps. 4 and 5.
110. Ronald C. Finucane, *Rescue of Innocents: Endangered Children in Medieval Miracles* (New York, 1997), p. 52. Didier Lett, *L'enfant des miracles: Enfance et société au Moyen Âge* (Paris, 1997), p. 361.
111. Sheila Ryan Johansson, "Deferred Infanticide: Excess Female Mortality during Childhood," in *Infanticide: Comparative and Evolutionary Perspectives*, ed. Glenn Hausfater and Sarah Blaffer Hrdy (New York, 1984), pp. 463–486. Female children were more likely to die after the age of one and into their teens. The cause was not violence against these girls but rather that they had poorer diets and less attentive care than male children, thus making them more vulnerable to disease and parasites. If menstruating girls have low iron intake, they are more susceptible to disease. Excessive female mortality, therefore, reflected a lower value placed on females. The cultural devaluing of females was coupled with an economic devaluation of female labor. The dowry was seen as a further drain on family resources.
112. *CCorR*, pp. 34–35.

113. Ernest Sabine, "City Cleaning in Medieval London," *Speculum* 12 (1937), pp. 335–353.

114. CLRO MC 11/1/5.

115. Richard Knox and Shane Leslie, trans., *The Miracles of King Henry VI* (Cambridge, 1923), pp. 164–166.

116. *CCorR*, pp. 30–31.

117. *CCorR*, pp. 25, 63, 170, 194, 238, 258 (boys); 30, 56, 183, 107, 250, 252 (girls).

118. *CCorR*, p. 250.

119. *CCorR*, pp. 56–57.

120. *LBG* 1352–74, p. 306.

Chapter 2

1. J. A. Burrow, *Ages of Man: A Study in Medieval Writing and Thought* (Oxford, 1988), p. 30. To the author, women's identity was formed by men as admirers, lovers, husbands, or disgusted observers of old women. In a recent collection of essays, Kim M. Phillips, "Maidenhood as the Perfect Age of Woman's Life," in *Young Medieval Women*, ed. Katherine J. Lewis, Noel James Nenuge, and Kim M. Phillips (New York, 1999), pp. 1–24, has argued that the period of maidenhood (midteens to early twenties) was considered in the Middle Ages as the most desirable period of a woman's life, comparable to adulthood for males. Whether virgin saints or heroines of romances or the poem, *The Pearl Maiden*, the female ideal was the slender, young, virginal figure. Spring, then, was the female glory.

2. Edith Rickert, ed. and trans., *The Babee's Book: Medieval Manners for the Young: Done into Modern English from Dr. Furnivall's Texts* (New York, 1966), p. 33. I have chosen to use the modern English rendition in order to make this book more readable to a larger public. Readers interested in the Middle English version should see Frederick J. Furnival, ed., *Early English Meals and Manners: John Russel's Boke of Nurture, Etc.*, EETS, o.s., vol. 32 (London, 1896). Felicity Riddy, "Mother Knows Best: Reading Social Change in a Courtesy Text," *Speculum* 71 (1996), pp. 66–86, has suggested that the poem was, perhaps, recorded by a Franciscan friar and that subsequent copies of it were meant for mistresses of young female servants from the countryside coming to town.

3. Kim M. Phillips, *Medieval Maidens: Young Women and Gender in England, 1270–1540* (Manchester, 2003), pp. 61–107, has discussed the education and cultural expectations for maidens.

4. See Rickert, *The Babee's Book*, and Furnival, *Early English Meals and Manners*, for examples.

5. The difference in behavior patterns between girls and boys can be clearly seen in the accidental deaths of peasant children. As early as two and three female children began to identify with the work of their mothers and had accidents around the home, such as playing with pots on the fire, while male children had more of their accidents outside, following their fathers. This early identity with the work roles of mothers and fathers persisted into the teenage years, as the peasant children

learned the tasks that the sexual division of labor in the peasant household economy dictated. The London coroners' inquests into accidental death are less well preserved and less conclusive, although they show a similar pattern. See Barbara A. Hanawalt, *The Ties That Bound: Peasant Families in Medieval England* (New York, 1986), chaps. 10, 11, and "Childrearing among the Lower Classes of Late Medieval England, *Journal of Interdisciplinary History* 8 (1977), pp. 1–22.

6. *Statutes of the Realm*, 7 Henry 4, c. 17.

7. Caroline M. Barron, "The Education and Training of Girls in Fifteenth-Century London," in *Courts, Counties, and the Capital in the Later Middle Ages*, ed. Diana E. S. Dunn (New York, 1996), pp. 139–153.

8. Sylvia L. Thrupp, *The Merchant Class of Medieval London* (Chicago, 1948), p. 171, thinks that most merchant-class girls had access to an education, but general literacy is hard to find. For the education of boys see Barbara A. Hanawalt, *Growing Up in Medieval London: The Experience of Childhood in History* (New York, 1993), pp 80–85.

9. Barron, "The Education and Training of Girls," p. 148.

10. Ibid., p. 147.

11. Thrupp, *Merchant Class*, p. 171.

12. *LBK 1422–61*, p. 118, TNA: PRO C1/150/28.

13. Hanawalt, *Growing Up in Medieval London*, pp. 82, 113, 136, 144. Barron, "The Education and Training of Girls," pp. 146–147, found that the four apprenticeship contracts for girls did not require education.

14. *LBI 1400–1422*, p. 36.

15. Steven Justice, *Writing and Rebellion: England in 1381* (Berkeley, 1994), chap. 1, "Insurgent Literacy," has discussed the active and passive knowledge of letters that English peasants and townspeople had.

16. Mary C. Erler, *Women, Reading, and Piety in Late Medieval England* (Cambridge, 2002). See in particular chap. 2, "The Library of a London Vowess, Margery de Nerford." Barron, "The Education and Training of Girls," pp. 150–152, lists women in London who are mentioned in connection with books in wills.

17. *Statutes of the Realm*, 7 Henry 4, c. 17. This statute was a reissue of the Statute of Laborers of 1351, which was designed to keep prices and labor at the 1347 level, that is, before the plague. It was hard to enforce, and the statute was continually reissued. In this later statute, the addition of a land value to the initial law was intended to further restrict those who wanted to take advantage of the labor shortage and move to positions of education or apprenticeship. For a discussion of the mobility of youth see P. J. P. Goldberg, "Migration, Youth and Gender in Later Medieval England," in *Youth in the Middle Ages*, ed. P. J. P. Goldberg and Felicity Riddy (York, England, 2004), pp. 85–100.

18. *LBK 1422–61*, pp. 87, 104–105.

19. *LBK 1422–61*, p. 8 (1423).

20. Barron, "The Education and Training of Girls," pp. 139–140. Judith M. Bennett, "Medieval Women, Modern Women: Across the Great Divide," in *Culture and History, 1350–1600: Essays on English Communities, Identities and Writing,*

ed. David Aers (London, 1992), pp. 59–60, has disputed women's access to apprenticeships on the whole. Participation in a craft does not necessarily imply guild membership, as Bennett has shown.

21. *LBI 1400–1422*, pp. 38, 134.

22. Listing is in *LBD 1309–14*, pp. 96–179. See also A. H. Thomas, introduction to *CPMR 1364–81*, vol. 2, pp. xxx–lxi, has a complete discussion of apprenticeship. He too notes the absence of women in the listing and likewise in that of the early sixteenth century.

23. Enfranchisement of women is difficult to find in medieval English towns. P. J. P. Goldberg, *Women, Work, and Life Cycle in a Medieval Economy: Women in York and Yorkshire c. 1300–1520* (Oxford, 1992), pp. 49–63, 334, found that women in York could be enfranchised by patrimony. He found that few cities extended citizenship to women but some licensed them to trade. Maryanne Kowaleski, *Local Markets and Regional Trade in Exeter* (Cambridge, 1995), pp. 95–99, 169–170, found that the franchise was limited to elite men and even many male apprentices did not enter into citizenship.

24. *CPMR 1413–37*, vol. 4, pp. 162, 166–167, 208, 227, and CLRO MC 1/2/171. CLRO MC 1/3/171, 1/1/13, 1/2A/68, 1/2A; *CPMR 1413–37*, vol. 4, pp. 42–43, 71, 162, 166–167, 176, 208, 227; *CPMR 1437–57*, vol. 5, p. 88.

25. CLRO MC 1/2A, 4 (1379). For the same case see MC 1/2 (1378–79), in which Robert, Isabel's husband, a chandler, sued. This suit alleged that Broke had not fed nor clothed the daughter properly and she should be returned to her parents.

26. *CPMR 1413–37*, vol. 4, pp. 42–43, *CPMR 1364–81*, vol. 2, p. 219.

27. Marci Sortor, "The Measure of Success: Evidence for Immigrant Networks in the Southern Low Countries, Saint-Omer 1413–1455," *Journal of Family History* 30 (April 2005), pp. 179–181.

28. Barron, "The Education and Training of Girls," p. 146.

29. Westminister Abbey Muniment Room, nos. 5959–5966.

30. Ibid., nos. 5966.

31. Ibid., nos. 5959.

32. Ibid., nos. 5960.

33. McIntosh, *Working Women in English Society, 1300–1620* (Cambridge, 2005), pp. 133–134, also makes this observation about female apprenticeship in the fourteenth and fifteenth centuries. But in the sixteenth century it was more common for women to enter apprenticeships.

34. Maryanne Kowaleski and Judith M. Bennett, "Crafts, Gilds, and Women in the Middle Ages: Fifty Years after Marian K. Dale," *Signs* 14 (1989), pp. 474–478. Judith M. Bennett, "Working Together: Women and Men in the Brewers' Gild of London, c. 1420," in *The Salt of Common Life: Individuality and Choice in the Medieval Town, Countryside and Church*, ed. Edwin DeWindt (Kalamazoo, Mich., 1995), p. 36. Although Barron, "The Education and Training of Young Girls," p. 145, found a late fifteenth-century guild ordinance that says that men and women could be admitted as apprentices, Judith Bennett does not find them in her more extensive study, *Ale, Beer, and Brewsters in England* (New York, 1996).

35. Phillips, *Medieval Maidens*, pp. 133–134, says that the silkwomen apprenticed girls in an organized and widespread manner, but her evidence for this is weak.

36. Heather Swanson, *Medieval Artisans: An Urban Class in Late Medieval England* (Oxford, 1989), p. 116, suggests that "the place of women in training a skilled workforce was crucial and makes a nonsense of much of the system of apprenticeship." Merry E. Wiesner, "Having Her Own Smoke: Employment and Independence for Singlewomen in Germany, 1400–1750," in *Singlewomen in the European Past, 1250–1800*, ed. Judith M. Bennett and Amy M. Froide (Philadelphia, 1999), p. 206, shows that home training was common in early modern Germany.

37. Some authors have conflated the position of servant and apprentice, but the apprentice contract was very different from the service contract. It was for a longer period, and it built in protections for the contracting parties. Jane Whittle, "Servants in Rural England c. 1450–1650: Hired Work as a Means of Accumulating Wealth and Skills before Marriage," in *The Marital Economy in Scandinavia and Britain, 1400–1900*, ed. Maria Ågren and Amy Louise Erickson (Aldershot, 2005), pp. 89–107, points out that "life-cycle" servants were able to learn skills and save money toward marriage.

38. Mary Bateson, ed., *Borough Customs*, SS, no. 18 (London, 1904), vol. 1, pp. 229–230.

39. A. H. Thomas, introduction to *CPMR 1364–81*, vol. 2, p. lx.

40. *CPMR 1413–37*, vol. 4, p. 176. *CPMR 1437–57*, vol. 5, p. 88. Other examples: *CPMR 1413–37*, vol. 4, pp. 42–43, 71, 162, 208.

41. CLRO MC 1/2A, and *CPMR 1413–37*, vol. 4, p. 166.

42. TNA: PRO C1/3/117, *CPMR 1413–37*, vol. 4, pp. 42–43. See also *CPMR 1364–81*, vol. 2, p. 107. *LBF 1337–52*, p. 142.

43. *LBG 1352–74*, p. 105. See also *LBI 1400–1422*, p. 76, *LBH 1375–99*, p. 182.

44. *CPMR 1437–57*, vol. 5, p. 65. See also TNA: PRO C1/155/10.

45. *CPMR 1413–37*, vol. 4, p. 53.

46. *CPMR 1413–37*, vol. 4, pp. 146–147.

47. *CPMR 1381–1412*, vol. 3, p. 240 (1397).

48. *LBD 1309–14*, p. ix.

49. See Hanawalt, *Growing Up in Medieval London*, pp. 129–181, for the male experience with apprenticeship. While the young men who were enrolled in the 1309–12 chamberlain's account shows that seven years was normal, about a third served a longer period. The service of male apprentices became ten years in the fifteenth century. Even in the earlier register, youths agreed to sixteen-year terms.

50. Six were said to have agreed to serve seven years, two each for eight and nine years, and then the spread is one for four years, one for five years, one for ten years, one for eleven years, one for fourteen, and one for fifteen.

51. *CPMR 1364–81*, vol. 2, p. 107 (1369).

52. *CPMR 1413–37*, vol. 4, p. 222. See also CLRO MC 1/2/141 (1392), in which the original bill suggested that Isabelle had been apprenticed when she was thirteen. But another man, who also claimed her as an apprentice, said that she was sixteen when apprenticed and would serve until she was nineteen.

53. *LBG 1352–74*, p. 105. Thrupp, *Merchant Class*, p. 172.

54. *CPMR 1413–37*, vol. 4, pp. 42–43. *CPMR 1323–64*, vol. 1, p. 274. See also *CPMR 1364–81*, vol. 2, p. 107, *CPMR 1437–57*, vol. 5, p. 65, CLRO MC 1/2/3. Charges of abuse might be made either by the apprentice herself or by the parents or kin.

55. See Hanawalt, *Growing Up in Medieval London*, pp. 157–163, for the abuses that were addressed regarding male apprentices and the intervention of family and friends.

56. *LBK 1422–61*, p. 17.

57. *CPMR 1413–37*, vol. 4, pp. 53–54.

58. *CPMR 1413–37*, vol. 4, p. 12.

59. *CPMR 1437–57*, vol. 5, pp. 14–15.

60. *CPMR 1364–81*, vol. 2, p. 219.

61. Darrel Amundsen and Carol Jean Dries, "The Age of Menarche in Medieval Europe," *Human Biology* 45 (1973), pp. 363–368.

62. James A. Brundage, *Law, Sex, and Christian Society in Medieval Europe* (Chicago, 1987), pp. 53, 91–92, 156, 199, 242, 283, 451, 508. Charles T. Wood, "The Doctor's Dilemma: Sin, Salvation, and the Menstrual Cycle," *Speculum* 56 (1981), pp. 710–727.

63. Burrow, *Ages of Man*, p. 27. Warren R. Dawson, ed., *A Leechbook or Collection of Medical Recipes of the Fifteenth Century* (London, 1934), pp. 123–124, 249, has recipes for curing pimples and for the flow of blood in menstruation. These cures must have been part of many household recipe books in fifteenth-century England.

64. Rickert, *The Babee's Book*, pp. 33–36, 4.

65. Ibid., pp. 34–36.

66. Wunderli, *London Church Courts and Society*, pp. 89–90.

67. Rossell Hope Robbins, ed., *Secular Lyrics of the Fourteenth and Fifteenth Centuries* (Oxford, 1952), pp. 16–19.

68. TNA: PRO C1/214/91. Some men were suspected of making a practice of deflowering virgins in their neighborhood (GL, Ms. 9064/2, fol. 159v.)

69. TNA: PRO C1/45/24. Of course, the case appeared in a Chancery petition because Philip did not pay and continued to vex the family.

70. John T. Appleby, ed. and trans., *The Chronicle of Richard of Devizes in the Time of Richard the First* (London, 1963), pp. 65–66, has a French Jew warning a younger man about the pitfalls of London that mentions pimps, prostitutes, and singing and dancing girls, but also "smooth-skin lads," "pretty boys," "effeminates, pederasts" and other bad people. But the secular records do not mention the sexual corruption of young boys and mention only one woman who dressed like a priest to practice prostitution.

71. *LBL 1461–1509*, p. 103. See also GL, Ms. 9064/1, fol. 55.

72. *LBL 1461–1509*, p. 103.

73. G. D. G. Hall, ed. and trans., *Tractatus de legibus et consuetudinibus regni Anglie qui Glanvilla vocatur* [The treatise on the laws and customs of the realm of England commonly called Glanville] (London, 1965), pp. 175–176. "In the crime of rape [*raptus crimen*] a woman charges a man with violating her by force in the peace

of the lord king. A woman who suffers in this way must go, soon after the deed is done, to the nearest vill and there show to trustworthy men the injury done to her, and any effusion of blood there may be and any tearing of her clothes. She should then do the same to the reeve of the hundred. Afterwards she should proclaim it publicly in the next county court." G.H. Boodbine and S. E. Thorne, eds., *Bracton on the Laws and Customs of England* (Cambridge, Mass., 1968–77), vol. 2, pp. 416–17. F. M. Nicholas, ed., *Britton* (London, 1865), bk. 1, pp. 17, 55. H. G. Richardson and G. O. Sayles, eds., *Fleta*, Seldon Society, no. 72 (London, 1955), bk. 1, p. 89, and William J. Whittaker, ed., *The Mirror of Justices*, SS, vol. 7 (London, 1895), p. 103. Frederick Pollock and Frederic William Maitland, *The History of English Law before the Time of Edward I*, 2nd ed. (Cambridge, 1898; reprint, Cambridge, 1968), vol. 2, pp. 490–491. The best analysis of the Statutes of Westminster, their provisions, and their enforcement is Harold N. Schneebach, "The Law of Felony in Medieval England from the Accession of Edward I until the Mid-fourteenth Century" (Ph.D. diss., University of Iowa, 1973), vol. 2, pp. 433–506. J. B. Post, "Ravishment of Women and the Statutes of Westminster," in *Legal Records and the Historian: Papers Presented to the Cambridge Legal History Conference 1975*, ed. J. H. Baker (London, 1978), pp. 150–164. Ruth Kittel, "Rape in Thirteenth-Century England: A Study of the Common-Law Courts," in *Women and the Law: The Social Historical Perspective*, ed. D. Kelly Weisberg (Cambridge, Mass., 1982), vol. 2, pp. 101–116. Barbara A. Hanawalt, *Crime and Conflict in English Communities* (Cambridge, Mass., 1979). The crime of rape became distinct from that of ravishment, which was directed at securing the property of a woman through carrying her off. The expert on this subject is Sue Sheridan Walker, "Common Law Juries and Feudal Marriage Customs in Medieval England: The Pleas of Ravishment," *University of Illinois Law Review* 3 (1984), pp. 705–718; "Punishing Convicted Ravishers: Statutory Strictures and Actual Practice in Thirteenth- and Fourteenth-Century England," *Journal of Medieval History* 13 (1987), pp. 237–50; "Wrongdoing and Compensation: The Pleas of Wardship in Thirteenth- and Fourteenth- Century England," *Journal of Legal History* 32 (1988), pp. 267–309.

74. Hanawalt, *Crime and Conflict in English Communities*, pp. 59–66, 153. In an eight-county survey, only 79 rape indictments were made out of 15,952, or only 0.2 percent of the cases. Only 10 percent of the indictments ended in conviction, and most of these were of young, virginal girls.

75. *CPMR 1437–57*, vol. 5, p. 162.

76. TNA: PRO C1/66/233.

77. Barbara A. Hanawalt, "Whose Story Was This? Rape Narratives in Medieval English Courts," in *"Of Good and Ill Repute": Gender and Social Control in Medieval England* (New York, 1998), pp. 124–141. This essay offers a complete analysis of the case and compares Joan's story to a crime-victim case from modern urban tales.

78. Helen M. Cam, ed., *The Eyre of London, 14 Edward II, A.D. 1321*, SS, no. 26, pt. 1 (London, 1968), pp. xxiii–xxiv, 87–91. Elsie Shanks, ed., *Novae Narrationes*,

with a legal introduction by S. F. C. Milsom, SS, vol. 80 (London, 1963), pp. 341–344.

79. For a complete discussion of prostitution in England see Ruth Mazo Karras, *Common Women: Prostitution and Sexuality in Medieval England* (New York, 1966).

80. *CPMR 1437–57*, vol. 5, pp. 13–14.

81. CLRO, Letter Book N, 1515–26, pp. 39–40. (This is an unpublished calendar.)

82. CLRO, Letter Book N, 1515–26, pp. 39–40. See also *LBK 1422–61*, pp. 216–217, in which a maiden in the service of a neighbor was enticed into a bawdy house and debauched against her will. In *CPMR 1437–57*, vol. 5, pp. 13–14 (1439), a woman sold a girl to unknown Lombards, who deflowered her against her will and then took her to the stews in Southwark on four occasions. For cases from the London ecclesiastical courts, see Richard Wunderli, *London Church Courts and Society on the Eve of the Reformation* (Cambridge, Mass., 1981), pp. 91–96.

83. GL, Ms. 9064/10.

84. Wunderli, *London Church Courts and Society*, pp. 91–92. In the Commissary court, the four cases were of "spiritual kin"—that is, godparents. None ended in conviction.

85. Henry Thomas Riley, ed., *Memorials of London and London Life in the Thirteenth, Fourteenth, and Fifteenth Centuries* (London, 1869), p. 140.

86. Arnold van Gennep, *The Rites of Passage*, trans. Monika B. Vizedom and Gabriella L. Caffee (1908; reprint, Chicago, 1960) chap. 6, "Initiation Rites," contains his distinction between physical puberty and social puberty. Victor W. Turner, *The Ritual Process: Structure and Anti-Structure* (New York, 1969).

Chapter 3

1. Edith Rickert, ed. and trans., *The Babee's Book: Medieval Manners for the Young: Done into Modern English from Dr. Furnivall's Texts* (New York, 1966), p. 41.

2. Mary Bateson, ed., *Borough Customs*, SS, no. 21 (London, 1904), vol. 2, p. lxxxviii. Both purchased and inherited property could be assigned to heirs in London.

3. Charles Phythian-Adams, *Desolation of a City: Coventry and the Urban Crisis of the Late Middle Ages* (Cambridge, 1979), pp. 84–85, found that in 1523, 43 percent of the female population over age fifteen was unmarried. Equivalent data do not exist for London.

4. Sylvia L. Thrupp, *The Merchant Class of Medieval London, 1300–1500* (Chicago, 1948), p. 196.

5. Information is scattered through the Letter Books. The ages are not usually given, but instead one can calculate age of marriage or inheritance if the age of entry into wardship is given as well as the date of exit. A few examples include *LBG 1352–74*, p. 10, age nineteen; p. 91, age nineteen; pp. 95–96, age twenty-seven, age thirty; p. 181, age sixteen; pp. 147–148, age nineteen; pp. 317–319, age eighteen. *LBH 1375–99*, p. 127 (1379), describes a girl as being "more than 15"; pp. 160–161, age twelve; p. 165, age seventeen and more; p. 186 (1403) describes

the inheritor as "well over 21"; and p. 357 says that the girl was fourteen when she married without the mayor's permission. *LBK 1422–61*, p. 42, age twenty-one. Sometimes the girl is simply described as married but under age (under sixteen presumably) when she died. Steve Rappaport, *Worlds within Worlds: Structures of Life in Sixteenth-Century London* (Cambridge, 1989), p. 68, thinks that in the sixteenth century women married in their midtwenties.

6. Barbara Megson, "Life Expectations of the Widows and Orphans of Freemen in London 1375–1399," *Local Population Studies* (1999), pp. 18–29, has made a thorough study of *LBH 1375–99*. She found (p. 26) that in eleven cases the girls were under twenty-one when they married with an average age of fifteen. Five of these were under the age of sixteen.

7. Ibid., p. 26. Those girls with an inheritance of over £100 tended to marry earlier.

8. David Nicholas, *The Domestic Life of a Medieval City: Women, Children, and the Family in Fourteenth-Century Ghent* (Lincoln, Neb., 1985), p. 24. The evidence is unclear about how common this age of marriage was or if it was simply permissible.

9. David Herlihy, *Medieval Households* (Cambridge, 1985), pp. 103, 110–111. Stanley Chojnacki, *Women and Men in Renaissance Venice: Twelve Essays on Patrician Society* (Baltimore, 2000), pp. 186–193, found variation in the age of marriage among the patricians. Maryanne Kowaleski, "Singlewomen in Medieval and Early Modern Europe: The Demographic Perspective," in *Singlewomen in the European Past, 1250–1800*, ed. Judith M. Bennett and Amy M. Froide (Philadelphia, 1999), pp. 39–44, has a summary of material on the age of first marriage from secondary literature.

10. *LBH 1375–99*, p. 384 (1385); *LBG 1352–74*, p. 181 (1364).

11. *LBK 1422–61*, p. 26.

12. *LBK 1422–61*, pp. 378, 380.

13. *LBK 1422–61*, p. 42 (1425). In *HW*, vol. 2, p. 5, Simon Fraunceys, a mercer, used his will to reiterate his provisions for his daughter's marriage: "And whereas he had already given to Alice his daughter and the heirs of her body his lands, tenements, and rents opposite la Ledenhalle, he wishes that in case she die without such heirs" that the property be sold for pious uses.

14. Megson, "Life Expectations," pp. 26–27, draws the same conclusion.

15. Bennett and Froide, "A Singular Past," pp. 1–37, and Kowaleski, "Singlewomen in Medieval and Early Modern Europe," pp. 38–81, in Bennett and Froide, *Singlewomen in the European Past, 1350–1800* (Philadelphia, 1999). Both these articles suggest that while marriage was a common assumption, there were, particularly in urban centers, a substantial portion of single women. Some of these would never marry, but some would eventually marry—a life-cycle pattern in which women delayed marriage until they had worked for a while. Shannon McSheffrey, *Love and Marriage in Late Medieval London*, Consortium for the Teaching of the Middle Ages (TEAMS): Documents and Practice Series (Kalamazoo, Mich., 1995), pp. 16–17, has used late fifteenth-century London ecclesiastical court depositions to investigate marriages of servants and laborers.

16. For a discussion of age of marriage in York, see P. J. P. Goldberg, "Marriage, Migration, Servanthood, and Life Cycle in Yorkshire Towns of the Later Middle Ages," *Continuity and Change* 1 (1986), pp. 153–154. Goldberg, "Female Labour, Service, and Marriage in Northern Towns during the Later Middle Ages," *Northern History* 22 (1986), pp. 25–26, has made much of very slim data (twenty-one couples) over a number of years, arguing that because the couples were closer together in age, they had "companionate marriages." His data, like other English data on the age of marriage for the lower classes, are minimal. See also P. J. P. Goldberg, *Women, Work and Life Cycle in a Medieval Economy: Women in York and Yorkshire, c. 1300–1520* (Oxford, 1992), pp. 225–230. The presumption of Goldberg and many other authors is that couples in the late Middle Ages tended to marry at a later age and that there were a number of single people in the society. John Hatcher, "Understanding the Population History of England 1450–1750," *Past and Present* 180 (2003), pp. 89–99, has argued against this view.

17. Vivien Brodsky Elliott, "Single Women in the London Marriage Market: Age, Status and Mobility, 1598–1619," in *Marriage and Society: Studies in the Social History of Marriage*, ed. P. D. Outhwaite (New York, 1982), pp. 81–100, found that there were two marriage patterns for first marriages. The upper classes tended to have a greater age disparity between the husband and wife than the lower-status couples.

18. GL, Ms. 9051/1, fols. 92, 85v. See also fols. 98v, 101v (80 marks toward marriage), and 207 (10 marks toward marriage). GL, Ms. 9171/1, fol. 60. A widow gave 10 marks to her goddaughter for her marriage. In another case in the same court, the daughter received 10 marks toward marriage, GL, Ms. 9171/5, fol. 21.

19. *LBK 1422–61*, p. 26 (1423–27). See also *LBH 1375–99*, p. 8 (1375) and p. 73 (1377), and *LBK 1422–61*, p. 12.

20. *LBG 1352–74*, p. 201 (1365, 1369).

21. *LBG 1352–74*, p. 158 (1363); *LBH 1375–99*, p. 8 (1375); *LBH 1375–99*, p. 73 (1377); *LBK 1422–61*, p. 12 (1423). Alice, daughter of Simon Herrward, went into wardship in 1423, but died in 1439 under the age of twenty-one. *LBK 1422–61*, p. 9.

22. *LBE 1314–37*, pp. 192–193.

23. *LBG 1352–74*, pp. 147–148.

24. Barbara A. Hanawalt, *Growing Up in Medieval London: The Experience of Childhood in History* (New York, 1993), pp. 202–203.

25. *LBK 1422–61*, p. 70.

26. *LBG 1352–74*, pp. 152–153 (1363).

27. CIPM 1361–65, vol. 11, pp. 462–463. Friends and neighbors took great care to see that property descended to rightful heirs. The two nieces of Master Richard Plescy in 1364 received substantial tenements, houses, shops, and gardens scattered throughout London. Both of these women were over forty. See also CIPM 1365–70, vol. 12, pp. 9–10, in which the niece of Walter Cobbe of London was also over forty when she received two small tenements with gardens,

and *CIPM 1405–13*, vol. 19, p. 50, in which Geoffrey Boure died in 1369 and left his property worth 10 marks yearly to his children. By 1405 the sole survivor was a woman who held the property because her siblings had all predeceased her.

28. Amy Louise Erickson, "The Marital Economy in Comparative Perspective," in *The Marital Economy in Scandinavia and Britain, 1400–1900*, ed. Maria Ågren and Amy Louise Erickson (Aldershot, 2005), p. 11. The information includes Sweden-Finland and Denmark-Norway in comparison to England-Scotland (excluding London).

29. Barbara Diefendorf, "Women and Property in *Ancien Régime* France: Theory and Practice in Dauphiné and Paris," in *Early Modern Conceptions of Property*, ed. John Brewer and Susan Staves (London, 1995), pp. 175–176. In Paris in the sixteenth and seventeenth centuries, the husband could not easily alienate inherited property. But property in the dowry that was communal could be alienated. For more information on the specific cases see Diefendorf, *Paris City Councillors in the Sixteenth Century: The Politics of Patrimony* (Princeton, 1983).

30. *HW*, vol. 1, p. 289.

31. *HW*, vol. 2, p. 9. In *LBF 1337–52*, pp. 76–77, Alice, granddaughter of Isabella Paas, inherited a brewery that had belonged to her. *CIPM 1374–77*, vol. 14, p. 35, expressed the legal limitations clearly: "long before his death he [John of Hengston] married Isabel daughter and heir of John Lorymer, she being seized of the above two messuages. He had no other estate therein save in her right."

32. *CPMR 1413–37*, vol. 4 (1432), pp. 265–266.

33. Frederick Pollok and Frederic William Maitland, *The History of English Law before the Time of Edward I*, 2nd ed. (Cambridge, 1968), vol. 2, pp. 83–84.

34. *CPMR 1364–81*, vol. 2, p. 132 (1371). In another case Marion Joynour won her suit and received her deed: *CPMR 1364–81*, vol. 2, p. 205 (1375). But Sara, wife of Robert Curson, was not as successful and did not get the deeds: *CPMR 1381–1412*, vol. 3, p. 241 (1396).

35. Helena M. Chew and Martin Weinbaum, eds., *The London Eyre of 1244*, LRS, vol. 6 (Leicester, 1970), p. 100. See also p. 88, indicating that Orfilia, daughter of Alan Ceyle of Laron, inherited a messuage in Gracechurch Street. She was denied the inheritance because her father was convicted of a felony and the king took it into his hands. But it was then discovered that Alan had died in prison before he was tried, and the land was returned to Orfilia. Jenny Kermode, *Medieval Merchants: York, Beverley and Hull in the Later Middle Ages* (Cambridge, 1998), pp. 91–92, shows that women in these northern boroughs were well aware of their rights in inheritance, but also sometimes had a struggle protecting their rights.

36. *CIPM 1365–70*, vol. 12, p. 43.

37. *CIPM 1370–74*, vol. 13, pp. 160–162. See also *CIPM 1365–70*, vol. 12, pp. 150–152, 235, 260; *CIPM 1413–18*, vol. 20, pp. 81, 259; *CIPM 1405–18*, vol. 19, p. 143; vol. 14, p. 205. *LBF 1337–52*, pp. 76–77. Alice, daughter of John de la March, did not get her inheritance until her father, who held by curtesy of England, died.

38. Henry Thomas Riley, ed., *Chronicles of the Mayors and Sheriffs of London, A.D. 1188–1274* (London, 1863), pp. 8–9.

39. CLRO, Husting Court Wills and Deeds, roll 30, Nov. 20, 1300–Nov. 19, 1301.

40. Ibid., roll 75 (1347–48) ms. 7, 8, 13, 15. Joseph P. Huffman, *Family, Commerce, and Religion in London and Cologne, Anglo-German Emigrants c. 1000–c. 1300* (Cambridge, 1998), pp. 67–70, suggests the possibility that these are mortgage tokens. Again, it is a way of keeping track of the real ownership of the property, although the token is a symbolic rather than a written transaction.

41. *HW*, vol.1, pp. 213–214.

42. *HW*, vol.1, p. 569.

43. *CIPM 1374–77*, vol. 14, p. 1.

44. *CIPM 1377–83*, vol. 15, p. 163. See also p. 129.

45. *CIPM 1352–61*, vol. 10, p. 142.

46. Frederick Furnivall, ed., *Political, Religious, and Love Poems from the Archbishop of Canterbury's Lambeth Ms. No. 306, and Other Sources*, EETS, o.s., vol. 15 (London, 1866; new ed. 1903), p. 44.

47. Lord John de Drokensford, for instance, bought up a number of contiguous properties, perhaps with the aim of building a town house for himself. He was in the service of the king and often in London. Even as bishop of Bath and Wells he frequented London. CLRO, Husting Court Wills and Deeds, roll 30, Nov. 30, 1300–Nov. 19, 1301. Kermode, *Medieval Merchants*, p. 102, observed a similar pattern in northern cities.

48. Bateson, *Borough Custom*, vol. 2, p. ci.

49. Michael M. Sheehan, *Marriage, Family, and Law in Medieval Europe: Collected Essays*, ed. James K. Farge (Toronto, 1996), p. 20.

50. Bateson, *Borough Customs*, vol. 2, p. xcix.

51. *HW*, vol. 2, pp. 90, 16, 103. GL, Ms. 9051/1, fol. 101v (1403), records a brewer who reserved for dowry of his daughter 80 marks sterling as well as a piece of silver with a lid of silver, six silver spoons, a mazer bound with silver, and two of his best beds with sheets and other such items, five brass pots of various sizes, one napkin and one towel. *CPMR 1381–1412*, vol. 3, p. 127 (1387), records a case of an orphan who married with a dowry of 100 marks, a small mazer with a covercle of mazer, bound with silver gilt, four plain pieces of silver, one set with a covercle to the same, and one second-best bed.

52. *CPMR 1364–81*, vol. 2, p. 185 (1375). See also *LBE 1314–37*, p. 23 (1314), and *LBI 1400–1422*, pp. 16, 199, 170, 264, 272.

53. Gudrun Andersson, "Forming the Partnership Socially and Economically: A Swedish Local Elite, 1650–1770," in *The Marital Economy in Scandinavia and Britain, 1400–1900*, ed. Maria Ågren and Amy Louise Erickson (Aldershot, 2005), pp. 58–73.

54. Susan Mosher Stuard, "Marriage Gifts and Fashion Mischief," in *The Medieval Marriage Scene: Prudence, Passion, Policy*, ed. Sherry Roush and Cristelle L. Baskin, Medieval and Renaissance Texts and Studies, vol. 299 (Tempe, Ariz., 2005), pp. 169–185.

55. CPMR *1381–1412*, vol. 3, p. 155 (1389). In a case in CPMR *1381–1412*, vol. 3, p. 103 (1385), three powerful men of London arranged for the purchase of property for a young couple worth £300, of which a third would come from the father of the groom and two-thirds from her inheritance. Death of the parties caused the bond to be nullified. See also CPMR *1413–37*, vol. 4, p. 47 (1416).

56. LBI *1400–1422*, pp. 253–254.

57. GL, Ms. 9051/2, fols. 207 and 98v.

58. GL, Ms. 9171/6, fol. 280v (1479).

59. HW, vol. 1, p. 243 (1313). See also CPMR *1437–57*, vol. 5, p. 25 (1439).

60. TNA: PRO C1/83/86, CI/31/351, C1/64/985, C1/33/71.

61. In TNA: PRO C1/32/334. CI/196/46, the groom was promised £100. In C1/216/68, the widow, the executor of her former husband, did not honor the dowry arrangement, which included £100, a gold ring, a horse called an Irish hoby, and the lease of a quay to hold for thirty-four years.

62. TNA: PRO C1/138/24.

63. Anne F. Sutton, *The Mercery of London: Trade, Goods and People, 1130–1578* (Aldershot, 2005), pp. 208–209.

64. Bateson, *Borough Customs*, vol. 2, p. xcvii. *Usufruct* is often the legal term used.

65. Bateson, *Borough Customs*, vol. 2, p. 126.

66. LBE *1314–37*, p. 33. For another case see CPMR *1381–1412*, vol. 3, pp. 177–178 (1391). The footnotes to this case involving Alice, widow of William Ancroft, explain the custom of London regarding the "widow's chamber" and the goods in it very clearly.

67. CPMR *1413–37*, vol. 4, p. 206 (1427).

68. HW, vol. 1, p. xli. Sharpe points out in his introduction to HW that the provisions for widows was better than in common law. Pollock and Maitland, *History of English Law*, vol. 2, pp. 374–375. The marriage did not need to take place at the church door, although it could, but the public announcement of the dower and dowry had to be made there. McSheffrey, *Love and Marriage*, pp. 47–48, found that the dower might be announced within the church.

69. HW, vol. 1, p. 45.

70. For common law, as opposed to borough law on dower see: Janet S. Loengard, "'Of the Gift of Her Husband': English Dower and Its Consequences in the Year 1200," in *Women in the Medieval World: Essays in Honor of John H. Mundy*, ed. J. Kirshner and S. F. Wemple (New York, 1985), pp. 215–237. Paul Brand, "'Deserving' and 'Undeserving' Wives: Earning and Forfeiting Dower in Medieval England," *Journal of Legal History* 22 (2001), pp. 1–20.

71. HW, vol. 1, p. 187.

72. HW, vol.1, p. 375.

73. HW, vol.1, p. xl.

74. GL, Ms. 9051/1 and Ms. 9051/2. The wills start in 1393 but are largely fifteenth-century.

75. For a brief summary of the common-law practice of jointure, which grew increasingly popular in the fourteenth century, see Mavis E. Mate, *Women in*

Medieval English Society (Cambridge, 1999), pp. 78–82. A fifteenth-century method of endowing widows with enfeoffment to "Use" was popular among the aristocracy, but in *HW*, vol. 1, p. xxiii, Sharpe points out that use, which became popular in common law, was exempted in the case of London and other cities because of borough tenure.

76. Bateson, *Borough Custom*, vol. 2, pp. lxxxviii, xciii.

77. *HW*, vol. 1, p. 287.

78. *HW*, vol. 1, p. 64.

79. *LBE 1314–37*, p. 108 (1319).

80. *LBH 1375–99*, p. 2 (1375).

81. *LBI 1400–1422*, p. 195 (1417–18).

82. Joel T. Rosenthal, *Patriarchy and Families of Privilege in Fifteenth-Century England* (Philadelphia, 1991), pp. 34, 106–111.

83. Barbara A. Hanawalt, *The Ties That Bound: Peasant Families in Medieval England* (New York, 1986), pp. 142–144.

84. Amy Louise Erickson, *Woman and Property in Early Modern England* (London, 1993), pp. 61–78, found that in the sixteenth and early seventeenth centuries, the practice in the countryside was to distribute property as equitably as possible.

85. Bateson, *Borough Customs*, vol. 2, p. cxiii.

86. Diefendorf, "Women and Property in *ancien régime* France," pp. 172–174, 177–182. Parisian widows had the right of return of lineage (inherited) property in addition to half of the community property. The other half was to be divided among the husband's nearest heirs. In statutory law regions, the wife received the return of dowry and the portion allotted to her in the marriage contract. Increasingly, the husband's will fixed the amount the widow received.

87. Nicholas, *Domestic Life*, pp. 26–27; see chap. 6 for Ghent's protection of wards. Again, the clan determined the wardship of children, rather than the mother.

88. Martha C. Howell, *The Marriage Exchange: Property, Social Place, and Gender in Cities of the Low Countries, 1300–1550* (Chicago, 1998), pp. 30–34.

89. Bateson, *Borough Customs*, vol. 2, pp. cvi–cvii.

90. Diane Owen Hughes, "From Brideprice to Dowry in Mediterranean Europe," *Journal of Family History* 3 (1978), pp. 262–296. Georges Duby, in *Medieval Marriage* (Baltimore, 1978), argued that about the same time in France the aristocratic families also switched to a dowry system.

91. Thomas Kuehn, *Law, Family, and Women: Toward a Legal Anthropology of Renaissance Italy* (Chicago, 1994), pp. 238–257. He sees some modification of the inheritance laws in favor of women over distant agnatic kin, but on the whole the system remained very much a male-dominated inheritance system. Ann Crabb, *The Strozzi of Florence: Widowhood and Family Solidarity in the Renaissance* (Ann Arbor, 2000), pp. 35–36. She found that wills modified the strict inheritance laws but women did not benefit in great numbers.

92. Chojnacki, *Women and Men in Renaissance Venice*, pp. 116–121.

93. Crabb, *The Strozzi of Florence*, pp. 37–38. Chojnacki, *Women and Men in Renaissance Venice*, pp. 117–118.
94. Nicholas, *Domestic Life in a Medieval City*, pp. 26–27.
95. Howell, *The Marriage Exchange*, p. 37. The bride's *portement* was listed in order to guarantee that as a widow she would receive the *reprise* or the return of the property she brought to the marriage.
96. Chojnacki, *Women and Men in Renaissance Venice*, p. 121.
97. Ibid., p. 132. Widows, with these lavish dowries, responded by increasing their bequests to their daughters and female kin to increase their dowries, p. 126.
98. David Herlihy and Christiane Klapisch-Zuber, *Tuscans and their Families: A Study of the Florentine Catasto of 1437* (New Haven, 1985), pp. 224–226. See also Christiane Klapisch-Zuber, *Women, Family, and Ritual in Renaissance Florence* (Chicago, 1885), pp. 221–224. Anthony Molho, *Marriage Alliance in Late Medieval Florence* (Cambridge, Mass., 1994), pp. 298–324, has the most complete discussion.
99. Molho, *Marriage Alliance in Late Medieval Florence*, pp. 27–79.

Chapter 4

1. Amy Louise Erickson, "The Marital Economy in Comparative Perspective," in *The Marital Economy in Scandinavia and Britain, 1400–1900*, ed. Maria Ågren and Amy Louise Erickson (Aldershot, 2005), p. 11, points out that England differed from the Scandinavian countries and France in requiring a wife to take the husband's name.
2. Shannon McSheffrey, "Men and Masculinity in Late Medieval London Civic Culture: Governance, Patriarchy and Reputation," in *Conflicted Identities and Multiple Masculinities*, ed. Jacqueline Murray (New York, 1999), pp. 243–278. She has discussed the formation of marriage, using the Consistory court of London for her source. She takes the point of view that marriage arrangement enhanced patriarchy. See also McSheffrey, *Love and Marriage in Late Medieval London*, TEAMS, Documents of Practice Series, Medieval Institute Publications (Kalamazoo, Mich., 1995). *Marriage, Sex, and Civic Culture in Late Medieval London* (Philadelphia, 2006). This book came out too late for inclusion in this book. See also Catherine Frances, "Making Marriages in Early Modern England: Rethinking the Role of Family and Friends," in *The Marital Economy in Scandinavia and Britain, 1400–1900*, ed. Maria Ågren and Amy Louise Erickson (Aldershot, 2005), pp. 40–55. Robert C. Palmer, "Contexts of Marriage in Medieval England: Evidence from the King's Court circa 1300," *Speculum* 59 (1984), pp. 42–67.
3. Elizabeth Ewan, "'To the Longer Liver': Provisions for the Dissolution of the Marital Economy in Scotland, 1470–1550," in *The Marital Economy in Scandinavia and Britain, 1400–1900*, ed. Maria Ågren and Amy Louise Erickson (Aldershot, 2005), pp. 191–206. While notarial records do not exist for London, there are some notarial protocol books in Scotland that clearly show the property arrangements of the marital economy.

4. Richard Helmholz, *Marriage Litigation in Medieval England* (Cambridge, 1974), pp. 72–87.

5. Helmholz, *Marriage Litigation*, pp. 25–73. Michael M. Sheehan, "The Formation and Stability of Marriage: Evidence of an Ely Register," *Mediaeval Studies* 33 (1971), pp. 228–237.

6. In "Mutatis Mutandis," the moralists deplore the misguidedness of the love match: "Self-will is taken for reason / True love for fancy choosth." Margot Adamson, ed., *A Treasury of Middle English Verse Selected and Rendered into Modern English* (London, 1930), p. 147.

7. Historians debate the point at which "love" became part of the expectation of a happy marriage. Alan Macfarlane, *Marriage and Love in England, 1300–1840* (Oxford, 1986), and Lawrence Stone, *The Family, Sex, and Marriage in England 1500–1800* (New York, 1977).

8. TNA: PRO C1/67/185. He was not alone. Richard "Goun" was apprenticed to a draper, but he ran away and married Alice, daughter of Simon Herward, late a mercer. She was apprenticed to a silkwoman and was a city orphan. Richard went to prison for his offense. See *LBK 1422–1461*, p. 208 (1436). See also *CEMCR 1298–1307*, p. 47 (1299). The Mercer's Company rule was that an apprentice who married had to finish his term, but he was allowed to receive wages for his work so that he could support his wife. Laetitia Lyell, ed., with F. D. Watney, *Acts of Court of the Mercer's Company, 1453–1527* (Cambridge, 1936), p. 186.

9. Christine Carpenter, ed., *Kingsford's Stonor Letters and Papers, 1290–1483* (Cambridge, 1996), vol. 2, no. 176. The original publication was C. L. Kingsford, ed., *The Stonor Letters and Papers, 1290–1483*, Camden Society, third series, vols. 29, 30, 34 (1919–24).

10. See McSheffrey, "Men and Masculinity," pp. 245–252.

11. Alison Hanham, *The Celys and Their World: An English Merchant Family of the Fifteenth Century* (Cambridge, 1985), p. 309.

12. *LBI 1400–1422*, p. 141 (1415). See TNA: PRO C1/6/89, in which John Welyngton, a young orphan, petitioned the chancellor about the sale of the rights over his marriage by William Brekspere of London for £20. In addition, £24 accrued to William from the residue of the sale.

13. TNA: PRO C1/20/137.

14. TNA: PRO C1/26/286. See also C1/43/65.

15. TNA: PRO C1/64/271.

16. GL, Ms. 9064/3, fol. 172v.

17. McSheffrey, "Men and Masculinity," pp. 243–244. In a complex case of 1489 that appeared in the Consistory court of London, witnesses were called to testify to the validity of a marriage. Thomas Wulley sued Margaret Isot to honor a contract they had made in 1471. The witnesses told a story of fornication and forced marriage. Thomas and Margaret had been lovers against the will of Thomas's parents. When his mother found him in bed with Margaret at Margaret's house, she stole his shoes so that he would have to walk home in Margaret's shoes.

But the parents were unable to stop the affair. Thomas's father went to a constable and asked him to catch the two lovers in the act. The constable did, and the couple were forced to exchange marriage vows. This early sexual adventure, against parental wishes, had not ended well for Wulley, who appealed to the Church court eighteen years later to honor the contract.

18. TNA: PRO C1/64/299.

19. "How the Wise Man Taught His Son," in Edith Rickert, ed. and trans., *The Babee's Book: Medieval Manners for the Young: Done into Modern English from Dr. Furnivall's Texts* (New York, 1966), pp. 45.

20. CLMC 1350–70, p. 161. See also *LBG, 1352–1374*, pp. 114–115.

21. LBC 1291–1309, pp. 18–19 (1293–1303).

22. TNA: PRO C1/22/144. See also some of the wardship cases previously cited.

23. McSheffrey, "Men and Masculinity," p. 247.

24. TNA: PRO C1/33/9.

25. TNA: PRO C1/166/45.

26. Eric Josef Carlson, *Marriage and the English Reformation* (Oxford, 1994), pp. 106–123.

27. McSheffrey, "Men and Masculinity," p. 248.

28. Ibid., pp. 248–249.

29. For the reading of the banns and the neglect thereof, see James A. Brundage, *Law, Sex, and Christian Society in Medieval Europe* (Chicago, 1987), pp. 441–443.

30. Kenneth Stevenson, *Nuptial Blessing: A Study of Christian Marriage Rites* (New York, 1983), pp. 76–80.

31. Ibid. pp. 237, 244–245. Helmholz, *Marriage Litigation*, p. 30, feels that it is fair to assume that most of the couples who had a private ceremony at home intended to have the church ceremony as well.

32. W. O. Hassall, *How They Lived: An Anthology of Original Accounts Written before 1485* (New York, 1962), p. 99.

33. LBH 1375–99, pp. 183–184.

34. Frederick J. Furnivall, ed., *Early English Meals and Manners: John Russel's Boke of Nurture, Etc.*, EETS, o.s., vol. 32 (London, 1896; reprint, Detroit, 1969), pp. 358–359.

35. For a discussion of the canon law of abstinence, see Brundage, *Law, Sex, and Christian Society*; see p. 164 for an amusing chart on the prohibitions found in penitential literature.

36. E. A. Wrigley and R. S. Schofield, *Population History of England, 1541–1871: A Reconstruction* (Cambridge, Mass., 1981). P. E. H. Hair, "Bridal Pregnancy in Earlier Rural England, further Examined," *Population Studies* 20 (1970), p. 67. Christine Peters, "Gender, Sacrament, and Ritual: The Making and Meaning of Marriage in Late Medieval and Early Modern England," *Past and Present* 169 (Nov. 2000), pp. 63–96.

37. LBE 1314–37, pp. 266–267. See also LBE 1314–37, pp. 47–48, LBF 1337–52, p. 181, LBG 1352–74, pp. 38–39, 163–164, 321–322, LBH 1375–99, p. 52, LBI 1400–1422, p. 141.

38. TNA: PRO C1/64/797. William Young, a gentleman, had agreed to marry a widow and claimed that she was his "well-willer and lover," but her brother objected and had him put into prison (C1/66/308). See also C1/67/199.

39. TNA: PRO C1/66/353.

40. TNA: PRO C1/64/935.

41. TNA: PRO C1/108/13.

42. TNA: PRO C1/47/102. See also C1/60/25, C1/46/457, C1/74/17.

43. TNA: PRO C1/71/7.

44. Richard M. Wunderli, *London Church Courts and Society on the Eve of the Reformation* (Cambridge, Mass., 1981), pp. 118–120. He found only one case of secret marriage, but forty-one people refused to solemnize their marriage.

45. GL, Ms. 9064/1, fol. 137. For other cases of marriages upheld see fols. 39, 40, 104.

46. GL, Ms. 9064/1, fols. 26, 26 d. In another case in the same roll, Joan Beckyn impeded the marriage of Margaret Harryson and George who was in the service of Lord St. John. They had already committed adultery (fol. 17).

47. Wunderli, *London Church Courts*, p. 120.

48. TNA: PRO C1/66/407.

49. TNA: PRO C1/19/459.

50. Alison Truelove, "Commanding Communications: the Fifteenth-Century Letters of the Stonor Women," in *Early Modern Women's Letter Writing, 1450–1700*, ed. James Daybell (New York, 2001), pp. 42–58. For a discussion of the Stonors and their role in fifteenth-century politics see Christine Carpenter, "The Stonor Circle in the Fifteenth Century," in *Rulers and Ruled in Late Medieval England: Essays Presented to Gerald Harris*, ed. Rowena E. Archer and Simon Walker (London, 1995), pp. 175–200.

51. Carpenter, *Kingsford's Stonor Letters and Papers*. A very short biography of Thomas Betson as well as his courtship of Katherine appears in Eileen Power, "Thomas Betson, a Merchant of the Staple in the Fifteenth Century," in Power, *Medieval People* (New York, 1963), pp. 120–151.

52. Hanham, *The Celys and Their World*.

53. It is remarkable how little information is preserved about even prominent London families such as the Ryche (or Riche) family. Possibly Thomas Riche, son of John Riche, was an orphan who was recorded in the mayor's court of orphans in 1460. John Riche left 500 marks to be divided among his four children. Thomas Riche had a sister Katherine, so this is possibly a family name. *LBK 1422–61*, pp. 400–401. Kingsford found that her mother's grandfather, William Gregory, left her 20 s. in his will dated November 6, 1485.

54. Power, *Medieval People*, pp. 125–126.

55. Carpenter, *Stonor Letters*, vol. 2, no. 172.

56. Power, *Medieval People*, pp. 129–131, *Stonor Letters*, vol. 2, no. 166.

57. Eileen Power, "The Ménagier's Wife: A Paris Housewife in the Fourteenth Century," in Power, *Medieval People*, pp. 96–119. The original text from which she took these quotations is Jérôme Pichone, ed., *Le Ménagier de Paris, Traité de Morale et d'Economie Domestique, compose ver 1393 par un Bourgeois Parisien*

public pour la premiè fois par la société des Bibliophiles Francois, 2 vols. (Paris, 1846). For the complete text see Tania Bayard, ed., *A Medieval Home Companion: Housekeeping in the Fourteenth Century* (New York, 1991).

58. Carpenter, *Stonor Letters*, vol. 2, no. 161. I have rendered the quotations throughout into modern English.

59. Ibid., no. 162.

60. Ibid., no. 162. The exchange of tokens was very popular in the late Middle Ages and later. The value might not be high, but they were a reminder of esteem and affection, and were used outside of courtship rituals as well. Barbara A. Hanawalt, "Lady Honor Lisle's Network of Influence," in *Women and Power in the Middle Ages*, ed. Mary Erler and Maryanne Kowaleski (Athens, Ga., 1988), pp. 188–212.

61. Carpenter, *Stonor Letters*, vol. 2, no. 166.

62. Ibid.

63. Ibid.

64. Carpenter, *Stonor Letters*, vol. 2, no. 185.

65. Ibid., no. 216.

66. Ibid., no. 217.

67. Susan Mosher Stuard, "Marriage Gifts and Fashion Mischief," in *The Medieval Marriage Scene: Prudence, Passion, Policy*, ed. Sherry Roush and Cristelle L. Baskins, Medieval and Renaissance Texts and Studies, vol. 299 (Tempe, Ariz., 2005), pp. 169–172. The girdle was just as important in Italy as in England. It was one of the symbolic items of women's dress.

68. Carpenter, *Stonor Letters*, vol. 2, no. 219.

69. Ibid., nos. 224, 229. In a letter dated July 31, he was still in London sending greetings to Katherine through Elizabeth. But a letter from Elizabeth to William Stonor dated October 5 states that Betson and his wife send their greetings.

70. Ibid., nos. 249, 250, 251.

71. Kingsford, introduction to *Stonor Letters*, pp. 56–57.

72. Hanham, *The Celys and Their World*.

73. Ibid., Hanham, *The Celys and Their World*, p. 16.

74. Ibid., pp. 32–33.

75. Letter quoted in ibid., p. 49.

76. Hanham, *The Celys and Their World*, p. 50.

77. Ibid., pp. 74–75.

78. Letter quoted in ibid., p. 16.

79. Hanham, *The Celys and Their World*, pp. 77–78.

80. Ibid., pp. 87–88.

81. Ibid., pp. 266–268.

82. Ibid., pp. 268–270, 414–417.

83. Ibid., p. 309.

84. Ibid., pp. 309–311.

85. Ibid., pp. 311–312.

86. Ibid., pp. 312–314.

87. Ibid., pp. 315–317.

88. Ibid., pp. 412–422.

89. Carpenter, *Stonor Letters*, vol. 2, no. 168.

90. Kay Lacey, "Margaret Croke (d. 1491)," in *Medieval London Widows 1300–1500*, ed. Caroline M. Barron and Anne F. Sutton (London, 1994), pp. 143–164. The mother of Elizabeth Stonor appears in the letters frequently and in other London records. Kay Lacey has given a full history of her and her family ties. She did not remarry but continued to administer family affairs.

Chapter 5

1. Charlotte Augusta Sneyd, trans., *A Relation or Rather a True Account of the Island of England; with Sundry Particulars of the Customs of These Peoples, and of the Royal Revenues under King Henry Seventh, about the Year 1500*, Camden Society, series 1, no. 37 (London, 1846), pp. 26–27.

2. Sylvia L. Thrupp, *The Merchant Class of Medieval London* (Chicago, 1949), chap. 5.

3. HW, vols. 1 and 2. Only medieval wills appear in this sample (until 1500). Of the 3,300 lay men's wills, 1,743 mention a surviving wife.

4. David Herlihy and Christiane Klapisch-Zuber, *Tuscans and Their Families: A Study of the Florentine Catasto of 1427* (New Haven, 1985), p. 216. For the widows' financial condition see Isabelle Chabot, "Widowhood and Poverty in Late Medieval Florence," *Continuity and Change* 3 (1988), pp. 291–311.

5. Paul Brand, "'Deserving' and 'Undeserving' Wives: Earning and Forfeiting Dower in Medieval England," *Journal of Legal History* 22 (2001), pp. 1–20. Brand found that in common law by the end of the thirteenth century, dower was considered a "reward" earned by the wife and not necessarily a binding agreement. The widow had to have sexual intercourse with the husband, and adultery could forfeit a dower. Jenny Kermode, *Medieval Merchants: York, Beverly, and Hull in the Later Middle Ages* (Cambridge, 1998), p. 91, found that most merchants left their widows at least their matrimonial home.

6. Caroline Barron, *London in the Later Middle Ages: Government and People 1200–1500* (Oxford, 2004), p. 128.

7. Luke 21:2: "And He saw also a certain poor widow casting in these two mites. And he said, Of a truth I say unto you that this poor widow hast cast in more than they all." Mark 12:42 adds: "For all they did cast in of their abundance, but she of her want did cast in that she had, even all her living." James A. Brundage, "Widows as Disadvantaged Persons in Medieval Canon Law," in *Upon My Husband's Death: Widows in the Literature and Histories of Medieval Europe*, ed. Louise Mirrer (Ann Arbor, 1992), pp. 193–206, discusses the widow and restitution of her property in canon law.

8. Charter of Henry III to the Widows of London (1268), LBC 1291–1309, pp. 36–7.

9. For a more complete discussion of recovery of dower and the figures and tables from the sample see: Barbara A. Hanawalt, "The Widow's Mite: Provisions for Medieval London Widows," in Mirrer, *Upon My Husband's Death*, pp. 21–46.

10. *Liber Albus*, pp. 165–166. "In Writ of Dower (*Unde nihil habet*) tenants shall have three summonses and after those one essoin. They shall have the View and after the View one essoin. Tenants shall have the View although they entered through the husband of the demandant, and also notwithstanding that the husband died seised. Tenants may vouch to warranty, and after each appearance may be essoined; and all the other process shall be made as in Writ of Right in Husting of Pleas of Land. And if the demandant recovers dower against the tenant by default made or by judgment of law on such Writ of Dower, and the said female demandant alleges in a Court of Record that her husband died seised, then the Mayor shall command the Sheriffs, by precept, to have summoned an Inquest of the venue where the tenements are, against the next Hustings of Common Pleas; for enquiry if the husband died seised, and as to the value of the tenements and the damages. And if she recovers upon Inquisition, enquiry shall be made as to the damages by the same Inquest."

11. CLRO, CP. The samples are for six-year periods taken roughly every twenty years. Some of the sample years were determined by interruptions in records. Reconstituting the cases meant following the widows through their initiation of the case to either the point at which the case dropped from the record or was resolved. In doing a sample, some of the cases could not be followed through to completion, and some appeared in their final stages. The sample includes 299 cases, 186 of which reached some sort of resolution, and 113 of which dropped out of the record.

12. My survey of the fifteenth-century rolls of the royal court of common pleas did not show that London women were taking their cases there instead. In general, London courts seem to have gone through a slump in the late fifteenth century, which is as yet unexplained.

13. 1301–6 (ninety-six cases), 1327–32 (sixty-eight cases), 1348–53 (forty-two cases), 1374–79 (thirty cases), 1400–1405 (eleven cases), 1427–33 (six cases).

14. Sue Sheridan Walker, "'Litigant Agency' in Dower Pleas in the Royal Common Law Courts in Thirteenth- and Early Fourteenth-Century England," *Journal of Legal History* 24 (2003), pp. 215–236. She found that women were very familiar with the courts, although they increasingly relied on attorneys.

15. Cases could run from for two to over five years. Hanawalt, "Widow's Mite," p. 28, table on the length of time cases took. Paul Brand, *Kings, Barons and Justices: The Making and Enforcement of Legislation in Thirteenth-Century England* (Cambridge, 2003), pp. 302–303, found that changes made in the royal courts sped up the process of suing for dower.

16. In 1301–6, 55 percent of the widows used attorneys, while only 34 percent of the defendants did. By 1327–32, the same percentage of widows was using attorneys, but 71 percent of the defendants did. In the immediate postplague years (1348–53), only 26 percent of the widows had attorneys, compared to 21 percent of the defendants. The number increased again by 1374–79, with 48 percent of the widows represented and 14 percent of the defendants. By 1400–1405, 75 percent of the widows had attorneys, and 19 percent of the defendants did.

For the thirteenth-century development of the legal profession see Paul Brand, *The Origins of the English Legal Profession* (Oxford, 1992).

17. In 1301–6 it is true that 61 percent of those widows who remained unmarried finally hired an attorney, and only 39 percent of those who remarried did so. But by 1327–32, 56 percent of the unmarried widows, compared to 55 percent of those who had remarried, hired attorneys, and by 1348–53 the balance shifts, with 19 percent of the unmarried widows represented by attorneys, compared to 38 percent of those who remarried. The balance remains similar through the rest of the century, for in 1374–79, 36 percent of the unmarried widows had an attorney, and 56 percent of the remarried did. In the fifteenth century the number of cases overall becomes very small, but in the majority of cases, both the widows and those who remarried used attorneys as a rule.

18. To the modern reader the word "tenant" may be confusing. It is not a simple renter but rather someone to whom the husband had granted the rent of property. As we shall see, it is not necessarily a relative, but rather someone whom the husband had sold or deeded the property.

19. CLRO CP 28, ms 2–16, CP 29, ms 1–12; many other cases as well.

20. 1301–6, 2.5; 1327–32, 2.03; 1348–53, 1.7; 1374–79, 2.2; 1400–1405, 2.6; 1427–33, 1.7.

21. Sue Sheridan Walker, "Litigation as Personal Quest: Suing for Dower in the Royal Courts, circa 1272–1350," in *Wife and Widow in Medieval England*, ed. Sue Sheridan Walker (Ann Arbor, Mich, 1993), pp. 81–108. Walker discusses widows pursuing their suits alone in royal courts but notes that by the end of the period she is covering, the use of attorneys increased.

22. In reading Husting court of common pleas cases, I looked up the wills of the various parties. The defendants were not executors of other people mentioned in the wills. The figure of 10 percent, therefore, is based on a more complete search than simply surname or relationship mentioned in the common pleas rolls.

23. See Hanawalt, "The Widow's Mite," p. 28, table 1.1. Average Length of Time for Dower Disputes (in months) p. 28. In 1301–6: fifty-one cases, or 44 percent, dropped out, and sixty-six cases, or 56 percent, reached resolution. In 1327–32: twenty-four cases, or 31 percent, dropped out, and fifty-three cases, or 69 percent, were resolved. In 1348–53: seventeen cases, or 33 percent, dropped out, and thirty-four, or 67 percent, reached resolution. In 1374–79: five cases, or 16 percent, dropped out, and twenty-seven cases, or 84 percent, reached resolution. In 1400–1405: twelve cases, or 75 percent, dropped out, and four cases, or 33 percent, were resolved. In 1427–33: four cases, or 67 percent, dropped out, and two cases, or 33 percent, were resolved.

24. The proportions were 38 percent (1301–6), 65 percent (1327–32), 69 percent (1348–53), 50 percent (1374–79), 100 percent (1400–1405 and likewise 1427–33).

25. CLRO CP 55, ms 3–19. See also CP 27, ms 4, CP 53, ms 7–20, CP 54, ms 1–8.

26. In 1301–6, six cases, or 21 percent; in 1327–32, three cases, or 23 percent; in 1348–53, two cases, or 12 percent; in 1374–79, one case, or 10 percent. This argument was not used in the fifteenth century.

27. CLRO CP 53, ms 15–24, CP 54, ms 1, CP 54, ms 3–15.

28. In 1301–6, five cases, or 17 percent; in 1327–32, three cases, or 23 percent; in 1348–53, one case, or 0.06 percent; in 1374–79, one case, or 10 percent.

29. CLRO CP 52, ms 5–12, CP 53, ms 1–14.

30. CLRO CP 74, ms 18, CP 74, ms 2–18, CP 77, ms. 1–3.

31. CLRO CP 52, ms 12–14, CP 53, 1–19, CP 54, ms 2–4. See also the case of Alice, widow of Elias de Braghyngge, who lost to Agnes, widow of John Russell, when she admitted that Agnes was right that she had lived in adultery the whole of Elias's life. She, too, claimed to have been reconciled with her husband before he died (CP 75, ms 10, CP 76, ms 9–13). Katherine, widow of John Arnald, was accused of adultery with Peter of Nealdon, chaplain. The jury said that she was never reconciled; CP30, ms 8–17, CP 31, ms 1–15. See Brand, "'Deserving' and 'Undeserving' Wives," pp. 1–20, for common law.

32. CPMR 1381–1412, vol. 3, pp. 151–153 (1388).

33. In 1301–6, six cases, or 21 percent. In 1327–32, five cases, or 38 percent. In 1348–53, one case, or 0.06 percent. In 1374–79, three cases, or 30 percent. CLRO CP 55, ms 15–19, CP 56, ms 1–16. For other cases, see CP 52, ms 1–11. Emma, widow of Godefred de Essex, had quitclaimed the tenement and did not deny it when confronted.

34. CPMR 1364–81, vol. 2, pp. 213–215.

35. Mary Bateson, ed., Borough Customs, SS, no. 21 (London, 1904), vol. 2, pp. ci–cii.

36. G. H. Martin, "The Registration of Deeds of Title in the Medieval Borough," in The Study of Medieval Records: Essays in Honour of Kathleen Major, ed. D. A. Bullough and R. L. Storey (Oxford, 1971), pp. 153–56.

37. See Hanawalt, "The Widow's 'Mite,'" p. 34, table 1.2, "Widows Recovering All or Part of Dower."

38. CLRO CP 52, ms 4–15, CP 53, ms 2. For another example see CP 28, ms 16, CP 29, ms 2–22, Johanna, widow of Nicholas le Lung.

39. CLRO CP 27, ms 15, CP 28, ms 2–15. CP 51, ms 3–8. CP 101, ms 1–6.

40. CLRO CP 51, ms 12. CP 53, ms 11–21, CP 54, ms 2. Another widow agreed to relinquish the one-half provision of the will in return for one-third, CLRO CP 54, ms 8–12, CP 55, ms 1–19.

41. James A. Brundage, "Widows and Remarriage: Moral Conflicts and Their Resolution in Classical Canon Law," in Wife and Widow in Medieval England, ed. Sue Sheridan Walker (Ann Arbor, 1993), pp. 17–31, discusses the ambiguity of the Church toward the remarriage of widows.

42. G. R. Owst, Literature and Pulpit in Medieval England, 3rd ed. (New York, 1961), p. 119. Ruth Kelso, Doctrine for the Lady of the Renaissance (Urbana, Ill., 1956), pp. 126–130.

43. Owst, Literature and Pulpit, pp. 388–389.

44. Kelso, Doctrine for the Lady of the Renaissance, pp. 131–132. Owst, Literature and Pulpit, p. 381.

45. Kermode, Medieval Merchants, pp. 91–92, observed that merchant widows faced considerable pressure to remarry.

46. R. S. Schofield and E. A. Wrigley, "Remarriage Intervals and the Effect of Marriage Order on Fertility," in *Marriage and Remarriage in Populations of the Past*, ed. J. Dupaquier, E. Helin, P. Laslett, M. Livi-Bacci, and S. Sogner (London, 1981), pp. 212, 214.

47. Joel T. Rosenthal, "Fifteenth-Century Widows and Widowhood: Bereavement, Reintegration, and Life Choices," in Walker, *Wife and Widow in Medieval England*, p. 37. See also Rosenthal, *Patriarchy and Families of Privilege in Fifteenth-Century England* (Philadelphia, 1991), pp. 175–256.

48. Michael M. Sheehan, "The Influence of Canon Law on the Property Rights of Married Women in England," *Mediaeval Studies* 25 (1963), p. 121. James A. Brundage, "Widows and Remarriage."

49. GL, Ms. 9051/1, fol. 105v.

50. CPMR 1323–64, vol. 1, p. 255 (1355). CPMR 1364–81, vol. 2, pp. 262–263 (1380).

51. See Barbara A. Hanawalt, "Remarriage as an Option for Urban and Rural Widows in Late Medieval England," in Walker, *Wife and Widow in Medieval England*, pp. 150–151, for tables giving numerical information.

52. Comparisons with early modern figures are useful here. Steve Rappaport, *Worlds within Worlds: Structures of Life in Sixteenth-Century London* (Cambridge, 1989), p. 40, quotes N. Adamson, "Urban Families: The Social Context of the London Elite, 1500–1603" (Ph.D. thesis, University of Toronto, 1983), showing that only a third of 208 widows of aldermanic families chose to marry again. Charles Carlton, *The Court of Orphans* (Leicester, 1974), discusses remarriage of widows appearing in the mayor's court but does not do a calculation.

53. John Hatcher, "Understanding the Population History of England, 1350–1750," *Past and Present* 180 (2003), pp. 83–130. The evidence, therefore, supports Hatcher's thesis of death being the determinant of low population in the fifteenth century rather than conditions that would lead to low fertility. The London widows were maximizing their fertility, often by marrying more than once or twice. P. J. P. Goldberg, *Women, Work, and Life Cycle in a Medieval Economy: Women in York and Yorkshire c. 1300–1520* (Oxford, 1992), pp. 267, found that only an average of 13 percent of widows remarried in York, but his numbers are small and are based on women's wills, which are not as accurate as the court cases.

54. The figures are: with one child, fifty-five remarried and thirty-six not; two children, twenty-nine yes and fifteen no; three children, twenty-one yes and seventeen no; and four or more, seventeen yes and sixteen no.

55. Thrupp, *Merchant Class*, p. 107.

56. Barron, *London in the Later Middle Ages*, pp. 101–115, has valuable graphs on London's wool exports.

57. Ariadne Schmidt, *Overleven na de dood: Wechuwen in Leiden in de Gouden Eeuw* (Amsterdam, 2001), p. 17, found that widows of craftsmen tended to marry someone of the same craft and that widows who had been left shops were much sought after. The remarriage of widows to men in the former husband's trade might have depended on the trade. Tanners in London did not

leave their businesses to their wives, and the possibility for women of surviving as processors in leather was limited. Some may have remarried outside the trade. Derek Keene, "Tanner's Widows, 1300–1350," in *Medieval London Widows 1300–1500*, ed. Caroline M. Barron and Anne F. Sutton (London, 1994), pp. 1–27.

58. Thrupp, *Merchant Class*, p. 28. Thomas F. Reddaway, *The Early History of the Goldsmiths' Company, 1327–1509* (London, 1975), pp. 275–321, has reconstructed biographies indicating marriages when known. Goldsmiths' widows seem to have preferred to marry other goldsmiths. Kermode, *Medieval Merchants*, pp. 87–88, found a similar pattern of remarriage in northern cities among the merchant class.

59. Rappaport, *Worlds within Worlds*, pp. 40–41.

60. TNA: PRO C1/158/35; C1/66/389; C1/43/65.

61. TNA: PRO C1/46/111.

62. TNA: PRO C1/61/485. This case is more fully discussed in chapter 6 as a case of prior contract.

63. TNA: PRO C1/66/308, C1/158/35, C1/66/389.

64. Mathew Davies, "Dame Thomasine Percyvale, 'The Maid of Week' (d. 1512)," in Barron and Sutton, *Medieval London Widows*, pp. 185–207. Her story was one of the popular ones from Cornwall, similar to the story of Dick Whittington. A colorful version of a rags-to-riches story appears in Charles M. Clode, *The Early History of the Guild of Merchant Taylors*, pt. 2 (London, 1888), pp. 11–13, 20–21.

65. TNA: PRO C1/123/6, C1/61/189.

66. LBG 1352–74, p. 250.

67. W. J. B. Crotch, ed. *The Prologues and Epilogues of William Caxton*, EETS, o.s., vol. 176 (London, 1928), p. 77.

68. Barbara Diefendorf, "Women and Property in *Ancien Régime* France: Theory and Practice in Dauphiné and Paris," in *Early Modern Conceptions of Property*, ed. John Brewer and Susan Staves (London, 1995), pp. 177–182. This study does not give the numbers of incidents of remarriage or of the different strategies used to support family. It also does not speculate on what the marriage and wardship arrangements did to the structure of Parisian and French society. The presumption is that patriarchy won out. For a more detailed discussion of the councillor families on which Diefendorf's initial study was based see Diefendorf, *Paris City Councillors in the Sixteenth Century: The Politics of Patrimony* (Princeton, 1983), chaps. 7, 8, 9. The small sample size of this group did not permit a statistical analysis, only case-by-case examples.

69. Marianne Danneel, "Orphanhood and Marriage in Fifteenth-Century Ghent," in *Marriage and Social Mobility in the Late Middle Ages*, ed. W. Prevenier, Studia Historica Gandensia, no. 274 (Ghent, 1989), pp. 99–111.

70. For problems with property in remarriage see David Nicholas, *The Domestic Life of a Medieval City: Women, Children, and Family in Fourteenth-Century Ghent* (Lincoln, Neb., 1985), pp. 27–32.

71. Martha C. Howell, *The Marriage Exchange: Property, Social Place, and Gender in Cities of the Low Countries, 1300–1550* (Chicago, 1998). This book is an excellent place to start looking at the complexities of medieval marriage contracts, dower, and dowry.

72. Schmidt, *Overleven na de drood: Weduwen in Leiden in de Gouden Eeuw*, pp. 318–320.

73. Christianae Klapisch-Zuber, *Women, Family, and Ritual in Renaissance Italy*, trans. Lydia G. Cochrane (Chicago, 1985), see particularly the essay "The 'Cruel Mother': Widowhood and Dowry in Florence in the Fourteenth and Fifteenth Centuries," pp. 117–131, and "The Griselda Complex: Dowry and Marriage Gifts in the Quattrocento," pp. 213–246. See also Anthony Molho, *Marriage Alliance in Late Medieval Florence* (Cambridge, Mass., 1994). Around 1100 in Italy and in the western European Mediterranean, dower was eliminated, and dowry became the sole exchange of property at marriage. See Dianne Owen Hughes, "From Brideprice to Dowry in Mediterranean Europe," *Journal of Family History* 3 (1978), pp. 262–296. Jane Fair Bestor, "Marriage Transactions in Renaissance Italy and Mauss's *Essay on the Gift*," *Past and Present* 164 (1999), pp. 6–46.

74. Stanley Chojnacki, "Dowries and Kinsmen in Early Renaissance Venice," in *Women in Medieval Society*, ed. Susan M. Stuard (Philadelphia, 1976), pp. 173–198, and "Patrician Women in Early Renaissance Venice," *Studies in the Renaissance* 21 (1974), pp. 176–203.

75. Keene, "Tanner's Widows, 1300–1350," pp. 14–22.

76. Reddaway, *The Early History of the Goldsmiths' Company*, pp. 275–231, found that goldsmith's widows tended to marry goldsmiths. Thrupp, *Merchant Class*, p. 28, found that 84 percent of the merchant's widows married merchants. Steve Rappaport, *Worlds within Worlds*, pp. 40–41.

Chapter 6

1. Helen V. Tauchen, Ann Dryden Witte, and Sharon K. Long, "Domestic Violence: A Non-random Affair," *International Economic Review* 32 (1991), pp. 491–511. Resource theory in modern terms usually applies when one of the couple has a higher paying job than the other or in some other way unbalances the economic relationship of the family.

2. Maria Ågren and Amy Louise Erickson, eds., *The Marital Economy in Scandinavia and Britain, 1400–1900* (Aldershot, 2005), use the concept of household economy of husband and wife and of partnership in the economy extensively, as do contributors to their collection of essays.

3. Sara M. Butler, "The Law as a Weapon in Marital Disputes: Evidence from the Late Medieval Court of Chancery, 1424–1529," *Journal of British Studies* 43 (2004), pp. 291–316, for a fine description of the problems of coverture and the types of cases that came into the Chancery.

4. Stanford B. Meech and Hope Emily Allen, eds., *The Book of Margery Kempe*, EETS, o.s., vol. 21 (London, 1940), pp. 6, 11–15, 21, 23–24. The vows do much to explain the marital discussion of Margery Kempe and her husband John. As they

sit sharing beer and cake, John wants her to honor her marriage vows to him by paying the conjugal debt (in sexual terms) and by taking her meals with him. While he agreed to live a celibate life with her, he does get the promise to be at least "boxom" at board and eat with him. And they do live together in sickness and health; she cares for him in his senility until he dies.

5. Katharina M. Wilson and Elizabeth M. Makowski, *Wykked Wyves and the Woes of Marriage: Misogamous Literature from Juvenal to Chaucer* (Albany, 1990). Chap. 4 is particularly relevant for the attitudes of the late Middle Ages toward women. Wilson and Makowski point to an increasing suspicion and disrespect of women in the fifteenth century. For a complete discussion of marital relations according to church writers see James A. Brundage, *Law, Sex, and Christian Society in Medieval Europe* (Chicago, 1987).

6. John Myrc, *Instructions for Parish Priests*, ed. Edward Peacock, EETS, o.s., vol. 209 (London, 1940), pp. 34, 42. See also John Shinners and William J. Dohar, eds., *Pastors and the Care of Souls* (Notre Dame, Ind., 1997), pp. 207–208.

7. Frederick C. Tubach, *Index Exemplorum: A Handbook of Medieval Religious Tales*, Folklore Fellows Communications, no. 204 (Helsinki, 1969). It gives a number of different parables for instructing husband and wife on forming a peaceful union.

8. H. Leith Spencer, *English Preaching in the Late Middle Ages* (Oxford, 1993), has a discussion of sermons and their audiences. David d'Avray, *Medieval Marriage Sermons: Mass Communication in a Culture without Print* (Oxford, 2001).

9. Tubach, *Index Exemplorum*, no. 2158.

10. Joan Young Gregg, *Devils, Women, and Jews: Reflections on the Other in Medieval Sermon Stories* (Binghamton, N.Y., 1997), pp. 117–119.

11. Tubach, *Index Exemplorum*, no. 3969.

12. Ibid., no. 4337.

13. Ibid., no. 5271.

14. Ibid, no. 2475.

15. Ibid., no. 5282. See also no. 3760, in which husband and wife argue over how to cook a hare; the wife has the husband beaten. In no. 3825, a drunken husband beats his wife with a plowshare, and in no. 4983, a man kills his wife and daughter for looking out of the window.

16. Ibid., no. 794. See also no. 3435, in which a woman kills her husband and burns down the house to conceal it. She chokes to death on the Host.

17. Frederick J. Furnivall, ed., *Manners and Meals in Olden Times*, EETS, o.s., vol. 32 (London, 1868), pp. 36–38. In addition to these English advice poems, by the late fifteenth century, Caxton had published *The Book of the Knight of La Tour-Landry* (ed. and trans. Thomas Wright, London, 1868). The French noble widower told a series of parables that warned his daughters about the dire things that could happen to them if they strayed from the path of virtue both before and after marriage. For an excellent collection of essays on advice for husbands and wives in conduct books see Kathleen Ashley and Robert L. A. Clark, eds., *Medieval Conduct* (Minneapolis, 2001).

18. Sharon Farmer, "Persuasive Voices: Clerical Images of Medieval Wives," *Speculum* 61 (1986), pp. 517–543.

19. Kay Lacey, "Margaret Croke," in *Medieval London Widows 1300–1500*, ed. Caroline M. Barron and Anne F. Sutton (London, 1994), pp. 155–161.

20. Christine Carpenter, ed., *Kingsford's Stonor Letters and Papers, 1290–1483* (Cambridge, 1996), vol. 2, nos. 168, 169, 170, 172.

21. Ibid., no. 208, in which she explains that she is staying in London to settle deeds in London and the suburbs.

22. Ibid., no. 169.

23. Ibid., no. 180.

24. Ibid., no. 172.

25. Ibid., no. 208.

26. Ibid., no. 226.

27. Alison Hanham, *The Celys and Their World: An English Merchant Family of the Fifteenth Century* (Cambridge, 1985), p. 315.

28. CPMR 1381–1412, vol. 3, p. 43 (July 14, 1383); CPMR 1364–81, vol. 2, p. 147 (August 18, 1372). The custom of leaving the wife in charge was also common in Flanders and the Netherlands. See James M. Murray, *Bruges, Cradle of Capitalism, 1280–1390* (Cambridge, 2005), p. 324.

29. CPMR 1381–1412, vol. 3, pp. 120–121 (May 10, 1386), p. 69.

30. CLRO, MC 1/1/56.

31. TNA: PRO C1/16/185. See also C1/64/434, C1/47/91, CPMR 1364–81, vol. 2, p. 147 (1372).

32. CPMR 1364–81, vol. 2, p. 270 (1380). See also p. 125 (1370).

33. CPMR 1364–81, vol. 2, p. 195 (1375).

34. William H. Hale, A *Series of Precedents and Proceedings in Criminal Causes Extracted from the Year 1475 to 1640. Extracted from the Act Books of Ecclesiastical Courts in the Diocese of London, Illustrative of the Discipline of the Church of England* (London, 1847), p. 27 (1491).

35. Judith Bennett, *Ale, Beer, and Brewsters in England,* (New York, 1996), pp. 60–76.

36. Heather Swanson, *Medieval Artisans: An Urban Class in Late Medieval England* (Oxford, 1989), pp. 35–36, 42–43, 51, 106, 116.

37. Derek Keene, "Tanner's Widows, 1300–1350," in *Medieval London Widows 1300–1500*, pp. 1–27.

38. Swanson, *Medieval Artisans*, p. 116, speculates that widows might have trained their new husbands in their craft. Murray, *Bruges, Cradle of Capitalism*, p. 325. Ariadne Schmidt, *Overleven na de dood: Wechuwen in Leiden in de Gouden Eeuw* (Amsterdam, 2001), pp. 318–319.

39. TNA: PRO C1/105/51.

40. TNA: PRO C1/172/1.

41. CLMC 1350–70, p. 88, letter 192.

42. Ralph B. Pugh, ed., *Calendar of London Trailbaston Trials under Commissions of 1305 and 1306* (London, 1975), p. 84.

43. TNA: PRO C1/102/60.

44. Barbara A. Hanawalt, *Growing Up in Medieval London: the Experience of Childhood in History* (New York, 1993), pp. 187–90.

45. TNA: PRO C1/4/116, C1/229/19.

46. *HW*, vol. 2, p. 132 (1369), p. 564.

47. Barbara A. Hanawalt, "Separation Anxieties in Late Medieval London: Gender in 'The Wright's Chaste Wife,'" in Hanawalt, *"Of Good and Ill Repute": Gender and Social Control in Medieval England* (Oxford, 1998), pp. 88–103. In that essay I was concerned about the female voice and authorship of the poem as well as the separation anxieties. The original appears in Lambeth Palace manuscript 306 and dates from 1460–70. It is a typical household book with recipes, some Lydgate, "Chronycullys of Englonde," devotional literature, and so on. The version I have used is Frederick J. Furnivall, ed., *The Wright's Chaste Wife; A Merry Tale by Adam of Cobsam*, EETS, o.s., vol. 12 (New York, 1969). A history of the analogues appears in a supplement to the tale written by W. A. Clouston, pp. 25–39. The author of this version declares himself in the poem to be Adam of Cobsam. The separation poems from India form a major genre of lyrical poems in the female voice. Tales in the Barahmasa tradition are the origins of the stories from which *The Wright's Chaste Wife* derives. See, for instance, Charlotte Vaudeville, *Barahmasa in Indian Literatures: Songs of the Twelve Months in Indo-Aryan Literatures* (Delhi, 1986).

48. Flax, or *linium usitassum*, was used extensively to make linen cloth, which was an essential, nonanimal fabric before the introduction of cotton into Europe. Hemp and nettles were also used. The process of rendering the plant into thread was an arduous one. The plant was pulled up by the roots to preserve long fibers. It was then dried. To separate the fiber from the plant, the plants were soaked, in a process called "retting." The bundles of flax straw were kept straight to prevent tangling. Next the flax was "beetled," or pounded, to remove the long fibers from the core. Apparently the wife had acquired the flax after it had been through this process. She set the lord to the next task, which was to pass the flax between the intermeshing wooden blades of a flax brake. This process let the inner core fall to the floor, while the fibers remained in the hands of the worker. The flax was passed through this process repeatedly. The next stage, that of "swingling," was also part of the lord's work, and the steward did this as well. The swingle board permitted the worker to draw a handful of the flax through the board and, with a wooden knife, remove the rest of the core and any coarse fibers remaining. The latter was "tow" and was used for sacking, etc. I am grateful to Dale Liles, who teaches linen cloth making and demonstrates the methods at Shakertown in Kentucky, for this information.

49. Charles Donahue, Jr., "Female Plaintiffs in Marriage Cases in the Court of York in the Later Middle Ages: What Can We Learn from the Number?," in *Wife and Widow in Medieval England*, ed. Sue Sheridan Walker (Ann Arbor, 1993), p. 186. In the York court in the fourteenth century, 78 percent of the actions were to enforce marriage, and only 19 percent were to dissolve or separate marriage. The rest concerned marital property. Donahue has 88 cases from the fourteenth century and 125 from the fifteenth century.

50. Richard Helmholz, *Marriage Litigation in Medieval England* (Cambridge, 1974), p. 74. He points out that "divorce" was commonly used in the Middle Ages, but that it normally meant annulment. The couple was usually separated and could not remarry. A recent study has pointed out that the Church balanced the rights of the husband with those of the wife and the heirs. Charles J. Reid, Jr., *Power over the Body, Equality in the Family: Rights and Domestic Relations in Medieval Canon Law*, Emory University Studies in Law and Religion (Grand Rapids, Mich., 2004).

51. Richard Wunderli, *London Church Courts and Society on the Eve of the Reformation* (Cambridge, Mass., 1981), pp. 120–121.

52. Ibid., pp. 194–203.

53. Richard Helmholz, *Marriage Litigation*, pp. 74–111.

54. Donahue, "Female Plaintiffs in Marriage Cases in the Court of York," pp. 188–195. Most of the cases in both centuries involved precontract. Donahue's evidence for better economic conditions for women is not strong, and the London evidence seems to contradict him.

55. Hale, *Precedent and Procedure*, pp. 9, 11. See also GL, Ms. 9064/1, fol. 9v.

56. TNA: PRO C1/61/485.

57. Wunderli, *London Church Courts*, pp. 121–122.

58. Helmholz, *Marriage Litigation*, pp. 88–89.

59. *CPMR 1364–81*, vol. 2, pp. 117–118, 173–174, 186, 206.

60. TNA: PRO C1/66/224.

61. *CLMC 1350–70*, p. 5.

62. TNA: PRO C1/64/223.

63. *CPMR 1364–81*, vol. 2, p. 90 (1386).

64. *CPMR 1364–81*, vol. 2, p. 23 (1365).

65. Sue Sheridan Walker, "Punishing Convicted Ravishers: Statutory Strictures and Actual Practice in Thirteenth and Fourteenth-Century England," *Journal of Medieval History* 13 (1987), pp. 237–250. See also Butler, "The Law as a Weapon in Marital Disputes," pp. 297–298.

66. Butler, "The Law as a Weapon in Marital Disputes," pp. 298–303. Butler makes extensive use of the Chancery petitions, but Londoners do not appear frequently in these cases of abduction. Her examples are drawn from all the late medieval petitions.

67. Hale, *Precedence and Procedure*, pp. 20, 2.

68. Butler, "The Law as a Weapon in Marital Disputes," pp. 306–315. She gives examples of the problems of support for abandoned wives.

69. CLRO MC 1/1/24.

70. Henry Ansgar Kelly, "Rule of Thumb and the Folklaw of the Husband's Stick," *Journal of Legal Education* 44 (1994), pp. 341–365. The rule of thumb was a measure of cloth. The phrase is not even mentioned in folklore indices. Anthony Fletcher, *Gender, Sex, and Subordination in England 1500–1800* (New Haven, 1995), pp. 192–203. Fletcher argues that the phrase was used in the Middle Ages, but it was not even used in the period he discusses. He assumes

that wife beating was very common, based on the cases that came into court. Actually, few cases of marital cruelty came into English ecclesiastical courts in the Middle Ages.

71. Ralph Houlbrooke, *Church Courts and the People during the English Reformation, 1520–1570* (Oxford, 1979), p. 85 and app. 3, found that in the period of his study, few marriages were annulled and most of those were for prior contact and only a scattering were for cruelty. R. Po-Chia Hsia, *Social Discipline in the Reformation: Central Europe, 1550–1750* (London, 1989), p. 125, found that matters of sexual misconduct were relatively few until after the 1650s. Martin Ingram, *Church Courts, Sex and Marriage in England, 1570–1640* (Cambridge, 1987), p. 125. J. M. Beattie, *Crime and the Courts in England, 1660–1800* (Princeton, 1988), p. 105, found that intrafamilial homicide was 36 percent of all homicide. Laura Gowing, *Domestic Dangers: Women, Words, and Sex in Early Modern England* (Oxford, 1996). In chapter 6, Gowing discusses adultery and violence. She found that in the church courts men were more successful in winning cases for separation for adultery than women were in winning on accusations of violence.

72. Ingram, *Church Courts, Sex and Marriage in England, 1570–1640*, pp. 126, 143, argues that while these ideas were discussed, historians have overemphasized their importance in daily life. Frances E. Dolan, *Dangerous Familiars: Representations of Domestic Crime in England, 1550–1700* (Ithaca, 1994), pp. 89–120, argues that around 1650 a change of attitude toward the acceptance of domestic violence is perceptible, in that literature and pamphlets began to fault husbands who were abusive.

73. Susan Cahn, *Industry of Devotion: The Transformation of Women's Work in England, 1500–1660* (New York, 1987), discusses how women's role in the family and economy changed from the Middle Ages to the early modern period.

74. *Statutes of the Realm*, 26 Edward III, c. 2.

75. Barbara A. Hanawalt, *Crime and Conflict in Medieval England, 1300–1348* (Cambridge, Mass., 1979), p. 159. The low incidence of intrafamilial violence in late medieval England deserves some discussion. Even if the figures represent considerable underreporting, they are still remarkably low. Of the 22,417 felony indictments appearing in "gaol" [English spelling of "jail" and the official name of the series] delivery rolls for eight counties from 1300 to 1348, only 0.7 percent were cases of one family member transgressing against another. In 92 percent of these cases, the felonious action involved homicide, but this was only 2 percent of the total homicides tried in gaol delivery. In the coroners' inquests of Northamptonshire for the whole of the fourteenth century, only 8 percent of the homicides reported were intrafamilial. The discrepancy between the coroners' rolls and gaol delivery is because the gaol delivery court records reflect those who were ultimately indicted for homicide, arrested, and tried. Coroners' inquests only indicate possible suspects. Even at the level of simple misbehavior, family seldom appear. Of the 2,774 cases tried in the first half of the century in the manor courts of Wakefield and Ingoldmells only sixty cases, or 2 percent, involved members of the same family: 57 percent were cases of

assault, and 40 percent debts and trespasses (the rest were a variety of other types of minor actions). James B. Given, *Society and Homicide in Thirteenth-Century England* (Stanford, 1977) found that in the thirteenth-century Eyre rolls, 4 percent (46) of the 1,251 homicide cases involved family (pp. 102–103). But on p. 55 he gives the figure of 6.5 percent. Elizabeth Pleck, *Domestic Tyranny: The Making of Social Policy Against Family Violence from Colonial Times to the Present* (New York, 1987), app. B, has tried to convert the medieval figures into modern figures per one hundred thousand population. The population of England that she posits is not adequately known, so these figures are not meaningful.

76. Donahue, "Female Plaintiffs in Marriage Cases in the Court of York," p. 187. Of 213 marital cases, only 5 were for cruelty and adultery.

77. Hanawalt, *Crime and Conflict in English Communities*, p. 160. The parent-child relationship accounted for 22 percent of the homicides in the gaol delivery rolls (11 percent in coroner's rolls) with the usual dynamic of the father killing the son. Sibling quarrels (brother killing brother) accounted for 11 percent of homicides in gaol delivery (22 percent in the coroners' rolls).

78. Paul Strohm, "Treason in the Household," in Strohm, *Hochon's Arrow: The Social Imagination of Fourteenth-Century Texts* (Princeton, 1992), pp. 121–144, has investigated a 1388 case of a woman of good family who leagued together with her lover to kill her husband as he lay in bed.

79. Butler, "The Law as a Weapon in Marital Disputes," pp. 310–313. The Chancery petitions, although they mention domestic violence or fear of it, are not a very reliable source for the problem.

80. *CPMR 1364–81*, p. 32 (1365).

81. Hanawalt, *The Ties That Bound: Peasant Families in Medieval England* (New York, 1986), p. 152.

82. *CCorR*, pp. 170–171.

83. *CCorR*, pp. 245–247.

84. *LBB 1275–1312*, p. 271.

85. *CCorR*, pp. 207–208. Martin Weinbaum, ed., *The London Eyre of 1276*, LRS, vol. 12 (Leicester, 1976), pp. 35.

86. Weinbaum, *London Eyre of 1276*, p. 25.

87. Guido Ruggerio, *Violence in Early Renaissance Venice* (New Brunswick, 1980), p. 72, shows 16.7 percent of interfamilial murder among nobles but only 5.4 percent among the workers. David Levinson, *Family Violence in Cross-cultural Perspective* (Newbury Park, Calif., 1989), pp. 24–38.

88. For a discussion of coverture from the sixteenth-century perspective see Frances E. Dolan, "Home-Rebels and House-Traitors: Murderous Wives in Early Modern England," *Yale Journal of Law and the Humanities* 4 (1992), pp. 1–31.

89. Susan D. Amussen, "Punishment, Discipline, and Power: The Social Meanings of Violence in Early Modern England," *Journal of British Studies* 34 (1995), p. 13, accepts violence as a category without evaluating its meaning in the contemporary context: "Violence within the household, as correction or otherwise, was a regular event in early modern society."

Chapter 7

1. Christopher Dyer, *Standards of Living in the Later Middle Ages: Social Change in England 1200–1520* (Cambridge, 1989), pp. 188–210, has some general comments on urban living but very little in the whole book on women. See also Michael Hicks, ed., *Revolution and Consumption in Late Medieval England* (Woodbridge, U.K., 2001). For a discussion of the literary side of possessions see D. Vance Smith, *Arts of Possession: The Middle English Household Imaginary* (Minneapolis, 2003). Lena Cowen Orlin, ed., *Material London, ca. 1600* (Philadelphia, 2000). Marjorie Keniston McIntosh, *Working Women in English Society, 1300–1620* (Cambridge, 2005), chap. 9.

2. William Fitzstephen, *Norman London,* with an essay by Sir Frank Stenton and introduction by F. Donald Logan (New York, 1990), pp. 48–60. John Scattergood, "Misrepresenting the City: Genre, Intertextuality and William Fitzstephen's Description of London (c. 1173)," in *London and Europe in the Later Middle Ages,* ed. Julia Boffery and Pamela King (London, 1995), pp. 1–34. Scattergood points out that Fitzstephen derived his description from a number of set pieces. This is, of course, true, but it is interesting that his personal observations did not modify his sources.

3. Caroline Barron, Christopher Coleman, and Claire Gobbi, eds., "The London Journal of Alessandro Magno 1562," *London Journal* 9 (1983), p. 144.

4. Frederick J. Furnival, ed., *Harrison's Description of England,* New Shakespeare Society Publications (London, 1877), pt. 1, p. lxiii.

5. The coroners' inquests are preserved or published in several places. TNA: PRO Just 2/94A, *LBB 1275–1312,* pp. 256–280, and *CCorR.* The figures given do not add up to 100 percent because I have left out such small categories such as churches, ditches, the Tower, and so on. Eighty-six percent of the men were murdered in streets or lanes, lots, and the river. Men were killed in their homes or gardens in only 16 percent of the cases, taverns in 8 percent, and shops in 5 percent. The other deaths were scattered in public places. Sixty-four percent of their fatal accidents were in streets, the river, and shops, and only 20 percent at their home. In other words, their homicidal interactions were oriented toward the outside and toward public places. Forty-one percent of the women were murdered in houses, 23 percent in streets, 12 percent in shops or bodies of water, and none in taverns. The accidental deaths, perhaps a more sensitive indicator of where people lived and worked, show that 50 percent of women's accidental deaths occurred in their homes, and 40 percent on streets or spaces outside the house and garden.

6. For a complete discussion of women's space see Barbara A. Hanawalt, "At the Margins of Women's Space in Medieval Europe," in *"Of Good and Ill Repute": Gender and Social Control in Medieval England* (New York, 1998), pp. 70–87.

7. John Schofield, *Medieval London Houses* (New Haven, 1994), pp. 34–41. Bishops, nobles, and wealthy merchants built houses between London and Westminster as London expanded.

8. Ibid., pp. 51–53.

9. Ibid., pp. 86–88. In 1384 a man leased a lot to build a range of houses on the Thames. The buildings were to face the street and were to be three stories high, with the individual stories measuring twelve feet by ten feet and reaching seven feet in height. Behind this street frontage, he was to build a hall measuring forty feet by twenty-three feet and a parlor, kitchen, and buttery. Underneath the structure, he was to have cellars seven feet high for merchandise storage. See also TNA: PRO, Ancient Deeds Catalogue, p. 210; and E40/A 1779 for another lease that specifies the dimensions of a property leased for one hundred years.

10. Charlotte Augusta Sneyd, trans., *A Relation or Rather a True Account of the Island of Englang; with Sundry Particulars of the Customs of These People, and of the Royal Revenues under King Henry Seventh, about the Year 1500*, Works of the Camden Society, series 1, no. 37 (New York, 1847), p. 42. The Venetian notes that the houses are of timber and brick in the French style, and he points out that there are no buildings in the Italian style. Henry Littlehales, ed., *The Medieval Records of a London City Church (St. Mary at Hill)*, pt. 1, EETS, o.s., vols. 125, 128 (London, 1904), pp. 28–29, describes a grand house that belonged to one of London's churches and was rented to a merchant of Venice in 1485. The church warden made a list of the amenities before it was leased. In addition to the chief chamber, it had eleven chambers with beds. A parlor was served by a buttery, kitchen, and larder house. A separate house for storing grain, a stable, and a well occupied the yard and garden area. With so many rooms, it is not surprising that the church warden noted a quantity of locks: thirty spring locks and keys, twenty-two stock locks and keys, four plate locks for the great wall cupboard and keys, five plate locks and keys with five bolts. The postern gate had a plate lock with bolt, iron, and two keys, and finally there were five other plate locks and five keys for them. All the windows were glass and in good repair.

11. *CIPM 1413–18*, vol. 20, p. 62.

12. *CIPM 1405–13*, vol. 19, p. 199.

13. *CIPM 1399–1405*, vol. 18, p. 9. John de Monte Acuto, knight, the Elder, held a tenement in his demesne, but it was by right of inheritance of his wife, Margaret, who was then sixty years old; *CIPM 1383–91*, vol. 16, p. 337.

14. CLRO, Bridge House Rental, 1460–86, vol. 3, pp. 1–9, 140–148, 282–290, 328–336, 422–430, 562–570, 710–719, 834–842, 1086, 1172.

15. Littlehales, *Medieval Records of a London City Church*, pp. 28–29, 65–76, 126.

16. *LBG 1352–74*, p. 203. See also pp. 327–328 for a similar lease to Geoffrey Chaucer.

17. *CLMC 1350–70*, pp. 47–48, TNA: PRO C1/67/38.

18. TNA: PRO C1/64/764.

19. Helena M. Chew and Martin Weinbaum, eds., *The London Eyre of 1244*, LRS, vol. 6 (Leicester, 1970), p. 20.

20. GL, 15–18 Edward VI, Ms. 1279, vol. 1. She paid "for her stondyng ate church dore for a hold yere 2 s." Although this record is later than our period, requiring payment for beggars was common practice in the Middle Ages as well.

21. TNA: PRO Just 2/94A, ms. 2 (1315).

22. Schofield, *Medieval London Houses*, pp. 56–57.

23. Carole Rawcliffe, "The Hospitals of Later Medieval London," *Medical History* 24 (1984), pp. 1–22. Nicholas Orme and Margaret Webster, *The English Hospital, 1070–1570* (New Haven, 1995), pp. 107–121. Rotha M. Clay, *The Medieval Hospitals of England* (London, 1909).

24. Susan M. B. Steuer, "Family Strategies in Medieval London: Financial Planning and the Urban Widow, 1123–1473," in *Essays in Medieval Studies: Children and the Family in the Middle Ages*, ed. Nicole Clifton, 1995 Proceedings of the Illinois Medieval Association, vol. 12 (Chicago, 1996), pp. 81–93. Her evidence comes from Nellie J. M. Kerling, ed. and trans., *Cartulary of St. Bartholomew's Hospital Founded 1123: A Calendar* (London, 1973). See P. H. Cullum, *Cremetts and Corodies: Care of the Poor and Sick at St. Leonard's Hospital, York, in the Middle Ages*, Borthwick Papers, no. 79 (York, England, 1991), for a full discussion of the use of corodies.

25. Steuer, "Family Strategies, pp. 85–86.

26. Ibid., pp. 82–84.

27. *CPMR 1381–1412*, vol. 3, pp. 4–5 (1381).

28. GL, Ms. 9064/1, fol. 40.

29. *CCorR*, pp. 68–69.

30. CLRO MC 1/2A/45.

31. *LBI 1400–1422*, pp. 49–50.

32. Schofield, *Medieval London Houses*, pp. 54–55. See Martha Carlin, *Medieval Southwark* (London, 1996), pp. 192–200, for inns on the south bank.

33. Adriadne Schmidt, *Overleven na de dood: Weduwen in Leidenin de Gouden Eeuw* (Amsterdam, 2001), p. 318, claims that all widows were poor because of the property division. Her observation is a good one, but did not apply to all widows in London.

34. Barbara A. Hanawalt, "Reading the Lives of the Illiterate: London's Poor," *Speculum* 80 (2005), pp. 1067–1086.

35. *Liber Albus*, pp. xxix–xxxii, 319–332.

36. Helena M. Chew and William Kellaway, eds., *London Assize of Nuisance, 1301–1431*, LRS, vol. 10 (London, 1973), p. 45 (1314). John Schofield, *The Building of London from the Conquest to the Great Fire* (London, 1984), p. 96; for a complete discussion see Earnest L. Sabine, "Latrines and Cesspools of Medieval London," *Speculum* 9 (1934), pp. 303–321.

37. *CCorR*, pp. 167–168 (1326). See Littlehales, *Medieval Records of a London Church*, pp. xi, xli, 249, for the cost of cleaning a privy in the late fifteenth century. The church wardens paid 2 s. a ton for cleaning of one privy. In addition, they had an annual expense of 10 s. plus 16 d. to have the muck carted off in a dung boat.

38. Sabine, "Latrines and Cesspools of Medieval London," pp. 303–321.

39. Ernest L. Sabine, "City Cleaning in Medieval London," *Speculum* 12 (1937), pp. 19–43.

40. *CPMR 1413–37*, vol. 4, p. 157.

41. Chew and Kellaway, *London Assize of Nuisance*, p. 79 (1333).

42. Ibid., p. 88 (1341). For a discussion of privacy see Diane Shaw, "The Construction of the Private in Medieval London," *Journal of Medieval and Early Modern Studies* 26 (1996), pp. 447–466.

43. *CEMCR 1298–1307*, p. 40.

44. *LBE 1314–37*, p. 8. Littlehales, *Medieval Records of a London Church*, pp. xxx, 86–87.

45. *CPMR 1413–37*, vol. 4, pp. 153, 157.

46. Helen M. Cam, ed., *The Eyre of London, 14 Edward II, A.D. 1321*, SS, no. 26, pt. 1 (London, 1968), pp. cxxiii–cxxiv, 87–89.

47. Sneyd, trans., *A Relation or Rather a True Account of the Island of England*, p. 43.

48. *LBG 1352–74*, p. 225.

49. *Rotuli Parliamentorum*, 2:447, as quoted by Margaret Curtis, "The London Lay Subsidy of 1332," in *Finance and Trade under Edward III*, ed. George Unwin (Manchester, 1919), p. 37.

50. Ibid., pp. 44–47. Poll taxes for 1381 do not exist. Those for Southwark are in Carlin, *Medieval Southwark*, pp. 136–143.

51. J. C. L. Stahlschmidt, ed., "Original Documents, Lay Subsidy Roll of 1411–1412," *Archaeological Journal* 44 (1871), pp. 56–83.

52. Curtis, "Lay Subsidy of 1332," pp. 51–56.

53. Lawrence M. Clopper, "Need Men and Women Labor? Langland's Wanderer and the Labor Ordinances," in *Chaucer's England: Literature in Historical Context*, ed. Barbara A. Hanawalt, Medieval Studies at Minnesota, vol. 4 (Minneapolis, 1992), pp. 110–132; and Caroline M. Barron, "William Langland: A London Poet," in Hanawalt, *Chaucer's England*, pp. 91–109.

54. George Economou, trans., *William Langland's Piers Plowman: The C Version* (Philadelphia, 1996), pp. 58–59.

55. *CPMR 1413–37*, vol. 4, pp. 151–154.

56. Curtis, "Lay Subsidy of 1332," p. 40.

57. For descriptions of rooms, their layout in various types of houses, fabric, and furnishing see Schofield, *Medieval London Houses*, pp. 61–133.

58. Tania Bayard, trans., *A Medieval Home Companion: Housekeeping in the Fourteenth Century* (New York: HarperCollins, 1991), p. 95.

59. Martha Howell provided this insight into the painting in a lecture at the John Paul Getty Museum in 1999.

60. *HW*, vol. 2, p. 131. Henry de Yerdelee left to Sabine, his wife, 1,000 marks sterling and her entire chamber, with jewels and all household goods.

61. TNA: PRO Prob. 2/8.

62. TNA: PRO Prob. 2/11, 2/15, 2/50, 2/137, 2/20, 2/22, 2/23, 2/93, 2/98, 2/143.

63. TNA: PRO Prob. 2/11, 137, 98.

64. *CCorR*, p. 41.

65. CLRO MC 1/3/232. A landlord claimed against his tenant that he had provided the basic amenities that a rental property worth 10 marks a year might cost. The landlord argued that the tenant had stripped the cellar and apartment on Cordwainer Street. From the parlor, the landlord charged, the tenant took one

bench of oak, an almery of timber from Norway, a mold board in the hall that was eighteen feet in length, a pavement of Flemish tile, a press of oak, and a barrel stand of oak. He also denuded the cellar and the yard, taking an entranceway to the cellar, an iron key for the pantry, a lead cistern weighing fifteen hundred pounds, two lead gutters weighing three hundred pounds, a lead pipe, a brewing trough weighing seven hundred pounds, and a brewing vat. In total, he stripped the house of £15 worth of goods. One wonders that the value was so low.

66. CLRO MC 1/2A/40.

67. CCorR, pp. 88–89.

68. LBK 1422–61, p. 86 (1428).

69. GL, Ms. 9051, and GL, Ms. 9171. The Archdeaconry court covers the period of 1393–1409 and the Commissary court that of 1377–1480.

70. Kristen M. Burkholder, "Threads Bared: Dress and Textiles in Late Medieval English Wills," in Medieval Clothing and Textiles, ed. Robin Netherton and Gale R. Owen-Crocker, vol. 1 (Woodbridge, U.K., 2005), pp. 133–153, has looked at 550 wills between 1327 and 1485. Only 17 percent of these were by women. The evidence comes from both the Husting court and the Prerogative court of Canterbury. She found that women and clerics were more likely to leave clothing (65 percent of the women and 63 percent of the clerics, and only 44 percent of lay men.) Furthermore, women were more likely to leave detailed descriptions.

71. HW, vol. 2, pp. 214–215 (1380), 259. See also pp. 216, 363.

72. HW, vol. 2, pp. 265–266 (1404).

73. GL, Ms. 9171/6, fol. 272v.

74. GL, Ms. 9171/3, fols. 152, 302v; GL, Ms. 9051/1, fols. 2, 4, 6v, 8, 9v, 10v, 12, 118v, 19, 21v. See Robert A. Wood, "Poor Widows, c. 1393–1415," in Medieval London Widows, 1300–1500, ed. Caroline M. Barron and Anne F. Sutton (London, 1994), pp. 55–70. Wood has used the Archdeaconry court alone and has used different categories than appear in the original. For a more complete analysis of the poor see Hanawalt, "Reading the Lives of the Illiterate: London's Poor."

75. CCorR, pp. 61–62.

76. Martin Weinbaum, ed., The London Eyre of 1276, LRS, vol. 12 (Leicester, 1976), pp. 8, 38.

77. HW, vol. 1, p. 227.

78. CPMR 1381–1412, pp. 3, 47–48.

79. CLMC 1350–70, pp. 47–48.

80. Barron et al., "Allesandro Magno," p. 143.

81. Ibid., p. 146. Sneyd, trans., A Relation or Rather a True Account of the Island of England, p. 21. The Venetian even observed that when the English soldiers were fighting the French, they insisted on eating even during the height of war.

82. Edith Rickert, ed. and trans., The Babee's Book: Medieval Manners for the Young: Done into Modern English from Dr. Furnivall's Texts (New York, 1966), pp. 34–35.

83. H. S. Bennett, England from Chaucer to Caxton (New York, 1928), pp. 134–138.

84. CCoR, pp. 68–69.

85. HW, vol. 2, pp. 214–215, 220–221.

86. Frances E. Baldwin, *Sumptuary Legislation and Personal Regulation in England*, Johns Hopkins University Studies in Social and Political Science, series 44 (Baltimore, 1926), pp. 47–50. Burkholder, "Threads Bared," has not only a quantitative description of the clothing left in wills but also a discussion of the conformity of this clothing to sumptuary legislation. Were people living beyond the law? She concludes, pp. 143–150, that Londoners and most people had possessions that were within the requirements of the legislation. Whether or not they were limited by budget, by their own preference for dressing according to their rank, or in accordance with the law is not shown in the wills.

87. *CPMR 1323–64*, vol. 1, p. 102 (1323).

88. *HW*, vol. 2, p. 114.

89. *HW*, vol. 2, pp. 214–215.

90. Paul Bailey, ed., *The Oxford Book of London* (Oxford, 1996), pp. 16–19.

91. Ibid., pp. 19–20.

92. Thomas F. Reddaway, *The Early History of the Goldsmith's Company, 1327–1509* (London, 1975), p. 83.

93. Derek Keene, "Shops and Shopping in Medieval London," in *Medieval Art, Architecture and Archaeology in London*, ed. Lindy Grant (Oxford, 1984), pp. 29–46.

94. Henry Thomas Riley, ed., *Memorials of London and London Life in the Thirteenth, Fourteenth, and Fifteenth Centuries* (London, 1869), pp. 203–204.

95. TNA: PRO C1/66/445. One widow complained that she had been robbed of 100s. and a gold bracelet. *CPMR 1323–64*, vol. 1, p. 120.

96. Bayard, *A Medieval Home Companion*, pp. 35–36.

97. "Bewte Will Shewe, Thow Hornys Be Away," in *Political, Religious, and Love Poems: From the Archhbishop of Canterbury's Lambeth Ms. No. 306 and Other Sources*, ed. Frederick J. Furnivall, EETS, o.s., vol. 15 (London, 1866), pp. 73–75. These attitudes confirm Burkholder's conclusion in "Threads Bared," pp. 149–150, that people might have chosen to dress according to their status.

98. Christine Carpenter, ed., *Kingsford's Stonor Letters and Papers, 1290–1483* (Cambridge, 1996), vol. 2, no. 211.

99. Ibid., nos. 217, 224, 227, 233.

100. Martha Carlin, "Fast Food and Urban Living Standards in Medieval England," in *Food and Eating in Medieval Europe*, ed. Martha Carlin and Joel T. Rosenthal (London, 1998), pp. 27–52.

101. Carlin, *Medieval Southwark*, pp. 49–50, 210–228.

102. *LBK 1422–61*, p. 95.

103. *LBK 1422–61*, pp. 75–76.

104. P. J. P. Goldberg, "Women in Fifteenth-Century Town Life," in *Towns and Townspeople in the Fifteenth Century*, ed. John A. F. Thomson (Wolfeboro Falls, N.H., 1988), pp. 105–128, discusses women's charitable giving in York.

105. *HW*, vol. 1, p. 277. *CIPM 1365–70*, vol. 12, pp. 269–270.

106. *CPMR 1381–1412*, vol. 3, pp. 43–45. For other examples of gifts to the parish church see *LBE 1314–37*, p. 259, *CPMR 1364–81*, vol. 2, p. 257 (1379), *CPMR 1381–1412*, vol. 3, p. 171.

107. GL, Ms. 9051/1, fol. 9v.

108. GL, Ms. 9171/3, fols. 152, 302v.

109. GL, Ms. 9051/1, fol. 9v.

110. GL, Ms. 9051/1, fols. 19, 20, 98.

111. Katherine L. French, "Women in the Late Medieval English Parish," in *Gendering the Master Narrative: Women and Power in the Middle Ages*, ed. Maryanne Kowaleski and Mary C. Erler (Ithaca, 2003), pp. 161–162.

112. Katherine L. French, "Maidens' Lights and Wives' Stores: Women's Parish Guilds in Late Medieval England," *Sixteenth-Century Journal* 29 (1998), pp. 399–425.

113. Katherine L. French, "'To Free Them from Binding': Women in the Late Medieval Parish," *Journal of Interdisciplinary History* 28 (1997), pp. 387–412.

114. French, "Women in the Late Medieval English Parish," pp. 162–165. French points out that many people still stood and that the sexes were divided in medieval churches. The prestige of seating meant more to women than to men.

115. George Unwin, *The Gilds and Companies of London* (1908; reprint, London, 1966), pp. 110–126.

116. Barbara A. Hanawalt, "Keepers of the Lights; Late Medieval English Parish Gilds," *Journal of Medieval and Renaissance History* 14 (1984), pp. 21–37.

117. Caroline M. Barron, "The Parish Fraternities of Medieval London," in *The Church in Pre-Reformation Society: Essays in Honour of F. R. H. DuBoulay*, ed. Caroline M. Barron and Christopher Harper-Bill (Woodbridge, U.K., 1985), pp. 13–37.

118. *CIPM 1383–91*, vol. 16, p. 200.

119. Clive Burgess, "Shaping the Parish: St. Mary at Hill, London, in the Fifteenth Century," in *The Cloister and the World: Essays in Medieval History in Honour of Barbara Harvey*, ed. John Blair and Brian Golding (Oxford, 1996), pp. 246–285. The accounts of St. Mary at Hill in London are particularly full. They show that elite men played the dominant role in donations to the church and, as church wardens, making decisions about its maintenance, building programs, and charitable organization. Women never appeared in church governance, but they did appear as donors and recipients of bequests. The parish formed a strong community bond for both men and women. The parishioners relied on each other in times of trouble and gave bequests at their death. The poor of the parish were given relief out of parish funds as well as individual wills.

120. Steuer, "Family Strategies in Medieval London," pp. 81–93. Mary C. Erler, "The Library of a London Vowess, Margery de Nerford," in *Women, Reading and Piety in Late Medieval England*, ed. Mary C. Erler (Cambridge, 2002), pp. 54–55.

121. *LBG 1352–74*, p. 210, *LBF 1337–52*, p. 228.

122. Matthew Davies, "Dame Thomasine Percyvale, 'The Maid of Week' (d. 1512)," in *Medieval London Widows, 1300–1500*, pp. 202–207.

123. Anne F. Sutton, "Lady Joan Bradbury (d. 1530)," in *Medieval London Widows, 1300–1500*, pp. 222–238.

Chapter 8

1. Annie Abram, *Social England in the Fifteenth Century: A Study in the Effects of Economic Conditions* (London, 1909), pp. 131–146. She assumed that women, because they had so many different occupations, were more highly skilled and versatile as laborers than were men. Eileen Power, *Medieval Women*, ed. M. M. Postan (London, 1975), pp. 34, 53–55, included single women in her view of women's opportunities in an expanding economy. Alice Clark, *Working Life of Women in the Seventeenth Century* (New York, 1920), wrote one of the most influential books, emphasizing the household economy. For a discussion of Clark, see Louise A. Tilly and Joan W. Scott, *Women, Work, and Family* (New York, 1978). Very much in the mold of Alice Clark and earlier writers is Kay E. Lacey, "Women and Work in Fourteenth- and Fifteenth-Century London," in *Women and Work in Pre-industrial England*, ed. Charles Kindsey and Lorna Duffin (Kent, England, 1985), pp. 24–82.

2. Caroline M. Barron, "'The Golden Age' of Women in Medieval London," *Reading Medieval Studies* 15 (1989), pp. 35–58. She has relied heavily on individual cases.

3. P. J. P. Goldberg, *Women, Work and Life Cycle in a Medieval Economy: Women in York and Yorkshire c. 1300–1520* (Oxford, 1992), pp. 345–361, for a summary. Goldberg's book relies heavily on the argument for a demographic shortfall giving single women more opportunities. He argues strongly that the "northern European marriage pattern" existed in medieval England and that women remained single and worked, thus delaying the age of marriage. He sees a number of single women enjoying considerable access to jobs and establishing an "economic enfranchisement." Unfortunately, he often relies on only fifteen to twenty cases. Heather Swanson, *Medieval Artisans: An Urban Class in Late Medieval England* (Oxford, 1989). She only mentions women as few or isolated examples. Judith M. Bennett, "History Stands Still: Women's Work in the European Past," *Feminist Studies* 19 (1988), pp. 269–283; "Medieval Women, Modern Women: Across the Great Divide," in *Culture and History, 1350–1600: Essays on English Communities, Identities and Writing*, ed. David Aers (Detroit, 1992), pp. 147–176; "Confronting Continuity," *Journal of Women's History* 9 (1997), pp. 73–94. These articles are critical of the "golden age" hypothesis.

4. Marjorie Keniston McIntosh, *Working Women in English Society* (Cambridge, 2005), pp. 28–36, has a very good discussion of the positions of historians writing on women in the economy in England.

5. Susan Cahn, *Industry of Devotion: The Transformation of Women's Work in England, 1500–1660* (New York, 1987). Peter Erle, *A City Full of People: Men and Women of London, 1640–1750* (London, 1994).

6. Martha Howell, *Women, Production, and Patriarchy in Late Medieval Cities* (Chicago, 1986). Katrina Honeyman and Jordan Goodman, "Women's Work, Gender Conflict, and Labour Markets in Europe, 1500–1900," *Economic History Review* 44 (1991), pp. 608–628. Judith C. Brown and Jordan Goodman,

"Women and Industry in Florence," *Journal of Economic History* 40 (1980), pp. 73–80, have shown that female employment, while low in the fifteenth century, increased in the seventeenth century as the Florentine economy changed.

7. David Herlihy, *Opera Muliebria: Women and Work in Medieval Europe* (New York, 1990), pp. 180–185.

8. See McIntosh, *Working Women*, pp. 37–42, for a concise statement of her thesis.

9. Maryanne Kowaleski, "Women's Work in a Market Town: Exeter in the Late Fourteenth Century," in *Women and Work in Preindustrial Europe*, ed. Barbara A. Hanawalt (Bloomington, Ind., 1986), pp. 145–164.

10. Olwen Hufton, "Women and the Family Economy in Eighteenth-Century France," *French Historical Studies* 9 (1975), pp. 1–22.

11. *Liber Albus*, p. 181. "Of hiring Houses: If a wife, as though a single woman, rents any house or shop within the said city, she shall be bound to pay the rent of the said house or shop, and shall be impleaded and sued as a single woman, by way of debt if necessary, notwithstanding that she is *coverte de baron* at the time of such letting, supposing that the lessor did not know thereof." London is in sharp contrast with Florence, in which a woman without a husband needed to have a *mundualdus* (a man who acted as her tutor) to make a legal transaction. The presumption was that a woman did not have a "legal persona." See Thomas Kuehn, "'Cum Consensu Mundualdi': Legal Guardianship of Women in Quatrocento Florence," *Viator* 13 (1982), pp. 309–333.

12. CLRO, Husting Court Wills and Deeds. The five-year samples were taken from the nineteenth-century handwritten calendar of the rolls compiled by W. T. Alchin and taken over by Reginald Sharpe, records clerk, and his assistants. This compilation is contained in reels 28 and 29 of the microfilm edition, *The Husting Rolls of Deeds and Wills, 1252–1485* (Cambridge, 1990). G. H. Martin provides a very helpful "Guide to the Microfilm Edition," pp. 5–25.

13. Martin, "Guide," p. 15, also notes that the volume decreased and the business of the court was reduced to four a year. He does not speculate on the reasons for the decrease, but it coincides with similar ones in the court of wards recorded in the Letter Books.

14. McIntosh, *Working Women*, pp. 114–116.

15. Helena M. Chew, *London Possessory Assizes: A Calendar*, LRS, vol. 1 (London, 1965). The suits brought under the possessory assizes were suits of novel disseisin, or who had rightful ownership of the land or rent. For a discussion of the history of this type of writ and court action see Donald W. Sutherland, *The Assize of Novel Disseisin* (Oxford, 1973). The action was a royal one, but in 1341 London purchased the right to hold the assizes in a London court (Chew, *London Possessory Assizes*, p. xvi).

16. Valerie Emanoil, "London Widows' Activities in the Late Medieval Land Market" (master's thesis, Clemson University, 1999), pp. 35–44. A widow acting alone as plaintiff was not unusual, since 200 of the 273 assizes were initiated by one person alone and an additional 48 by husband and wife.

17. TNA: PRO C1/216/68.

18. Emanoil, "London Widows' Activities," p. 45.

19. *LBE 1314–37*, pp. 117 and 114. See p. 107.

20. *LBE 1314–37*, p. 107 (1319).

21. *LBF 1337–52*, p. 236 (1351). In another case, the new husband and the widow rented a tenement to the heir, and he was to get the reversion when she died, p. 220. *LBG 1352–74*, pp. 285–286. *LBE 1314–37*, pp. 37, 174, 184, 190, 204–205, 286, *LBF 1337–52*, pp. 31, 104, 113.

22. *LBE 1314–37*, pp. 255, 114.

23. *LBE 1314–37*, p. 135.

24. *LBE 1314–37*, p. 174 (1322).

25. *LBH 1375–99*, p. 2. In *LBE 1314–37*, p. 134, a husband and wife leased a mercer a chamber in their seld with chests and cupboards there in for 13 s. 4 d. See also *LBG 1352–74*, p. 309.

26. *LBF 1337–52*, p. 171.

27. *LBF 1337–52*, p. 235. *LBG 1352–74*, p. 27; and pp. 37–38.

28. *LBE 1314–37*, pp. 67–68. For another case see *LBI 1400–1422*, pp. 153–55.

29. *LBF 1337–52*, p. 63. See also p. 117. *CPMR 1413–143*, vol. 4 (1422), p. 144.

30. *LBF 1337–52*, pp. 56–57. See also p. 31. In *LBG 1352–74*, p. 70, a husband and wife give certain quitrents to Johanna Wiggemor of Hertforshire for a term of 30 years to pay back a commercial loan of £40. See also *CPMR 1364–81*, vol. 2, p. 139 (1372).

31. *CPMR 1364–81*, vol. 2, p. 67 (1366).

32. *CPMR 1413–37*, vol. 4, p. 207 (1426).

33. *CPMR 1364–81*, vol. 2, p. 114 (1370).

34. *CPMR 1364–81*, vol. 2, p. 157 (1379).

35. *LBE 1314–37*, p. 74 (1320).

36. In *CPMR 1364–81*, vol. 2, p. 284 (1381), has another case in which the widow of a knight appealed to the king's council to get back a box of muniments relating to her and her husband's lands and debts. The king referred to the city, and a return was requested. Delivery of a chest of deeds from one woman to another appears in *LBE 1314–37*, p. 34 (1314).

37. *CPMR 1364–81*, vol. 2, pp. 286–286 (1381). For other mention of written deeds in women's private possession see *LBG 1352–74*, pp. 183–184, *CPMR 1381–1412*, vol. 3, pp. 84, 190 (1387, 1391). *LBH 1375–99*, pp. 104–105, 143–144.

38. Brigitte Bedos Rezak, "Women, Seals, and Power in Medieval France, 1150–1350," in *Women and Power in the Middle Ages*, ed. Mary Erler and Maryanne Kowaleski (Athens, Ga., 1988), pp. 61–82.

39. Helena M. Chew and William Kellaway, eds., *London Assize of Nuisance, 1301–1431: A Calendar*, LRS, vol. 10 (London, 1973), p. 6.

40. Ibid., p. 12.

41. Ibid., p. 141. On the other hand, Idonea de Cambridge complained about a leaning stone wall that endangered her tenants, p. 28.

42. Amy Louise Erickson, *Women and Property in Early Modern England* (London, 1993), has looked at early modern England and the practice of common law and

customary law in regard to women's property rights. Her study does not include London. Her conclusion is that the situation did not become really dire for women until the late seventeenth century. On the other hand, she did not draw a comparison of the sixteenth century to the medieval laws.

43. Barron, "Golden Age," pp. 42–43.

44. *Liber Albus*, p. 181. "And where a woman *coverte de baron* follows any craft within the said city by herself apart, with which the husband in no way intermeddles, such woman shall be bound as a single woman as to all that concerns her said craft. And if the husband and wife are impleaded, in such case, the wife shall plead as a single woman in a Court of Record, and shall have her law and other advantages by way of plea just as a single woman." If condemned in court, she will go to prison, and "neither the husband or his goods shall in such a case be charged or interfered with." The *Liber Albus* also specified that if a plaint of trespass is made against a husband and wife, the woman alone shall make answer. In the case of debt, if both of the couple enter into a contract, and a plaint is made, the husband shall have the aid of his wife and be given time to consult with her (p. 182).

45. *CPMR 1381–1412*, vol. 3, p. 51.

46. *CPMR 1381–1412*, vol. 3, p. 19.

47. Marjorie K. McIntosh, "The Benefits and Drawbacks of *Femme Sole* Status in England, 1300–1630," *Journal of British Studies* 44 (2005), pp. 410–438.

48. In *CIPM 1347–52*, vol. 9, pp. 301–302. *CIPM 1347–52*, vol. 9, pp. 458–459, marriage of a widow of a former office of engraver gave her new husband the position and dower. *LBG 1352–74*, p. 5, suggests that the king's valet and his wife were given the office of gauging wine in 1352, but one assumes that this would be something that they would receive payment from but not do themselves.

49. *CPMR 1413–37*, vol. 4, pp. 138–139 (1421).

50. CLRO MC 1/2, MC 1/2A, MC 1/3, MC 1/3A. The bills were equity petitions made to the mayor. They are not published, although there is a handwritten calendar. I used the calendar and compared it with the original bills. For MC 1/3A, I used the originals. The bundles include materials from 1366 to 1471. Most of them come from the late fourteenth century and the first half of the fifteenth century. I did not use sampling for these bundles. Although both a graduate assistant and I checked the figures, they showed some discrepancies. The number of women is accurate, but the number of men may not be completely accurate. The total number of persons appearing in court was 1,900, with 890 men appearing as plaintiffs and 901 as defendants. The total number of cases was 1,710. Inaccuracies in the count of males are not great enough to change the overall percentages. McIntosh, "*Femme Sole* Status," p. 436, table A4, groups the bills by date and includes later bills as well. I have used only those listed above and did not try to group them by date. McIntosh's data show considerable variations, but the overall results are the same. She also did the Sheriff's court and a sample derived from the *CPMR*. See pp. 43–48. Because we used different approaches, her data and mine are hard to compare. I found twelve cases in

which the woman was specifically stated as trading *femme sole*, but her samples might not have included these.

51. CLRO MC 1/3 (1421). She brought the case with her husband.

52. In CLRO MC 1/2, Margery Notyngham and her husband, a mercer, were sued for a debt of £21 by a Fleming. In MC 1/2 (1391), Isabelle, a silkwoman and wife of Alan Senerur, had a debt of £6 17s. 6d. and was sued for retaining silk she got from the wife of the plaintiff. The man, a skinner, also wanted 100s. in damages. In MC 1/2 (1393), Alice, wife of Nicholas, trading *femme sole*, contracted a debt of 40s. She paid 36s. In MC 1/2 (1379), a woman failed to return a coffer. In MC 1/3 (1436), Alice, widow of John Worwell, owed a brewer 5 marks from the time she was trading *femme sole* as a huckster. In MC 1/3 (1441), Katherine, wife of William Sergeant, traded *sole* out of her house as an upholdster [dealer in secondhand clothes] and received furs from the plaintiff but did not pay him. In MC 1/3 (1442), Agnes, wife of Thomas Atte Wode, a brewer, had incurred a debt of £14 for sixty quarters of malt while she was trading *femme sole*. In MC 1/3 (1444), Katherine, wife of Edward Frank, incurred a debt for 10s. 10d. She did not appear, and the plaintiff received 3s. in damages, and she was fined. In MC 1/3 (1444), Katherine, a huckster, and wife of Thomas Clerk, incurred a debt of 14s. 9d. for white bread. In MC 1/3 (1456), Elizabeth, a huckster, and wife of Richard Bulk, owed a debt of 13s. 4d. for beer. In MC 13A, Margery, wife of William Bailey, owed a debt of 19s. 6d.

53. TNA: PRO C1/80/12. See also C1/131/68.

54. TNA: PRO C1/67/174. For a similar case, see (C1/64/883).

55. McIntosh, "*Femme Sole* Status," pp. 434–435. The total number of women appearing in court is small, as in the original bills. Common suits were for debt, withholding goods, and broken covenants.

56. *CPMR 1381–1412*, vol. 3, pp. 19–21 (1382).

57. McIntosh, *Working Women*, p. 121.

58. *CPMR 1364–81*, vol. 2, p. 78 (1367). See also *CPMR 1381–1412*, vol. 3, p. 297 (1409), in which William Crane, a haberdasher, tried to collect on a debt against John Frenssh and his wife, who was trading *sole*; he finally confessed that the couple knew nothing of the matter, and he took the loan himself.

59. CLRO, MC 1/2A, 5; MC 1/2, 79, 163, 245; MC 1/3A, 12; MC 1/3, 59, 80, 87, 237, 373. See also *CPMR 1437–57*, vol. 5, p. 97 (1447). *CPMR 1413–37*, vol. 4, p. 144 (1422).

60. *CPMR 1437–57*, vol. 5, pp. 101–102 (1447).

61. *CPMR 1437–57*, vol. 5, p. 35 (1441).

62. *LBG 1352–74*, p. 169, *CPMR 1364–81*, vol. 2, p. 69 (1367). William C. Jordan, *Women and Credit in Pre-industrial and Developing Societies* (Philadelphia, 1993), pt. 2, overemphasizes the role of women in the credit markets for the late medieval period. He uses little evidence for his sweeping claims.

63. *CPMR 1364–81*, vol. 2, pp. 90–91 (1368), p. 217 (1380).

64. *CPMR 1364–81*, vol. 2, pp. 107–108. Assault and slander and an accusation of a miscarriage also appeared on p. 41 (1365).

65. *CPMR 1364–81*, vol. 2, pp. 30, 35 (1365).

66. TNA: PRO C1/16/45.

67. McIntosh, *Working Women*, pp. 85–98. Women in suits over debt appear in a variety of cases: *CPMR 1364–81*, vol. 2, pp. 66–67 (1366), TNA: PRO C1/33/353, CLRO MC 1/1/188.

68. One of the success stories of a widow collecting debts owed to her husband was that of Margaret Croke. See Kay Lacey, "Margaret Croke (d. 1491)," in *Medieval London Widows, 1300–1500*, ed. Caroline M. Barron and Anne F. Sutton (London, 1994), pp. 143–164. *CPMR 1381–1412*, vol. 3, pp. 253–255 (1398). Naveryna, widow and executrix of John Thornbury, knight, along with Thornsbury's son, recovered money from Matheu de Magname of Bologna and Gerard de Ferrar, who were executors of the will of an Englishman, William Gold. The amount claimed included a third part of 6,000 marks in gold, silver, silk, jewels, precious stones, letters, and accounts. She, or her fellow executors, did get the third part.

69. *CPMR 1364–81*, vol. 2, pp. 218–219 (1376).

70. *CPMR 1364–81*, vol. 2, p. 171 (1374). See also pp. 216–217 (1376), *CPMR 1413–37*, vol. 4, p. 186 (1425) and p. 188 (1426). In an interesting case in *CPMR 1381–1412*, vol. 3, p. 72 (1384), a widow came to court saying that her husband had repeatedly tried to pay 500 marks in a loan. No one came to collect it, so she deposited the sum with the chamberlain, who would pay should the party appear.

71. *CPMR 1323–64*, vol. 1, p. 114 (1339).

72. A. Abram, "Women Traders in Medieval London," *Economic Journal* 26 (1916), pp. 276–285. Marian K. Dale, "The London Silkwomen of the Fifteenth Century," *Economic History Review*, 1st series, 4 (1933), pp. 324–335. Lacey, "Women and Work in Fourteenth and Fifteenth Century London," pp. 24–82. Jenny Kermode, *Medieval Merchants: York, Beverley and Hull in the Later Middle Ages* (Cambridge, 1998), p. 304, found that few widows took over from their former husbands.

73. Martha Carlin, *Medieval Southwark* (London, 1996), pp. 174–177. Of the 137 female householders, 10 to 14 were servants, and 4 were described as widows and, according to tax records, were fairly well off. She speculates that many of the other female householders were also widows. Only a few of these women had servants living with them. These women paid 35 percent lower taxes than couples, whereas single men paid only 7 percent less.

74. GL, Ms. 9051/1.

75. *LBF 1337–52*, pp. 91–92, *CPMR 1413–37*, vol. 4, p. 10 (1413).

76. See McIntosh, *Working Women*, pp. 107–114, on pawning.

77. *LBH 1375–99*, pp. 32–33, is a case of the orphaned daughter of Nicholas Donat, a spicer and brother to John. His daughter became an orphan of the city, so he apparently had citizenship.

78. *CPMR 1381–1412*, vol. 3, pp. 185–187, 217–218, 265–266.

79. Derek Keene, "Tanners' Widows, 1300–1350," in Barron and Sutton, *Medieval London Widows, 1300–1500*, pp. 1–28.

80. Elspeth Veale, "Matilda Penne, Skinner (d. 1392–3)," in Barron and Sutton, *Medieval London Widows, 1300–1500*, pp. 47–54.

81. Caroline M. Barron, "Johanna Hill (d. 1441) and Johanna Sturdy (d. c. 1460), Bell-Founders," in Barron and Sutton, *Medieval London Widows, 1300–1500*, pp. 99–111.

82. CPMR 1364–81, vol. 2, p. 46 (1365).

83. TNA: PRO C1/7/263, C1/7/283.

84. CPMR 1413–37, vol. 4, pp. 230–231 (1429).

85. CPMR 1413–37, vol. 4, p. 280 (1434).

86. Thomas F. Reddaway, *The Early History of the Goldsmiths' Company, 1327–1509* (London, 1975), p. 147.

87. CPMR 1364–81, vol. 2, p. 128 (1371).

88. Heather Swanson, "Illusion of Economic Structure: Craft Guilds in Late Medieval English Towns," *Past and Present* 121 (1988), pp. 45–46.

89. Barbara A. Hanawalt, *Growing Up in Medieval London: The Experience of Childhood in History* (New York, 1993), pp. 155–171.

90. CPMR 1364–81, vol. 2, pp. 99–103, 110–111 (1368–69).

91. Annie Abram, "Women Traders in Medieval London," pp. 276–285. Dale, "The London Silkwomen of the Fifteenth Century," pp. 324–335. Dale's article was reprinted with comments by Judith Bennett and Maryann Kowaleski in *Signs* 14 (Chicago, 1989), pp. 489–501.

92. Dale, "The London Silkwomen," pp. 495–497.

93. For a summary of women and their relationship to craft and merchant guilds see Maryanne Kowaleski and Judith M. Bennett, "Crafts, Gilds, and Women in the Middle Ages: Fifty Years after Marian K. Dale," *Signs*, 14 (1989), pp. 474–488. As Howell observed in *Women, Production and Patriarchy*, the women's guilds of Cologne lost their official status in government. In Paris, women were never the masters of their guilds.

94. CPMR 1364–81, vol. 2, pp. 99–106.

95. Dale, "The London Silkwomen," pp. 489–500. For references to London silkwomen in addition to Dale's article, see CLRO MC 1/2/92, CPMR 1413–37, vol. 4, p. 146 (1422), LBF 1337–52, p. 187, LBK 1422–61, pp. 127, 378. CLRO, Bridge House Rental 1460–86, vol. 3, pp. 3, 560, 1152, shows that silkwomen set up shops on one of the main thoroughfares of the city. Dale used the Chancery petitions to good effect. Many of these cases are about uncollected debts: C1/64/735, 808, 1161, and TNA: PRO C1/110/125.

96. Anne F. Sutton, "Alice Claver, Silkwoman (d. 1489)," in Barron and Sutton, *Medieval London Widows, 1300–1500*, pp. 129–142.

97. The wills of these two men are not recorded. A William Hull was active as master of the masons and carpenters and served as a viewer of nuisances between 1457 and 1467. CPMR 1438–82, vol. 6, pp. 3, 8, 14, 17, 31, 32, 34, 37, 41, 42. Sutton, "Alice Claver," p. 134, was prominent among the silkwomen connected with Alice Claver.

98. TNA: PRO C1/43/219.

99. Anne F. Sutton, "The Shop-Floor of the London Mercery Trade, c. 1200–c. 1500: The Marginalization of the Artisan, the Itinerant Mercer, and the Shopholder," *Nottingham Medieval Studies* 45 (2001), pp. 12–50.

100. Judith M. Bennett, *Ale, Beer, and Brewsters in England: Women's Work in a Changing World, 1300–1600* (New York, 1996), chap. 3.

101. Ibid., chap. 4.

102. Ibid., chap. 5.

103. Ibid., chap. 8. McIntosh, *Working Women*, pp. 140–181, has looked at women in brewing in other towns in England, as has Bennett. She concludes that women continued to prosper in brewing in the late fourteenth and fifteenth centuries in these market towns, but that this decreased in the sixteenth century. She would not call this a "golden age" but feels that Bennett's conclusion that brewsters were always marginal and poorly paid is inaccurate. The corrective, however, is for married women whose husbands were prominent in other trades or in government.

104. Bennett, "Working Together." Henry Thomas Riley, ed., *Memorials of London and London Life in the Thirteenth, Fourteenth, and Fifteenth Centuries* (London, 1869), p. 182. Only two women were among the twenty-nine taverners who shut their shops and would not sell wine in protest of a city ordinance (1331) that all wine be sold from taverns with doors and windows open to the daylight.

105. McIntosh, *Working Women*, pp. 202–209, for women innkeepers.

106. *CPMR 1413–37*, vol. 4, p. 122 (1422), *CPMR 1381–1412*, vol. 3, p. 282 (1406), *CPMR 1364–81*, vol. 2, p. 198 (1375).

107. *CPMR 1323–64*, vol. 1, p. 233 (1350).

108. *CPMR 1364–81*, vol. 2, pp. 203–204 (1375), TNA: PRO C1/67/146.

109. Gervase Rosser, "London and Westminster: The Suburb in the Urban Economy in the Later Middle Ages," in *Towns and Townspeople in the Fifteenth Century*, ed. John A. F. Thomson (Gloucester, U.K., 1988), p. 53, observes that women in Westminster ran rooming houses. In Thomas, *CEMCR 1298–1307*, p. 12, a foreign woman is accused of running a lodging house as a foreigner and buying and selling Rhine wine to foreigners. McIntosh, *Women's Work*, pp. 61–71, discusses the role of women as landladies for boarders and for room rentals.

110. Barbara A. Hanawalt, "The Widow's Mite: Provisions for Medieval London Widows," in *Upon My Husband's Death: Widows in the Literature and Histories of Medieval Europe*, ed. Louise Mirrer (Ann Arbor, 1992), pp. 21–45.

111. The deficiencies of the English evidence are apparent when one reads chap. 8 of James M. Murray, *Bruges, Cradle of Capitalism, 1280–1390* (Cambridge, 2005). He is able to point to women in the money-changing business, banking, cloth making, and a number of other trades. But he shows that the majority of women taking part in business belonged to households headed by men; occasionally, a widow was the household head.

112. McIntosh, *"Femme Sole* Status," pp. 429–431.

113. Sheilagh Ogilvie, "How Does Social Capital Affect Women? Guilds and Communities of Early Modern Germany," *American Historical Review* 109 (2004), pp. 325–359. Ogilvie has demonstrated how guilds and communities effectively excluded women from participating in the social capital or social and economic networks. She does not find that the earlier period was a golden age for women.

Chapter 9

1. Marjorie Keniston McIntosh, *Working Women in English Society* (Cambridge, 2005).

2. Rodney H. Hilton, "Women Traders in Medieval England," *Women's Studies* 2 (1984), p. 149, found that three-fourths of the immigrants in the market town were single women. P. J. P. Goldberg, *Women, Work, and Life Cycle in a Medieval Economy: Women in York and Yorkshire c. 1300–1520* (Oxford, 1992), chap. 6, gives no more than a general causation of movement into towns and anecdotal information of some women and couples who did. David Herlihy, *Opera Muliebria: Women and Work in Medieval Europe* (New York, 1990), pp. 135–142, has offered an admittedly crude measure for Paris drawn from the rolls of 1292 and 1313. He found that four out of ten Parisian males and three out of four females were possibly immigrants. Immigrants from the Paris basin showed 438 men per 100 women. But these figures are from tax records and would not necessarily represent young women coming in for service. In Florence in 1427, more than one-third of the women heading households were listed as servants, pp. 142–148, 159. Madonna J. Hettinger, "Defining the Servant: Legal and Extra-legal Terms of Employment in Fifteenth-Century England," in *The Work of Work: Servitude, Slavery, and Labor in Medieval England*, ed. Allen J. Frantzen and Douglas Moffat (Glasgow, GB, 1994), pp. 206–228. For a more complete discussion of servants in London, including male servants, see Barbara A. Hanawalt, *Growing Up in Medieval London: The Experience of Childhood in History* (New York, 1993), chap. 10. James M. Murray, *Bruges, Cradle of Capitalism, 1280–1390* (Cambridge, 2005), p. 329, thinks that a large number of single women came to Bruges and that many went into casual prostitution. For a summary of arguments on the presence of single women see Maryanne Kowaleski, "Singlewomen in Medieval and Early Modern Europe: The Demographic Perspective," in *Singlewomen in the European Past, 1250–1800*, ed. Judith M. Bennett and Amy M. Froide (Philadelphia, 1999), pp. 38–81.

3. P. J. P. Goldberg, "Migration, Youth, and Gender in Later Medieval England," in *Youth in the Middle Ages*, ed. P. J. P. Goldberg and Felicity Riddy (York, U.K., 2004), pp. 87–88.

4. Goldberg, "Migration, Youth, and Gender," pp. 91–99.

5. McIntosh, *Working Women*, pp. 47–48.

6. P. J. P. Goldberg, "What Is a Servant?" in *Concepts and Patterns of Service in the Later Middle Ages*, ed. Anne Curry and Elizabeth Matthew (Woodbridge, U.K., 2000), pp. 1–20. He has an extended discussion of the use of these terms.

7. Barbara A. Hanawalt, "The Host, the Law, and the Ambiguous Space of Medieval London Taverns," in *"Of Good and Ill Repute": Gender and Social Control in Medieval England* (New York, 1998), pp. 104–123. For a discussion of the use of the term, see David Herlihy, *Medieval Households* (Cambridge, Mass., 1948), pp. 2–5.

8. *LBF 1337–52*, p. 157 (1346).

9. Caroline M. Barron, "The Fourteenth-Century Poll Tax Returns for Worcester," *Midland History* (1989), pp. 1–29. Goldberg, *Women, Work and Life Cycle*, p. 161.

10. Martha Carlin, *Medieval Southwark* (London, 1996), pp. 137–139, found that in the 1381 poll tax returns, 5.5 percent of the people listed (n=1,060) were female live-in servants and 1.6 percent were female live-out servants. Only eight of the female-headed households in the 1381 poll tax had servants (p. 177). Carlin shows that in Flemish and other alien households in 1440, there were 101 male single male live-in servants and 15 female live-in servants, pp. 152–153. Other servants again show a predominance of males (seventy-three) over females (twenty-one). Five of the male servants were married, and seven of the females were.

11. In Sylvia L. Thrupp, *The Merchant Class of Medieval London, 1300–1500* (Ann Arbor, 1948), p. 151, a man specified in a retirement contract that he would have servants to accompany him and his wife when they went out into the streets.

12. McIntosh, *Working Women*, pp. 53–55.

13. CLRO MC 1/1/12. LBG 1352–74, p. 105 (1358).

14. TNA: PRO C1/46/64 and C1/46/84.

15. McIntosh, *Working Women*, p. 53.

16. In *HW*, vol. 2, p. 75, an uncle leaves money toward marriage; in another case, a man has both his niece and his nephew in the household, p. 89.

17. *LBH 1375–99*, p. 297 (1386–87).

18. CLRO MC 1/2A/14 (1382).

19. The Statute of Laborers (1351) was legislation designed to fix wages and prices at the preplague levels. Many of the cases that involve servants, such as Sir John's, were brought for stealing servants and paying a higher wage. TNA: PRO C1/31/493.

20. CLRO, 1515–26, p. 92. (This is an unpublished calendar.)

21. TNA: PRO C1/46/387.

22. CLRO MC 1/2/28 (1380).

23. CPMR 1364–81, vol. 2, p. 37 (1365).

24. The London information on the pay of domestic servants or even female laborers is very poor. London has nothing compared to the information in Ghent; see Marianne Danneel, "Quelques aspects du service domestique féminin à Gand d'après les registres et les manuels échevinaux des Parchons," in *Sociale strucuren en topografie van armoede en rijkdom in de 14de en 15de eeuw, Methodologische aspecten en resultaten van recent orderzoek, Handelingen van het colloquium gehouden te Gent op 24 mei 1985*, Studia Historica Gandensia, no. 267 (Ghent, 1986), pp. 51–72. Judith C. Brown and Jordan Goodman, "Women and Industry in Florence," *Journal of Economic History* 40 (1980), pp. 73–80. Simon A. C. Penn and Christophen Dyer, "Wages and Earnings in Late Medieval England: Evidence from the Enforcement of the Labor Laws," *Economic History Review*, 2nd ser., 43 (1990), pp. 356–376.

25. CLRO MC 1/2A/14 (1382).

26. CPMR 1364–81, vol. 2, pp. 145–146 (1372), Joan Rawe, however, petitioned the lord chancellor that she had worked for a mercer under contract for a year and they had agreed on the wages she would receive. She was not given them,

and when she asked to be released from service, he had her arrested (TNA: PRO C1/46/117).

27. TNA: PRO C1/66/390. In TNA: PRO C1/124/32, a master owed 33 s. 4 d. to a former servant and the husband was now suing him for damages at £59.

28. CLRO MC 1/1/1.

29. *CCorR*, pp. 40–4.

30. *CPMR 1364–81*, vol. 2, p. 25 (1365).

31. TNA: PRO C1/11/114.

32. TNA: PRO C1/64/1158.

33. Frederick C. Tubach, *Index Exemplorum: A Handbook of Medieval Religious Tales*, Folklore Fellows Communications, vol. 86, no. 204 (Helsinki, 1969), nos. 4295, 3155.

34. Thomas F. Reddaway, *The Early History of the Goldsmith's Company, 1327–1509* (London, 1975), p. 151.

35. *Lists of Early Chancery Proceedings in the Public Record Office*, 2 vols. (New York, 1963), p. 130.

36. *LBK 1422–61*, pp. 216–217.

37. Hanawalt, *Growing Up in Medieval London*, 186–199. Susan D. Amussen, "Punishment, Discipline, and Power: The Social Meanings of Violence in Early Modern England," *Journal of British Studies* 34 (1995), pp. 1–34, also speaks of the sexual vulnerability of female servants and the lack of recourse they had in courts. Their position in the household and in law was as ambiguous in the seventeenth century as it was in the fourteenth and fifteenth centuries.

38. TNA: PRO C1/66/369.

39. GL, Ms. 9064/3, fol. 10v. See also GL, Ms. 9064/2, fol. 175.

40. Barbara A. Hanawalt, "The Host, the Law, and the Ambiguous Space of Medieval London Taverns," pp. 104–123. Peter Clark, *The English Alehouse: A Social History 1200–1830* (London, 1983), p. 5. The distinctions among alehouses, taverns, and inns were not made until a statute was established in the sixteenth century that described alehouses as the lower end of the social scale (existing primarily for drink and perhaps some lodging), taverns as selling wine, and inns as being at the upper end of the scale, providing respectable wine, ale, beer, food, and chambers. In the Middle Ages, taverns sold both ale and wine, while alehouses sold only ale.

41. Judith M. Bennett, *Ale, Beer, and Brewsters* (New York, 1996), pp. 122–144.

42. *LBA 1275–98*, p. 220.

43. GL, Ms. 9064/1, fols. 5, 5v, 6, 26v, 30, 31, 64v, 65, 66, 81v, 114, 116, 116v, 119, 119v, 122v, 155v. In TNA: PRO C1/136/79, John Godwynn and Agnes, his wife, were accused in the wardmote of Billingsgate of keeping misrule in an inn called the Mermaid, held on lease from the chamberlain of London.

44. GL, Ms. 9064/1, fols. 68, 83, 84, 91v.

45. TNA: PRO C1/148/67. On the slavery of female domestics in Italy, see Susan Mosher Stuard, "To Town to Serve: Urban Domestic Slavery in Medieval Ragusa," in *Women and Work in Preindustrial Europe*, ed. Barbara A. Hanawalt (Bloomington, Ind., 1986), pp. 39–55.

46. In TNA: PRO C1/66/210. In C1/66/390, a female servant worked for six years and did not receive pay. Her master would not pay her and threatened an action of trespass to compel her to serve. In C1/64/1053, a servant took away two silver spoons and goods worth 100s., which her kinsman said were owed to her.

47. CLMC 1350–70, p. 63 (1352), TNA: PRO C1/45/401, C1/46/271, CPMR 1364–81, vol. 2, p. 35 (1365).

48. Edith Rickert, ed. and trans., "How the Good Wife Taught Her Daughter," pp. 37–38, and "How the Wise Man Taught His Son," p. 46, in *The Babee's Book: Medieval Manners for the Young: Done into Modern English from Dr. Furnivall's Texts* (New York, 1966).

49. Rickert, trans., "How the Good Wife Taught Her Daughter," p. 38.

50. TNA: PRO C1/32/355, C1/32/386.

51. TNA: PRO C1/61/554.

52. *HW*, vol. 1, p. 221; *HW*, vol. 2, pp. 4, 5, 8, 9, 35, 48, 72, 86, 111, 123, 178, 252, 270, 292, 306, 323, 332.

53. TNA: PRO C1/11/114. They claimed that the executors deprived them of it.

54. Barbara A. Hanawalt, "Reading the Lives of the Illiterate: London's Poor," *Speculum* 80 (2004), pp. 1067–1086.

55. CPMR 1364–81, vol. 2, p. 252, pp. 66–67 (1366). LBH 1375–99, p. 121. TNA: PRO C1/33/253. CLRO MC 1/1/188. McIntosh, *Working Women*, pp. 130–132.

56. LBK 1422–61, p. 85.

57. LBH 1375–99, p. 215.

58. LBI 1400–1422, p. 50, pp. 97–98.

59. LBG 1352–74, p. 123, LBH 1375–99, p. 121. LBI 1400–1422, p. 71.

60. LBK 1422–61, p. 293; see n. 122 for reference to Thomas Catworth's injunction that "Sunday should be hold high and holy."

61. LBE 1314–37, pp. 156–159, 161–162, LBG 1352–74, p. 248.

62. LBH 1375–99, pp. 244–245.

63. Figures from CPMR 1413–37, vol. 4, pp. 115–146, 150–159. In 1421–23, six men were charged with extortion as porters, two as regraters, fourteen as hucksters (mostly selling ale that was not of correct measure), ten as "foreigners" acting as free, and two as forestallers. Women were charged mostly with being hucksters (forty-eight), regraters (sixteen), and a scattering of scolds, forstallers, and persons acting free of the city while foreigners. It was the married couples who did all of the above. Only one couple was accused of being a bawd. The figures are interesting compared to Portsoken from 1465 to 1482. Either the concerns of the court and society had changed or Portsoken was quite different as a ward. But Portsoken was included in the earlier records that are preserved. Perhaps social concerns had changed.

64. LBG 1352–74, pp. 175, 269. See also CPMR 1413–37, vol. 4, p. 159

65. LBF 1337–52, pp. 91–93.

66. LBF 1337–52, pp. 91–93 (1343).

67. LBG 1352–74, p. 259.

68. CPMR 1413–37, vol. 4, p. 138 (1422).

69. *LBE 1314–37*, p. 120. See also *CPMR 1323–64*, vol. 1, pp. 161–166 (1338), for forestalling at the corn market; *CPMR 1364–81*, vol. 2, p. 21 (1365), for buying poultry before the market opened; *CPMR 1413–37*, vol. 4, pp. 124, 129, 136.

70. *CEMCR 1323–64*, vol. 1, p. 193 (1344).

71. *CPMR 1364–81*, vol. 2, p. 67 (1366).

72. *LBH 1375–99*, pp. 18–19. Hucksters were not allowed to buy ale and sell it again under penalty of forfeiting the ale. Gelde was pretending to be an official who could take the ale as payment for enforcing the law. See *LBG 1352–74*, p. 124. A restatement of the law appears in *LBH 1375–99*, p. 215.

73. *CEMCR 1298–1307*, p. 62. in *CPMR 1364–81*, vol. 2, p. 32 (1365), eight women were charged with assault and one "huxtere" went to prison for drawing blood from a constable and beating a beadle of the ward.

74. *LBE 1314–37*, pp. 179–180, 184–185, 109–191 (1323)

75. Richard M. Wunderli, *London Church Courts and Society on the Eve of the Reformation* (Boston, 1981), pp. 103–108.

76. GL, Ms. 9064/3.

77. Wunderli, *London Church Courts*, p. 105.

78. Leah Lydia Otis, *Prostitution in Medieval Society: The History of an Urban Institution in Languedoc* (Chicago, 1985), and Jacques Rossiaud, *Medieval Prostitution*, trans. Lydia G. Cochrane (Oxford, 1988), and Murray, *Cradle of Capitalism*, pp. 328–343. He notes that prostitution was tolerated in late medieval Bruges. The city did not try to organize prostitution, but it did fine establishments where prostitution occurred. It is striking that the fines increased dramatically after 1349. Murray suggests that this indicates the increased presence of foreign merchants in Bruges and is another indication of capital growth.

79. E. J. Burford, *Bawds and Lodgings: A History of the London Bankside Brothels, c. 1000–1675* (London, 1976). Martha Carlin, *Medieval Southwark*, pp. 209–229, for stews and prostitution. Because Ruth Mazo Karras, *Common Women: Prostitution and Sexuality in Medieval England* (New York, 1996), discusses medieval English prostitution, including London, the matter does not need extensive discussion here. See also McIntosh, *Working Women*, pp. 75–77. McIntosh points out that in the sixteenth century, the condemnation of prostitution also became associated with venereal disease.

80. GL, Ms. 9064/1, fols. 4v, 22v, 47v, 58v.

81. CLRO, Repetories 5, fols. 52–52v.

82. CLRO, Repetories 5, fols. 110v, 114v.

83. GL, Ms. 9064/1, fols. 143, 43, 32.

84. *CPMR, 1413–37*, vol. 4, p. 138.

85. Karras, *Common Women*, pp. 66–76.

86. Karras, *Common Women*, p. 70. For a complete account of the case see Ruth Mazo Karras and David Lorenzo Boyd, "'Ut cum Muliere': A Male Transvestite Prostitute in Fourteenth-Century London," in *The Pleasures of History: Reading Sexualities in Premodern Europe*, ed. Louise Fredenburt and Carla Freccero (London, 1996), pp. 99–116.

87. CLRO, Portsoken, Ward Presentations, Ms. 242A, 1, 3–7 (1465–83).

88. Wunderli, *Church Courts of London*, p. 100. See also p. 147, table 5.

89. Ibid., pp. 92–93.

90. Ibid., pp. 92–96.

91. Ibid., pp. 99–100.

92. Ibid., p. 98.

93. GL, Ms. 9064/1, fols. 59, 50, 113, Ms. 9064/3, fol. 217.

94. CPMR *1437–57*, vol. 5, p. 14.

95. GL, Ms. 9064/1, fol. 101. See Karras, *Common Women*, p. 79, for further information.

96. GL, Ms. 9064/1, fol. 58v.

97. CPMR *1413–37*, vol. 4, pp. 189–190. Also in *LBK 1422–61*, pp. 16, 24.

98. *Lists of Early Chancery Proceedings*, p. 41.

99. GL, Ms. 9064/1, fol. 125v. CPMR *1381–1412*, vol. 3, p. 304.

100. CPMR *1323–64*, vol. 1, p. 50 (1329).

101. *LBF 1337–52*, pp. 266–267. But Desiderata de Toryntone was found guilty of taking £40 in silver plate belonging to her mistress (*LBE 1314–37*, p. 290), as was Alice Littleglenne of Leicestershire county for having in her possession two women's robes, three mazer cups, and other goods worth 100 s. (*LBE 1314–37*, p. 279).

102. GL, Ms. 9064/1, fol. 23.

103. McIntosh, *Working Women*, has demonstrated this thesis in her book with many examples.

Bibliography

Manuscript Sources

Corporation of London Record Office
    Bridge House Rental
    Court of Common Pleas: CP
    Husting Court Wills and Deeds
    Letter Books
    Mayor's Court, Original Bills: MC
    Portsoken, Ward Presentments, 1465–83
    Repetories

Guildhall Library Archives
    Archdeaconry Court: Ms. 9051
    Churchwardens' Accounts
      St. Andrew Hubbard: Ms. 1279
    Commissary Court: Ms. 9064
    Commissary Court: Ms. 9171

Public Record Office
    Ancient Deeds Catalogue
    Coroners' Roll: Just 2/94A
    Early Chancery Proceedings: C1

Probate: Prob. 2

Westminister Abbey Muniment Room

Primary Sources

Adamson, Margot, ed. *A Treasury of Middle English Verse Selected and Rendered into Modern English*. London, 1930.

Alchin, W. T., and Sharpe, Reginald. *Husting Court Wills and Deeds*, Microfilm Edition.

Appleby, John T., ed. and trans. *The Chronicle of Richard of Devizes in the Time of Richard the First*. London, 1963.

Barron, Caroline, Christopher Coleman, and Claire Gobbi, eds. "The London Journal of Alessandro Magno 1562." *London Journal* 9 (1983), pp. 136–152.

Bateson, Mary, ed. *Borough Customs*. Selden Society. 2 vols. London, 1904.

Bayard, Tania, ed. *A Medieval Home Companion: Housekeeping in the Fourteenth Century*. New York, 1991.

Calendar of Inquisitions Post Mortem. 14 vols. London, 1904–54.

Cam, Helen M., ed. *The Eyre of London, 14 Edward II, A.D. 1321*. Selden Society, vol. 26, pt. 1. London, 1968.

Carpenter, Christine, ed. *Kingsford's Stonor Letters and Papers, 1290–1483*. Cambridge, 1996.

Chew, Helena, ed. *London Possessory Assizes: A Calendar*. London Record Society, vol. 1. London, 1965.

Chew, Helena M., and William Kellaway, eds. *London Assize of Nuisance, 1301–1431*. London Record Society, vol. 10. London, 1973.

Chew, Helena M., and Martin Weinbaum, eds. *The London Eyre of 1244*. London Record Society, vol. 6. Leicester, 1970.

Crotch, W. J. B., ed. *The Prologues and Epilogues of William Caxton*. Early English Text Society, o.s., vol. 176. London, 1928.

Dawson, Warren R., ed. *A Leechbook or Collection of Medical Recipes of the Fifteenth Century*. London, 1934.

Economou, George, trans. *William Langland's Piers Plowman: The C Version*. Philadelphia, 1996.

Fitzstephen, William. *Norman London*. With an essay by Sir Frank Stenton and introduction by F. Donald Logan. New York, 1990.

Furnival, Frederick J., ed. *Early English Meals and Manners: John Russel's Boke of Nurture, Etc.* Early English Text Society, o.s., vol. 32. London, 1868.

———. *Harrison's Description of England*. New Shakespeare Society Publications, pt. 1. London, 1877.

———. *Political, Religious, and Love Poems from the Archbishop of Canterbury's Lambeth Ms. No. 306, and Other Sources*. Early English Text Society, o.s., vol. 15. London, 1866; new ed., 1903.

————. *The Wright's Chaste Wife; A Merry Tale by Adam of Cobsam*. Early English Text Society, o.s., vol. 12. New York, 1969.

Hale, William H., ed. *A Series of Precedents and Proceedings in Criminal Causes Extracted from the Year 1475 to 1640. Extracted from the Act Books of Ecclesiastical Courts in the Diocese of London, Illustrative of the Discipline of the Church of England.* London, 1847.

Hall, G. D. G., ed. and trans. *Tractatus de legibus et consuetudinibus regni Anglie qui Glanvilla vocatur* [The treatise on the laws and customs of the realm of England commonly called Glanville] London, 1965.

Hassall, W. O. *How They Lived: An Anthology of Original Accounts Written before 1485.* New York, 1962.

Kerling, Nellie J. M., ed. and trans. *Cartulary of St. Bartholomew's Hospital Founded 1123: A Calendar.* London, 1973.

Knox, Ronald, and Shane Leslie, trans. *The Miracles of King Henry VI.* Cambridge, 1923.

Lists of Early Chancery Proceedings in the Public Record Office. 2 vols. New York, 1963.

Littlehales, Henry, ed. *The Medieval Records of a London City Church.* Early English Text Society, o.s., vols. 125, 128. London, 1905.

Lyell, Laetitia, ed., with F. D. Watney. *Acts of Court of the Mercer's Company, 1453–1527.* Cambridge, 1936.

Meech, Stanford B., and Hope Emily Allens, eds. *The Book of Margery Kempe.* Early English Text Society, o.s., vol. 21. London, 1940.

Nicholas, F. M., ed. *Britton.* 2 vols. London, 1865.

Peacock, Edward, ed. *John Myrc's Instructions for Parish Priests.* Early English Text Society, o.s., vol. 209. London, 1940.

Pichon, Jérôme, ed. *Le Ménagier de Paris, Traité de Morale et d'Economie Domestique, compose ver 1393 par un Bourgeois Parisien publié pour la premié fois par la Société des Bibliographiles Français..* 2 vols. Paris, 1846.

Pugh, Ralph B., ed. *Calendar of London Trailbaston Trials under Commissions of 1305 and 1306.* London, 1975.

Richardson, H. G., and G. O. Sayles, eds. *Fleta.* Selden Society, vol. 72. London, 1953.

Rickert, Edith, ed. and trans. *The Babee's Book: Medieval Manners for the Young: Done into Modern English from Dr. Furnivall's Texts.* New York, 1966.

Riley, Henry Thomas, ed. *Chronicles of the Mayors and Sheriffs of London, A.D. 1188–1274.* London, 1863.

————. *Liber Albus: The White Book of the City of London.* London, 1861.

————. *Memorials of London and London Life in the Thirteenth, Fourteenth, and Fifteenth Centuries.* London, 1869.

Robbins, Rossell Hope, ed. *Secular Lyrics of the Fourteenth and Fifteenth Centuries.* Oxford, 1952.

Shanks, Elsie, ed. *Novae Narrationes.* With a legal introduction by S. F. C. Milsom. Selden Society, vol. 80. London, 1963.

Sharpe, R. R., ed. *Calendar of Coroners' Rolls of the City of London*, 1300–1378. London, 1913.

——. *Calendar of Letter Books of the City of London, A–L (1275–1497)*. 11 vols. London, 1899–1912.

——. *Calendar of Letters from the Mayor and Corporation of the City of London*. London, 1885.

——. *Calendar of Wills Proved and Enrolled in the Court of Husting, London, A.D. 1258–A.D. 1688*. 2 vols. London, 1890.

Shinners, John, and William J. Dohar, eds. *Pastors and the Care of Souls*. Notre Dame, Ind., 1997.

Sneyd, Charlotte Augusta, trans. *A Relation or Rather a True Account of the Island of England; With Sundry Particulars of the Customs of These People, and of the Royal Revenues under the King Henry the Seventh, about the year 1500*. Works of the Camden Society, series 1, no. 37. New York, 1847.

Stahlschmidt, J. C. L., ed. "Original Documents, Lay Subsidy Roll of 1411–1412." *Archaeological Journal* 44 (1871), pp. 56–83.

The Statutes of the Realm (1225–1713). 9 vols. London, 1810–22.

Thomas, A. H., ed. *Calendar of Early Mayor's Court Rolls of the City of London, 1298–1307*. London, 1924.

Thomas, A. H. (vols. 1–4), and P. E. Jones (vols. 5–6), eds. *Calendar of Plea and Memoranda Rolls of the City of London, 1323–1482*. Cambridge, 1926–61.

Tubach, Frederick C. *Index Exemplorum: A Handbook of Medieval Religious Tales*. Folklore Fellows Communications, vol. 86, no. 204. Helsinki, 1969.

Weinbaum, Martin, ed. *The London Eyre of 1276*. London Record Society, vol. 12. Leicester, 1976.

Whittaker, William J., ed. *The Mirror of Justices*. Selden Society, vol. 7. London, 1895.

Wright, Thomas, ed. and trans. *The Book of the Knight of La Tour-Landry*. London, 1868.

Secondary Sources

Abram, Annie. *Social England in the Fifteenth Century: A Study in the Effects of Economic Conditions*. London, 1909.

——. "Women Traders in Medieval London." *Economic Journal* 26 (1916), pp. 276–285.

Adamson, N. "Urban Families: The Social Context of the London Elite, 1500–1603." Ph.D. diss., University of Toronto, 1983.

Ågren, Maria, and Amy Louise Erickson, eds. *The Marital Economy in Scandinavia and Britain, 1400–1900* (Aldershot, 2005).

Amundsen, Darrel, and Carol Jean Dries. "The Age of Menarche in Medieval Europe." *Human Biology* 45 (1973), pp. 363–368.

Amussen, Susan D. "Punishment, Discipline, and Power: The Social Meanings of Violence in Early Modern England." *Journal of British Studies* 34 (1995), pp. 1–34.

Bibliography

Andersson, Gudrun. "Forming the Partnership Socially and Economically: A Swedish Local Elite, 1650–1770." In *The Marital Economy in Scandinavia and Britain*, 1400–1900, pp. 58–73. Ed. Maria Ågren and Amy Louise Erickson. Aldershot, 2005.

Ashley, Kathleen, and Robert L. A. Clark, eds. *Medieval Conduct*. Minneapolis, 2001.

Bailey, Paul, ed. *The Oxford Book of London*. Oxford, 1996.

Baldwin, Frances E. *Sumptuary Legislation and Personal Regulation in England*. Johns Hopkins University Studies in Social and Political Science, series 44. Baltimore, 1926.

Barron, Caroline M. "The Education and Training of Girls in Fifteenth-Century London." In *Courts, Counties, and the Capital in the Later Middle Ages*, pp. 139–153. Ed. Diana E. S. Dunn. New York, 1996.

———. "The Fourteenth Century Poll Tax Returns for Worcester." *Midland History* (1989), pp. 1–29.

———. "'The Golden Age' of Women in Medieval London." *Reading Medieval Studies* 15 (1989), pp. 35–58.

———. "Johanna Hill (d. 1441) and Johanna Sturdy (d. c. 1460), Bell-Founders." In *Medieval London Widows, 1300–1500*, pp. 99–111. Ed. Caroline M. Barron and Anne F. Sutton. London, 1994.

———. *London in the Later Middle Ages: Government and People, 1200–1500*. Oxford, 2004.

———. "The Parish Fraternities of Medieval London." In *The Church in Pre-Reformation Society: Essays in Honour of F. R. H. DuBoulay*, pp. 13–37. Ed. Caroline M. Barron and Christopher Harper-Bill. Woodbridge, U.K., 1985.

———. "William Langland: A London Poet." In *Chaucer's England: Literature in Historical Context*, pp. 91–109. Ed. Barbara A. Hanawalt. Medieval Studies at Minnesota, vol. 4. Minneapolis, 1992.

Beattie, J. M. *Crime and the Courts in England, 1660–1800*. Princeton, 1988.

Bennett, H. S. *England from Chaucer to Caxton*. New York, 1928.

Bennett, Judith M. *Ale, Beer, and Brewsters in England*. New York, 1996.

———. "Confronting Continuity." *Journal of Women's History* 9 (1997), pp. 73–94.

———. *History Matters: Patriarchy and the Challenge of Feminism*. Philadelphia, 2006.

———. "History Stands Still: Women's Work in the European Past." *Feminist Studies* 19 (1988), pp. 269–283.

———. "Medieval Women, Modern Women: Across the Great Divide." In *Culture and History, 1350–1600: Essays on English Communities, Identities and Writing*, pp. 47–76. Ed. David Aers. London, 1992.

———. "Working Together: Women and Men in the Brewers' Gild of London, c. 1420." In *The Salt of Common Life: Individuality and Choice in the Medieval Town, Countryside and Church*, pp. 181–232. Ed. Edwin DeWindt. Kalamazoo, Mich., 1995.

Bennett, Judith M., and Amy M. Froide. "A Singular Past." *Singlewomen in the European Past, 1250–1800*, pp. 1–37. Ed. Judith M. Bennett and Amy M. Froide. Philadelphia, 1999.

Bestor, Jane Fair. "Marriage Transactions in Renaissance Italy and Mauss's *Essay on the Gift.*" *Past and Present* 164 (1999), pp. 6–46.

Brand, Paul. "'Deserving' and 'Undeserving' Wives: Earning and Forfeiting Dower in Medieval England." *Journal of Legal History* 22 (2001), pp. 1–20.

———. *Kings, Barons and Justices: The Making and Enforcement of Legislation in Thirteenth-Century England.* Cambridge, 2003.

———. *The Origins of the English Legal Profession.* Oxford, 1992.

Brown, Judith C., and Jordan Goodman. "Women and Industry in Florence." *Journal of Economic History* 40 (1980), pp. 73–80.

Brundage, James A. *Law, Sex, and Christian Society in Medieval Europe.* Chicago, 1987.

———. Widows and Remarriage: Moral Conflicts and Their Resolution in Classical Canon Law." In *Wife and Widow in Medieval England,* pp. 17–31. Ed. Sue Sheridan Walker. Ann Arbor, 1993.

———. "Widows as Disadvantaged Persons in Medieval Canon Law." In *Upon My Husband's Death: Widows in the Literature and Histories of Medieval Europe,* pp. 193–206. Ed. Louise Mirrer. Ann Arbor, 1992.

Burford, E. J. *Bawds and Lodgings: A History of the London Bankside Brothels, c.* 1000–1675. London, 1976.

Burgess, Clive. "Shaping the Parish: St. Mary at Hill, London, in the Fifteenth Century." In *The Cloister and the World: Essays in Medieval History in Honour of Barbara Harvey,* pp. 246–285. Ed. John Blair and Brian Golding. Oxford, 1996.

Burkholder, Kristen M. "Threads Bared: Dress and Textiles in Late Medieval English Wills." In *Medieval Clothing and Textiles,* vol. 1, pp. 133–153. Ed. Robin Netherton and Gale R. Owen-Crocker. Woodbridge, U.K., 2005.

Burrow, J. A. *The Ages of Man: A Study in Medieval Writing and Thought.* Oxford, 1988.

Butler, Sara M. "The Law as a Weapon in Marital Disputes: Evidence from the Late Medieval Court of Chancery, 1424–1529." *Journal of British Studies* 43 (2004), pp. 291–316.

Cadden, Joan. *Meanings of Sex Difference in the Middle Ages.* Cambridge, 1993.

Cahn, Susan. *Industry of Devotion: The Transformation of Women's Work in England, 1500–1660.* New York, 1987.

Campbell, B. M. S., J. A. Galloway, D. Keen, and M. Murphy. *A Medieval Capital and Its Grain Supply: Agrarian Production and Distribution in the London Region c.* 1300. Belfast, 1993.

Carlin, Martha. "Fast Food and Urban Living Standards in Medieval England." In *Food and Eating in Medieval Europe,* pp. 27–52. Ed. Martha Carlin and Joel T. Rosenthal. London, 1998.

———. *Medieval Southwark.* London, 1996.

Carlson, Eric Josef. *Marriage and the English Reformation.* Oxford, 1994.

Carlton, Charles. *The Court of Orphans.* Leicester, 1974.

Carpenter, Christine. "The Stonor Circle in the Fifteenth Century." In *Rulers and Ruled in Late Medieval England: Essays Presented to Gerald Harris,* pp. 175–200. Ed. Rowena E. Archer and Simon Walker. London, 1995.

Chabot, Isabelle. "Widowhood and Poverty in Late Medieval Florence." *Continuity and Change* 3 (1988), pp. 291–311.

Chojnacki, Stanley. "Dowries and Kinsmen in Early Renaissance Venice." In *Women in Medieval Society*, pp. 173–198. Ed. Susan M. Stuard. Philadelphia, 1976.

———. "Patrician Women in Early Renaissance Venice." *Studies in the Renaissance* 21 (1974), pp. 176–203.

———. *Women and Men in Renaissance Venice: Twelve Essays on Patrician Society.* Baltimore, 2000.

Clark, Alice. *Working Life of Women in the Seventeenth Century.* New York, 1920.

Clark, Elaine. "City Orphans and Custody Laws in Medieval England." *American Journal of Legal History* 34 (1990), pp. 168–187.

Clark, Peter. *The English Alehouse: A Social History* 1200–1830. London, 1983.

Clay, Rotha M. *The Medieval Hospitals of England.* London, 1909.

Clode, Charles M. *The Early History of the Guild of Merchant Taylors.* 2 vols. London, 1888.

Clopper, Lawrence M. "Need Men and Women Labor? Langland's Wanderer and the Labor Ordinances." In *Chaucer's England: Literature in Historical Context*, pp. 110–132. Ed. Barbara A. Hanawalt. Medieval Studies at Minnesota, vol. 4. Minneapolis, 1992.

Crabb, Ann. *The Strozzi of Florence: Widowhood and Family Solidarity in the Renaissance.* Ann Arbor, 2000.

Cressy, David. *Birth, Marriage and Death: Ritual, Religion, and the Life-Cycle in Tudor and Stuart England.* Oxford, 1997.

Cullum, P. H. *Cremetts and Corodies: Care of the Poor and Sick at St. Leonard's Hospital, York, in the Middle Ages.* Borthwick Papers, no. 79. York, England, 1991.

Curtis, Margaret. "The London Lay Subsidy of 1332." In *Finance and Trade under Edward III*, pp. 35–60. Ed. George Unwin. Manchester, 1919.

Dale, Marian K. "The London Silkwomen of the Fifteenth Century." *Economic History Review*, 1st ser., 4 (1933), pp. 324–335.

Danneel, Marianne. "Orphanhood and Marriage in Fifteenth-Century Ghent." In *Marriage and Social Mobility in the Late Middle Ages*, pp. 99–111. Ed. W. Prevenier. Studia Historica Gandensia, no. 274. Ghent, 1989.

———. "Quelques aspects du service domestique féminin à Gand d'après les registres et les manuels échevinaux des Parchons." In *Sociale strucuren en topografie van armoede en rijkdom in de 14de en 15de eeuw. Methodologische aspecten en resultaten van recent orderzoek. Handelingen van het colloquium gehouden te Gent op 24 mei 1985*, pp. 51–72. Ed. W. Prerenier,R. Van Uytren, and E. Van Cauwenberghe. Studia Historica Gandensia, no. 267. Ghent, 1986.

Davies, Mathew. "Dame Thomasine Percyvale, 'The Maid of Week' (d. 1512)." In *Medieval London Widows*, 1300–1500, pp. 185–207. Ed. Caroline M. Barron and Anne F. Sutton. London, 1994.

d'Avray, David. *Medieval Marriage Sermons: Mass Communication in a Culture without Print.* Oxford, 2001.

Diefendorf, Barbara. *Paris City Councillors in the Sixteenth Century: The Politics of Patrimony*. Princeton, 1983.

————. "Women and Property in *Ancien Régime* France: Theory and Practice in Dauphiné and Paris." In *Early Modern Conceptions of Property*, pp. 177–182. Ed. John Brewer and Susan Staves. London, 1995.

Dolan, Frances E. *Dangerous Familiars: Representations of Domestic Crime in England, 1550–1700*. Ithaca, 1994.

————. "Home-Rebels and House-Traitors: Murderous Wives in Early Modern England." *Yale Journal of Law and the Humanities* 4 (1992), pp. 1–31.

Donahue, Charles, Jr. "Female Plaintiffs in Marriage Cases in the Court of York in the Later Middle Ages: What Can We Learn from the Numbers." In *Wife and Widow in Medieval England*, pp. 183–213. Ed. Sue Sheridan Walker. Ann Arbor, 1993.

Dove, Mary. *The Perfect Age of Man's Life*. Cambridge, 1986.

Duby, Georges. *Medieval Marriage*. Baltimore, 1978.

Dyer, Christopher. *Standards of Living in the Later Middle Ages: Social Change in England 1200–1520*. Cambridge, 1989.

Ekwall, Eilert. *Studies on the Population of Medieval London*. Stockholm, 1956.

Elliott, Vivien Brodsky. "Single Women in the London Marriage Market: Age, Status and Mobility, 1598–1619." In *Marriage and Society: Studies in the Social History of Marriage*, pp. 81–100. Ed. P. D. Outhwaite. New York, 1982.

Emanoil, Valerie. "London Widows' Activities in the Late Medieval Land Market." Master's thesis, Clemson University, 1999.

Erickson, Amy Louise. "The Marital Economy in Comparative Perspective." In *The Marital Economy in Scandinavia and Britain 1400–1900*, pp. 3–22. Ed. Maria Ågren and Amy Louise Erickson. Aldershot, 2005.

————. *Woman and Property in Early Modern England*. London, 1993.

Erle, Peter. *A City Full of People: Men and Women of London, 1640–1750*. London, 1994.

Erler, Mary C. *Women, Reading and Piety in Late Medieval England*. Cambridge, 2002.

Ewan, Elizabeth. "'To the Longer Liver': Provisions for the Dissolution of the Marital Economy in Scotland, 1470–1550." In *The Marital Economy in Scandinavia and Britain, 1400–1900*, pp. 191–206. Ed. Maria Ågren and Amy Louise Erkckson. Aldershot, 2005.

Farmer, Sharon. "Persuasive Voices: Clerical Images of Medieval Wives." *Speculum* 61 (1986), pp. 517–543.

Finucane, Ronald C. *Rescue of Innocents: Endangered Children in Medieval Miracles*. New York, 1997.

Fletcher, Anthony. *Gender, Sex, and Subordination in England 1500–1800*. New Haven, 1995.

Frances, Catherine. "Making Marriages in Early Modern England: Rethinking the Role of Family and Friends." In *The Marital Economy in Scandinavia and Britain, 1400–1900*, pp. 40–55. Ed. Maria Ågren and Amy Louise Erickson. Aldershot, 2005.

French, Katherine L. "Maidens' Lights and Wives' Stores: Women's Parish Guilds in Late Medieval England." *Sixteenth-Century Journal* 29 (1998), pp. 399–425.

———. "'To Free Them from Binding': Women in the Late Medieval Parish." *Journal of Interdisciplinary History* 28 (1997), pp. 387–412.

———. "Women in the Late Medieval English Parish." In *Gendering the Master Narrative: Women and Power in the Middle Ages*, pp. 156–173. Ed. Maryanne Kowaleski and Mary C. Erler. Ithaca, 2003.

Given, James B. *Society and Homicide in Thirteenth-Century England*. Stanford, 1977.

Goldberg, P. J. P. "Female Labour, Service, and Marriage in Northern Towns during the Later Middle Ages." *Northern History* 22 (1986), pp. 18–38.

———. "Marriage, Migration, Servanthood, and Life Cycle in Yorkshire Towns of the Later Middle Ages." *Continuity and Change* 1 (1986), pp. 141–169.

———. "Migration, Youth and Gender in Later Medieval England." In *Youth in the Middle Ages*, pp. 85–100. Ed. P. J. P. Goldberg and Felicity Riddy. York, U.K., 2004.

———. "What Is a Servant?" In *Concepts and Patterns of Service in the Later Middle Ages*, pp. 1–20. Ed. Anne Curry and Elizabeth Matthew. Woodbridge, U.K., 2000.

———. "Women in Fifteenth-Century Town Life." In *Towns and Townspeople in the Fifteenth Century*, pp. 105–128. Ed. John A. F. Thomson. Wolfeboro Falls, N.H., 1988.

———. *Women, Work, and Life Cycle in a Medieval Economy: Women in York and Yorkshire c. 1300–1520*. Oxford, 1992.

Gowing, Laura. *Domestic Dangers: Women, Words, and Sex in Early Modern England*. Oxford, 1996.

Gregg, Joan Young. *Devils, Women, and Jews: Reflections on the Other in Medieval Sermon Stories*. Binghamton, N.Y., 1997.

Haas, Louis. *The Renaissance Man and His Children: Childbirth and Early Childhood in Florence, 1300–1600*. New York, 1998.

Hair, P. E. H. "Bridal Pregnancy in Earlier Rural England, further Examined." *Population Studies* 20 (1970), pp. 59–70.

Hanawalt, Barbara A. "At the Margins of Women's Space in Medieval Europe." In *"Of Good and Ill Repute": Gender and Social Control in Medieval England*, pp. 70–87. New York, 1998.

———. "Childrearing among the Lower Classes in Late Medieval England." *Journal of Interdisciplinary History* 8 (1977), pp. 1–22.

———. *Crime and Conflict in English Communities, 1300–1348*. Cambridge, Mass., 1979.

———. *Growing Up in Medieval London: The Experience of Childhood in History*. New York, 1993.

———. "The Host, the Law, and the Ambiguous Space of Medieval London Taverns." In *"Of Good and Ill Repute": Gender and Social Control in Medieval England*, pp. 104–123. New York, 1998.

———. "Keepers of the Lights; Late Medieval English Parish Gilds." *Journal of Medieval and Renaissance History* 14 (1984), pp. 21–37.

Hanawalt, Barbara A. "Lady Honor Lisle's Network of Influence." In *Women and Power in the Middle Ages*, pp. 188–212. Ed. Mary Erler and Maryanne Kowaleski. Athens, Ga., 1988.

———. "Reading the Lives of the Illiterate: London's Poor." *Speculum* 80 (2005), pp. 1067–1086.

———. "Remarriage as an Option for Urban and Rural Widows in Late Medieval England." In *Wife and Widow in Medieval England*, pp. 141–164. Ed. Sue Sheridan Walker. Ann Arbor, 1993.

———. "Separation Anxieties in Late Medieval London: Gender in "The Wright's Chaste Wife." In Barbara Hanawalt, *"Of Good and Ill Repute": Gender and Social Control in Medieval England*, pp. 88–103. Oxford, 1998.

———. *The Ties That Bound: Peasant Families in Medieval England*. New York, 1986.

———. "The Widow's Mite: Provisions for Medieval London Widows." In *Upon My Husband's Death: Widows in the Literature and Histories of Medieval Europe*, pp. 21–46. Ed. Louise Mirrer. Ann Arbor, 1992.

———. "Whose Story Was This? Rape Narratives in Medieval English Courts." In *"Of Good and Ill Repute": Gender and Social Control in Medieval England*, pp. 124–141. New York, 1998.

Hanham, Alison. *The Celys and Their World: An English Merchant Family of the Fifteenth Century*. Cambridge, 1985.

Hatcher, John. "Understanding the Population History of England 1450–1750." *Past and Present* 180 (2003), pp. 83–130.

Helmholz, Richard H. "Infanticide in England in the Later Middle Ages." *History of Childhood Quarterly* 1 (1974–75), pp. 282–340.

———. *Marriage Litigation in Medieval England*. Cambridge, 1974.

Herlihy, David. *Medieval Households*. Cambridge, 1985.

———. *Opera Muliebria: Women and Work in Medieval Europe*. New York, 1990.

Herlihy, David, and Christiane Klapisch-Zuber. *Tuscans and Their Families: A Study of the Florentine Catasto of 1427*. New Haven, 1985.

Hettinger, Madonna J. "Defining the Servant: Legal and Extra-legal Terms of Employment in Fifteenth-Century England." In *The Work of Work: Servitude, Slavery, and Labor in Medieval England*, pp. 206–228. Ed. Allen J. Frantzen and Douglas Moffat. Glasgow, U.K., 1994.

Hicks, Michael, ed., *Revolution and Consumption in Late Medieval England*. Woodbridge, U.K., 2001.

Hilton, Rodney H. "Women Traders in Medieval England." *Women's Studies* 2 (1984), pp. 138–155.

Honeyman, Katrina, and Jordan Goodman. "Women's Work, Gender Conflict, and Labour Markets in Europe, 1500–1900." *Economic History Review* 44 (1991), pp. 608–628.

Houlbrooke, Ralph. *Church Courts and the People during the English Reformation, 1520–1570*. Oxford, 1979.

Howell, Martha C. *The Marriage Exchange: Property, Social Place, and Gender in Cities of the Low Countries, 1300–1550*. Chicago, 1998.

Bibliography

————. *Women, Production, and Patriarchy in Late Medieval Cities*. Chicago, 1986.

Hsia, R. Po-Chia. *Social Discipline in the Reformation: Central Europe, 1550–1750*. London, 1989.

Huffman, Joseph P. *Family, Commerce, and Religion in London and Cologne, Anglo-German Emigrants c. 1000–c. 1300*. Cambridge, 1998.

Hufton, Olwen. "Women and the Family Economy in Eighteenth-Century France." *French Historical Studies* 9 (1975), pp. 1–22.

Hughes, Diane Owen. "From Brideprice to Dowry in Mediterranean Europe." *Journal of Family History* 3 (1978), pp. 262–296.

Hurnard, Naomi D. *The King's Pardon for Homicide before 1307*. Oxford, 1969.

Ingram, Martin. *Church Courts, Sex and Marriage in England, 1570–1640*. Cambridge, 1987.

Johansson, Sheila Ryan. "Deferred Infanticide: Excess Female Mortality during Childhood." In *Infanticide: Comparative and Evolutionary Perspectives*, pp. 463–488. Ed. Glenn Hausfater and Sarah Blaffer Hrdy. New York, 1984.

Jordan, William C. *Women and Credit in Pre-industrial and Developing Societies*. Philadelphia, 1993.

Justice, Steven. *Writing and Rebellion: England in 1381*. Berkeley, 1994.

Karras, Ruth Mazo. *Common Women: Prostitution and Sexuality in Medieval England*. New York, 1966.

Karras, Ruth Mazo, and David Lorenzo Boyd. "'Ut cum Muliere': A Male Transvestite Prostitute in Fourteenth-Century London." In *The Pleasures of History: Reading Sexualities in Premodern Europe*, pp. 99–116. Ed. Louise Fredenburt and Carla Freccero. London, 1996.

Keene, Derek. "Shops and Shopping in Medieval London." In *Medieval Art, Architecture and Archaeology in London*, pp. 29–46. Ed. Lindy Grant. Oxford, 1984.

————. "Tanners' Widows, 1300–1350." In *Medieval London Widows, 1300–1500*, pp. 1–27. Ed. Caroline M. Barron and Anne F. Sutton. London, 1994.

Kelly, Henry Ansgar. "Rule of Thumb and the Folklaw of the Husband's Stick." *Journal of Legal Education* 44 (1994), pp. 341–365.

Kelso, Ruth. *Doctrine for the Lady of the Renaissance*. Urbana, Ill., 1956.

Kermode, Jenny. *Medieval Merchants: York, Beverley and Hull in the Later Middle Ages*. Cambridge, 1998.

Kittel, Ruth. "Rape in Thirteenth-Century England: A Study of the Common-Law Courts." In *Women and the Law: The Social Historical Perspective*, vol. 2, pp. 101–116. Ed. D. Kelly Weisberg. Cambridge, Mass., 1982.

Klapisch-Zuber, Christiane. *Women, Family, and Ritual in Renaissance Italy*. Trans. Lydia Cochrane. Chicago, 1985.

Kowaleski, Maryanne. *Local Markets and Regional Trade in Exeter*. Cambridge, 1995.

————. "Singlewomen in Medieval and Early Modern Europe: The Demographic Perspective." In *Singlewomen in the European Past, 1250–1800*, pp. 38–81. Ed. Judith M. Bennett and Amy M. Froide. Philadelphia, 1999.

————. "Women's Work in a Market Town: Exeter in the Late Fourteenth Century." In *Women and Work in Preindustrial Europe*, pp. 145–164. Ed. Barbara A. Hanawalt. Bloomington, Ind., 1986.

Bibliography

Kowaleski, Maryanne, and Judith M. Bennett. "Crafts, Gilds, and Women in the Middle Ages: Fifty Years after Marian K. Dale." *Signs* 14 (1989), pp. 474–487.

Kuehn, Thomas. "'*Cum Consensu Mundualdi*': Legal Guardianship of Women in Quatrocento Florence." *Viator* 13 (1982), pp. 309–333.

———. *Law, Family, and Women: Toward a Legal Anthropology of Renaissance* Italy. Chicago, 1994.

Lacey, Kay E. "Margaret Croke (d. 1491)." In *Medieval London Widows 1300–1500*, pp. 143–164. Ed. Caroline M. Barron and Anne F. Sutton. London, 1994.

———. "Women and Work in Fourteenth and Fifteenth Century London." In *Women and Work in Pre-industrial England*, pp. 24–82. Ed. Charles Kindsey and Lorna Duffin. Kent, England, 1985.

Lett, Didier. *L'enfant des miracles: Enfance et société au Moyen Âge.* Paris, 1997.

Levinson, David. *Family Violence in Cross-cultural Perspective.* Newbury Park, Calif., 1989.

Loengard, Janet S. "'Of the Gift of her Husband': English Dower and Its Consequences in the Year 1200." In *Women in the Medieval World: Essays in Honor of John H. Mundy*, pp. 215–237. Ed. J. Kirshner and S. F. Wemple. New York, 1985.

Lynch, Joseph H. *Godparents and Kinship in Early Medieval Europe.* Princeton, 1986.

Macfarlane, Alan. *Marriage and Love in England, 1300–1840.* Oxford, 1986.

Martin, G. H. *The Husting Rolls of Deeds and Wills, 1252–1485: Guide to the Microfilm Edition.* Cambridge, 1990.

———. "The Registration of Deeds of Title in the Medieval Borough." In *The Study of Medieval Records: Essays in Honour of Kathleen Major*, pp. 151–173. Ed. D. A. Bullough and R. L. Storey. Oxford, 1971.

Mate, Mavis E. *Women in Medieval English Society.* Cambridge, 1999.

McIntosh, Marjorie Keniston. "The Benefits and Drawbacks of *Femme Sole* Status in England, 1300–1630." *Journal of British Studies* 44 (2005), pp. 410–438.

———. *Working Women in English Society, 1300–1620.* Cambridge, 2005.

McSheffrey, Shannon. *Love and Marriage in Late Medieval London.* Comsortium for the Teaching of the Middle Ages: Documents and Practice Series. Kalamazoo, Mich., 1995.

———. *Marriage, Sex, and Civic Society in Late Medieval London.* Philadelphia, 2006.

———. "Men and Masculinity in Late Medieval London Civic Culture: Governance, Patriarchy and Reputation." In *Conflicted Identities and Multiple Masculinities*, pp. 243–278. Ed. Jacqueline Murray. New York, 1999.

Megson, Barbara. "Life Expectations of the Widows and Orphans of Freemen in London, 1375–1399." *Local Population Studies* (1996), pp. 18–29.

Molho, Anthony. *Marriage Alliance in Late Medieval Florence.* Cambridge, Mass., 1994.

Murray, James M. *Bruges, Cradle of Capitalism, 1280–1390.* Cambridge, 2005.

Nicholas, David. *The Domestic Life of a Medieval City: Women, Children, and the Family in Fourteenth-Century Ghent.* Lincoln, Neb., 1985.

Ogilvie, Sheilagh. "How Does Social Capital Affect Women? Guilds and Communities of Early Modern Germany." *American Historical Review* 109 (2004), pp. 325–359.

Bibliography

Orlin, Lena Cowen, ed. *Material London, ca. 1600.* Philadelphia, 2000.

Orme, Nicholas, and Margaret Webster. *The English Hospital, 1070–1570.* New Haven, 1995.

Otis, Leah L. "Municipal Wet Nurses in Fifteenth-Century Montpellier." In *Women and Work in Preindustrial Europe,* pp. 83–93. Ed. Barbara A. Hanawalt. Bloomington, Ind., 1986.

———. *Prostitution in Medieval Society: The History of an Urban Institution in Languedoc.* Chicago, 1985.

Owst, G. R. *Literature and Pulpit in Medieval England.* 3rd ed. New York, 1961.

Palmer, Robert C. "Contexts of Marriage in Medieval England: Evidence from the King's Court circa 1300." *Speculum* 59 (1984), pp. 42–67.

Pendrill, Charles. *London Life in the Fourteenth Century.* London, 1925; reprint, Port Washington, N.Y., 1977.

Penn, Simon A. C., and Christophen Dyer. "Wages and Earnings in Late Medieval England: Evidence from the Enforcement of the Labor Laws." *Economic History Review,* 2nd series., 43 (1990), pp. 356–376.

Peters, Christine. "Gender, Sacrament, and Ritual: The Making and Meaning of Marriage in Late Medieval and Early Modern England." *Past and Present* 169 (Nov. 2000), pp. 63–96.

Phillips, Kim M. "Maidenhood as the Perfect Age of Woman's Life." In *Young Medieval Women,* pp. 1–24. Ed. Katherine J. Lewis, Noel James Nenuge, and Kim M. Phillips. New York, 1999.

———. *Medieval Maidens: Young Women and Gender in England, 1270–1540.* Manchester, 2003.

Phythian-Adams, Charles. *Desolation of a City: Coventry and the Urban Crisis of the Late Middle Ages.* Cambridge, 1979.

Pleck, Elizabeth. *Domestic Tyranny: The Making of Social Policy against Family Violence from Colonial Times to the Present.* New York, 1987.

Pollock, Frederick, and Frederic William Maitland. *The History of English Law before the Time of Edward I.* 2nd ed. 2 vols. Cambridge, 1898; reprint, Cambridge, 1968.

Post, J. B. "Ravishment of Women and the Statutes of Westminster." In *Legal Records and the Historian: Papers Presented to the Cambridge Legal History Conference,* pp. 150–164. Ed. J. H. Baker. London, 1978.

Power, Eileen. *Medieval People.* New York, 1963.

———. *Medieval Women.* Ed. M. M. Postan. London, 1975.

Rappaport, Steve. *Worlds within Worlds: Structure of Life in Sixteenth-Century London.* Cambridge, 1989.

Rawcliffe, Carole. "The Hospitals of Later Medieval London." *Medical History* 24 (1984), pp. 1–22.

Reddaway, Thomas F. *The Early History of the Goldsmiths' Company, 1327–1509.* London, 1975.

Reid, Charles J., Jr. *Power over the Body, Equality in the Family: Rights and Domestic Relations in Medieval Canon Law.* Emory University Studies in Law and Religion. Grand Rapids, Mich., 2004.

Bibliography

Riddy, Felicity. "Mother Knows Best: Reading Social Change in a Courtesy Text." *Speculum* 71 (1996), pp. 66–86.

Röhrkasten, Jens. "Trends in Mortality in Late Medieval London (1348–1400)." *Nottingham Medieval Studies* 45 (2001), pp. 172–209.

Rosenthal, Joel T. "Fifteenth-Century Widows and Widowhood: Bereavement, Reintegration, and Life Choices." In *Wife and Widow in Medieval England*, pp. 33–58. Ed. Sue Sheridan Walker. Ann Arbor, 1993.

———. *Old Age in Late Medieval England*. Philadelphia, 1996.

———. *Patriarchy and Families of Privilege in Fifteenth-Century England*. Philadelphia, 1991.

Rosser, Gervase. "London and Westminster: The Suburb in the Urban Economy in the Later Middle Ages." In *Towns and Townspeople in the Fifteenth Century*, pp. 45–61. Ed. John A. F. Thomson. Gloucester, U.K., 1988.

Rossiaud, Jacques. *Medieval Prostitution*. Trans. Lydia G. Cochrane. Oxford, 1988.

Ruggerio, Guido. *Violence in Early Renaissance Venice*. New Brunswick, 1980.

Sabine, Ernest. "City Cleaning in Medieval London." *Speculum* 12 (1937), pp. 335–353.

———. "Latrines and Cesspools of Medieval London." *Speculum* 9 (1934), pp. 303–321.

Scattergood, John. "Misrepresenting the City: Genre, Intertextuality and William Fitzstephen's Description of London (c. 1173)." In *London and Europe in the Later Middle Ages*, pp. 1–34. Ed. Julia Boffery and Pamela King. London, 1995.

Schmidt, Ariadne. *Overleven na de dood: Wechuwen in Leiden in de Gouden Eeuw*. Amsterdam, 2001.

Schmidt, Jean-Claude. *Holy Greyhound: Guinefort, Healer of Children since the Thirteenth Century*. Trans. Martin Thom. Cambridge Studies in Oral and Literate Culture, no. 6. Cambridge, 1983.

Schneebach, Harold N. "The Law of Felony in Medieval England from the Accession of Edward I until the Mid–fourteenth Century." 2 vols. Ph.D. diss., University of Iowa, 1973.

Schofield, John. *The Building of London from the Conquest to the Great Fire*. London, 1984.

———. *Medieval London Houses*. New Haven, 1994.

Schofield, R. S., and E. A. Wrigley. "Remarriage Intervals and the Effect of Marriage Order on Fertility." In *Marriage and Remarriage in Populations of the Past*, pp. 211–227. Ed. J. Dupaquier, E. Helin, P. Laslett, M. Livi-Bacci, and S. Sogner. London, 1981.

Shaw, Diane. "The Construction of the Private in Medieval London." *Journal of Medieval and Early Modern Studies* 26 (1996), pp. 447–466.

Sheehan, Michael M. "The Formation and Stability of Marriage: Evidence of an Ely Register." *Mediaeval Studies* 33 (1971), pp. 228–237.

———. "The Influence of Canon Law on the Property Rights of Married Women in England." *Mediaeval Studies* 25 (1963), pp. 109–124.

———. *Marriage, Family, and Law in Medieval Europe: Collected Essays*. Ed. James K. Farge. Toronto, 1996.

Smith, D. Vance. *Arts of Possession: The Middle English Household Imaginary*. Minneapolis, 2003.

Sortor, Marci. "The Measure of Success: Evidence for Immigrant Networks in the Southern Low Countries, Saint-Omer 1413–1455." *Journal of Family History* 30 (April 2005), pp. 179–181.

Spencer, H. Leith. *English Preaching in the Late Middle Ages.* Oxford, 1993.

Steuer, Susan M. B. "Family Strategies in Medieval London: Financial Planning and the Urban Widow, 1123–1473." In *Essays in Medieval Studies: Children and the Family in the Middle Ages*, pp. 81–93. Ed. Nicole Clifton. 1995 Proceedings of the Illinois Medieval Association, vol. 12. Chicago, 1996.

Stevenson, Kenneth. *Nuptial Blessing: A Study of Christian Marriage Rites.* New York, 1983.

Stone, Lawrence. *The Family, Sex, and Marriage in England 1500–1800.* New York, 1977.

Strohm, Paul. "Treason in the Household." In *Hochon's Arrow: The Social Imagination of Fourteenth-Century Texts*, pp. 121–144. Princeton, 1992.

Stuard, Susan Mosher. "Marriage Gifts and Fashion Mischief." In *The Medieval Marriage Scene: Prudence, Passion, Policy*, pp. 169–185. Ed. Sherry Roush and Cristelle L. Baskin. Medieval and Renaissance Texts and Studies, vol. 299. Tempe, Ariz., 2005.

———. "To Town to Serve: Urban Domestic Slavery in Medieval Ragusa." In *Women and Work in Preindustrial Europe*, pp. 29–55. Ed. Barbara A. Hanawalt. Bloomington, Ind., 1986.

Sutherland, Donald W. *The Assize of Novel Disseisin.* Oxford, 1973.

Sutton, Anne F. "Alice Claver, Silkwoman (d. 1489)." In *Medieval London Widows, 1300–1500*, pp. 129–142. Ed. Caroline M. Barron and Anne F. Sutton. London, 1994.

———. "Lady Joan Bradbury (d. 1530)." In *Medieval London Widows, 1300–1500*, pp. 209–238. Ed. Caroline M. Barron and Anne F. Sutton. London, 1994.

———. *The Mercery of London: Trade, Goods and People, 1130–1578.* Aldershot, 2005.

———. "The Shop-Floor of the London Mercery Trade, c. 1200–c. 1500: The Marginalization of the Artisan, the Itinerant Mercer, and the Shopholder." *Nottingham Medieval Studies* 45 (2001), pp. 12–50.

Swabey, Ffiona. *Medieval Gentlewoman: Life in a Widow's Household in the Later Middle Ages.* New York, 1999.

Swanson, Heather. "Illusion of Economic Structure: Craft Guilds in Late Medieval English Towns." *Past and Present*, no. 121 (1988), pp. 45–46.

———. *Medieval Artisans: An Urban Class in Late Medieval England.* Oxford, 1989.

Tauchen, Helen V., Ann Dryden Witte, Sharon K. Long. "Domestic Violence: A Non-random Affair." *International Economic Review* 32(1991), pp. 491–511.

Thrupp, Sylvia. *The Merchant Class of Medieval London.* Ann Arbor, 1948.

Tilly, Louise A., and Scott, Joan A. *Women, Work, and Family.* New York, 1978.

Truelove, Alison. "Commanding Communications: The Fifteenth-Century Letters of the Stonor Women." In *Early Modern Women's Letter Writing, 1450–1700*, pp. 42–58. Ed. James Daybell. New York, 2001.

Turner, Victor W. *The Ritual Process: Structure and Anti-structure.* New York, 1969.

Unwin, George. *The Guilds and Companies of London.* 1908; reprint. London, 1966.

van Gennep, Arnold. *The Rites of Passage.* Trans. Monika B. Vizedom and Gabriella L. Caffee. 1908; reprint, Chicago, 1960.

Vaudeville, Charlotte. *Barahmasa in Indian Literatures: Songs of the Twelve Months in Indo-Aryan Literatures.* Delhi, 1986.

Veale, Elspeth. "Matilda Penne, Skinner (d. 1392–3)." In *Medieval London Widows, 1300–1500,* pp. 47–54. Ed. Caroline M. Barron and Anne F. Sutton. London, 1994.

Walker, Sue Sheridan. "Common Law Juries and Feudal Marriage Customs in Medieval England: The Pleas of Ravishment." *University of Illinois Law Review* 3 (1984), pp. 705–718.

———. "'Litigant Agency' in Dower Pleas in the Royal Common Law Courts in Thirteenth- and Early Fourteenth-Century England." *Journal of Legal History* 24 (2003), pp. 215–236.

———. "Litigation as Personal Quest: Suing for Dower in the Royal Courts, circa 1272–1350." In *Wife and Widow in Medieval England,* pp. 81–108. Ed. Sue Sheridan Walker. Ann Arbor, 1993.

———. "Punishing Convicted Ravishers: Statutory Strictures and Actual Practice in Thirteenth- and Fourteenth-Century England." *Journal of Medieval History* 13 (1987), pp. 237–250.

———. "Wrongdoing and Compensation: The Pleas of Wardship in Thirteenth- and Fourteenth-Century England." *Journal of Legal History* 32 (1988), pp. 267–309.

Whittle, Jane. "Servants in Rural England c. 1450–1650: Hired Work as a Means of Accumulating Wealth and Skills before Marriage." In *The Marital Economy in Scandinavia and Britain, 1400–1900,* pp. 89–107. Ed. Maria Ågren and Amy Louise Erickson. Aldershot, 2005.

Wiesner, Merry E. "Having Her Own Smoke: Employment and Independence for Singlewomen in Germany, 1400–1750." In *Singlewomen in the European Past, 1250–1800,* pp. 192–216. Ed. Judith M. Bennett and Amy M. Froide. Philadelphia, 1999.

Williams, Gwyn A. *Medieval London: From Commune to Capital.* London, 1963.

Wilson, Katharina M., and Elizabeth M. Makowski. *Wykked Wyves and the Woes of Marriage: Misogamous Literature from Juvenal to Chaucer.* Albany, 1990.

Wood, Charles T. "The Doctor's Dilemma: Sin, Salvation, and the Menstrual Cycle." *Speculum* 56 (1981), pp. 710–727.

Wood, Robert A. "Poor Widows, c. 1393–1415." In *Medieval London Widows, 1300–1500,* pp. 55–70. Ed. Caroline M. Barron and Anne F. Sutton. London, 1994.

Woodbine, G. H., and S. E. Thorne, eds. *Bracton on the Laws and Customs of England.* Cambridge, Mass., 1968–77.

Wrigley, E. A., and R. S. Schofield. *Population History of England, 1541–1871: A Reconstruction.* Cambridge, Mass., 1981.

Wunderli, Richard. *London Church Courts and Society on the Eve of the Reformation.* Cambridge, Mass, 1981.

Index

Index

Index

Index

Index

Index

Index

Index

Index

Index

Index

Index

Wynton, Thomas de, 63
Wyntonia, Petronilla, daughter of William de, 33

Yakeslee, John, 167
  Margery, widow of, 167
Yerdele, John, 172
  Isabella, wife of, 171–172, 174

Yerdele, Sabina, 157
Yieveneye, John de, 27
  Theophania, wife of John and widow of
    William de Medelane, 27
Yong, William, 110
York, 49, 128, 130, 188
Ypres, 124